TOMARE!

[STOP!]

You're going the wrong way!

Manga is a completely different type of reading experience.

To start at the *beginning*, go to the *end*!

at's right! Authentic manga is read the traditional Japanese way—om right to left, exactly the *opposite* of how American books are ad. It's easy to follow: Just go to the other end of the book and read ch page—and each panel—from right side to left side, starting at e top right. Now you're experiencing manga as it was meant to be!

A Kodansha Comics Trade Paperback Original.

Fairy Girls volume 4 copyright © 2016 Hiro Mashima / BOKU
English translation copyright © 2016 Hiro Mashima / BOKU

Published in the United States by Kodansha Comics, an imprint of Kodansha USA Publishing, LLC, New York.

Publication rights for this English edition arranged through Kodansha Ltd., Tokyo.

First published in Japan in 2016 by Kodansha Ltd., Tokyo
ISBN 978-1-63236-333-6

Printed in the United States of America.

www.kodanshacomics.com

9 8 7 6 5 4 3 2 1

Translation: William Flanagan
Lettering: AndWorld Design
Editing: Megan McPherson
Kodansha Comics edition cover design: Phil Balsman

FAIRY GIRLS

"I'm pleasantly surprised to find modern shojo using cross-dressing as a dramatic device to deliver social commentary... Recommended."

-Otaku USA Magazine

The prince in his dark days

By **Hico Yamanal**

A drunkard for a father, a household of poverty... For 17-year-old Atsu misfortune is all she knows and believes in. Until one day, a char encounter with Itaru–the wealthy heir of a huge corporation–chang everything. The two look identical, uncannily so. When Itaru curiou goes missing, Atsuko is roped into being his stand-in. There, in his sh Atsuko must parade like a prince in a palace. She encounters many experiences, but at what cost…?

iry Tail takes place in a world filled with magic. 17-year-old Lucy is
wizard-in-training who wants to join a magic guild so that she can
come a full-fledged wizard. She dreams of joining the most famous guild,
own as Fairy Tail. One day she meets Natsu, a boy raised by a dragon
ich vanished when he was young. Natsu has devoted his life to finding
dragon father. When Natsu helps Lucy out of a tricky situation, she
covers that he is a member of Fairy Tail, and our heroes' adventure
gether begins.

FAIRY TAIL

MASTER'S EDITION

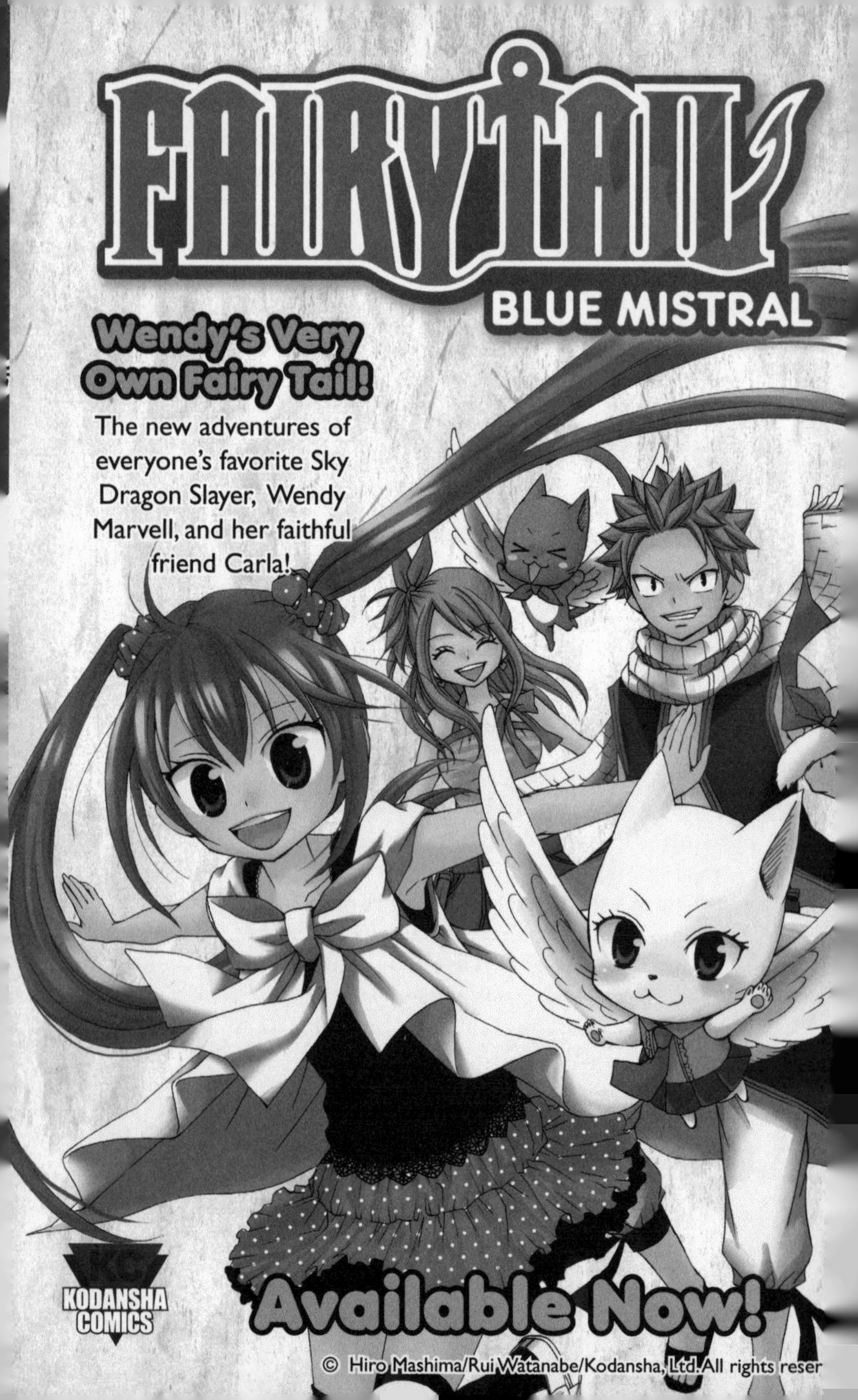
FAIRY TAIL
BLUE MISTRAL
Wendy's Very Own Fairy Tail!
The new adventures of everyone's favorite Sky Dragon Slayer, Wendy Marvell, and her faithful friend Carla!
KODANSHA COMICS
Available Now!
© Hiro Mashima/Rui Watanabe/Kodansha, Ltd. All rights reser

New action series from Takei Hiroyuki, creator of the classic shonen franchise Shaman King!

medieval Japan, a bell hanging on the collar is a sign that a cat as a master. Norachiyo's bell hangs from his katana sheath, but he is onetheless a stray — a ronin. This one-eyed cat samurai travels across a ishonest world, cutting through pretense and deception with his blade.

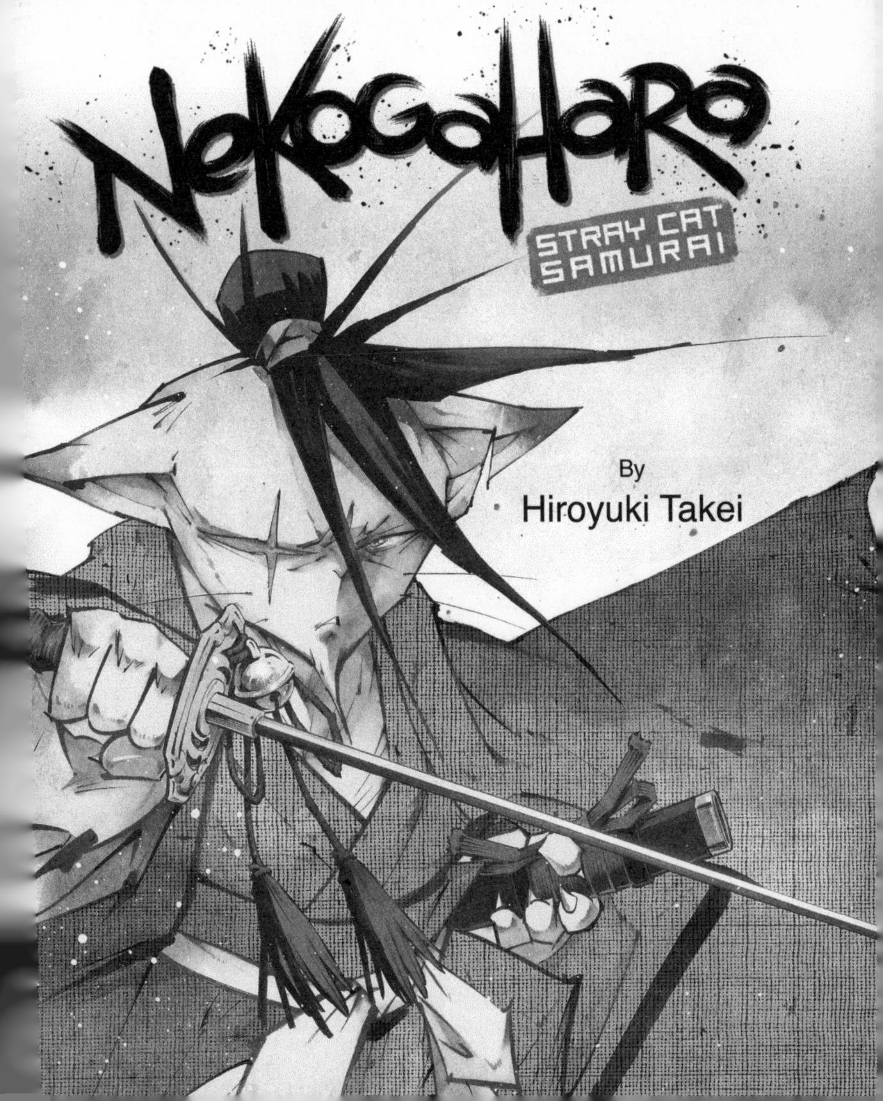
NekoGaHara
STRAY CAT
SAMURAI
By
Hiroyuki Takei

HAPPINESS

ハピネス

By **Shuzo Oshimi**

From the creator of *Flowers of Evil*

Nothing interesting in happening in Makoto Ozaki's first year of hig school. HIs life is a serise of quiet humiliations: low-grade bullie unreliable friends, and the constant frustration of his adolescent lust. Bu one night, a pale, thin girl knocks him to the ground in an alley and offe him a choice.

Now everything is different. Daylight is searingly bright. Food taste awful. And worse than anything is the terrible, consuming thirst...

Praise for Shuzo Oshimi's *Flowers of Evil*

"A shockingly readable story that vividly—one might even say queasily—evokes the fe and confusion of discovering one's own sexuality. Recommended." —The Manga Critic

"A page-turning tale of sordid middle school blackmail." —Otaku USA Magazine

"A stunning new horror manga." —Third Eye Comics

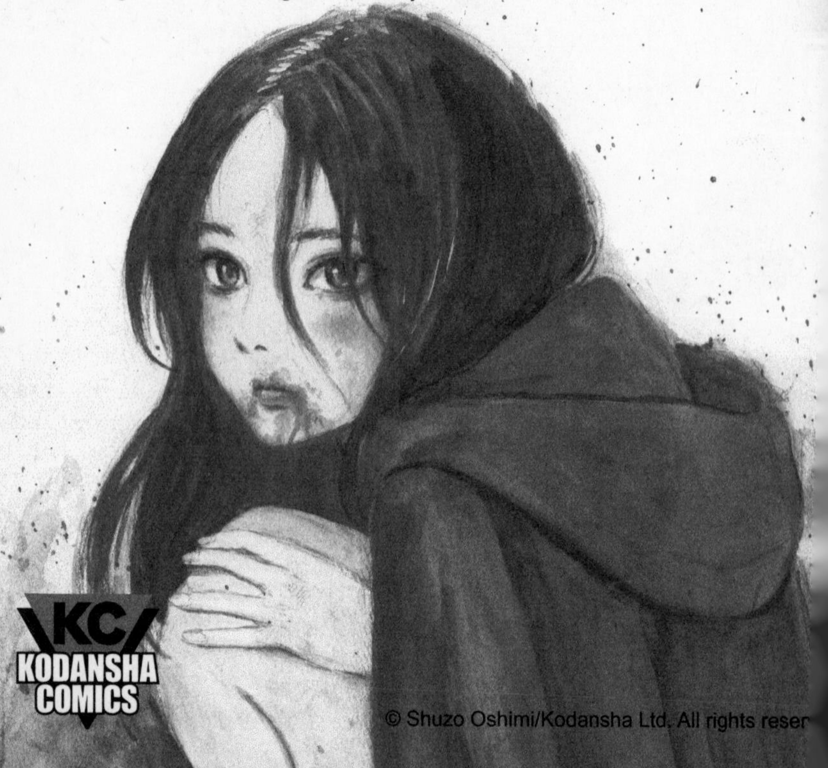

KC KODANSHA COMICS

The Black Museum The Ghost and the Lady

By Kazuhiro Fujita

…ep in Scotland Yard in London sits an evidence room, where artifacts of the …atest mysteries in London history are kept. In this "Black Museum" sits two …lets, fused together after a head-on collision. This was the key piece of evidence … a case that brought together a supernatural Man in Gray and the famous nurse … activist Florence Nightingale — the only person who can see him. Surrounded … war and suffering, the lady enters into a desperate pact with this ghostlike man...

Praise for Kazuhiro Fujita's *Ushio and Tora*

…harming revival that combines a classic look with modern depth and pacing... **Essential viewing … for curmudgeons and new fans alike."** — Anime News Network

…**EAT!** The first episode of Ushio and Tora captures the essence of '90s anime." — IGN

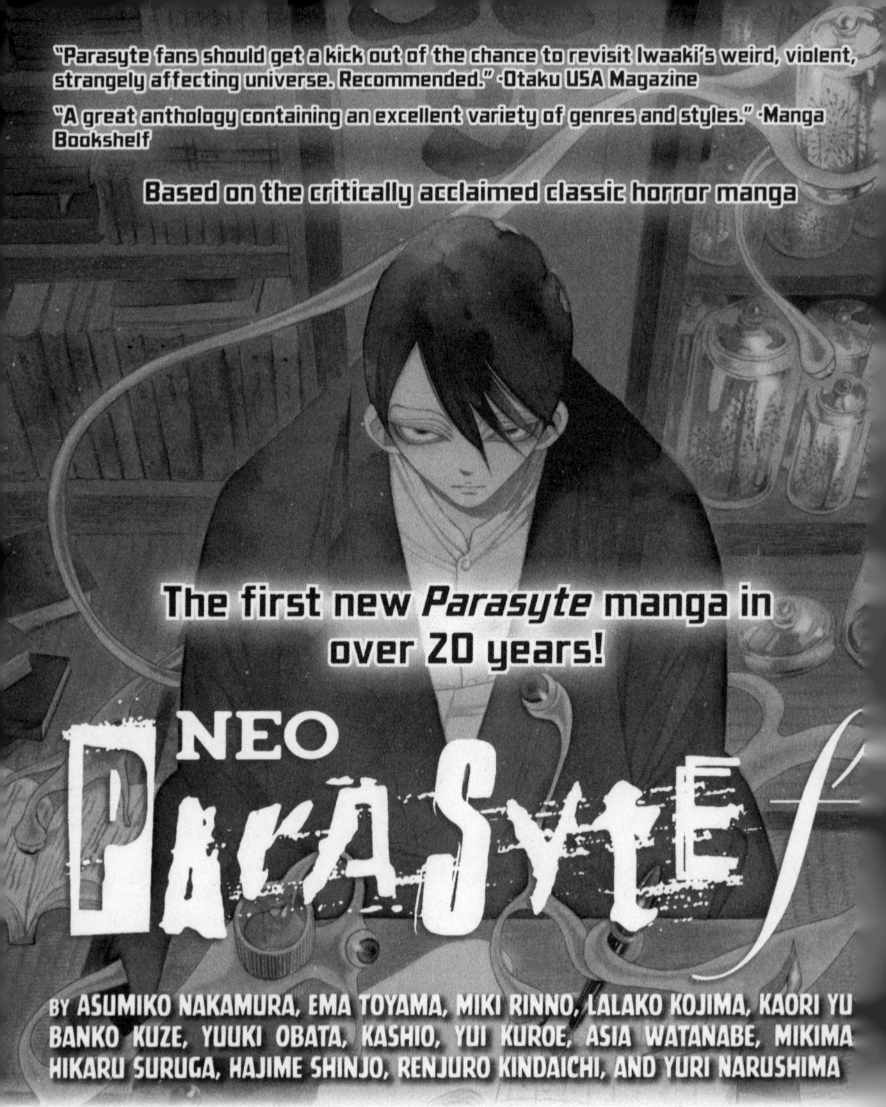

Based on the critically acclaimed classic horror manga

The first new *Parasyte* manga in over 20 years!

NEO PARASYTEf

BY ASUMIKO NAKAMURA, EMA TOYAMA, MIKI RINNO, LALAKO KOJIMA, KAORI YU
BANKO KUZE, YUUKI OBATA, KASHIO, YUI KUROE, ASIA WATANABE, MIKIMA
HIKARU SURUGA, HAJIME SHINJO, RENJURO KINDAICHI, AND YURI NARUSHIMA

A collection of chilling new *Parasyte* stories from Japan's top shojo artis

Parasites: shape-shifting aliens whose only purpose is to assimilate with and consu the human race... but do these monsters have a different side? A parasite become prince to save his romance-obsessed female host from a dangerous stalker. Anoth hosts a cooking show, in which the real monsters are revealed. These and 13 m stories, from some of the greatest shojo manga artists alive today, together make up a chilling, funny, and entertaining tribute to one of manga's horror classics!

KC
KODANSH
COMICS

The award-winning manga about what happens inside you!

"Far more entertaining than it ought to be... what kid doesn't want to think that every time they sneeze a torpedo shoots out their nose?"
—Anime News Network

Strep throat! Hay fever! Influenza! The world is a dangerous place for a red blood cell just trying to get her deliveries finished. Fortunately, she's not alone. She's got a whole human body's worth of cells ready to help out! The mysterious white blood cell, the buff and brash killer T cell, the nerdy neuron, even the cute little platelets — everyone's got to come together if they want to keep you healthy!

Cells at Work!

はたらく細胞

By Akane Shimizu

KC
KODANSHA
COMICS

Japan's most powerful spirit medium delves into the ghost world's greatest mysteries!

Story by Kyo Shiradaira, famed author of mystery fiction and creator of Spiral, Blast of Tempest, and The Record of a Fallen Vampire.

Both touched by spirits called yoka Kotoko and Kuro have gained uniqu superhuman powers. But to gain h powers Kotoko has given up an ey and a leg, and Kuro's person life is in shambles. S when Kotoko sugges they team up to de with renegades fro the spirit world, Ku doesn't have many oth choices, but Kotoko might ju have a few ulterior motives...

IN/SPECTRE

STORY BY **KYO SHIRODAIF**
ART BY **CHASHIBA KATAS**

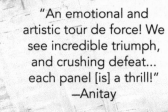

"An emotional and artistic tour de force! We see incredible triumph, and crushing defeat... each panel [is] a thrill!"
—Anitay

"A journey that's instantly compelling."
—Anime News Network

WELCOME
TO THE BALLROOM

By Tomo Takeuchi

ckless high school student Tatara Fujita wants to be good at
nething—anything. Unfortunately, he's about as average as a slouchy
en can bee. The local bullies know this, and make it a habit to hit him up
cash, but all that changes when the debonair Kaname Sengoku sends
m packing. Sengoku's not the neighborhood watch, though. He's a
fessional ballroom dancer. And once Tatara Fujita gets
led into the world of competitive dancesport, his life will
er be the same.

KC KODANSHA COMICS

A new series from the creator of *Soul Eater*, the megahit manga and anime seen on Toonami!

"Fun and lively... a great start!"
    -Adventures in
     Poor Taste

FIRE FORCE

By Atsushi Ohkubo

The city of Tokyo is plagued by a deadly phenomenon: spontaneo human combustion! Luckily, a special team is there to quench inferno: The Fire Force! The fire soldiers at Special Fire Cathedra are about to get a unique addition. Enter Shinra, a boy who possess the power to run at the speed of a rocket, leaving behind the famo "devil's footprints" (and destroying his shoes in the proces Can Shinra and his colleagues discover the source of this stran epidemic before the city burns to ashes?

aving lost his wife, high school teacher Kohei Inuzuka is doing his best to raise his young
aughter Tsumugi on his own. He's a pretty bad cook and doesn't have a big appetite to begin
ith, but chance brings his little family together with one of his students, the lonely Kotori.
e three of them are anything but comfortable in the kitchen, but the healing power of home
oking might just work on their grieving hearts.

'his season's number-one feel-good anime!" —Anime News Network

. beautifully-drawn story about comfort food and family and grief. Recommended." —Otaku
5A Magazine

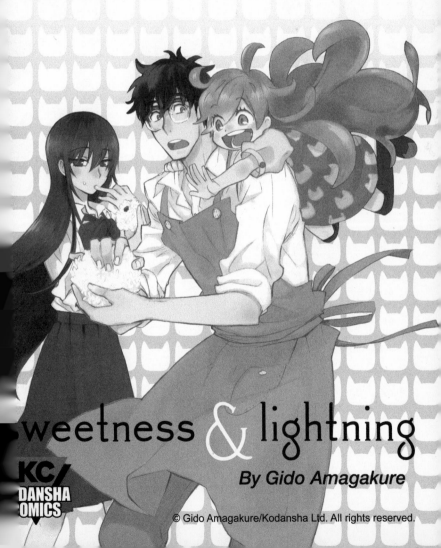

weetness & lightning

By Gido Amagakure

KC/
DANSHA
OMICS

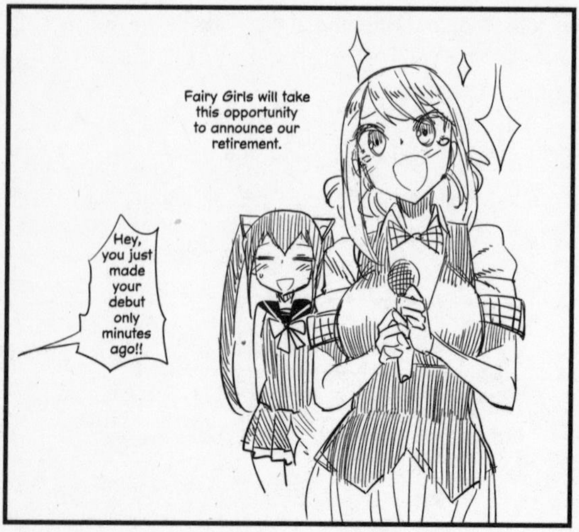
Fairy Girls will take this opportunity to announce our retirement.
Hey, you just made your debut only minutes ago!!

Page 156, Retirement

Within the past ten or 15 years, it has become customary for someone in the entertainment industry who wants to (or has to) leave either a group, or the industry itself, to refer to this as "graduating," rather than "quitting" or "being fired." This is especially true for idol groups for which this "graduation" can be an event itself. But the upshot is the same. For whatever reason, the idol is on their way out, and is putting the best face on the matter.

Page 167, Rice gruel

What is it that most Japanese people want when they're sick? It's a simple dish made of cooked rice, milk, usually a few mild herbs and spices, and maybe some meats and veggies in it. Although in English, they call it "rice gruel," in Japanese it is called *o-kayu*, and it's a comfort food that recalls the feeling of mothered while you were sick as a child. In many ways, both in meaning and nuance, rice gruel is to the Japanese as chicken soup is to many Western readers.

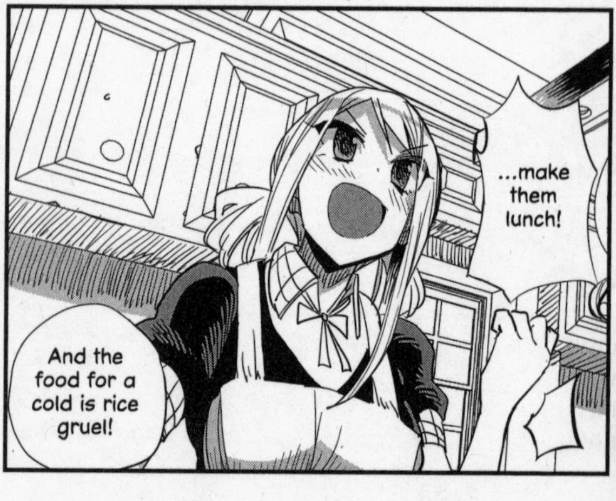
...make them lunch!
And the food for a cold is rice gruel!

FAIRY GIRLS

4

MANGA BY BOKU

BASED ON A STORY BY HIRO MASHI

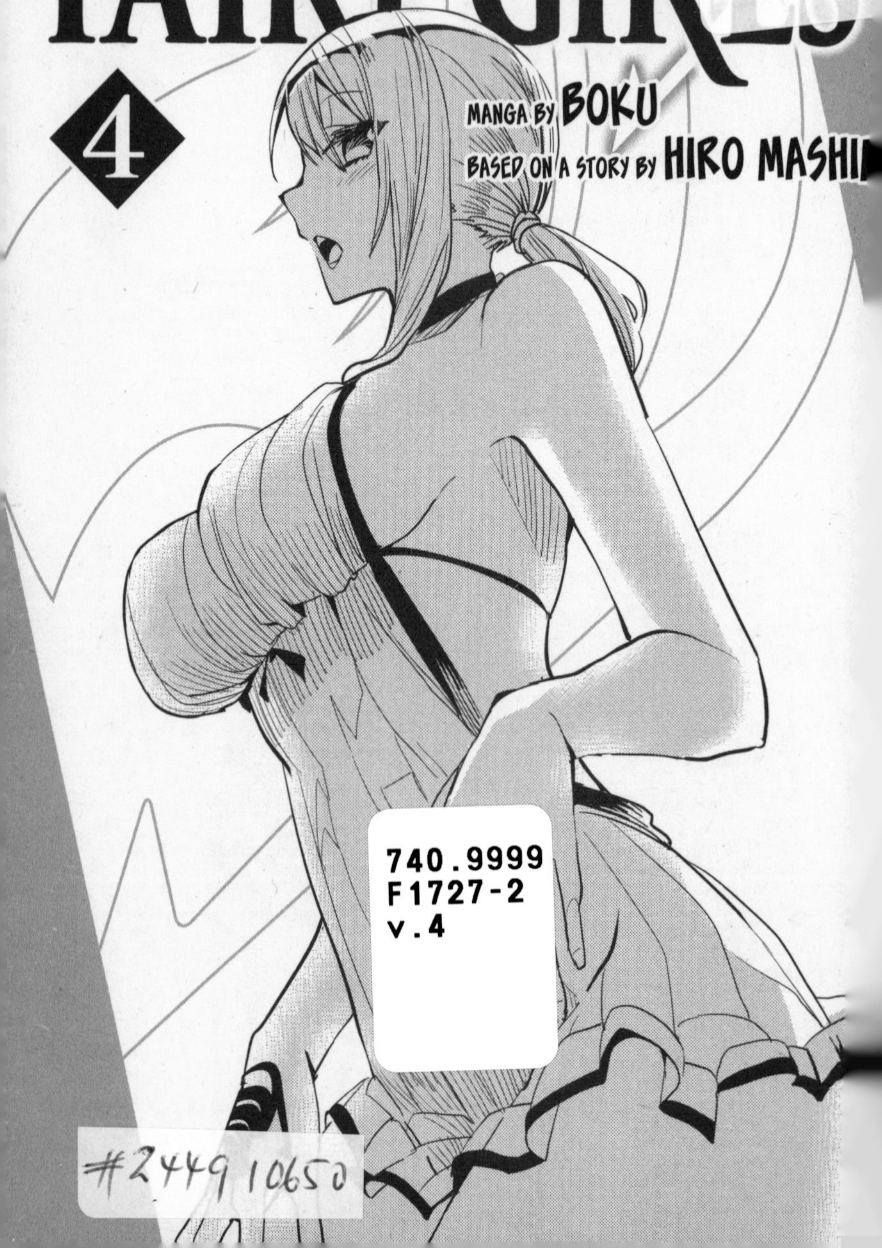

CONTENTS

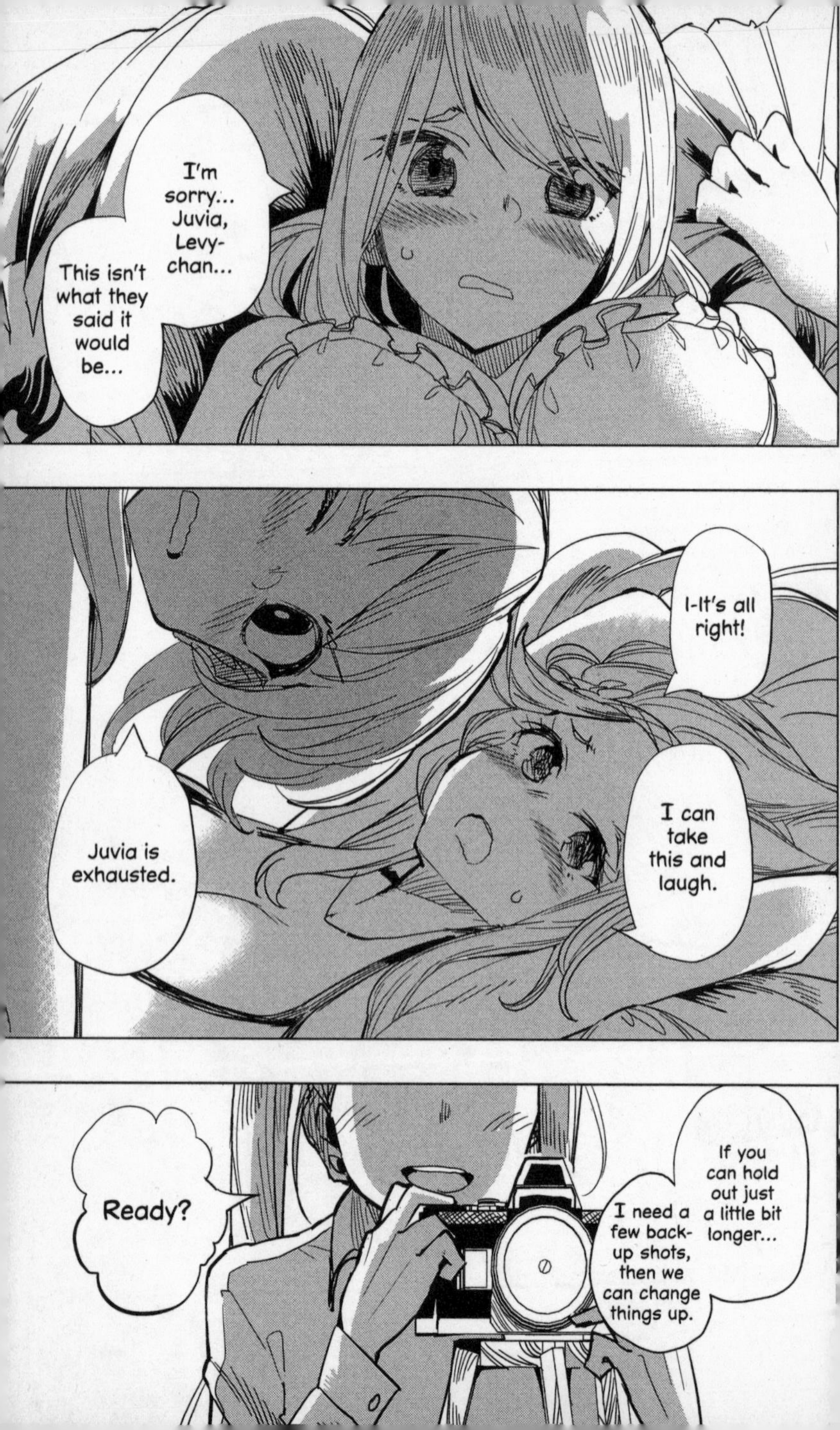
I'm sorry... Juvia, Levy-chan...
This isn't what they said it would be...
I-It's all right!
I can take this and laugh.
Juvia is exhausted.
If you can hold out just a little bit longer...
I need a few back-up shots, then we can change things up.
Ready?

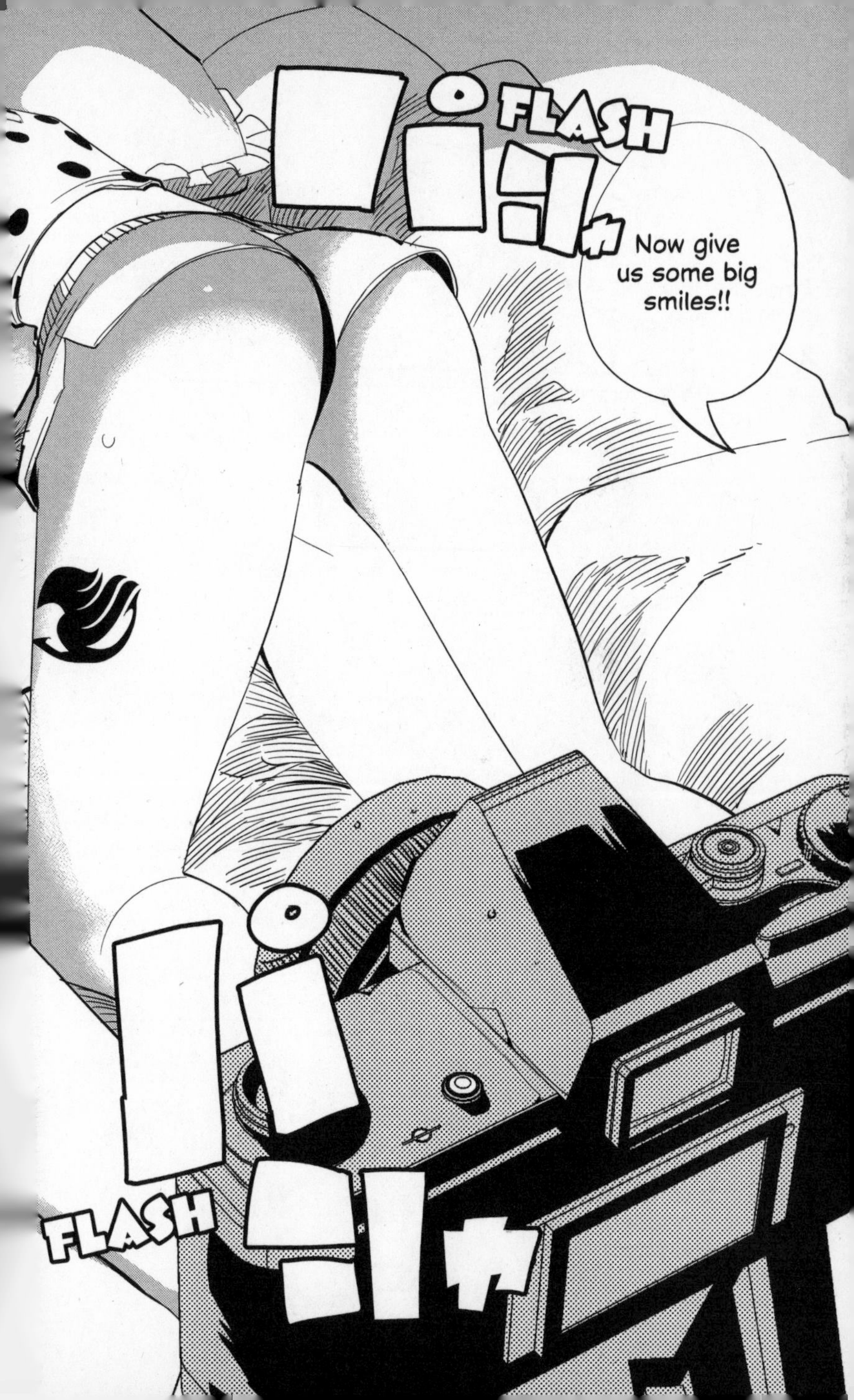
FLASH
Now give us some big smiles!!
FLASH

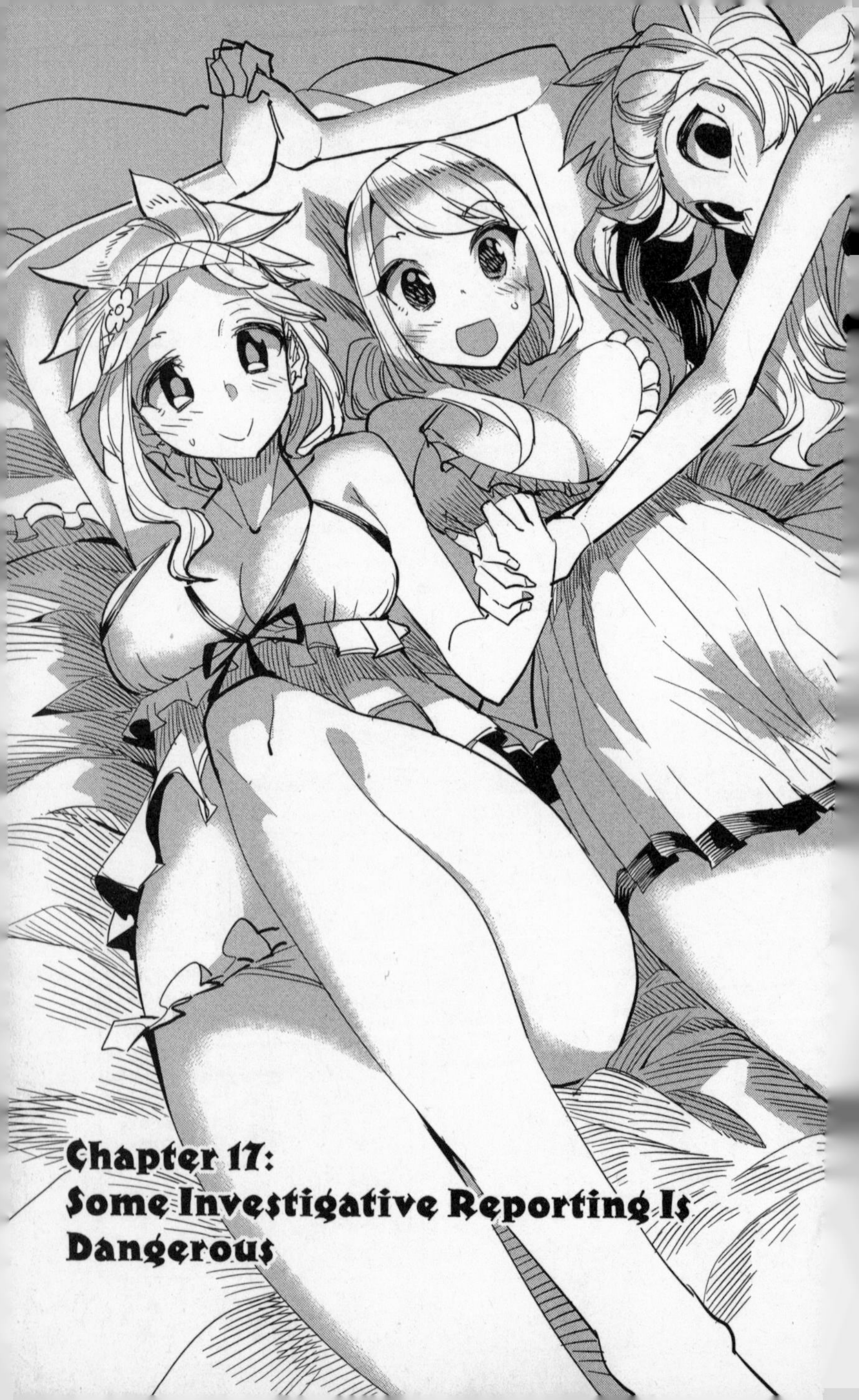
Chapter 17:
Some Investigative Reporting Is Dangerous

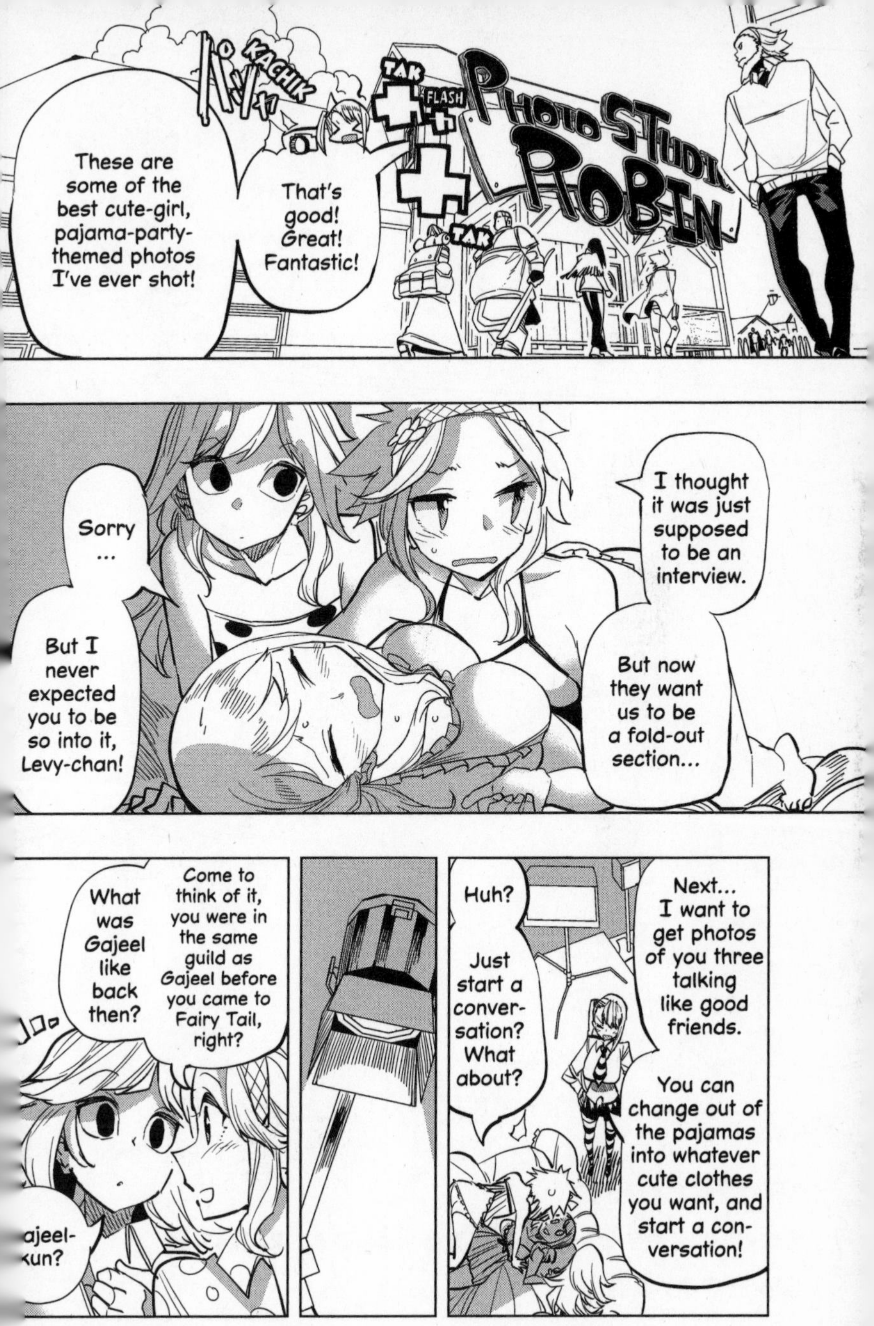

PHOTO STUDIO ROBIN
TAK
FLASH
KACHIK
That's good! Great! Fantastic!
These are some of the best cute-girl, pajama-party-themed photos I've ever shot!
TAK
I thought it was just supposed to be an interview.
But now they want us to be a fold-out section...
Sorry ...
But I never expected you to be so into it, Levy-chan!
Next... I want to get photos of you three talking like good friends.
You can change out of the pajamas into whatever cute clothes you want, and start a con-versation!
Huh?
Just start a conver-sation? What about?
Come to think of it, you were in the same guild as Gajeel before you came to Fairy Tail, right?
What was Gajeel like back then?
ajeel-kun?

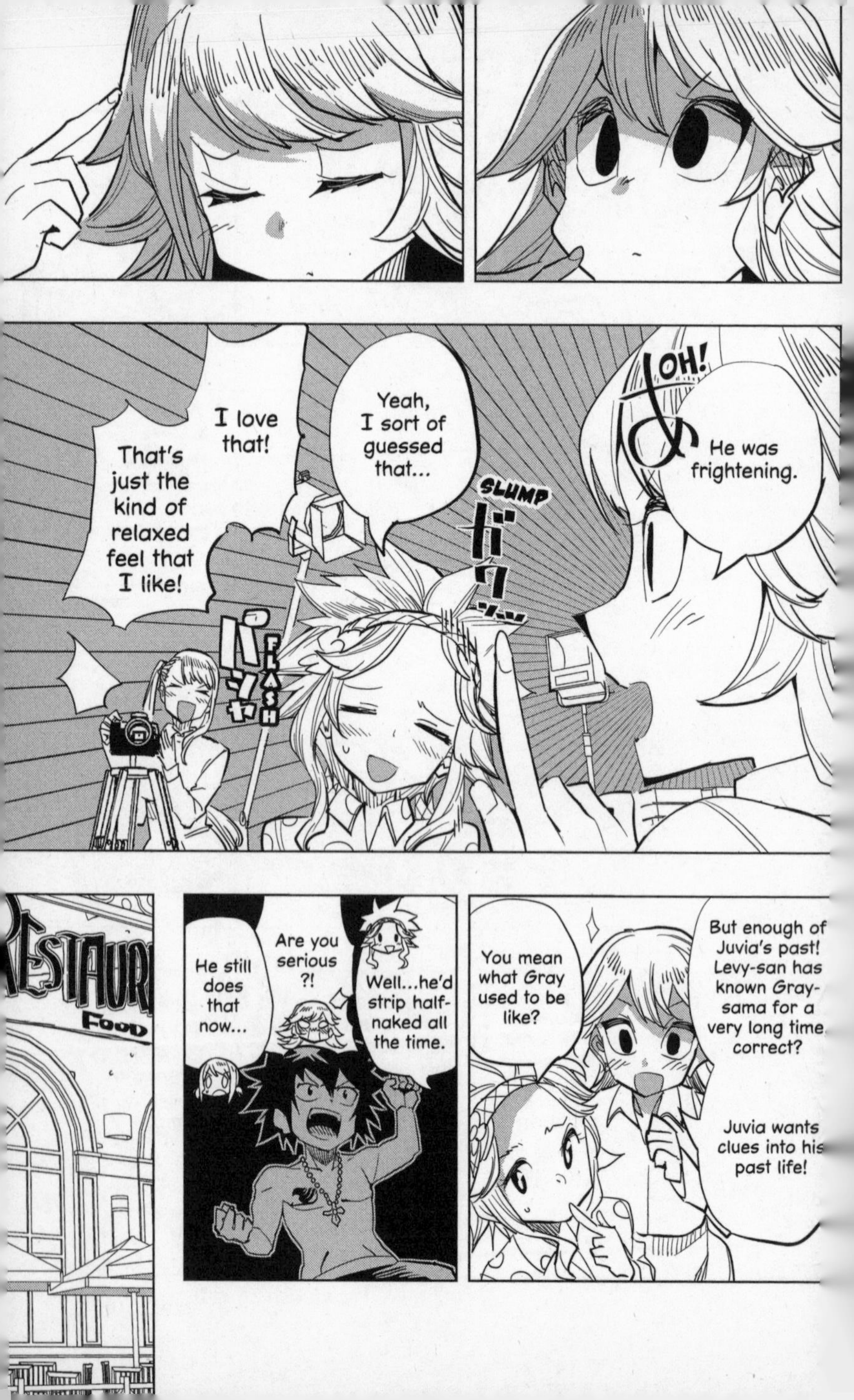
OH!
He was frightening.
SLUMP
Yeah, I sort of guessed that...
I love that!
That's just the kind of relaxed feel that I like!
FLASH
But enough of Juvia's past! Levy-san has known Gray-sama for a very long time, correct?
Juvia wants clues into his past life!
You mean what Gray used to be like?
Well...he'd strip half-naked all the time.
Are you serious?!
He still does that now...
FOOD

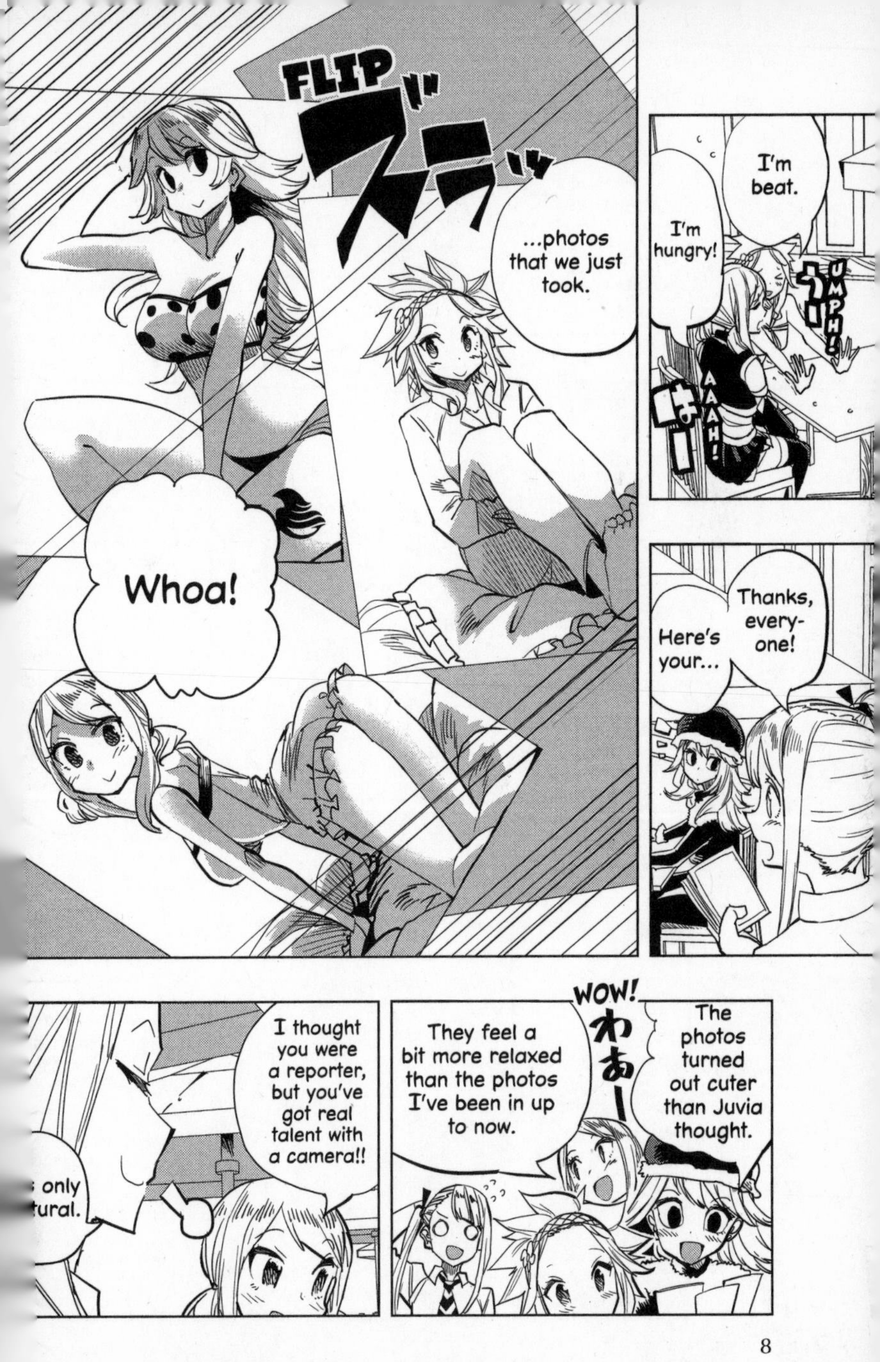
I'm beat.
I'm hungry!
UMPH!
AAAH!
Thanks, everyone!
Here's your...
FLIP
...photos that we just took.
Whoa!
WOW!
わぁー
The photos turned out cuter than Juvia thought.
They feel a bit more relaxed than the photos I've been in up to now.
I thought you were a reporter, but you've got real talent with a camera!!
only tural.

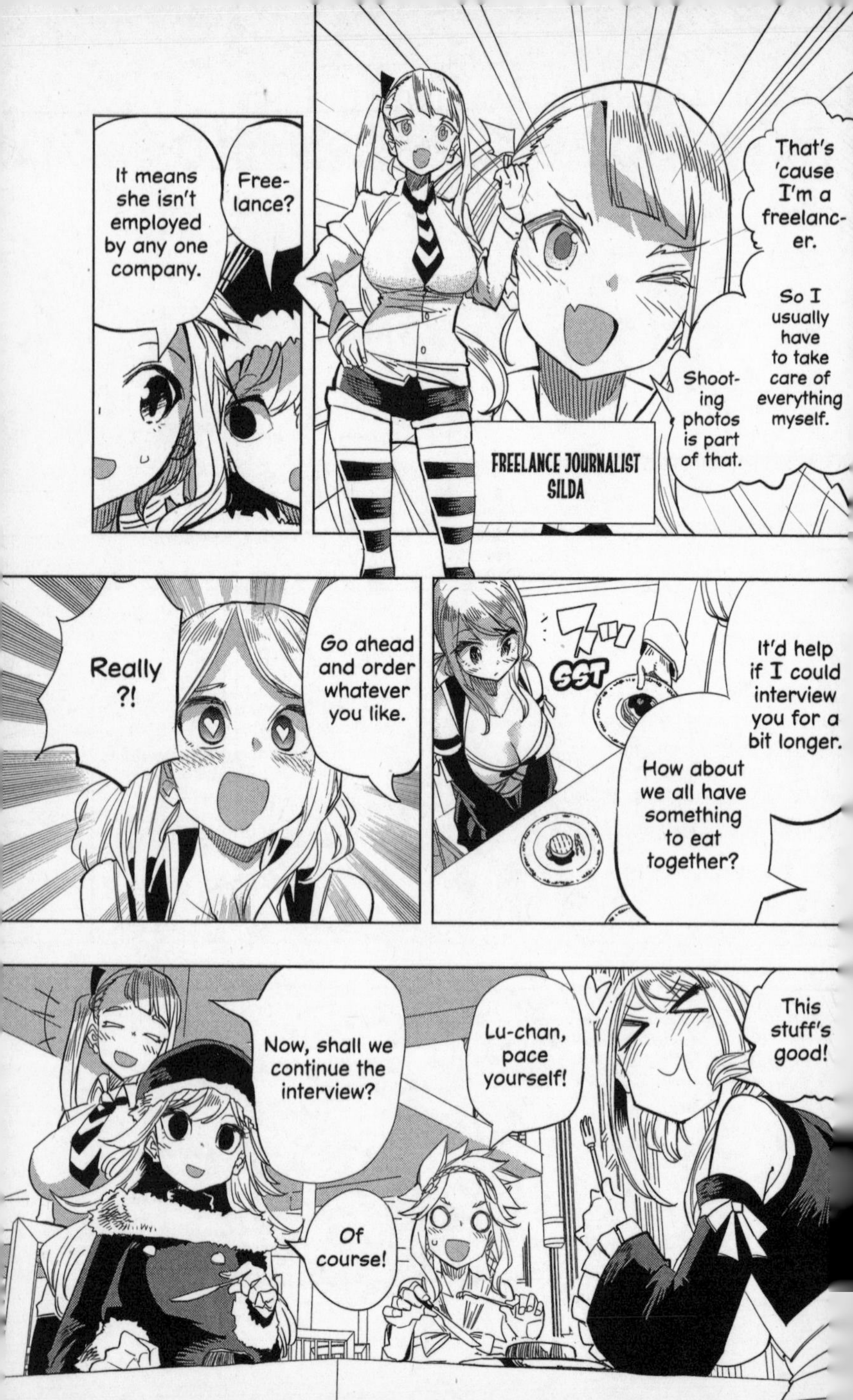

That's 'cause I'm a freelancer.
So I usually have to take care of everything myself.
Shooting photos is part of that.
FREELANCE JOURNALIST SILDA
Free-lance?
It means she isn't employed by any one company.
SST
It'd help if I could interview you for a bit longer.
How about we all have something to eat together?
Go ahead and order whatever you like.
Really?!
This stuff's good!
Lu-chan, pace yourself!
Now, shall we continue the interview?
Of course!

WHAT ARE YOUR FAVORITE THINGS TO EAT?

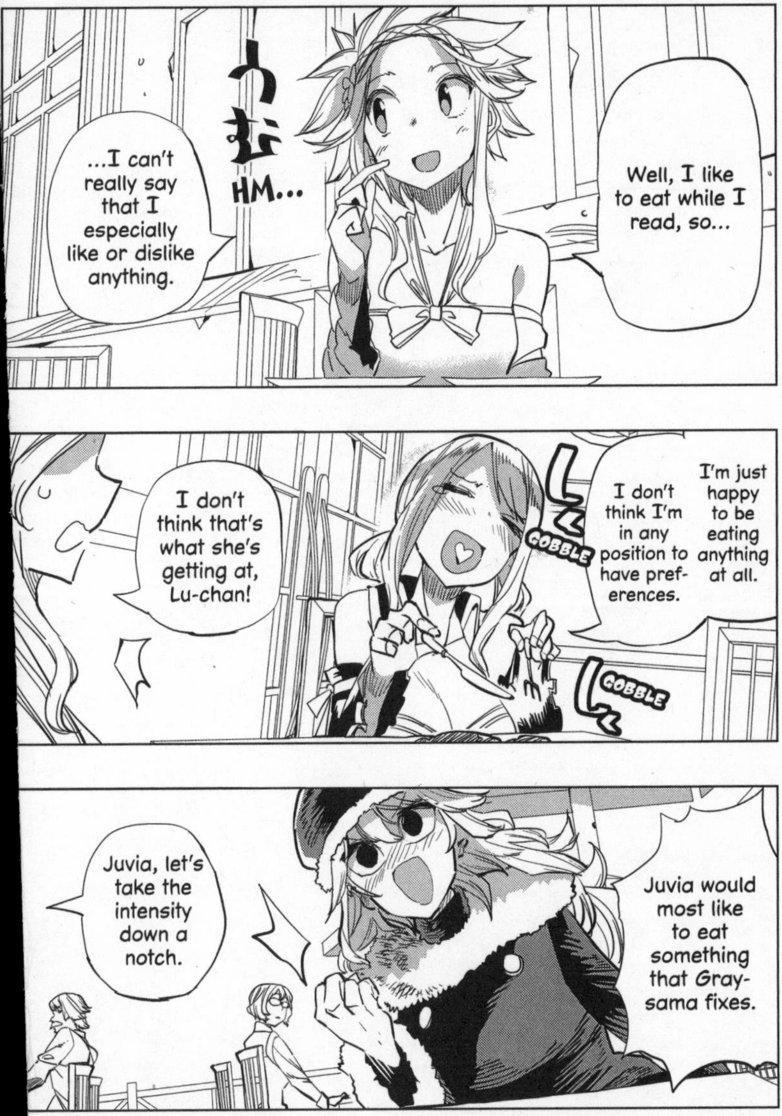

Well, I like to eat while I read, so...
うむ
HM...
...I can't really say that I especially like or dislike anything.
I'm just happy to be eating anything at all.
I don't think I'm in any position to have preferences.
COBBLE
COBBLE
I don't think that's what she's getting at, Lu-chan!
Juvia would most like to eat something that Gray-sama fixes.
Juvia, let's take the intensity down a notch.

WHO DO YOU FEEL CLOSEST TO IN THE GUILD?

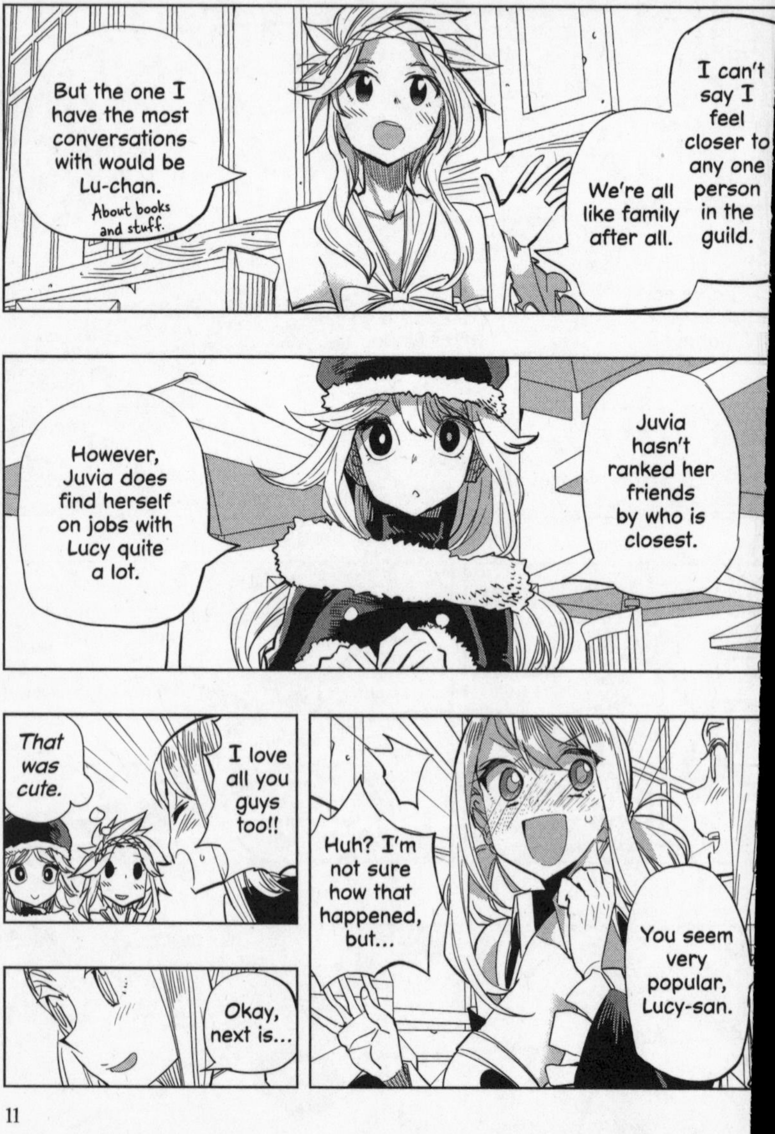
I can't say I feel closer to any one person in the guild.
We're all like family after all.
But the one I have the most conversations with would be Lu-chan.
About books and stuff.
Juvia hasn't ranked her friends by who is closest.
However, Juvia does find herself on jobs with Lucy quite a lot.
You seem very popular, Lucy-san.
Huh? I'm not sure how that happened, but...
I love all you guys too!!
That was cute.
Okay, next is...

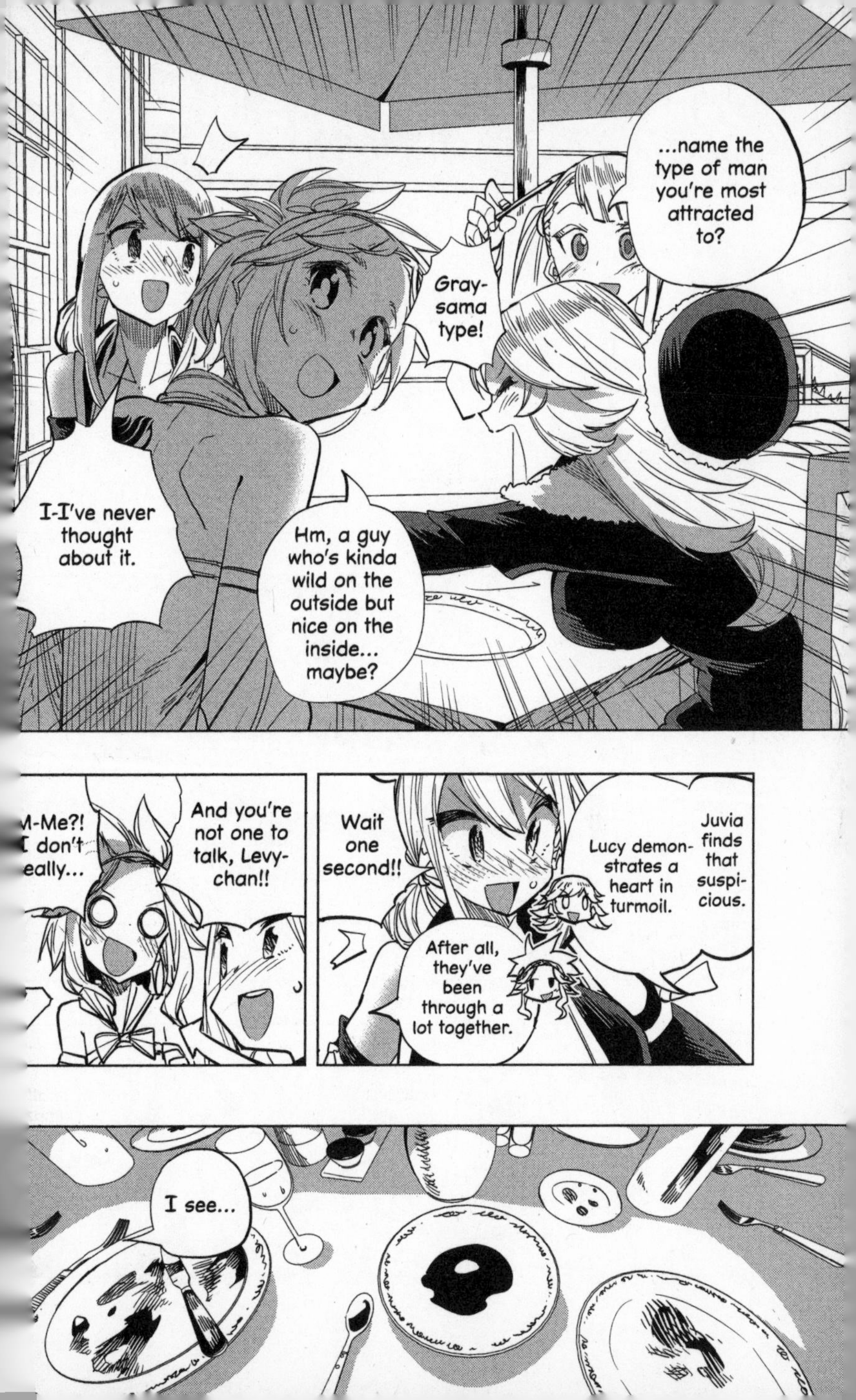
...name the type of man you're most attracted to?
Gray-sama type!
Hm, a guy who's kinda wild on the outside but nice on the inside... maybe?
I-I've never thought about it.
Juvia finds that suspicious.
Lucy demonstrates a heart in turmoil.
Wait one second!!
After all, they've been through a lot together.
And you're not one to talk, Levy-chan!!
M-Me?! I don't eally...
I see...

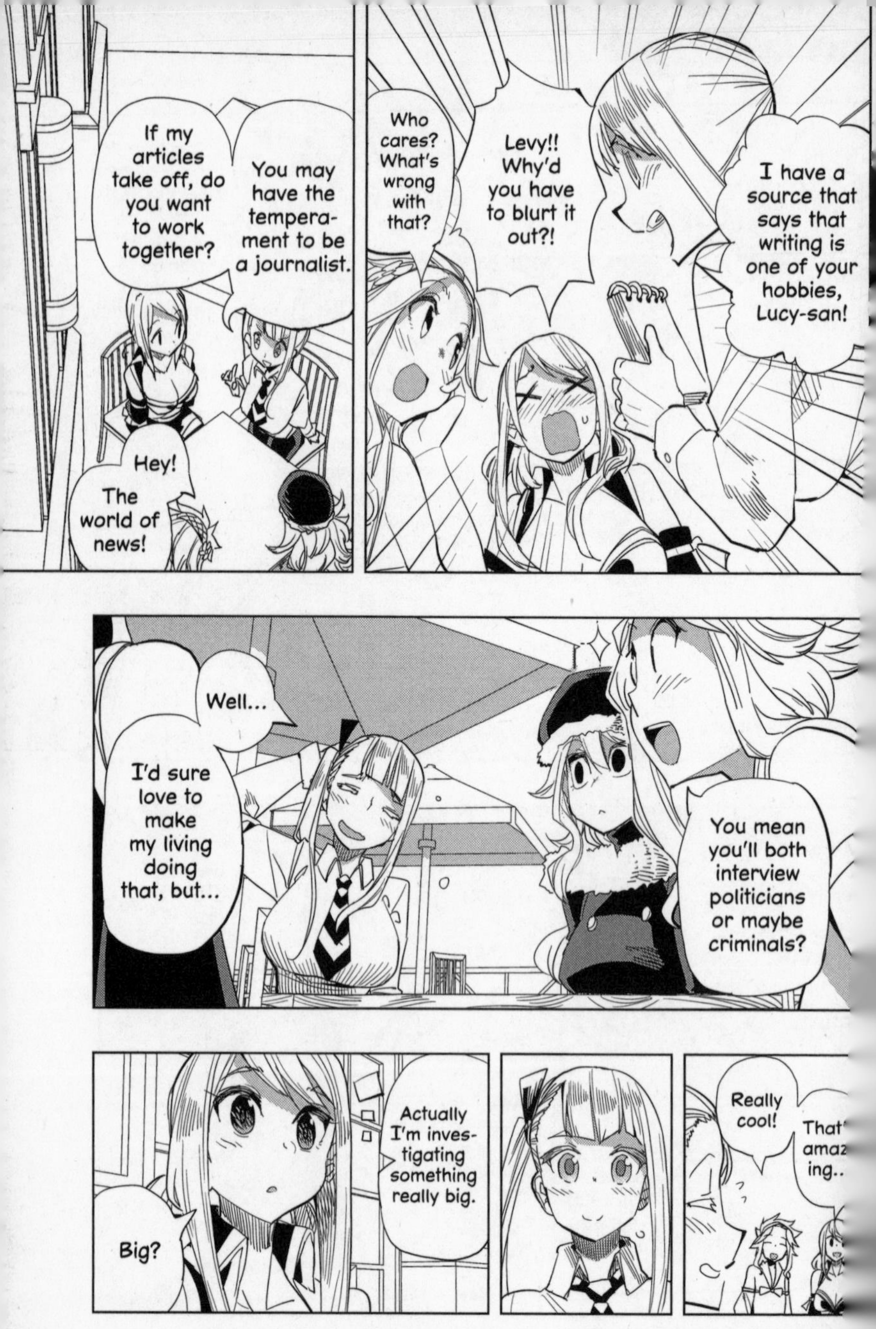
I have a source that says that writing is one of your hobbies, Lucy-san!
Levy!! Why'd you have to blurt it out?!
Who cares? What's wrong with that?
You may have the tempera-ment to be a journalist.
If my articles take off, do you want to work together?
Hey! The world of news!
You mean you'll both interview politicians or maybe criminals?
Well...
I'd sure love to make my living doing that, but...
Really cool!
Actually I'm inves-tigating something really big.
Big?

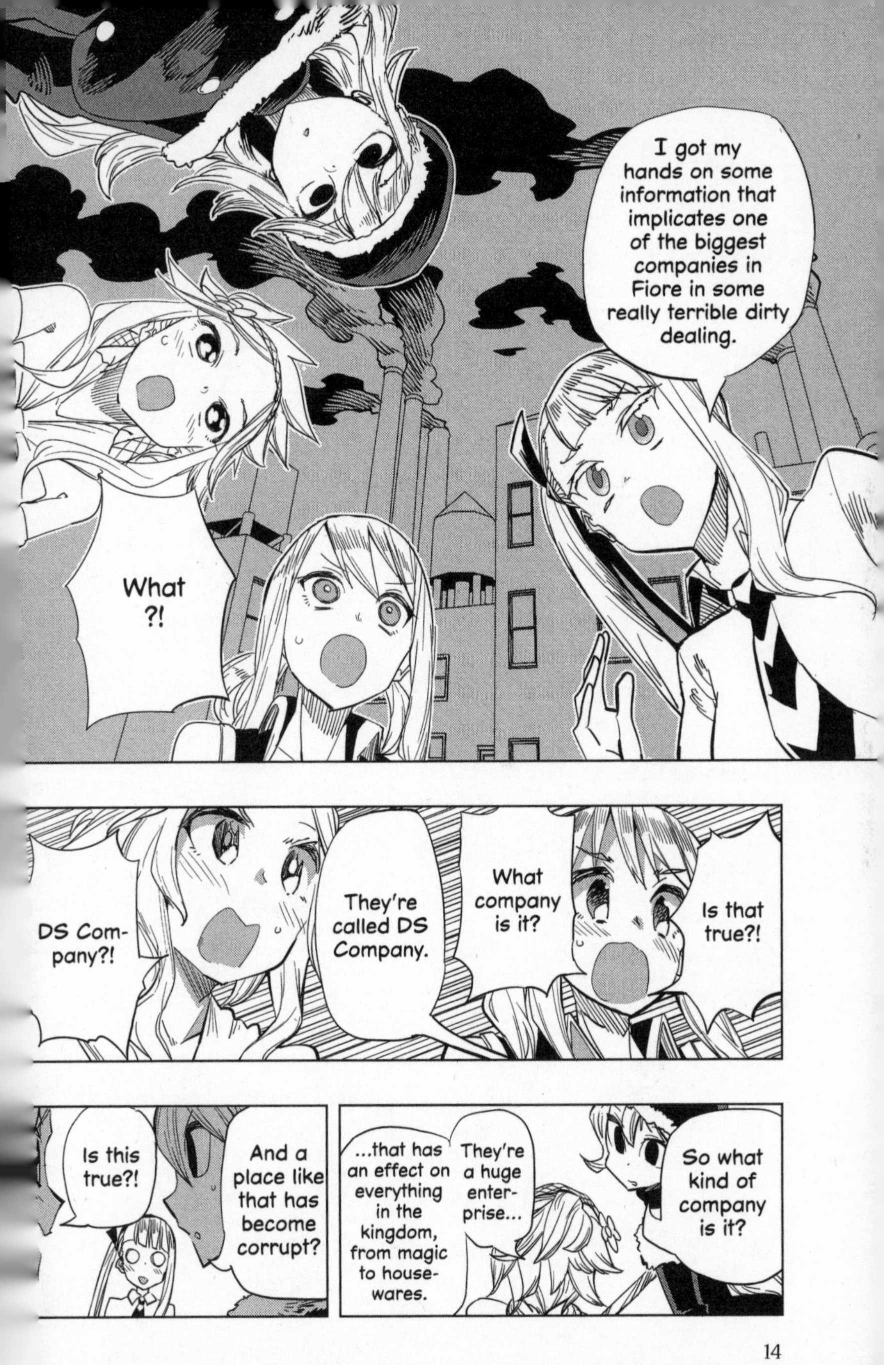
I got my hands on some information that implicates one of the biggest companies in Fiore in some really terrible dirty dealing.
What ?!
Is that true?!
What company is it?
They're called DS Company.
DS Com-pany?!
So what kind of company is it?
They're a huge enter-prise...
...that has an effect on everything in the kingdom, from magic to house-wares.
And a place like that has become corrupt?
Is this true?!

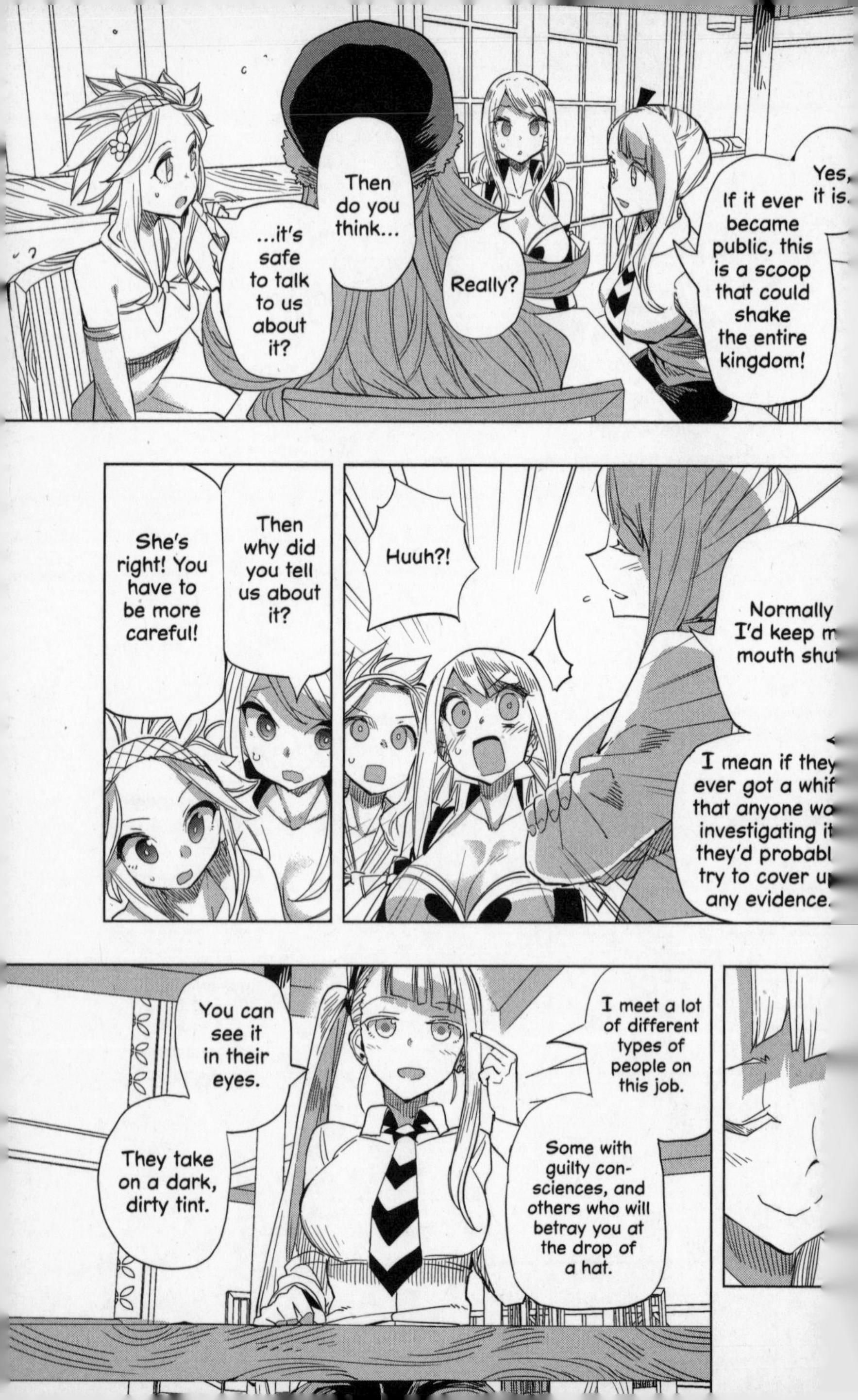
Yes, it is.
If it ever became public, this is a scoop that could shake the entire kingdom!
Really?
Then do you think...
...it's safe to talk to us about it?
Normally I'd keep m mouth shu
I mean if they ever got a whif that anyone wa investigating it they'd probabl try to cover u any evidence.
Huuh?!
Then why did you tell us about it?
She's right! You have to be more careful!
I meet a lot of different types of people on this job.
Some with guilty con- sciences, and others who will betray you at the drop of a hat.
You can see it in their eyes.
They take on a dark, dirty tint.

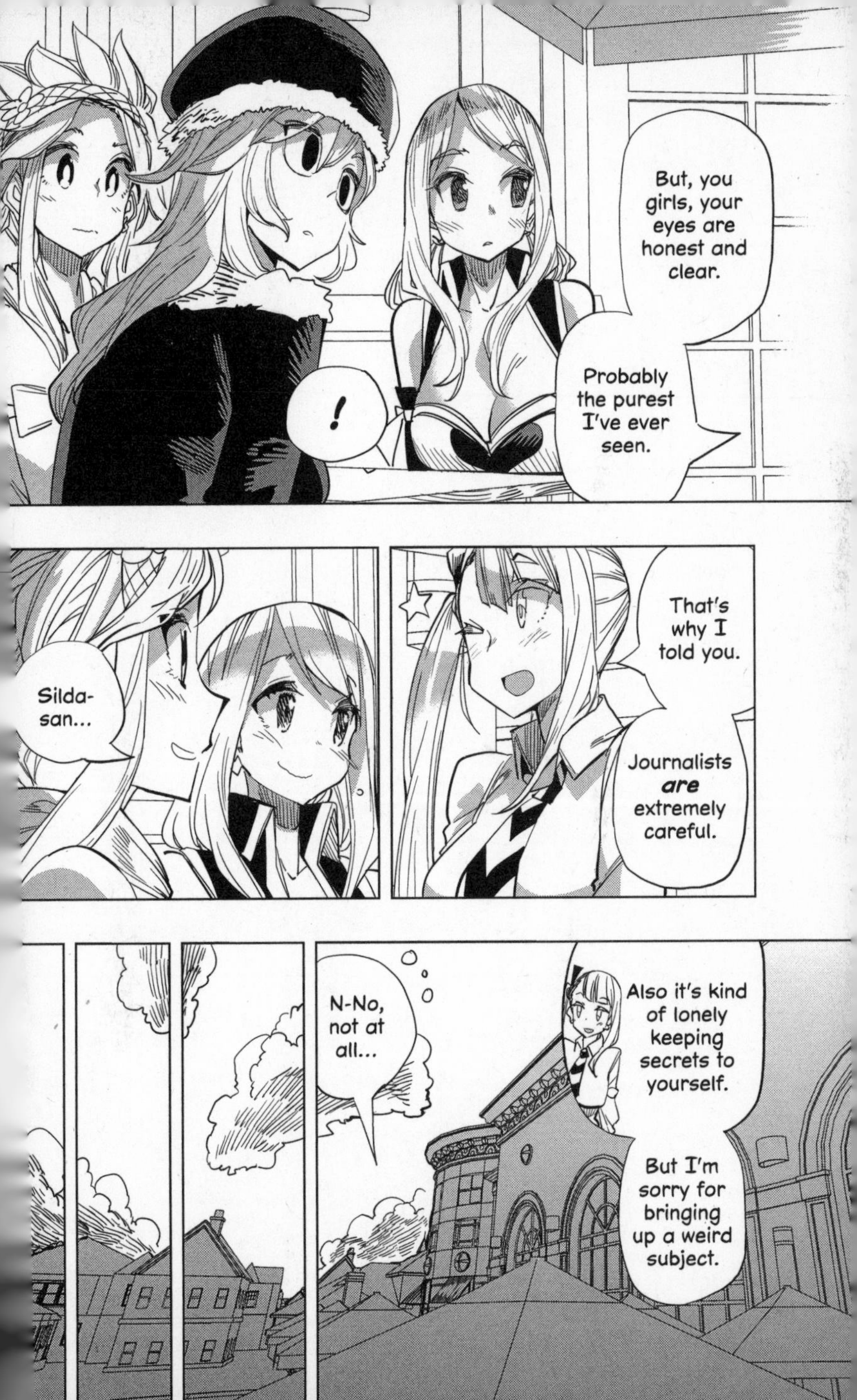
But, you girls, your eyes are honest and clear.
Probably the purest I've ever seen.
!
That's why I told you.
Journalists ***are*** extremely careful.
Silda-san...
Also it's kind of lonely keeping secrets to yourself.
But I'm sorry for bringing up a weird subject.
N-No, not at all...

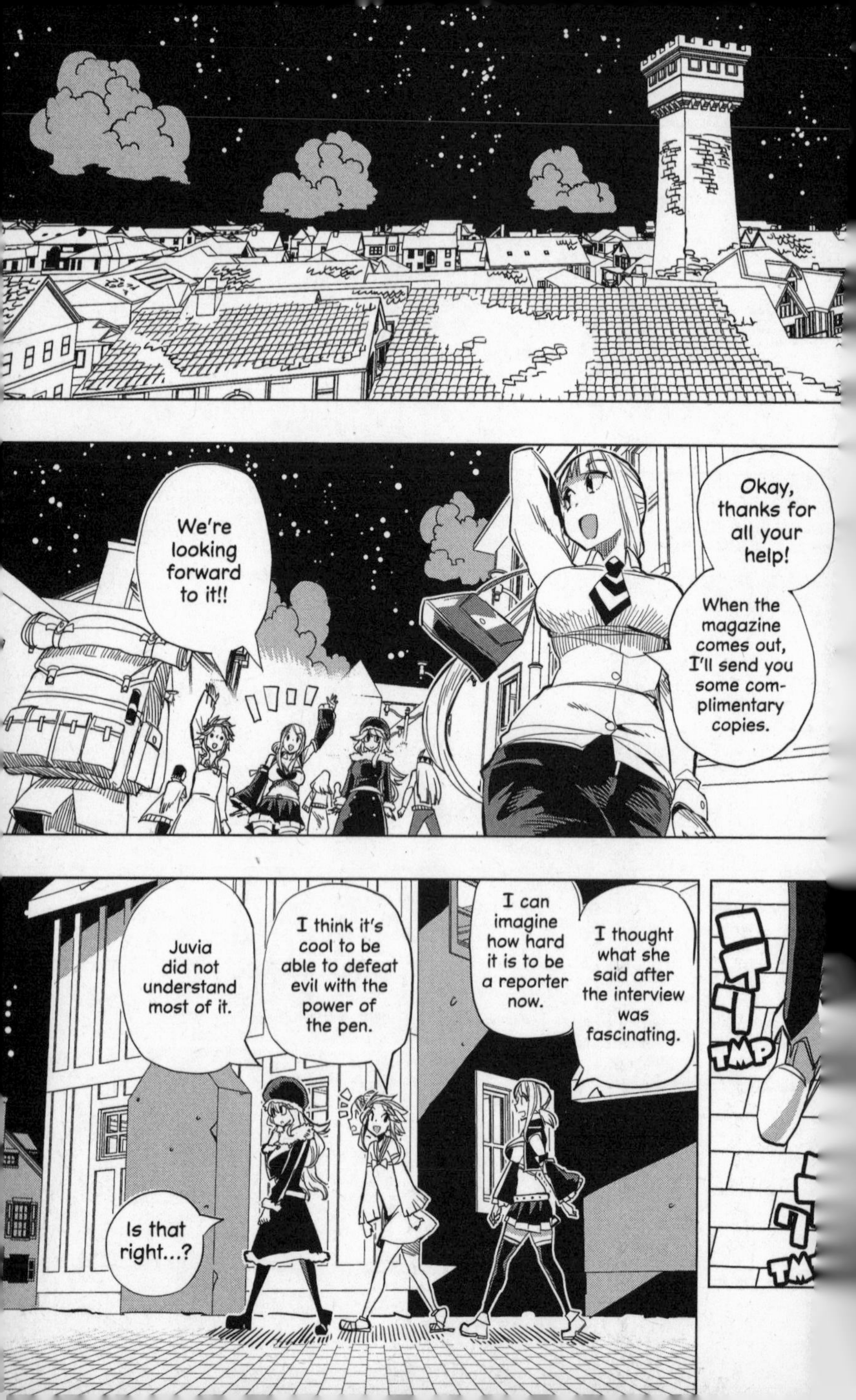
Okay, thanks for all your help!
When the magazine comes out, I'll send you some complimentary copies.
We're looking forward to it!!
TMP
TM
I thought what she said after the interview was fascinating.
I can imagine how hard it is to be a reporter now.
I think it's cool to be able to defeat evil with the power of the pen.
Juvia did not understand most of it.
Is that right...?

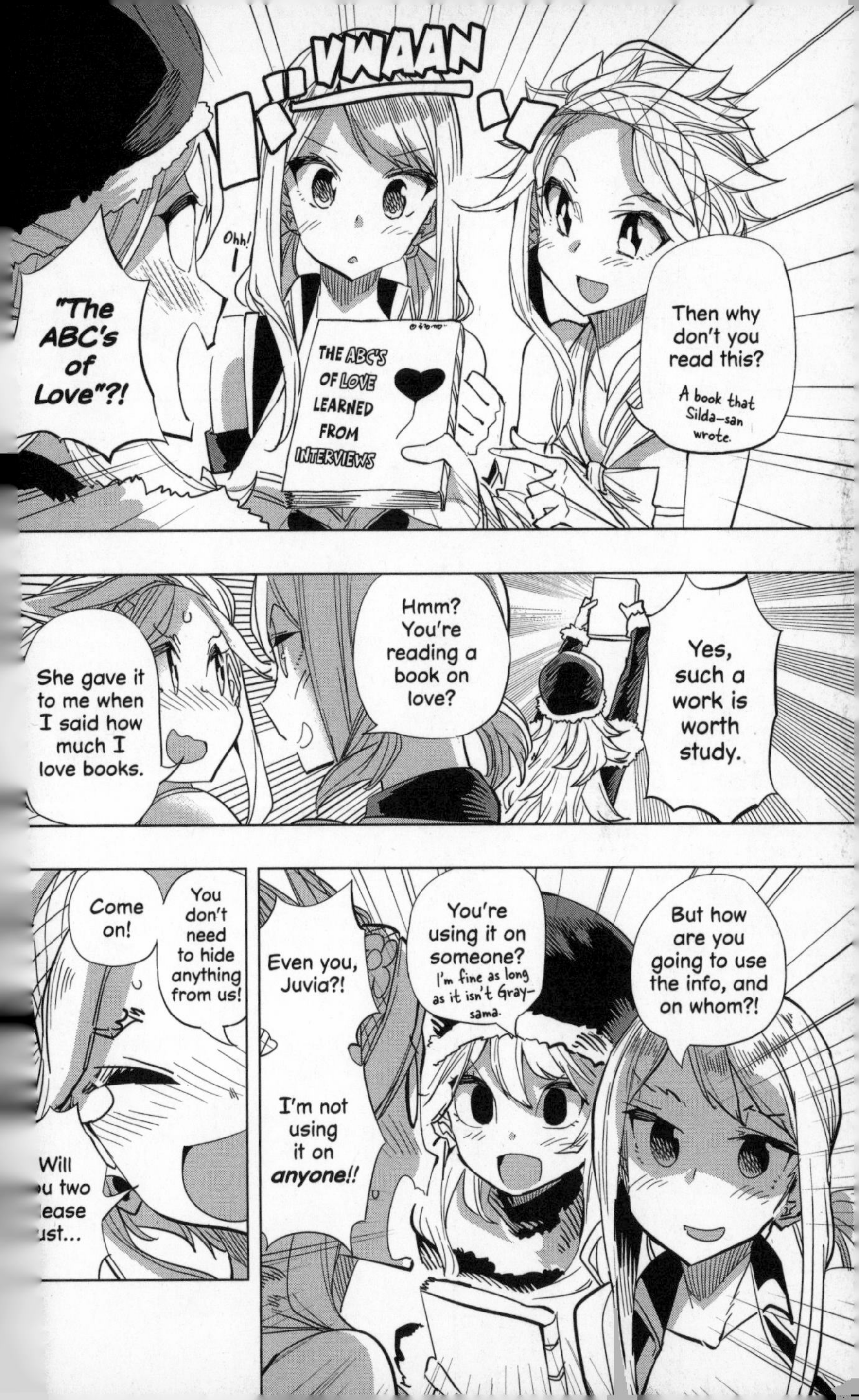
...VWAAN
Then why don't you read this?
A book that Silda-san wrote.
THE ABC'S OF LOVE LEARNED FROM INTERVIEWS
Ohh!
"The ABC's of Love"?!
Yes, such a work is worth study.
Hmm? You're reading a book on love?
She gave it to me when I said how much I love books.
But how are you going to use the info, and on whom?!
You're using it on someone?
I'm fine as long as it isn't Gray-sama.
Even you, Juvia?!
I'm not using it on *anyone*!!
You don't need to hide anything from us!
Come on!
Will
u two
ease
ust...

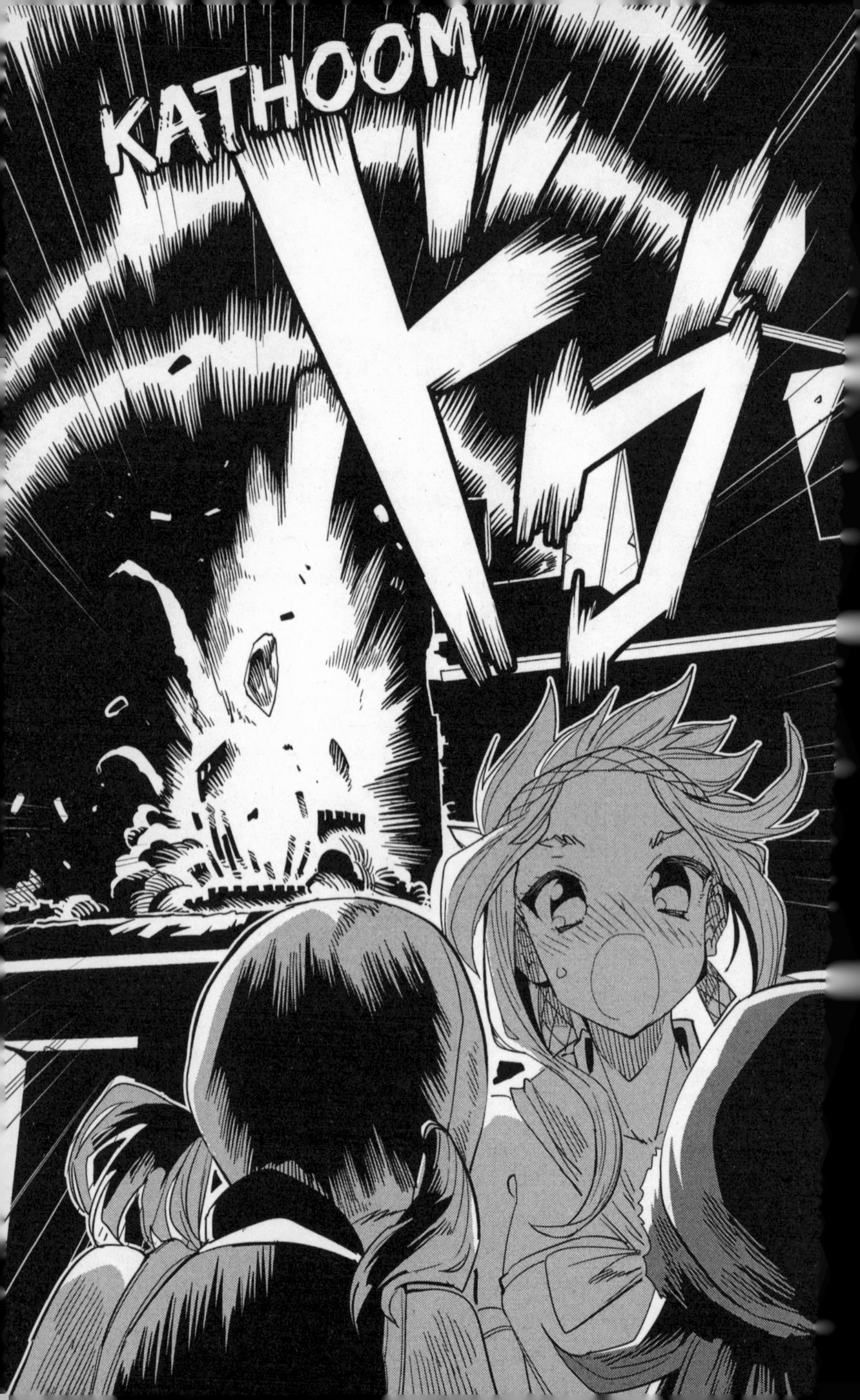
KATHOOM

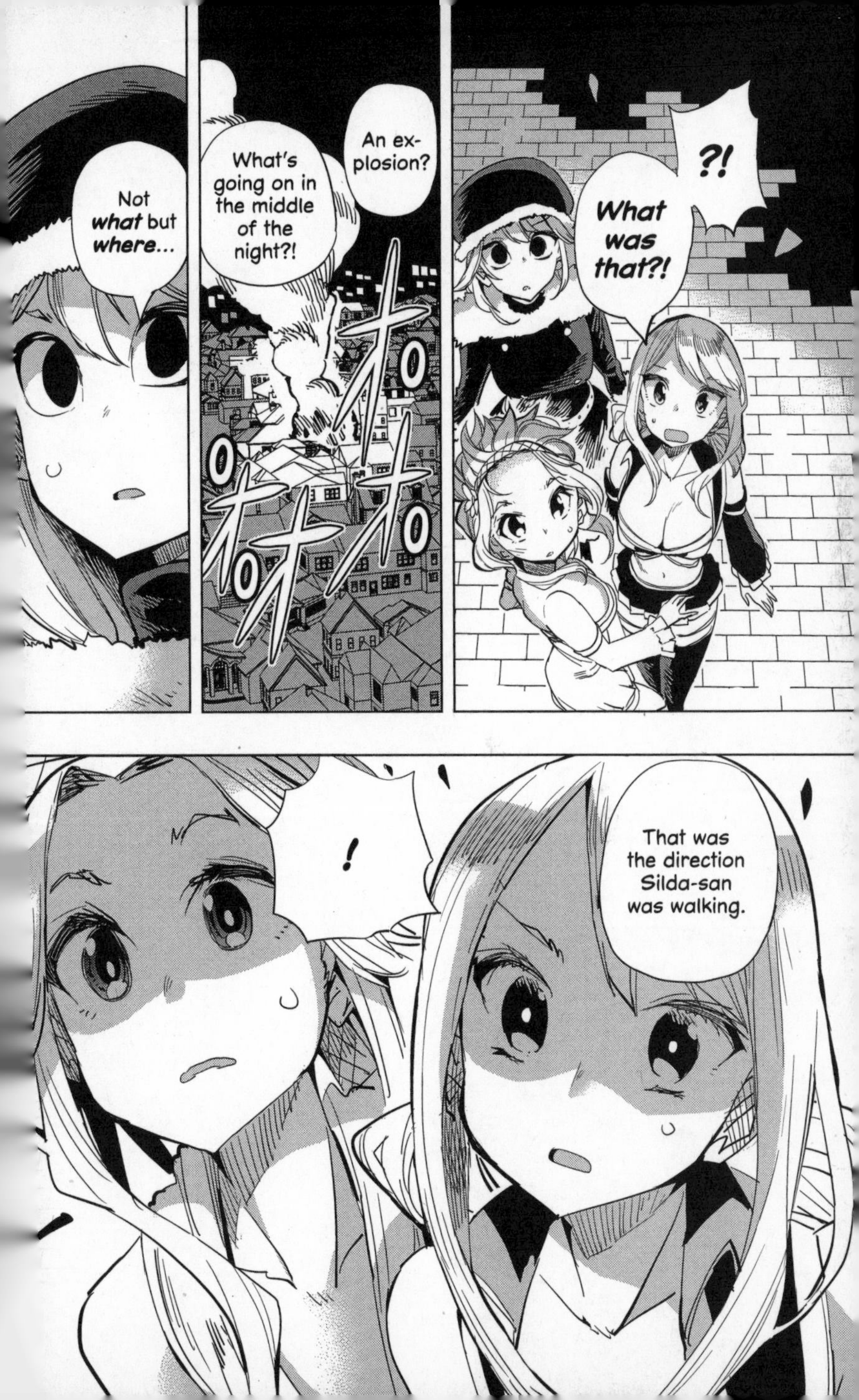

?!
What was that?!
An explosion?
What's going on in the middle of the night?!
Not *what* but *where...*
That was the direction Silda-san was walking.
!

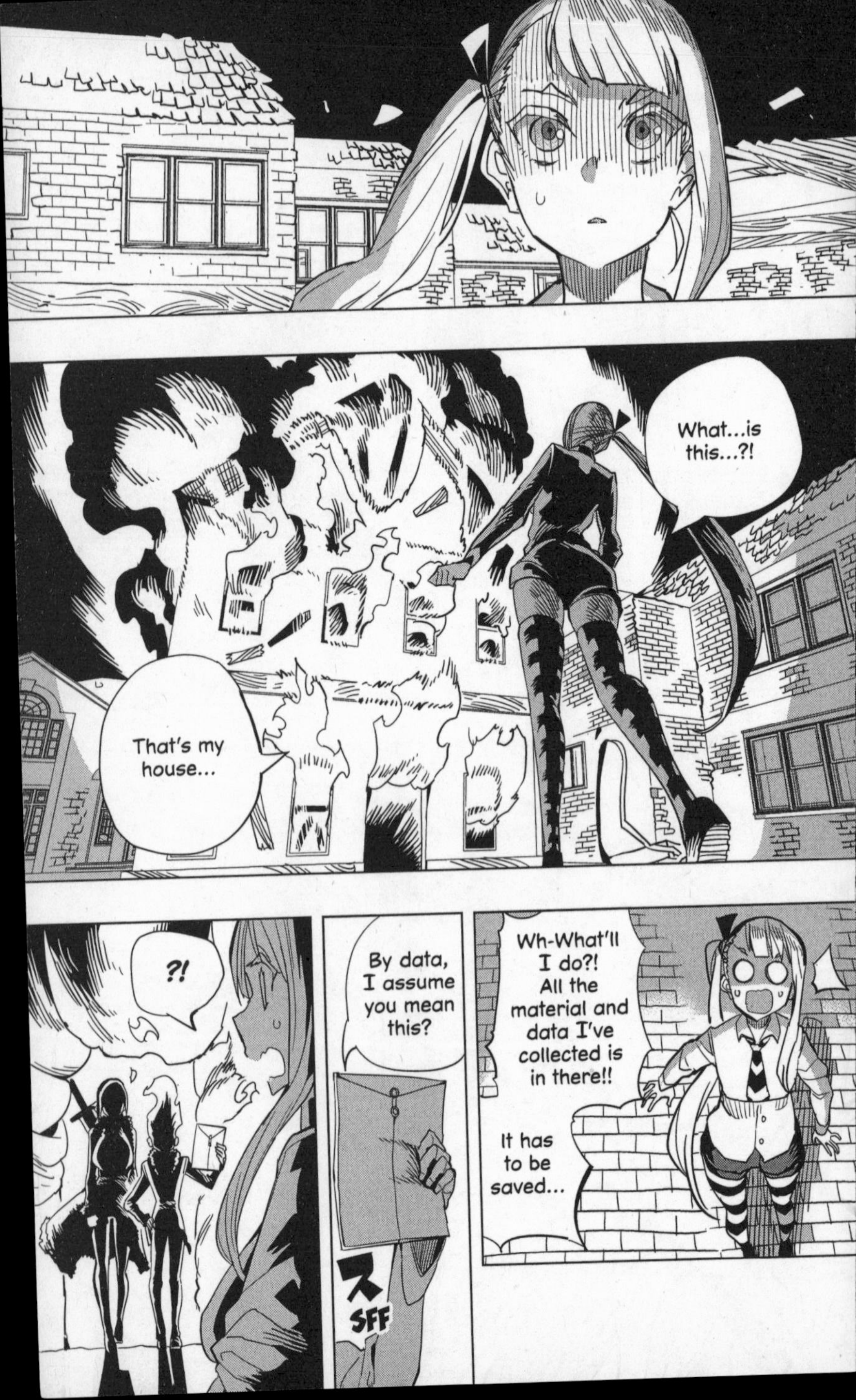
What...is this...?!
That's my house...
Wh-What'll I do?! All the material and data I've collected is in there!!
It has to be saved...
By data, I assume you mean this?
ス
SFF
?!

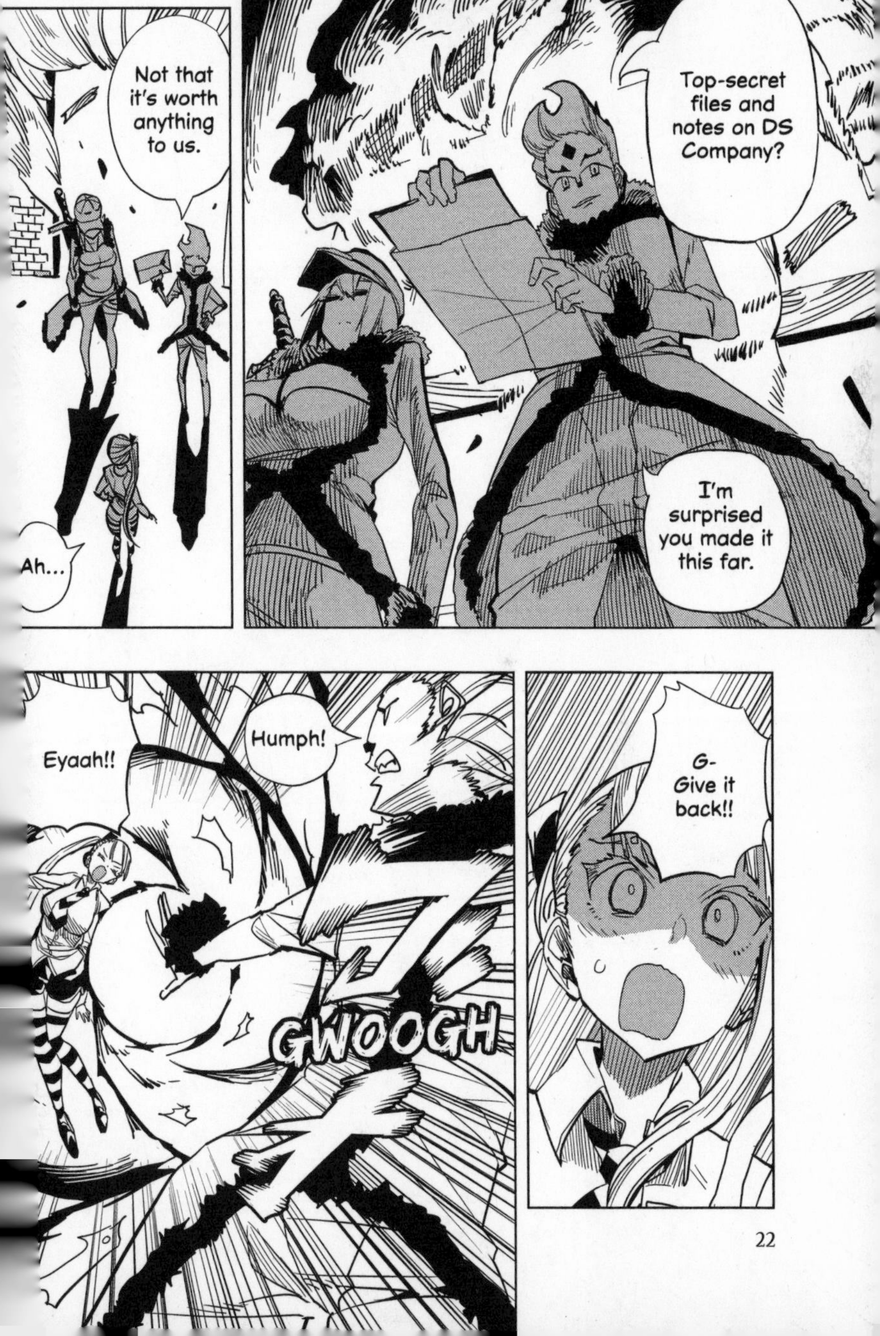
Top-secret files and notes on DS Company?
I'm surprised you made it this far.
Not that it's worth anything to us.
Ah...
G- Give it back!!
Humph!
Eyaah!!
GWOOGH

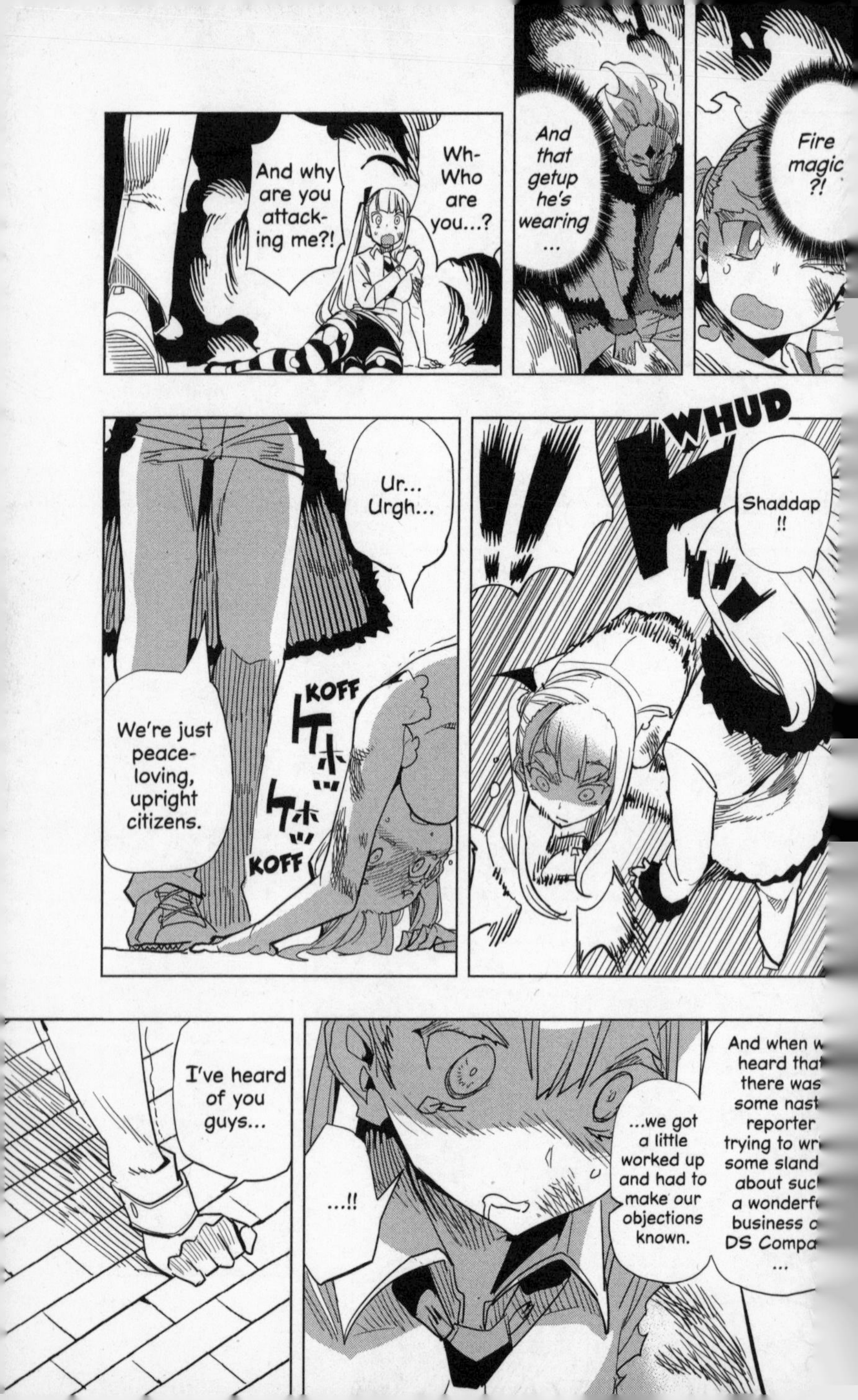
Fire magic?!
And that getup he's wearing ...
Wh- Who are you...?
And why are you attack-ing me?!
WHUD
Shaddap!!
Ur... Urgh...
KOFF
We're just peace-loving, upright citizens.
KOFF
And when w heard tha there was some nast reporter trying to wr some sland about suc a wonderf business c DS Compa ...
...we got a little worked up and had to make our objections known.
...!!
I've heard of you guys...

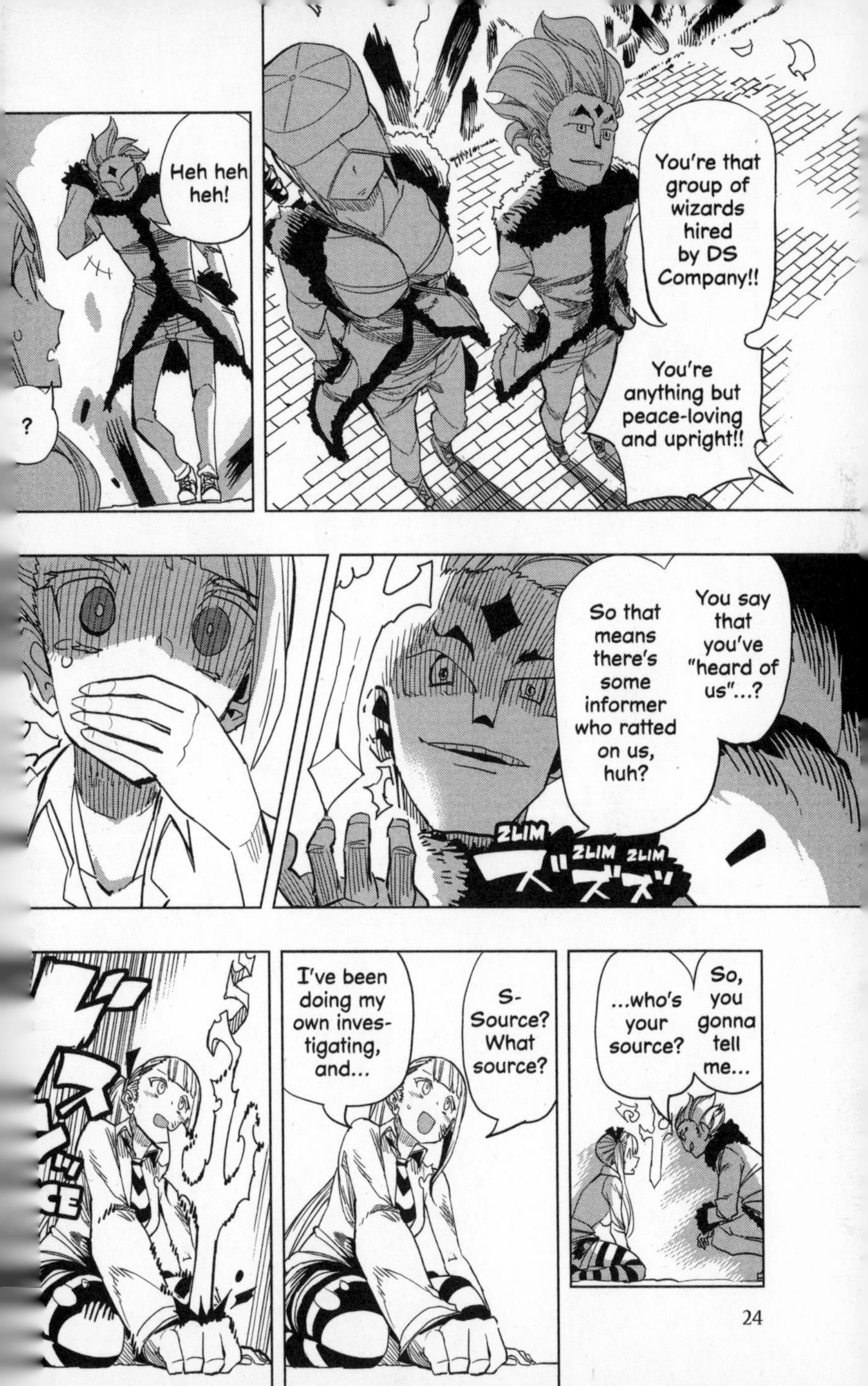
You're that group of wizards hired by DS Company!!
You're anything but peace-loving and upright!!
Heh heh heh!
?
You say that you've "heard of us"...?
So that means there's some informer who ratted on us, huh?
ZLIM
ZLIM ZLIM
So, you gonna tell me...
...who's your source?
S-Source? What source?
I've been doing my own inves-tigating, and...

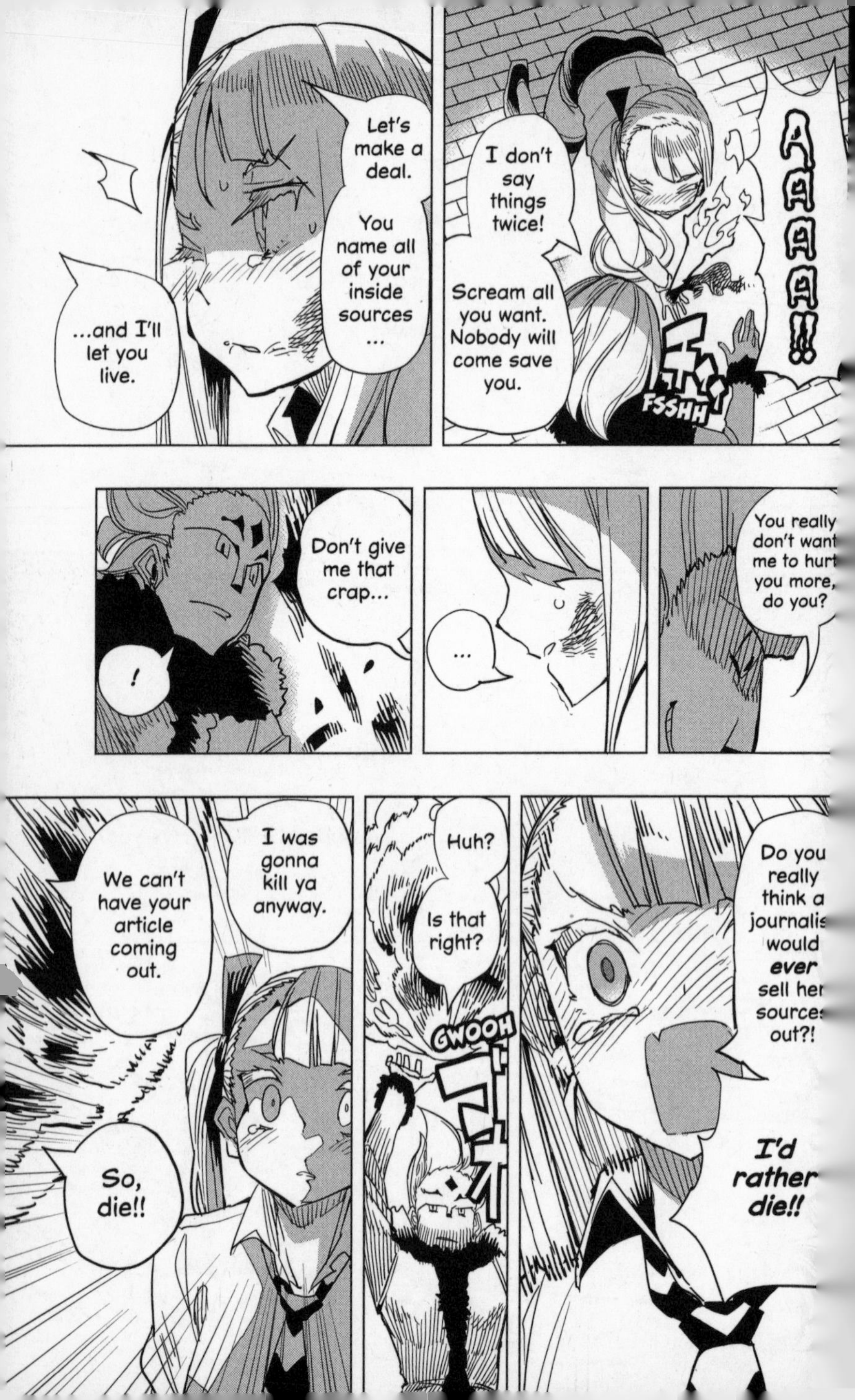
AAAAA!!
FSSHH
I don't say things twice!
Scream all you want. Nobody will come save you.
Let's make a deal.
You name all of your inside sources ...
...and I'll let you live.
You really don't want me to hurt you more, do you?
...
Don't give me that crap...
!
Do you really think a journalist would *ever* sell her sources out?!
I'd rather die!!
Huh?
Is that right?
GWOOH
I was gonna kill ya anyway.
We can't have your article coming out.
So, die!!

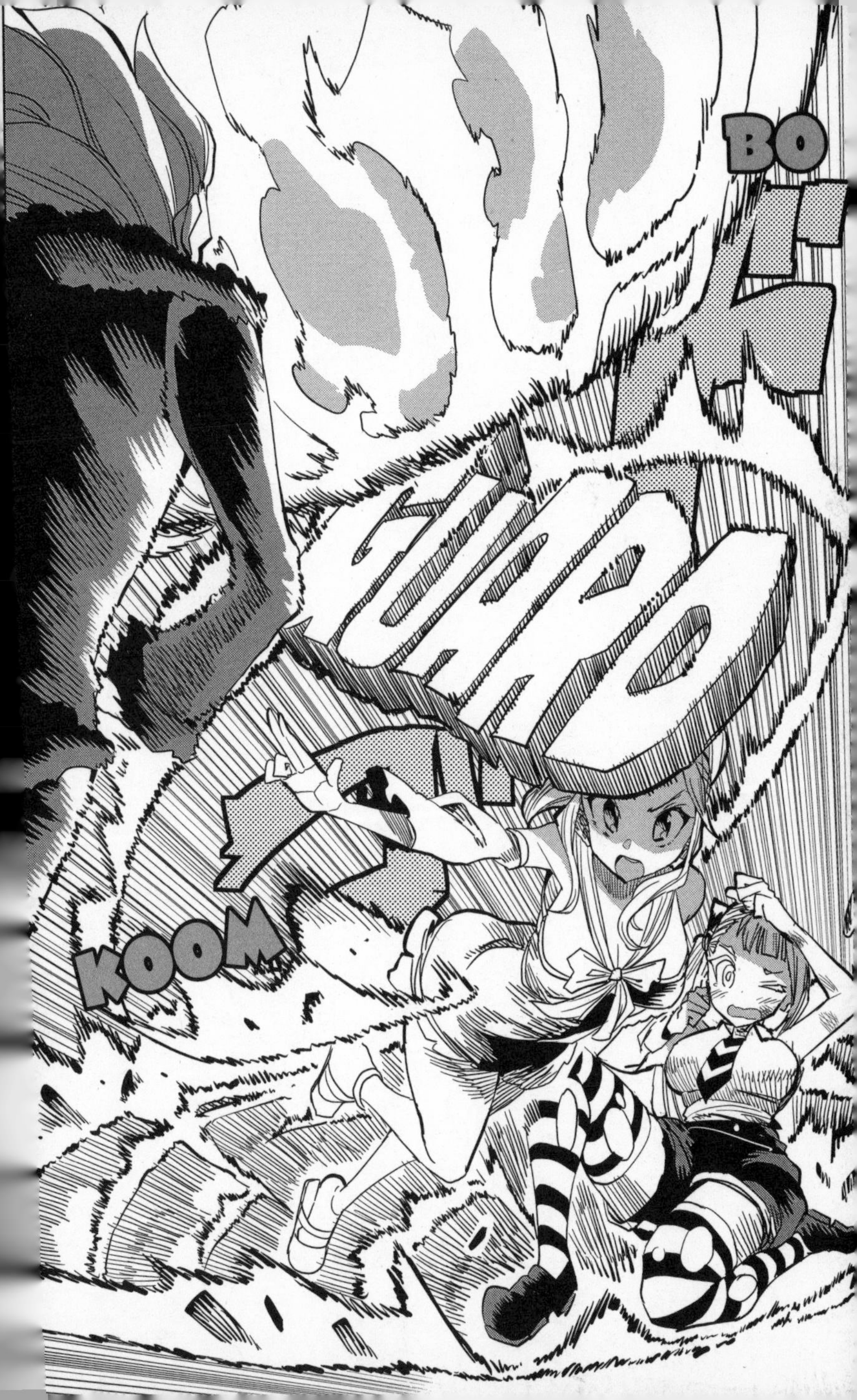
BO
KOOM

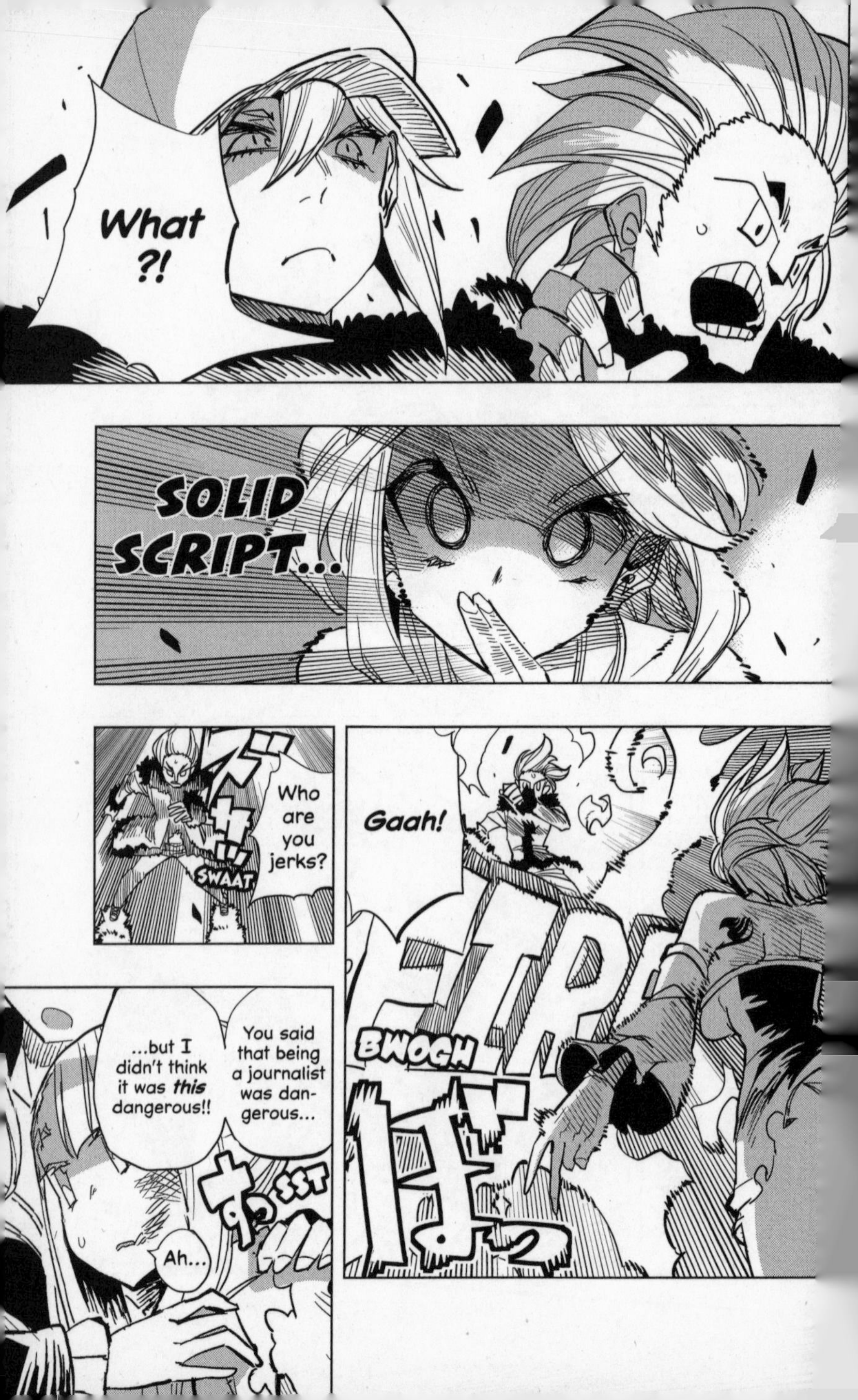
What ?!
SOLID SCRIPT...
Gaah!
BWOGH
Who are you jerks?
SWAAT
You said that being a journalist was dangerous...
...but I didn't think it was *this* dangerous!!
SST
Ah...

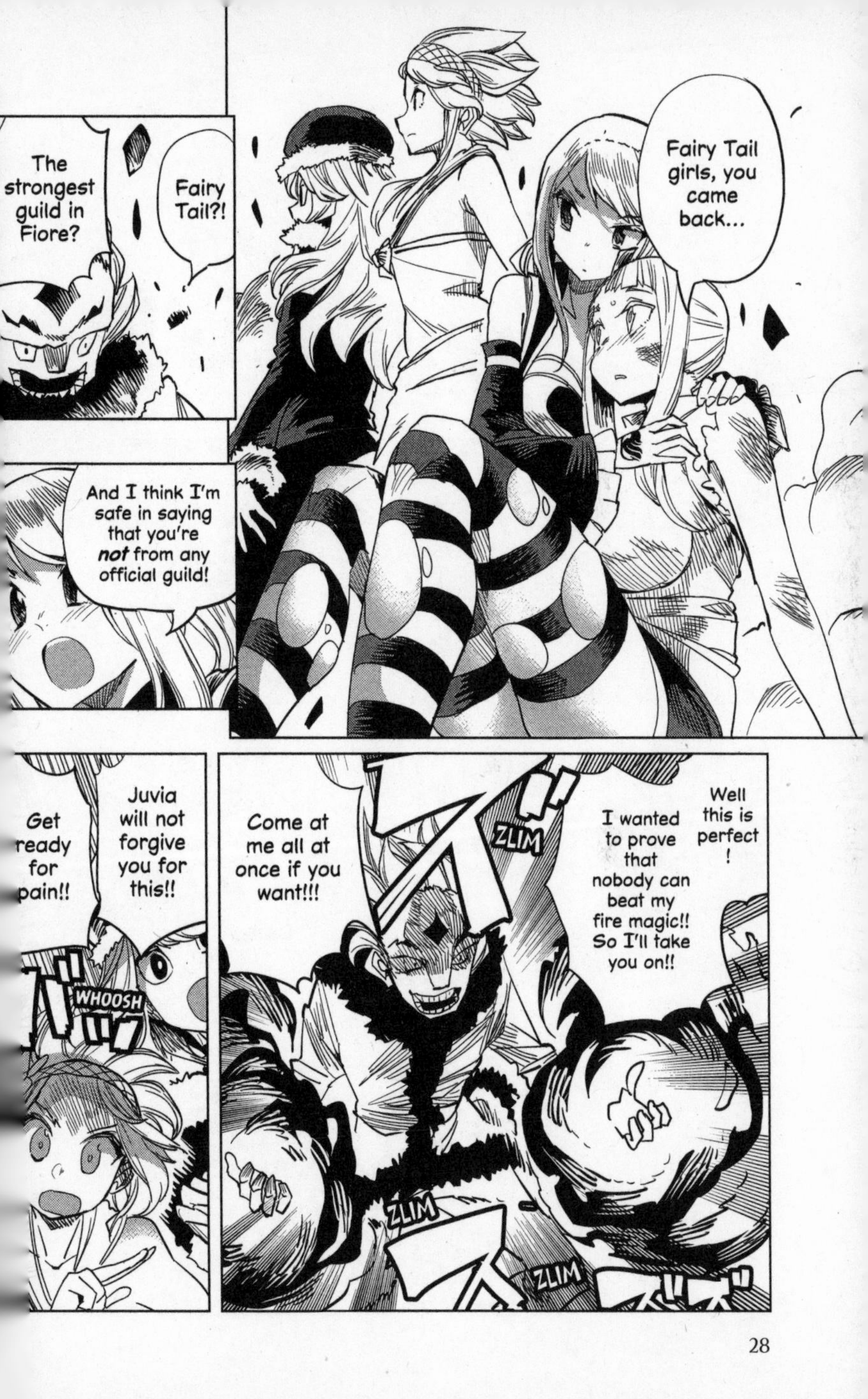
Fairy Tail girls, you came back...
Fairy Tail?!
The strongest guild in Fiore?
And I think I'm safe in saying that you're **not** from any official guild!
Well this is perfect!
I wanted to prove that nobody can beat my fire magic!! So I'll take you on!!
Come at me all at once if you want!!!
ZLIM
ZLIM
ZLIM
Juvia will not forgive you for this!!
Get ready for pain!!
WHOOSH

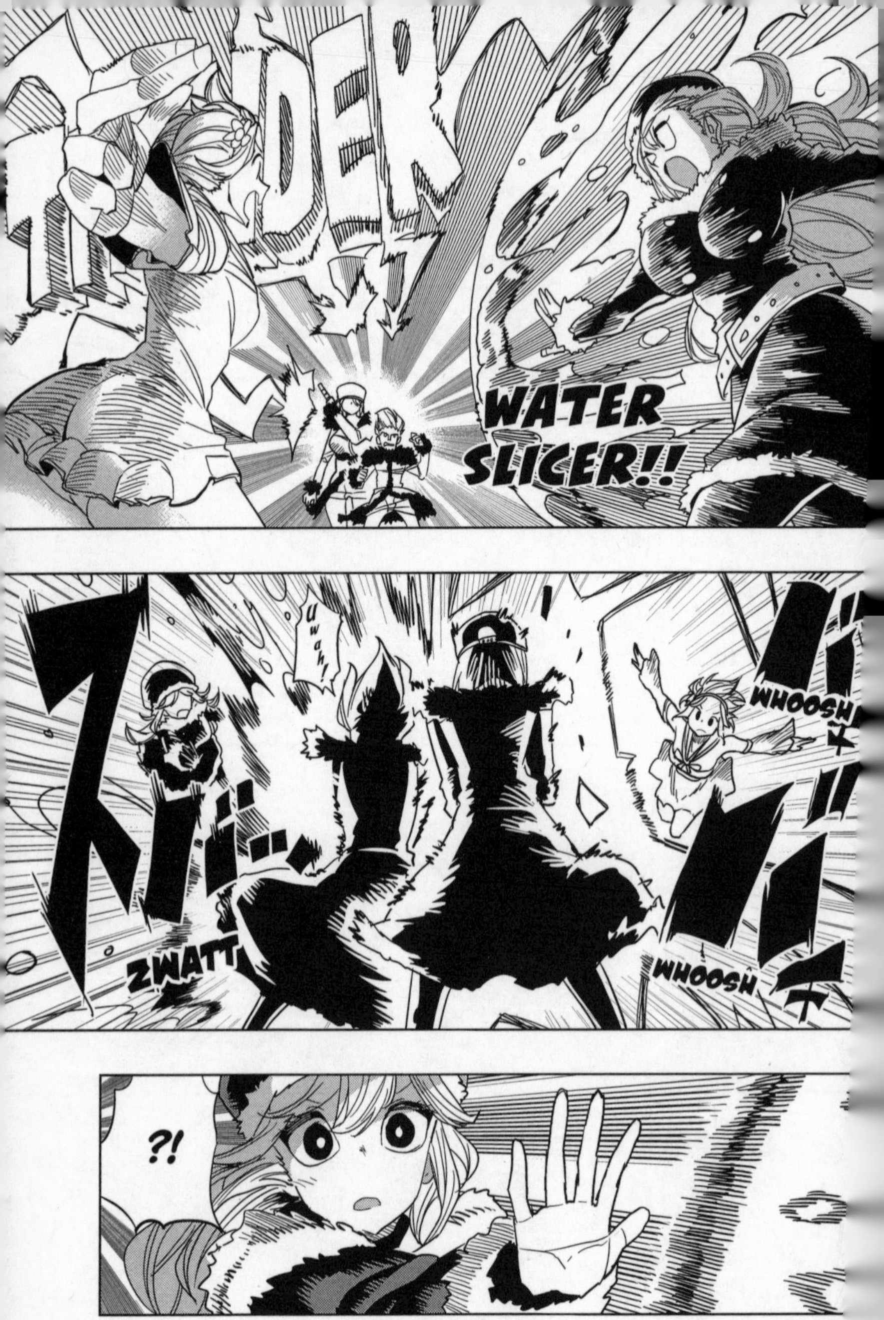
WATER SLICER!!
WHOOSH
WHOOSH
Uwah!
ZWATT
?!

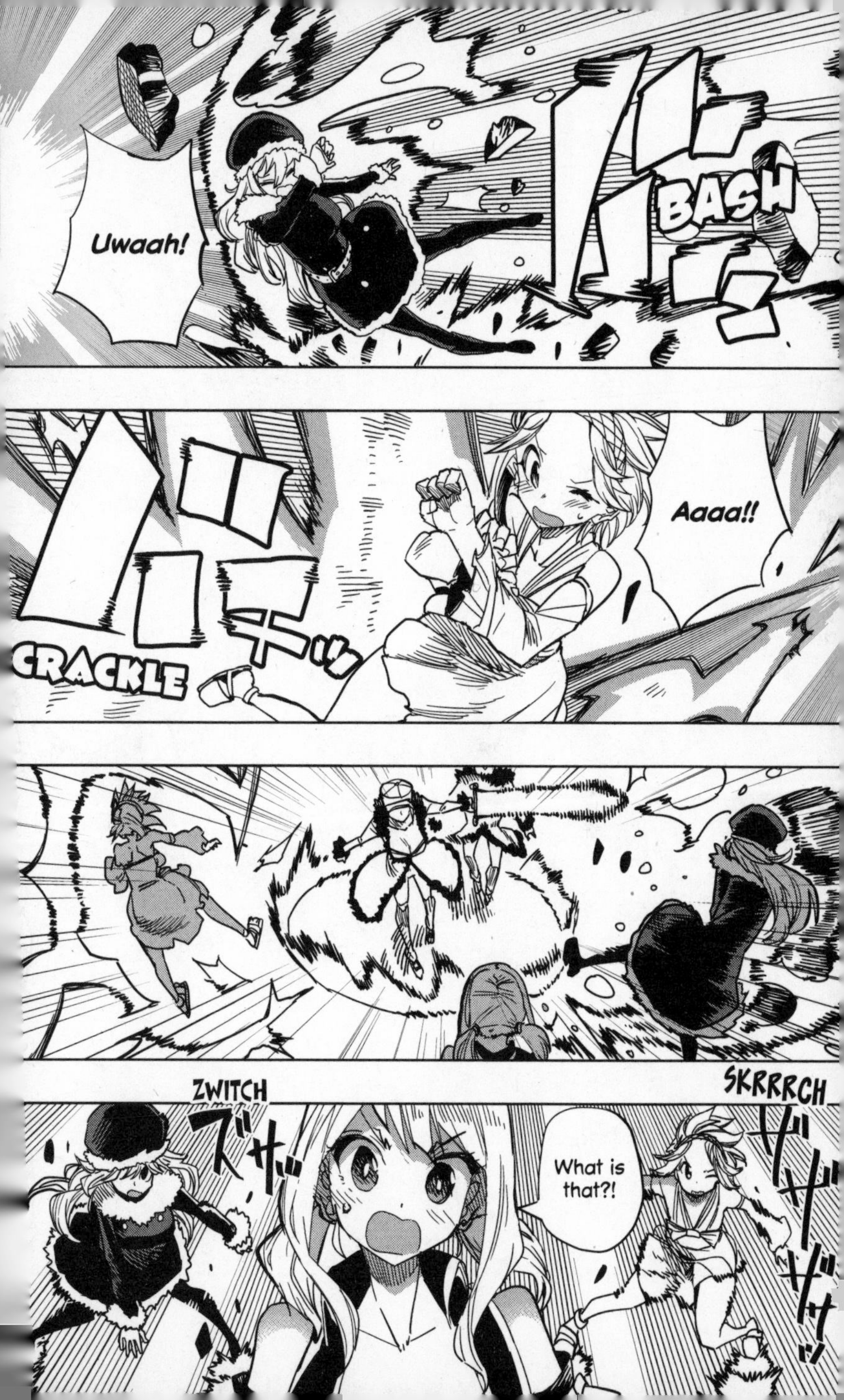
BASH
Uwaah!
Aaaa!!
CRACKLE
SKRRRCH
What is that?!
ZWITCH

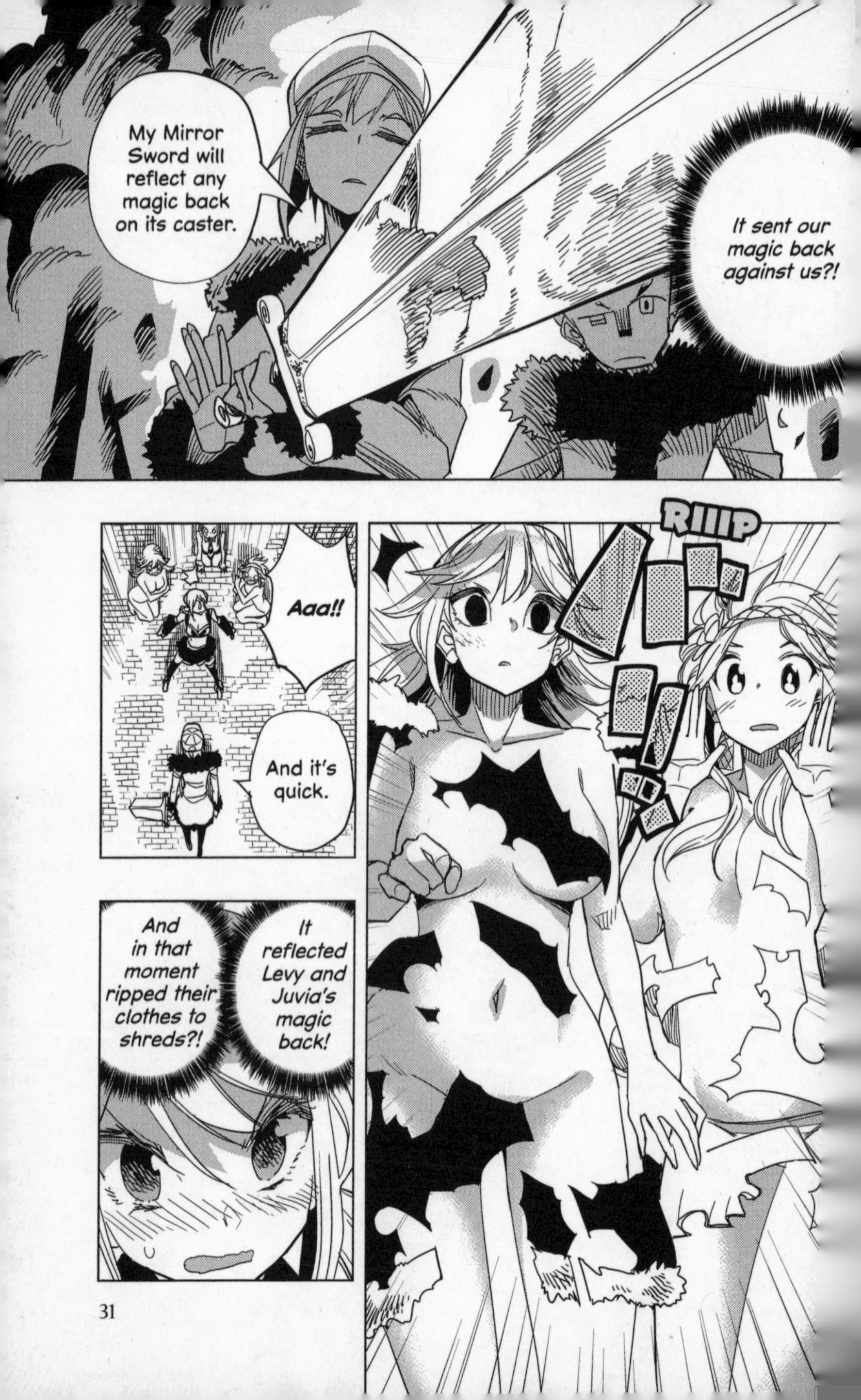
My Mirror Sword will reflect any magic back on its caster.
It sent our magic back against us?!
RIIIP
Aaa!!
And it's quick.
It reflected Levy and Juvia's magic back!
And in that moment ripped their clothes to shreds?!

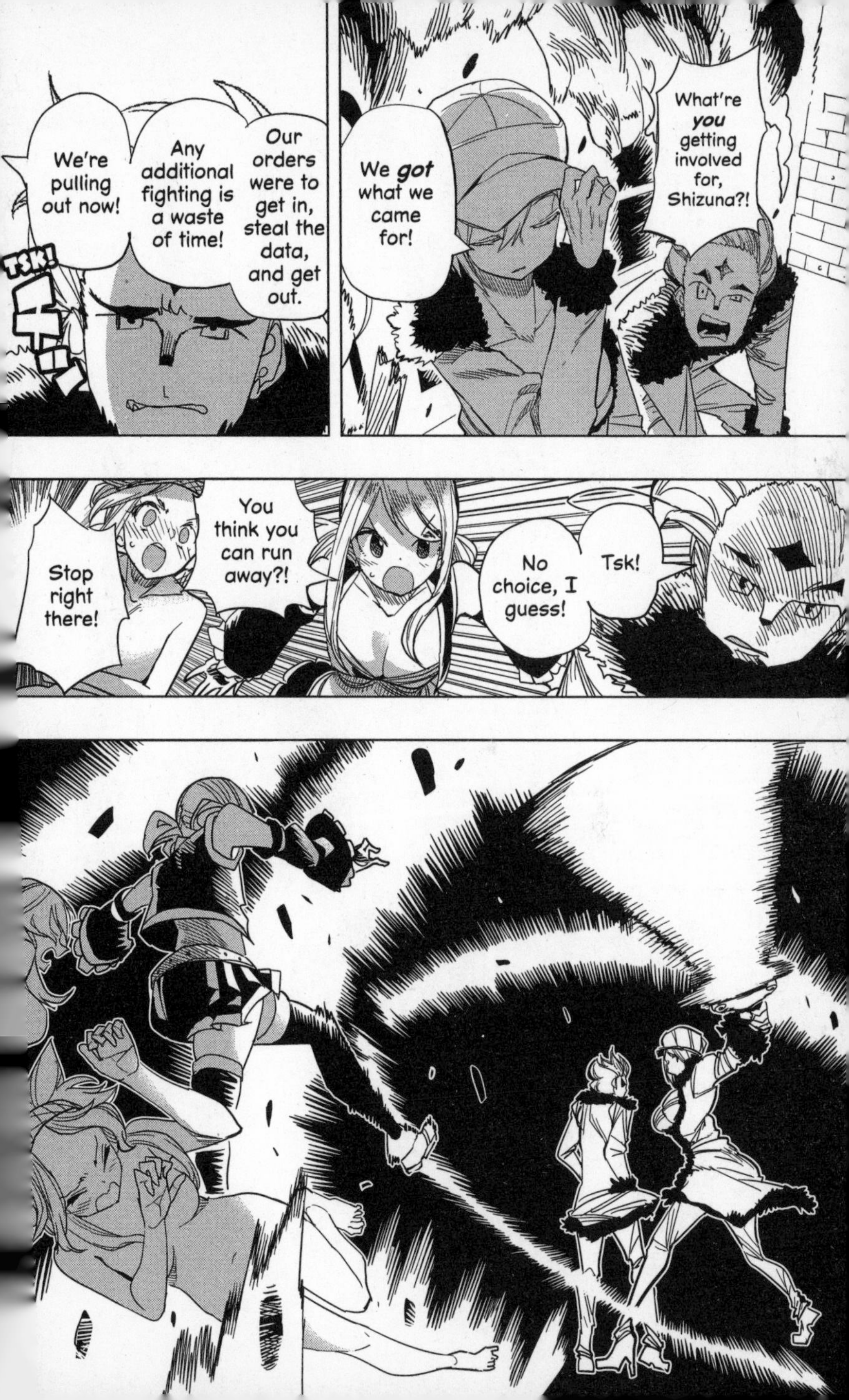
What're *you* getting involved for, Shizuna?!
We *got* what we came for!
Our orders were to get in, steal the data, and get out.
Any additional fighting is a waste of time!
We're pulling out now!
TSK!
Tsk!
No choice, I guess!
You think you can run away?!
Stop right there!

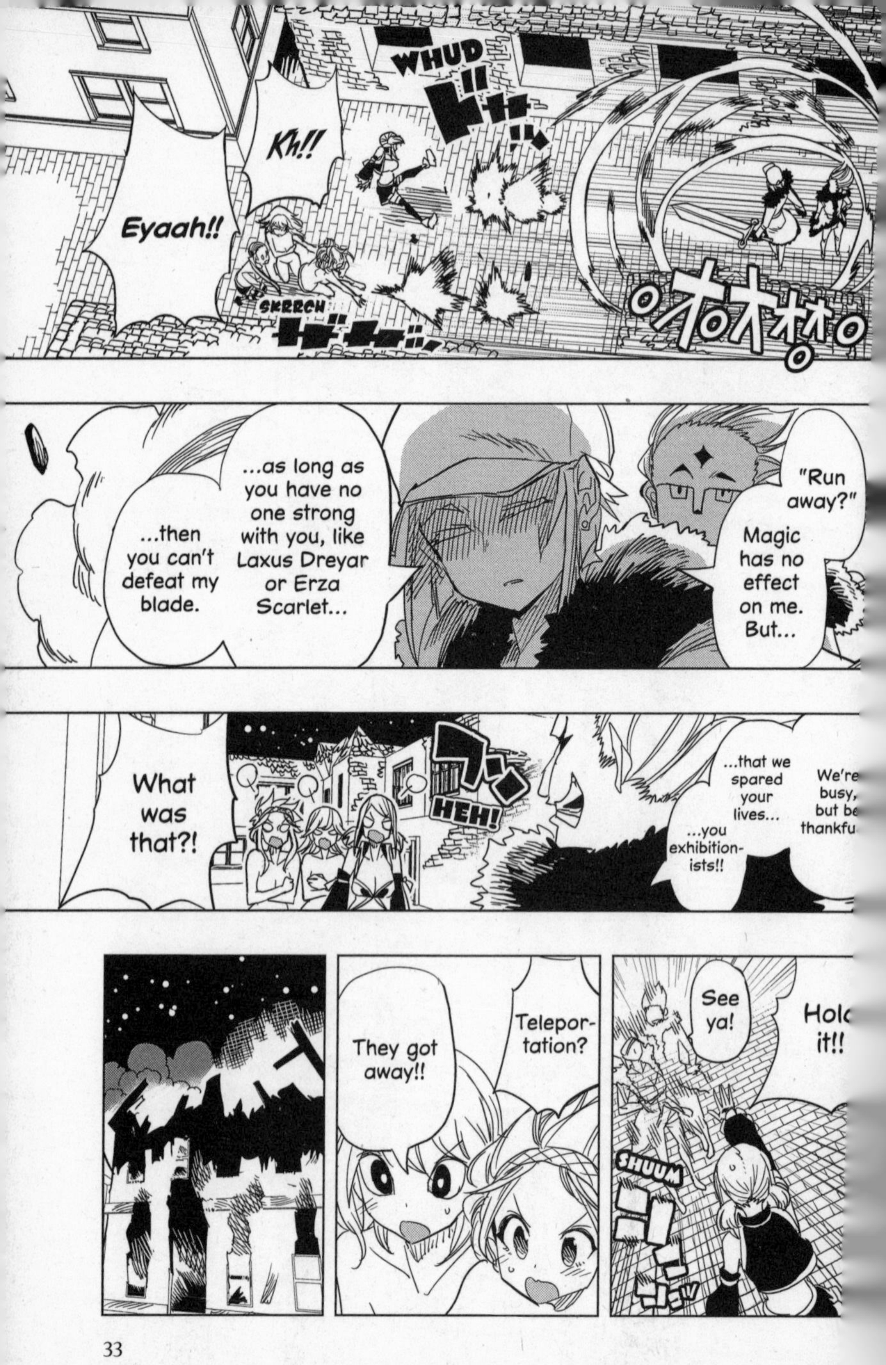

WHUD
Kh!!
Eyaah!!
SKRRCH
"Run away?" Magic has no effect on me. But...
...as long as you have no one strong with you, like Laxus Dreyar or Erza Scarlet...
...then you can't defeat my blade.
We're busy, but be thankfu
...that we spared your lives...
...you exhibition-ists!!
HEH!
What was that?!
Hol it!!
See ya!
SHUUM
Telepor-tation?
They got away!!

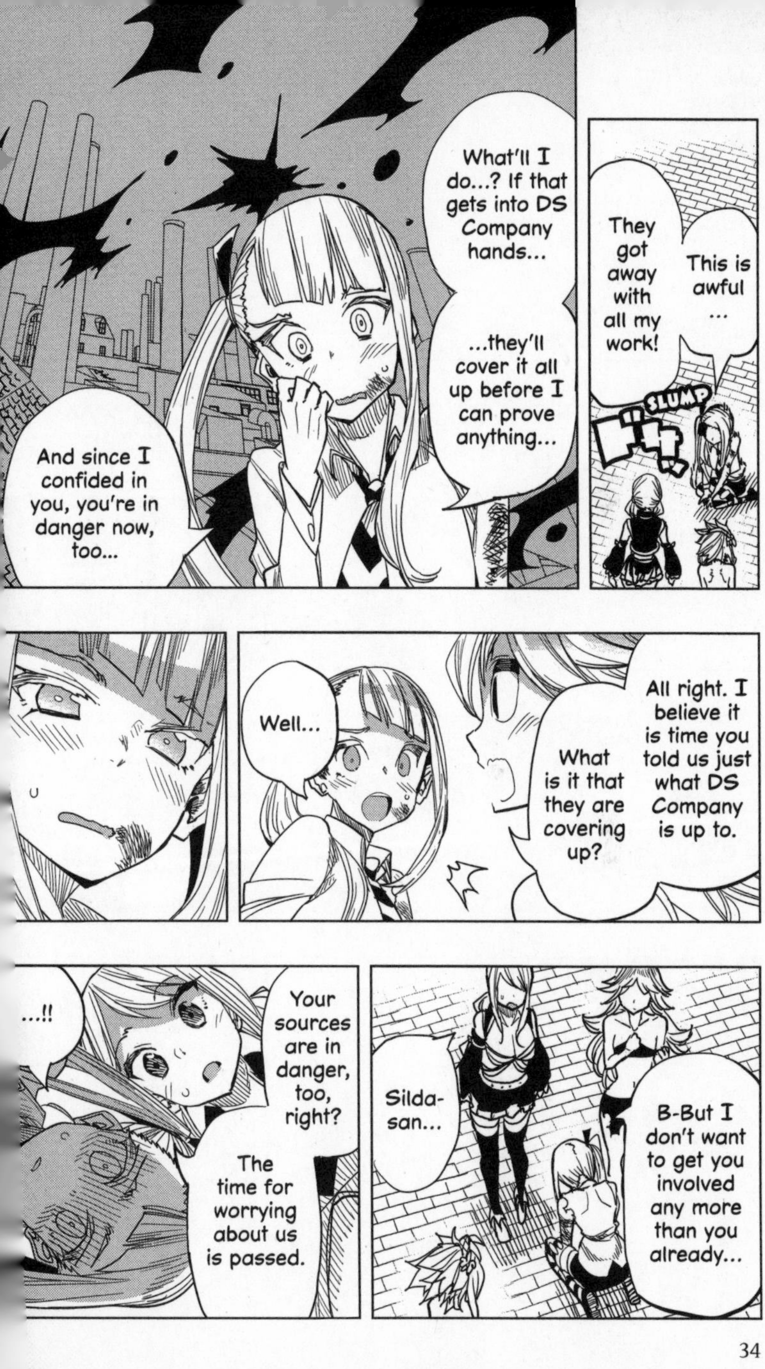
This is awful ...
They got away with all my work!
SLUMP
What'll I do...? If that gets into DS Company hands...
...they'll cover it all up before I can prove anything...
And since I confided in you, you're in danger now, too...
All right. I believe it is time you told us just what DS Company is up to.
What is it that they are covering up?
Well...
B-But I don't want to get you involved any more than you already...
Silda-san...
Your sources are in danger, too, right?
The time for worrying about us is passed.
...!!

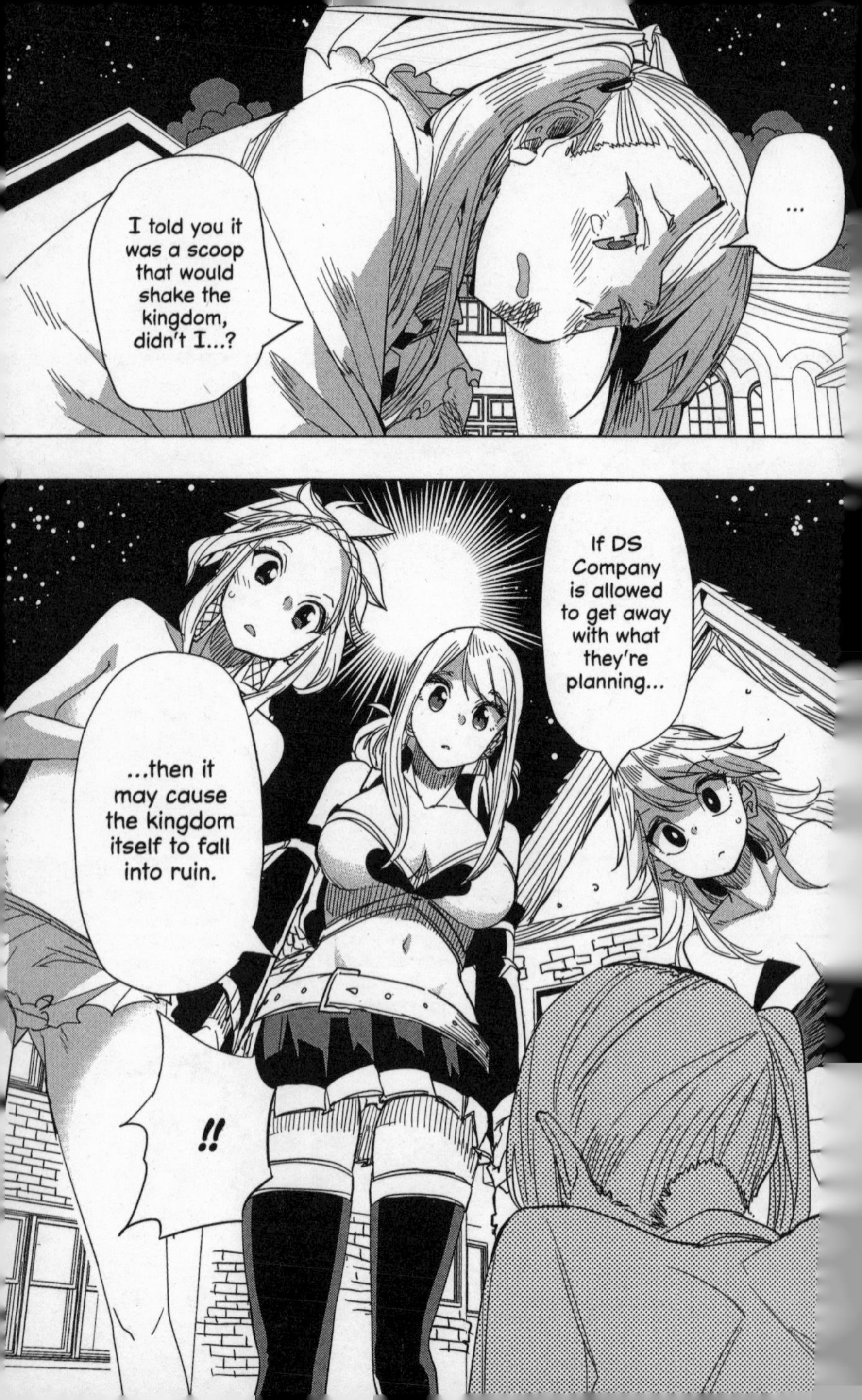
...
I told you it was a scoop that would shake the kingdom, didn't I...?
If DS Company is allowed to get away with what they're planning...
...then it may cause the kingdom itself to fall into ruin.
!!

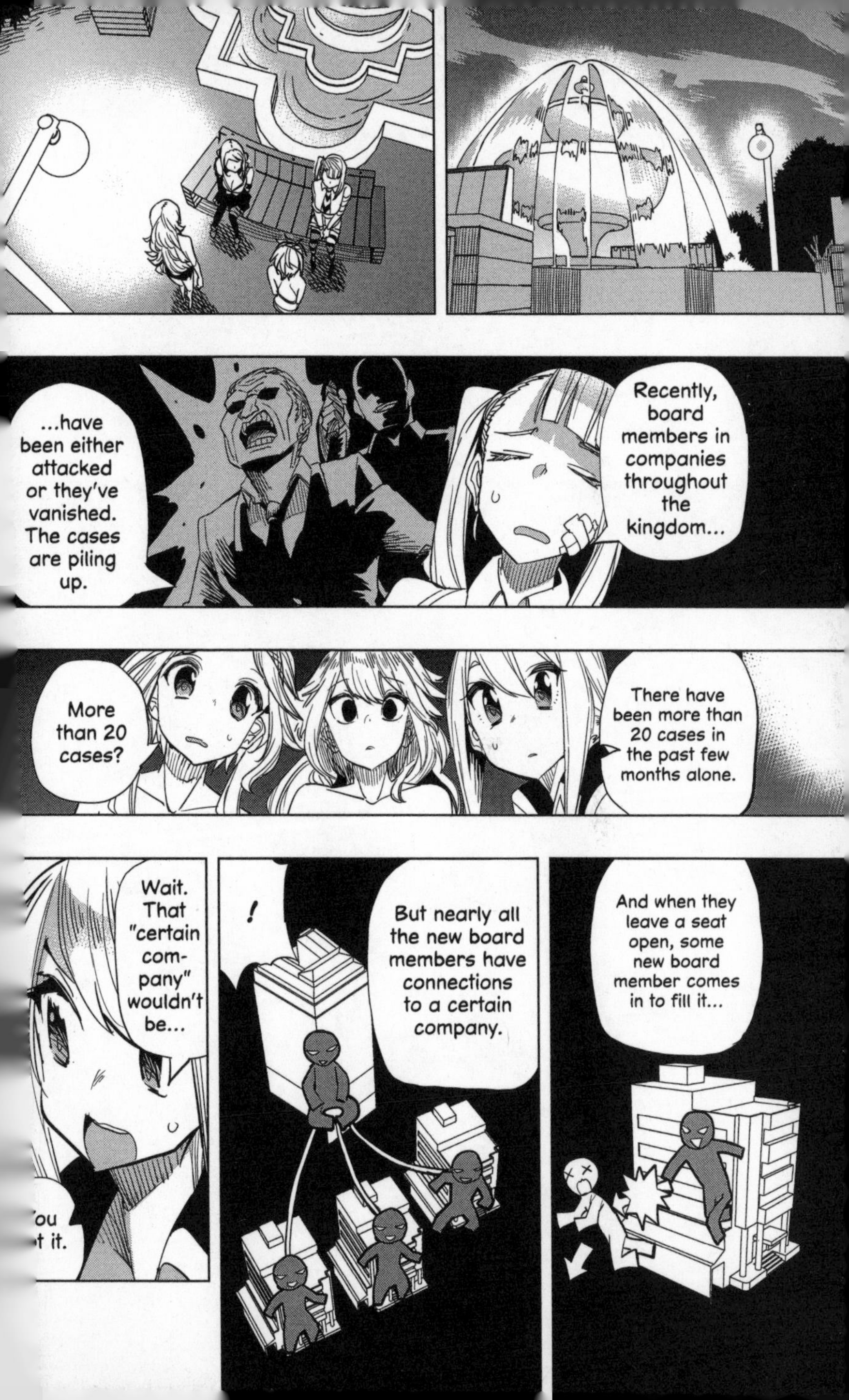
Recently, board members in companies throughout the kingdom...
...have been either attacked or they've vanished. The cases are piling up.
There have been more than 20 cases in the past few months alone.
More than 20 cases?
And when they leave a seat open, some new board member comes in to fill it...
But nearly all the new board members have connections to a certain company.
!
Wait. That "certain company" wouldn't be...

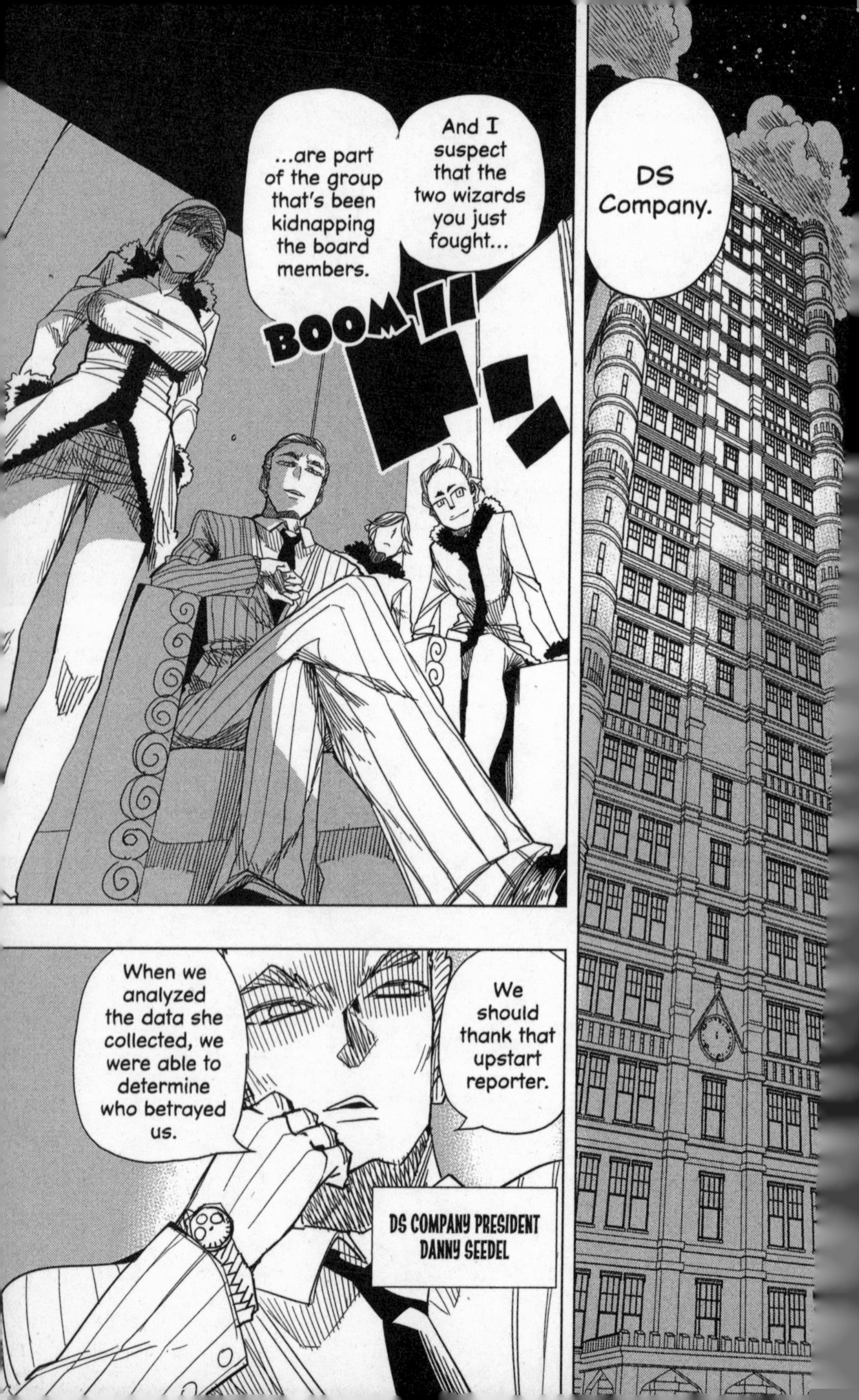
DS Company.
And I suspect that the two wizards you just fought...
...are part of the group that's been kidnapping the board members.
BOOM!!
We should thank that upstart reporter.
When we analyzed the data she collected, we were able to determine who betrayed us.
DS COMPANY PRESIDENT DANNY SEEDEL

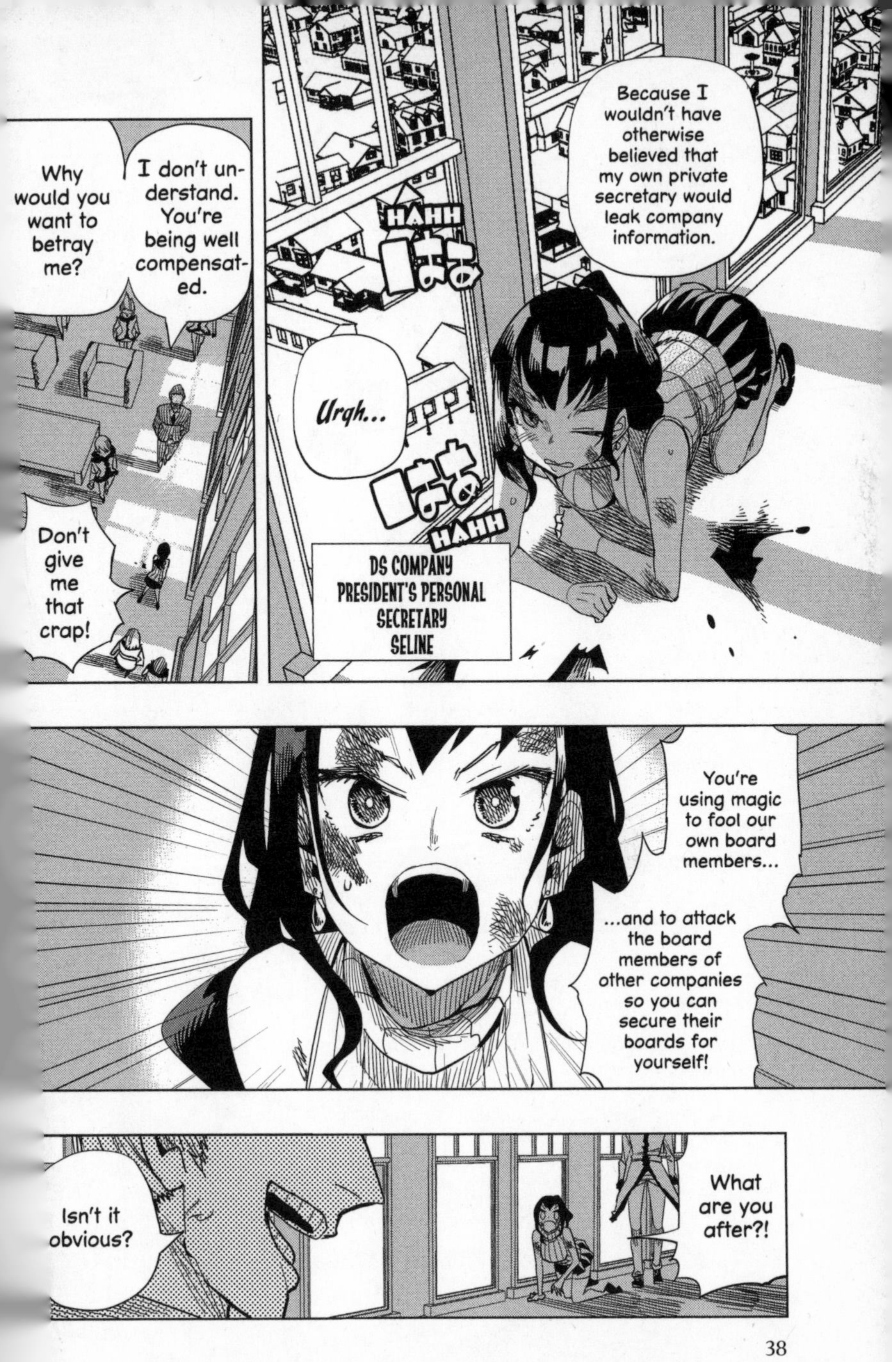

Because I wouldn't have otherwise believed that my own private secretary would leak company information.
HAHH
Urgh...
HAHH
DS COMPANY PRESIDENT'S PERSONAL SECRETARY SELINE
I don't understand. You're being well compensated.
Why would you want to betray me?
Don't give me that crap!
You're using magic to fool our own board members...
...and to attack the board members of other companies so you can secure their boards for yourself!
What are you after?!
Isn't it obvious?

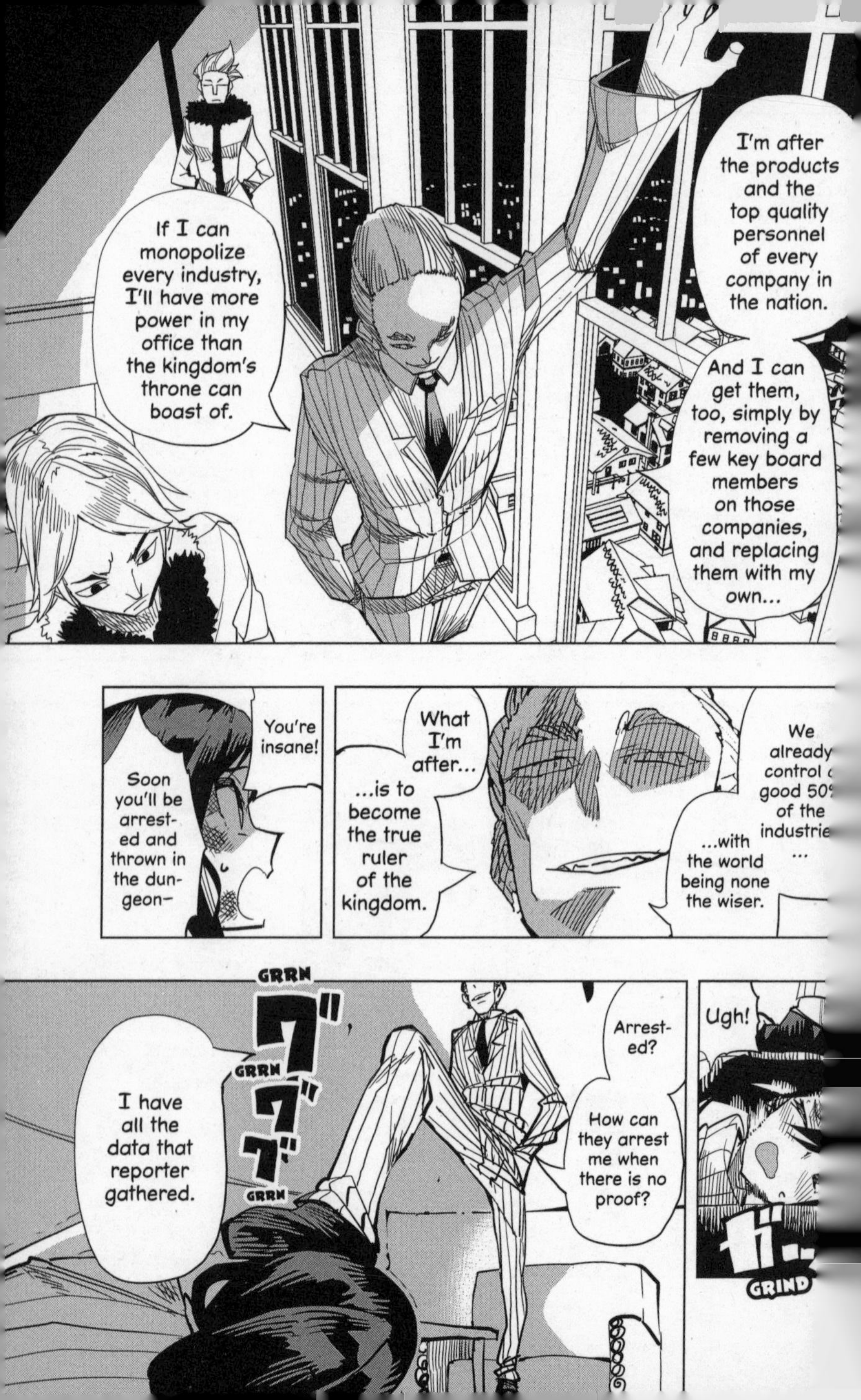
I'm after the products and the top quality personnel of every company in the nation.
And I can get them, too, simply by removing a few key board members on those companies, and replacing them with my own...
If I can monopolize every industry, I'll have more power in my office than the kingdom's throne can boast of.
We already control good 50 of the industrie ...
...with the world being none the wiser.
What I'm after...
...is to become the true ruler of the kingdom.
You're insane!
Soon you'll be arrest-ed and thrown in the dun-geon–
Ugh!
GRIND
Arrest-ed?
How can they arrest me when there is no proof?
GRRN
GRRN
GRRN
I have all the data that reporter gathered.

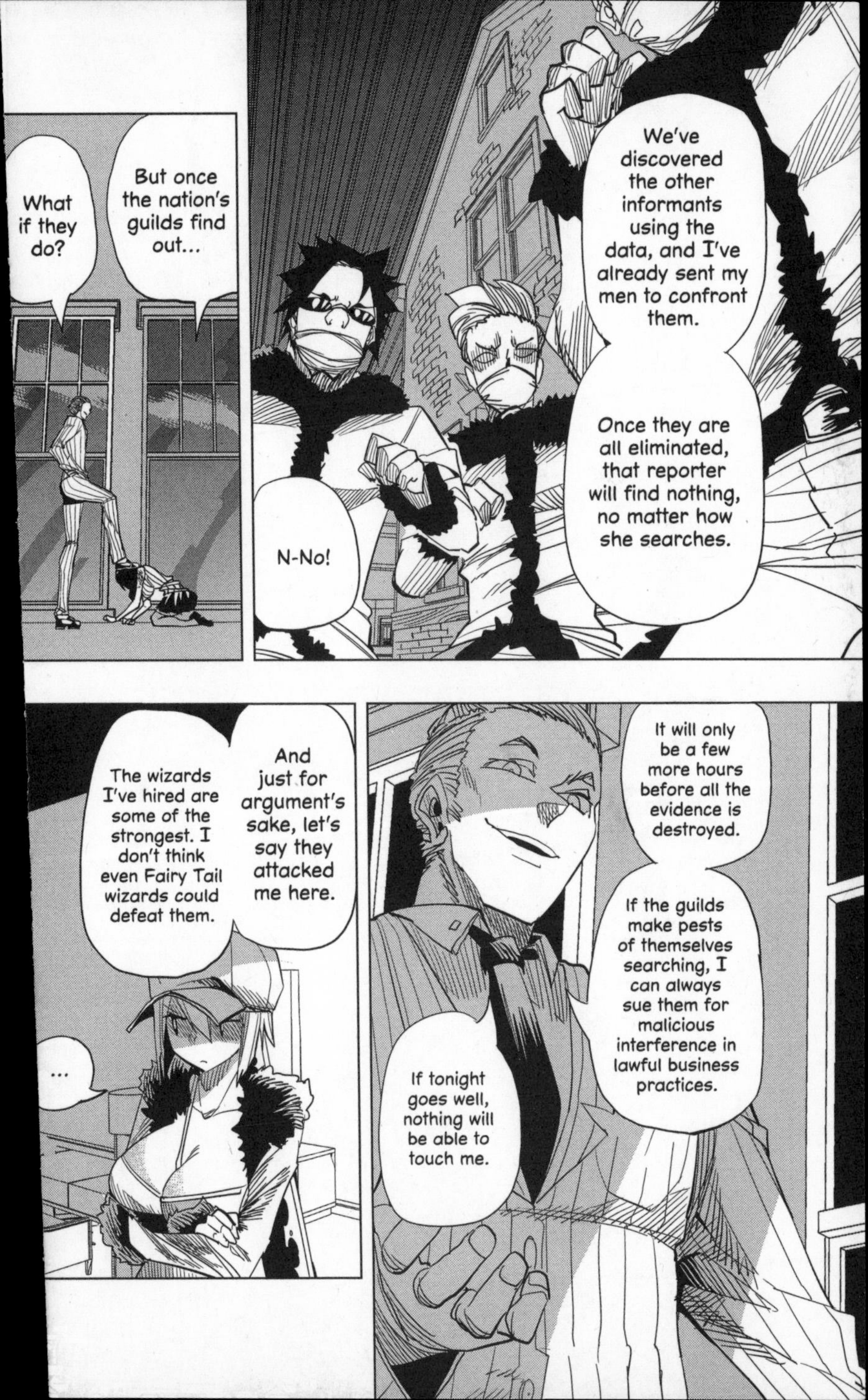
We've discovered the other informants using the data, and I've already sent my men to confront them.
Once they are all eliminated, that reporter will find nothing, no matter how she searches.
N-No!
But once the nation's guilds find out...
What if they do?
It will only be a few more hours before all the evidence is destroyed.
If the guilds make pests of themselves searching, I can always sue them for malicious interference in lawful business practices.
If tonight goes well, nothing will be able to touch me.
And just for argument's sake, let's say they attacked me here.
The wizards I've hired are some of the strongest. I don't think even Fairy Tail wizards could defeat them.
...

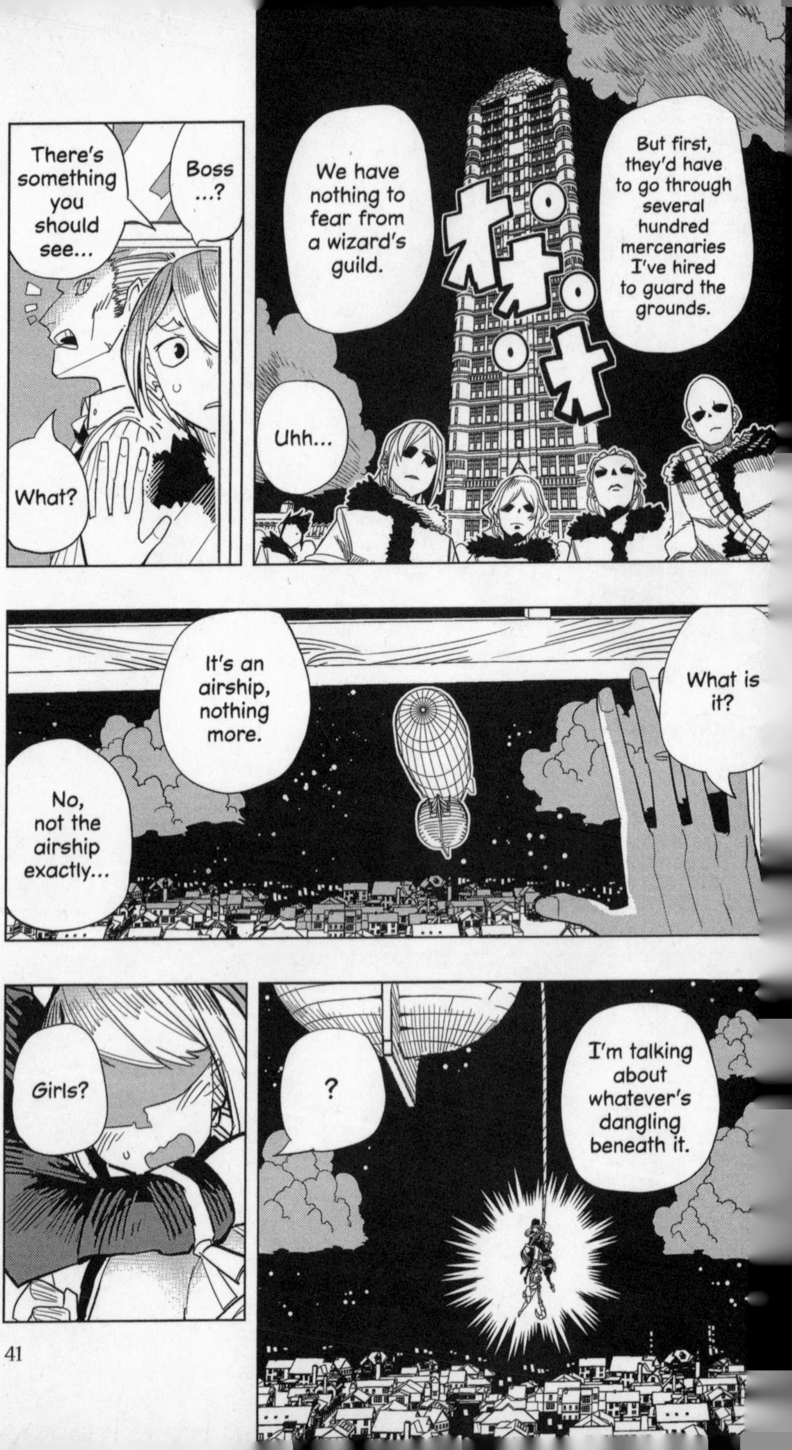
We have nothing to fear from a wizard's guild.
But first, they'd have to go through several hundred mercenaries I've hired to guard the grounds.
Uhh...
Boss ...?
There's something you should see...
What?
What is it?
It's an airship, nothing more.
No, not the airship exactly...
I'm talking about whatever's dangling beneath it.
?
Girls?

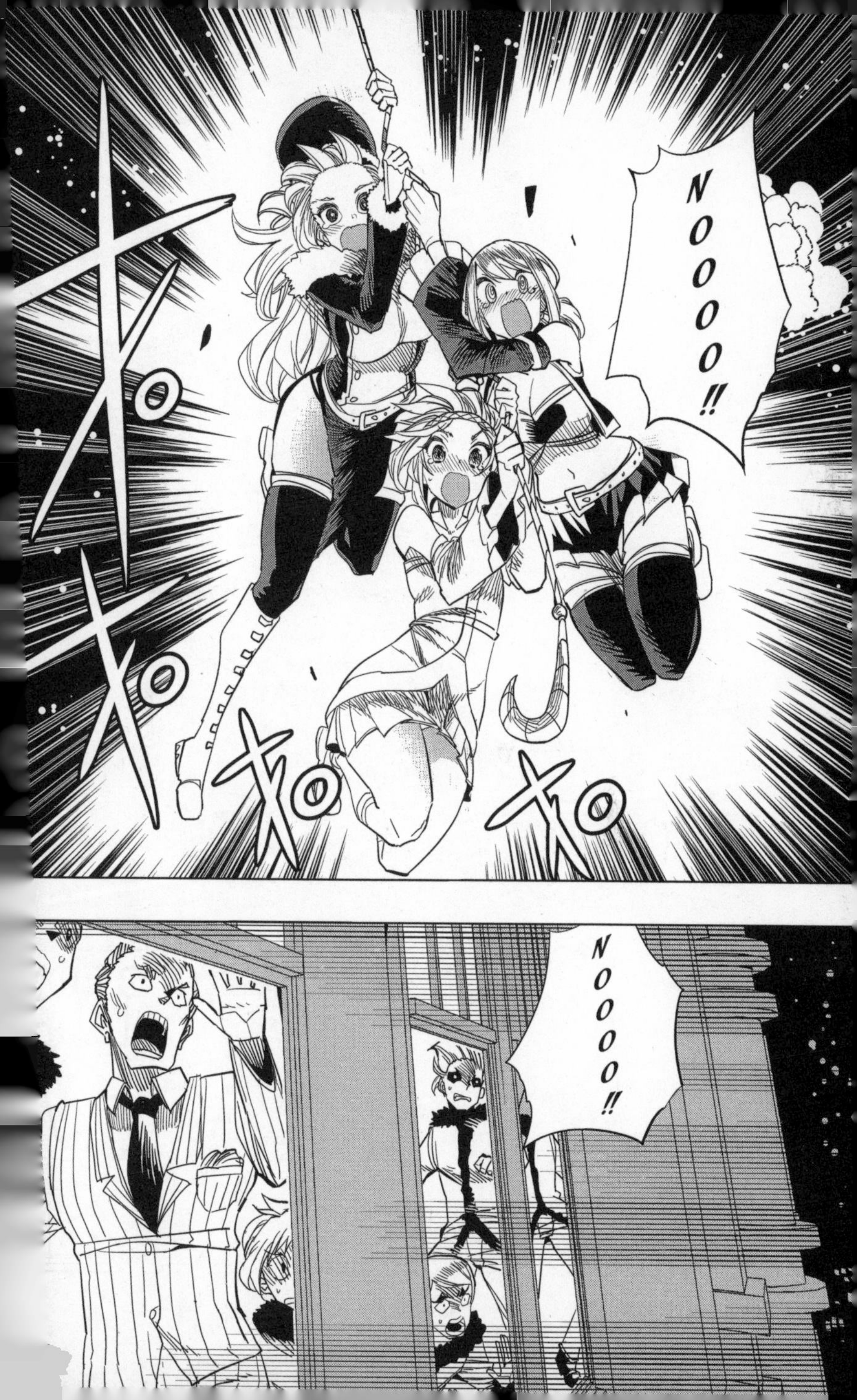
NOOOOO!!
NOOOOO!!

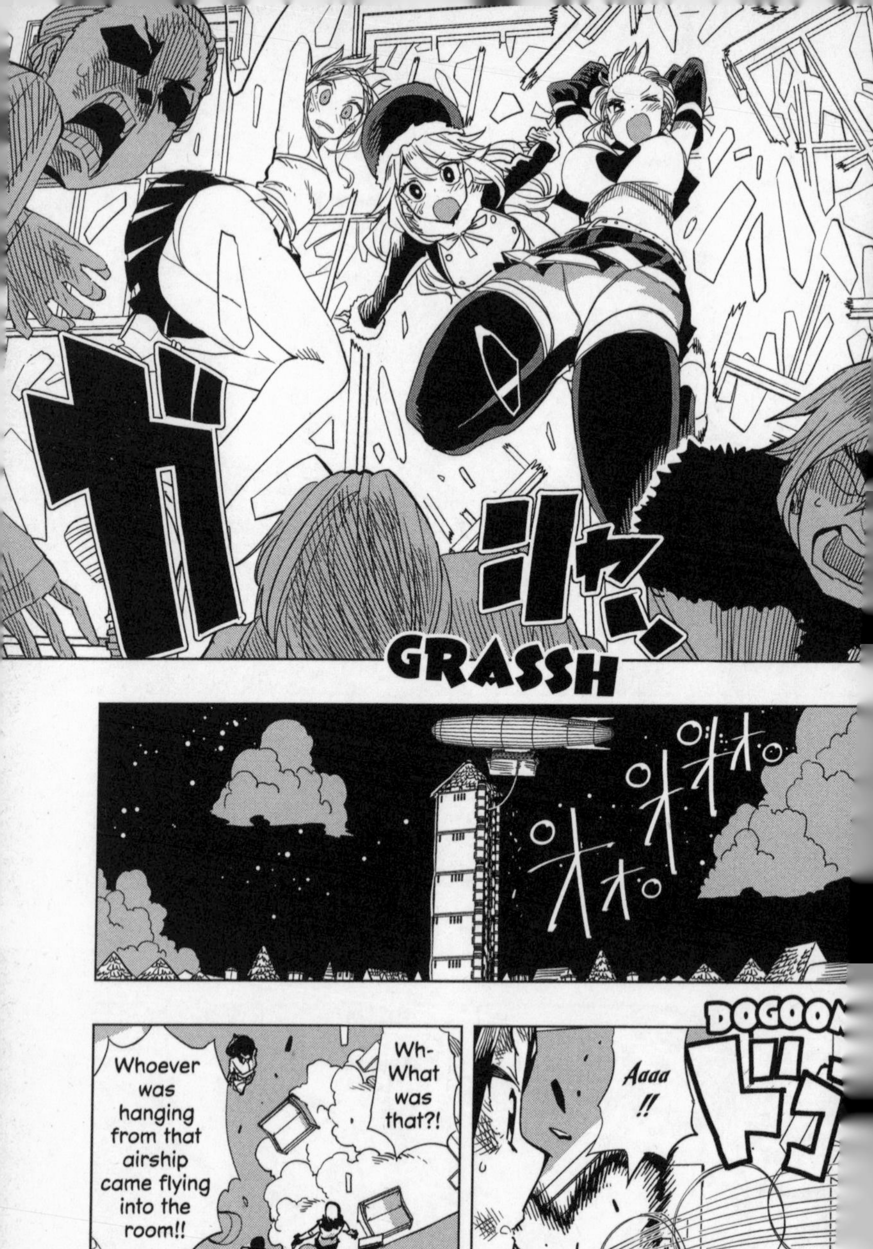
GRASSH
DOGOON
Aaaa!!
Wh- What was that?!
Whoever was hanging from that airship came flying into the room!!

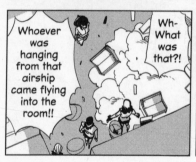

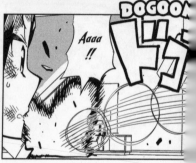

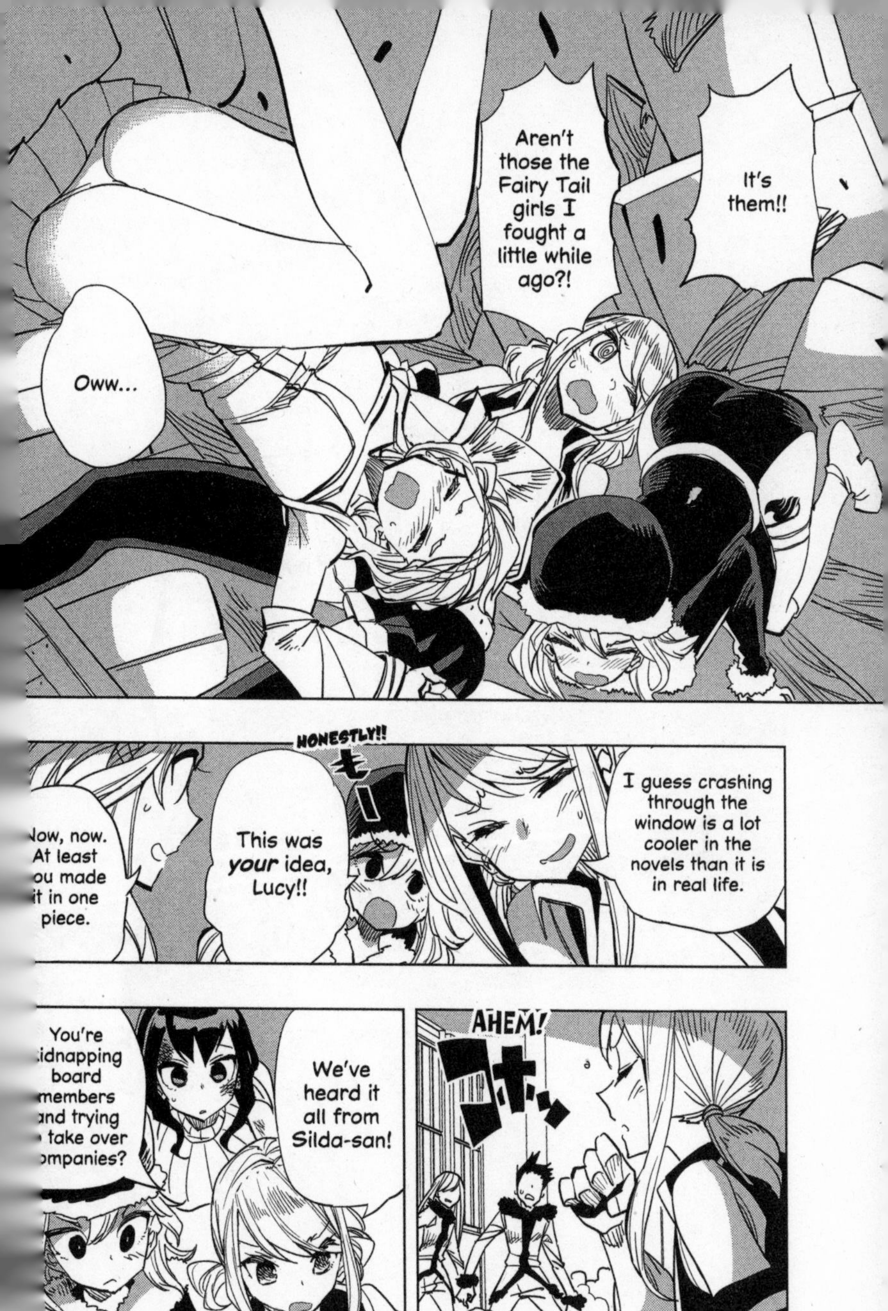
It's them!!
Aren't those the Fairy Tail girls I fought a little while ago?!
Oww...
I guess crashing through the window is a lot cooler in the novels than it is in real life.
HONESTLY!!
This was *your* idea, Lucy!!
Now, now. At least ou made it in one piece.
AHEM!
We've heard it all from Silda-san!
You're idnapping board members and trying take over ompanies?

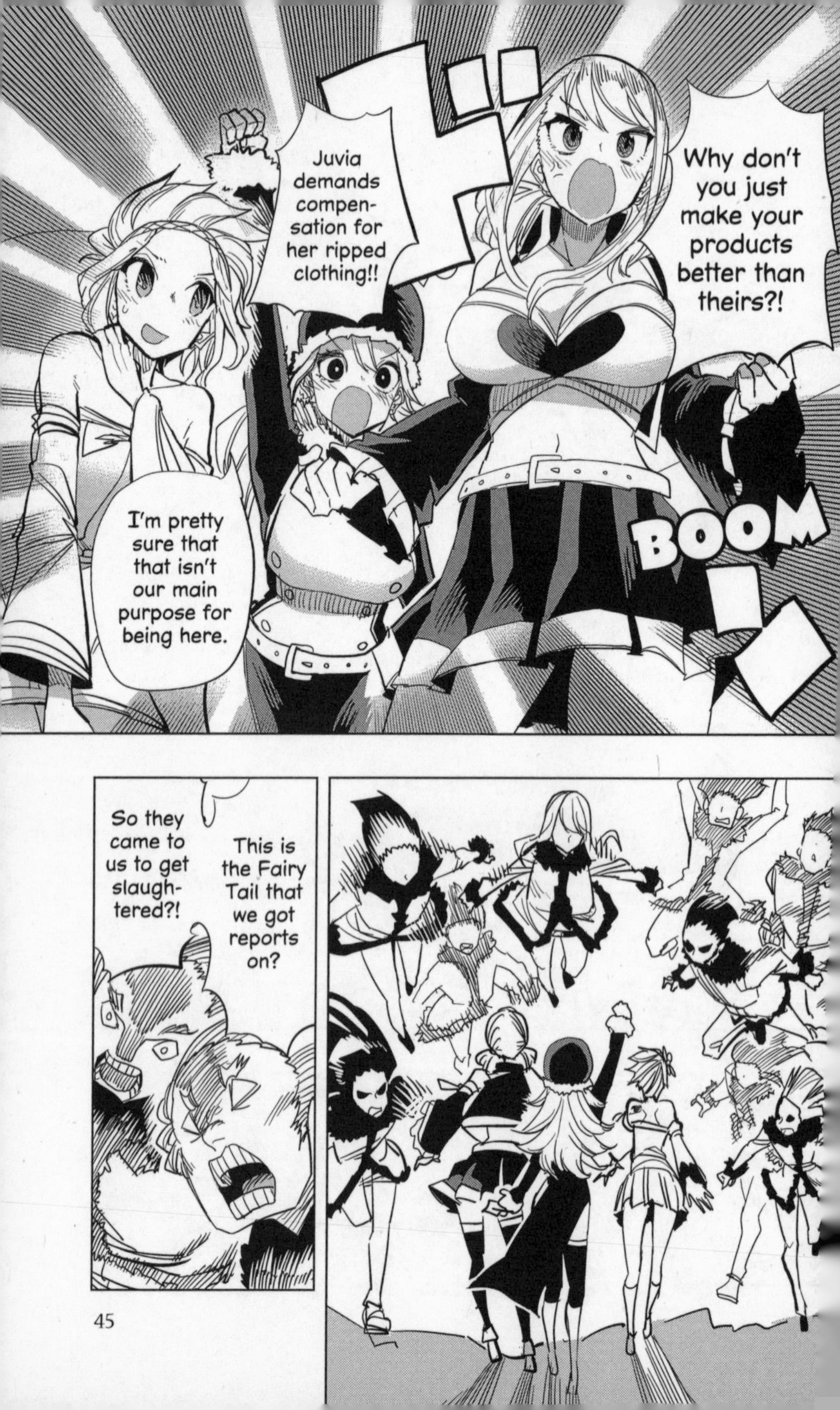
Why don't you just make your products better than theirs?!
Juvia demands compen-sation for her ripped clothing!!
BOOM
I'm pretty sure that that isn't our main purpose for being here.
This is the Fairy Tail that we got reports on?
So they came to us to get slaugh-tered?!

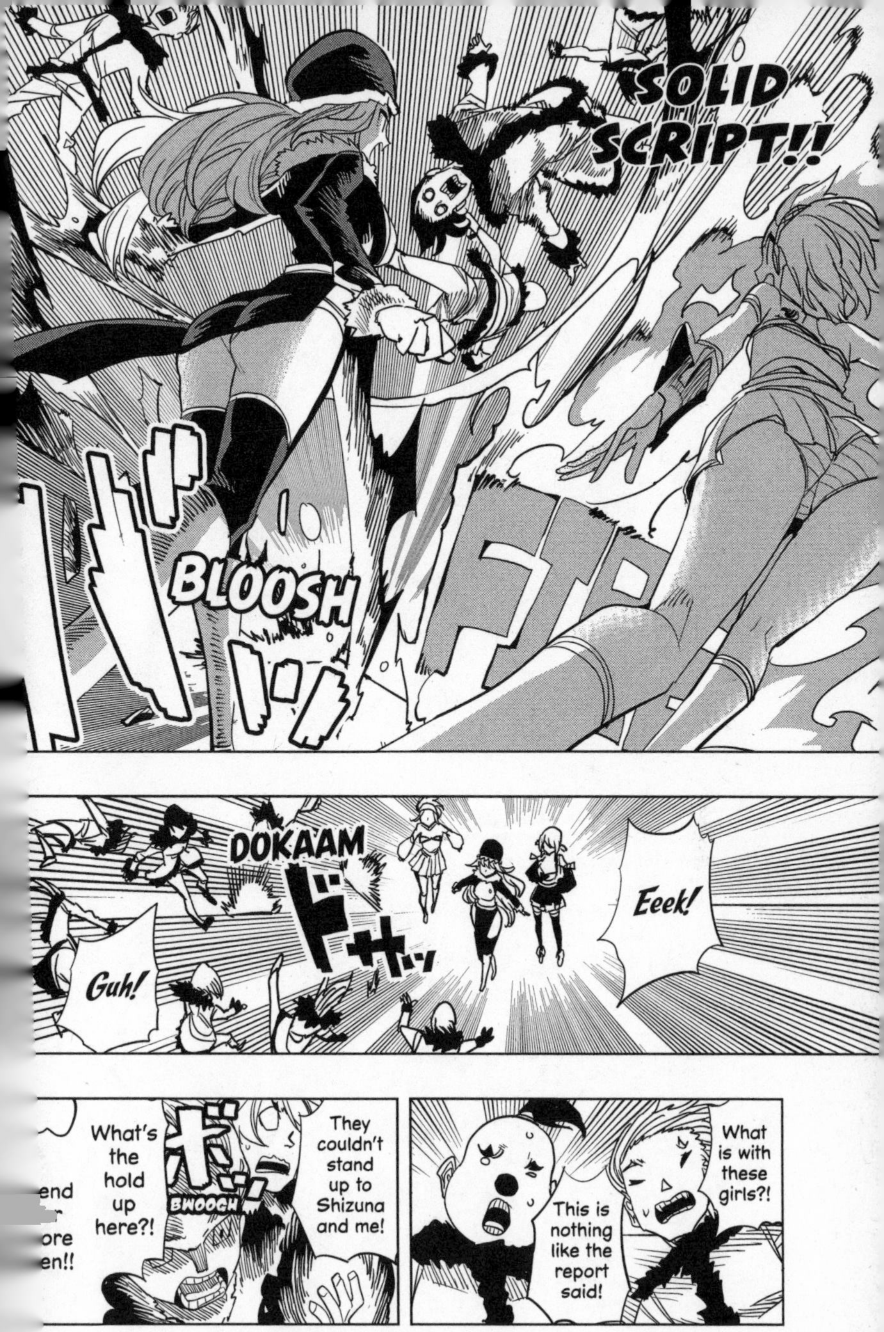
SOLID SCRIPT!!
BLOOSH
Eeek!
DOKAAM
Guh!
What is with these girls?!
This is nothing like the report said!
They couldn't stand up to Shizuna and me!
What's the hold up here?!
BWOOGH

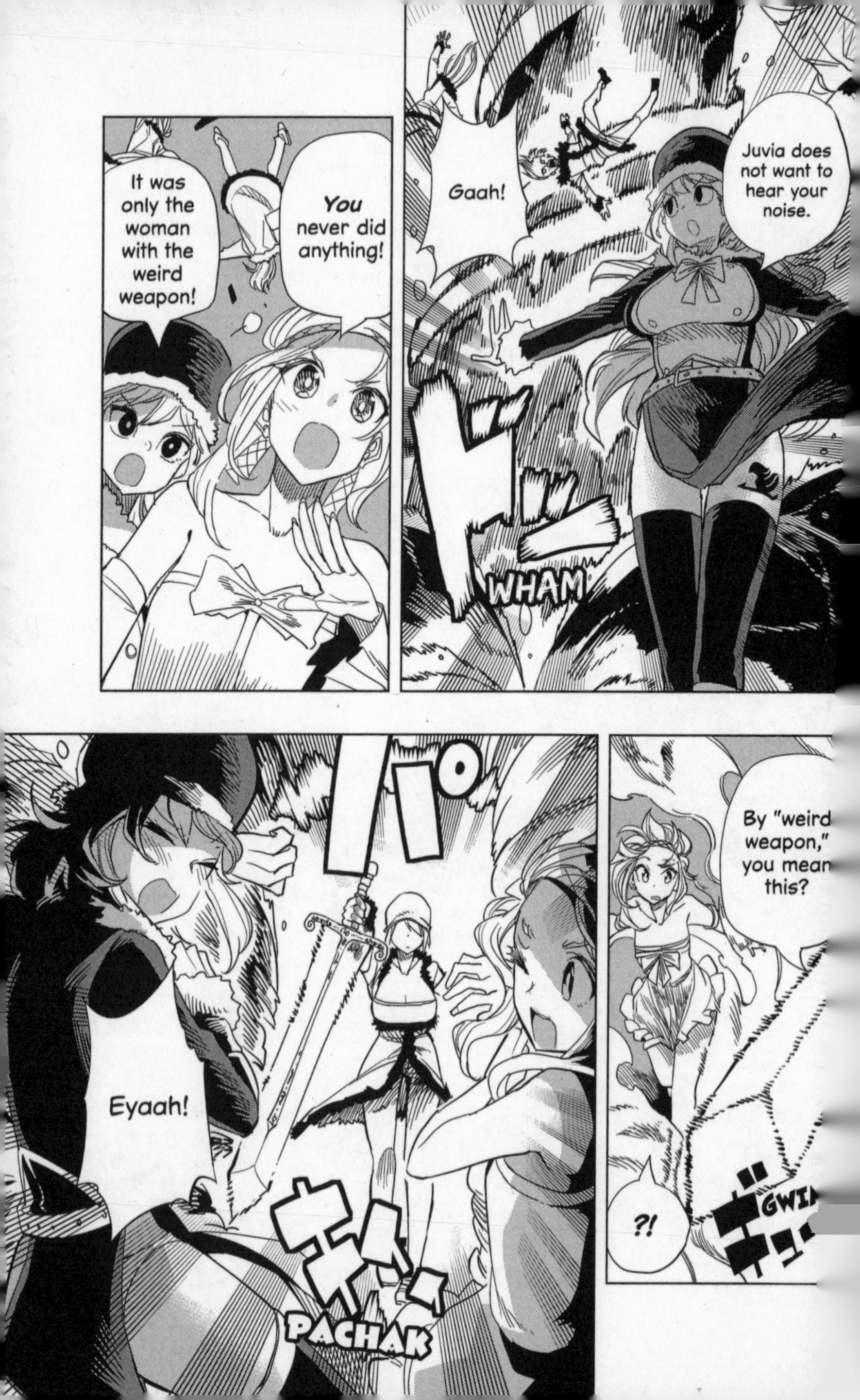
Juvia does not want to hear your noise.
Gaah!
WHAM
You never did anything!
It was only the woman with the weird weapon!
By "weird weapon," you mean this?
?!
GWI
Eyaah!
PACHAK

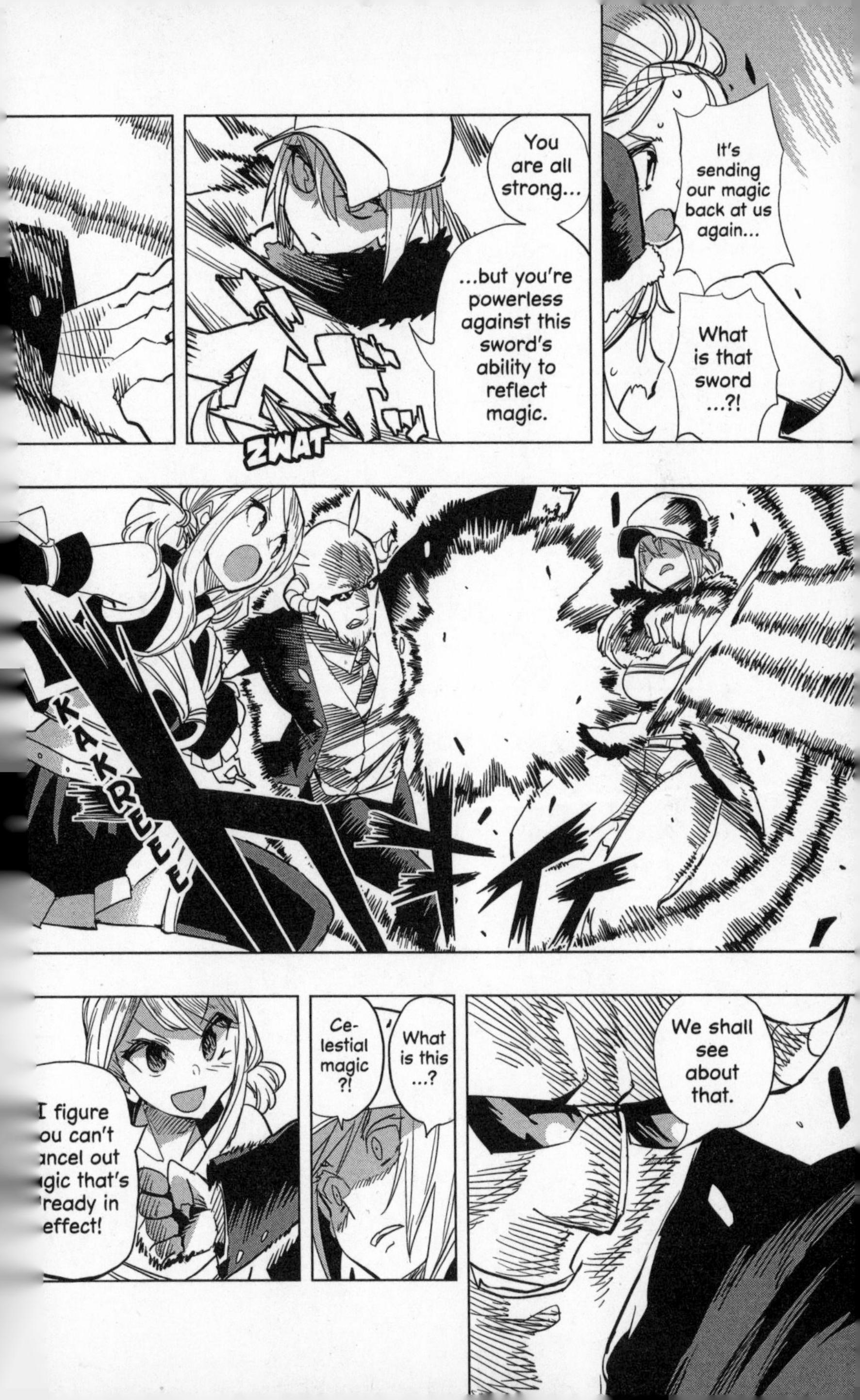
It's sending our magic back at us again...
What is that sword ...?!
You are all strong...
...but you're powerless against this sword's ability to reflect magic.
ZWAT
KAKREEEE
We shall see about that.
What is this ...?
Ce-lestial magic ?!
I figure ou can't ancel out gic that's ready in effect!

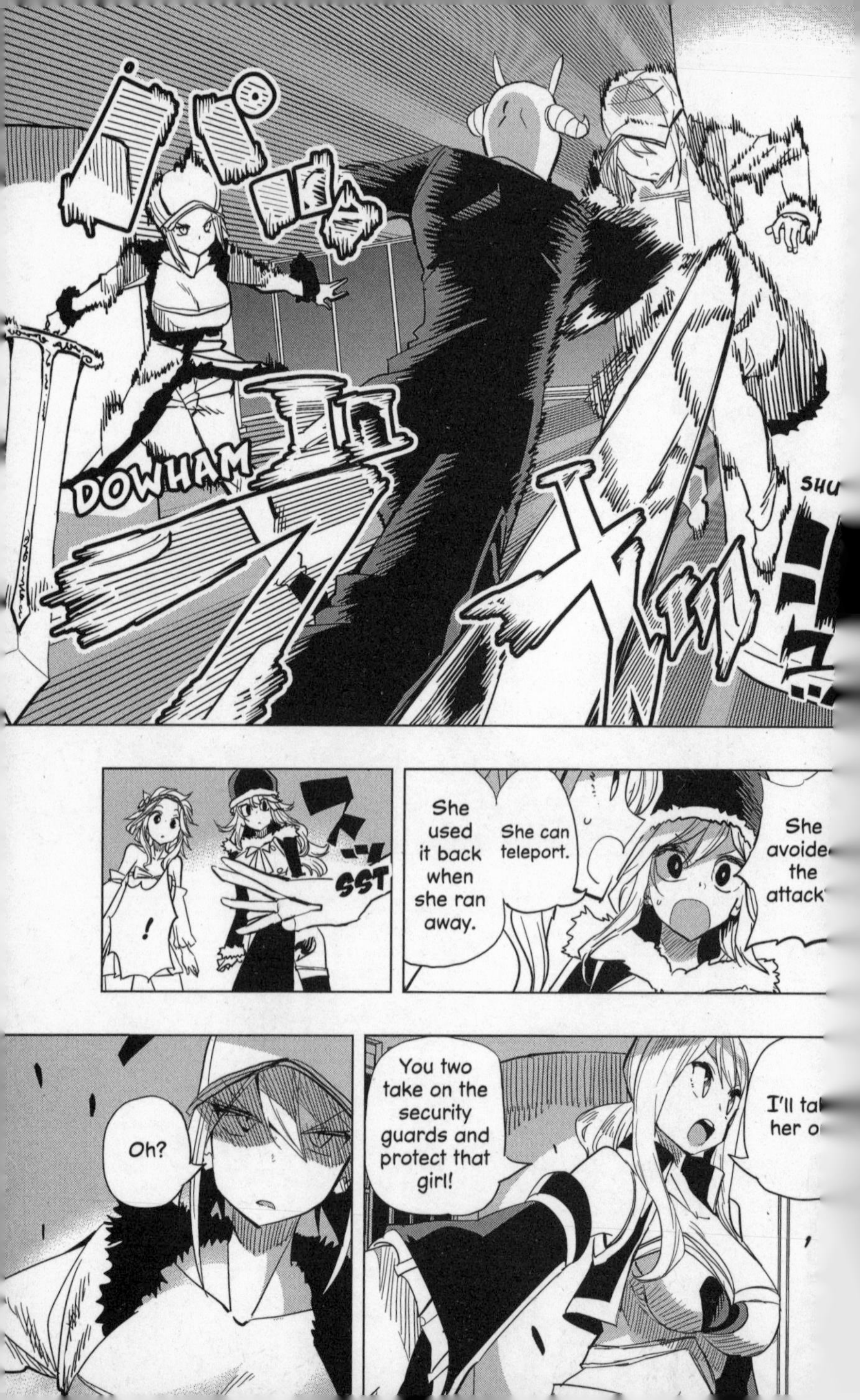
SHU
DOWHAM
She avoide the attack
She can teleport.
She used it back when she ran away.
SST
I'll ta her o
You two take on the security guards and protect that girl!
Oh?

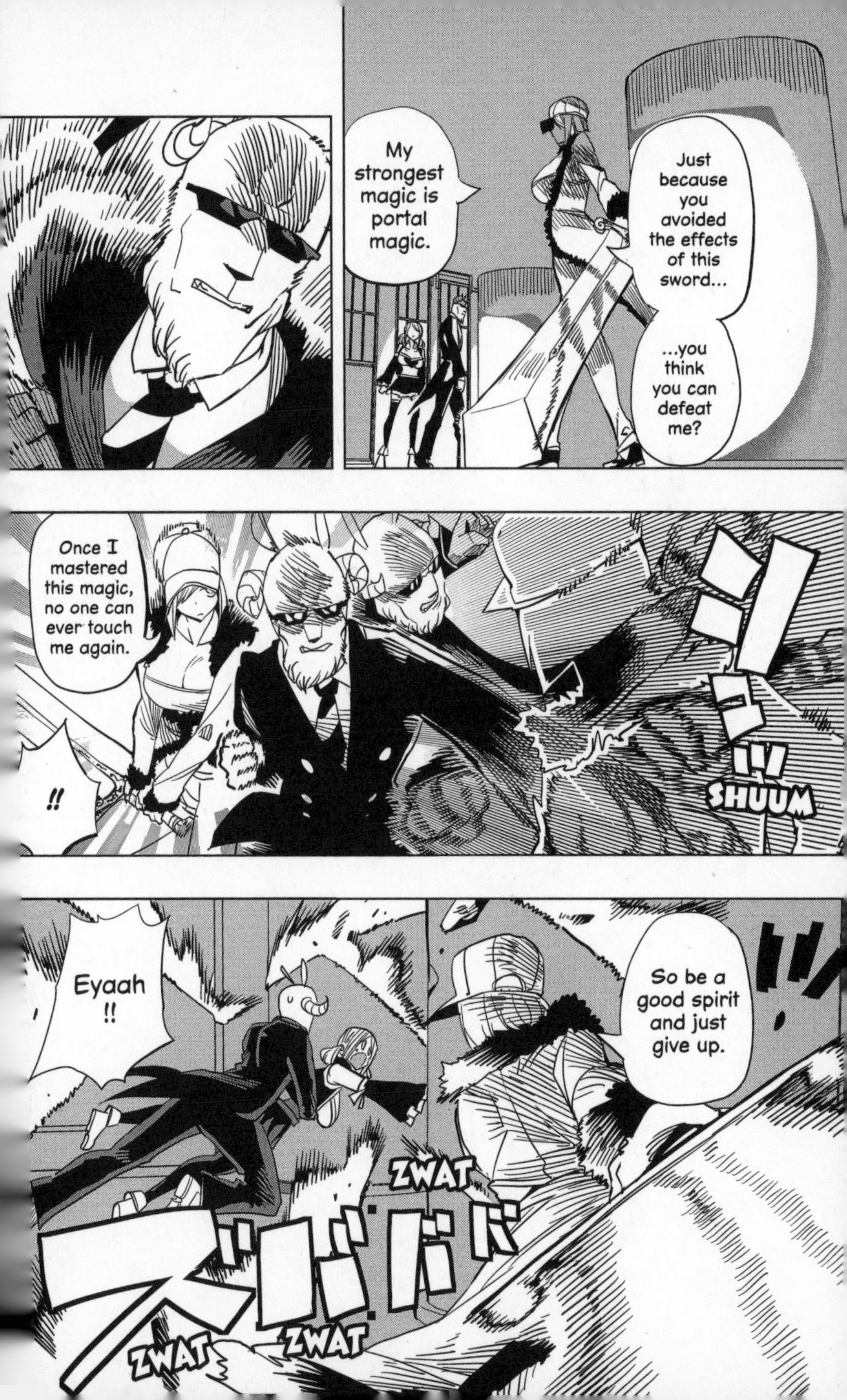
Just because you avoided the effects of this sword...
...you think you can defeat me?
My strongest magic is portal magic.
SHUUM
Once I mastered this magic, no one can ever touch me again.
!!
So be a good spirit and just give up.
ZWAT
ZWAT
ZWAT
Eyaah !!

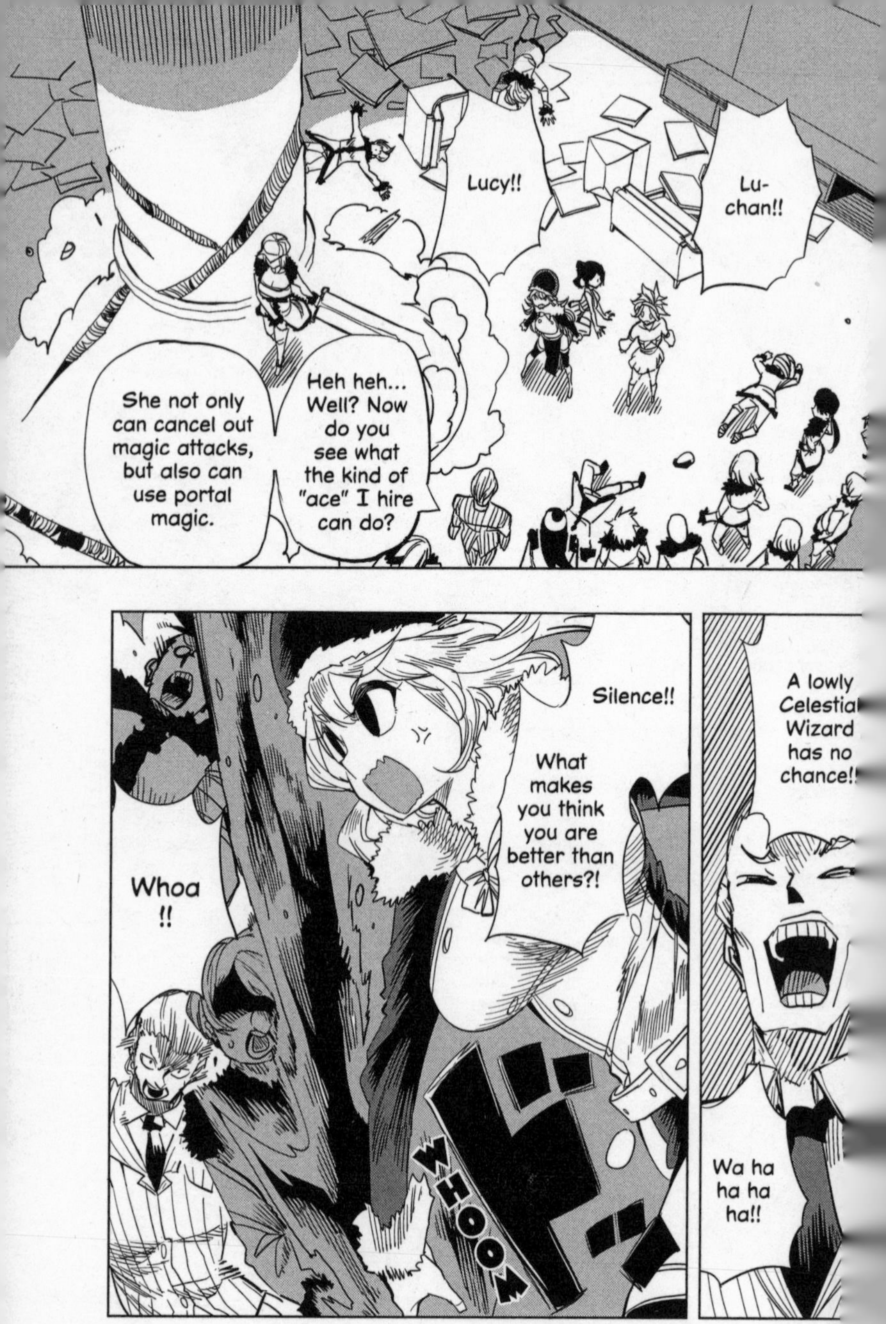
Lu-chan!!
Lucy!!
Heh heh... Well? Now do you see what the kind of "ace" I hire can do?
She not only can cancel out magic attacks, but also can use portal magic.
A lowly Celestial Wizard has no chance!!
Wa ha ha ha ha!!
Silence!!
What makes you think you are better than others?!
WHOOM
Whoa!!

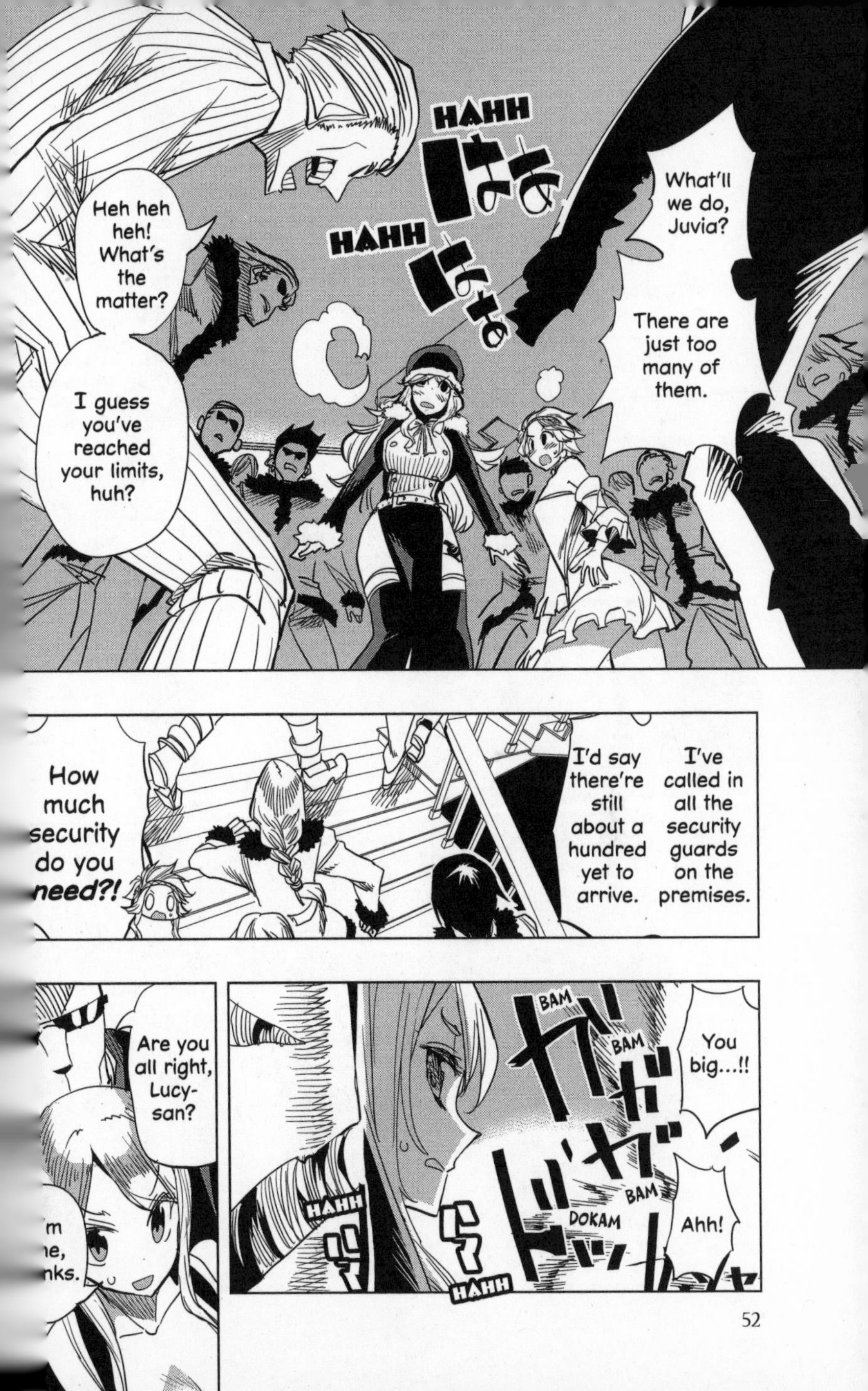
What'll we do, Juvia?
There are just too many of them.
HAHH
HAHH
Heh heh heh! What's the matter?
I guess you've reached your limits, huh?
I've called in all the security guards on the premises.
I'd say there're still about a hundred yet to arrive.
How much security do you *need?!*
You big...!!
BAM
BAM
BAM
DOKAM
Ahh!
HAHH
HAHH
Are you all right, Lucy-san?

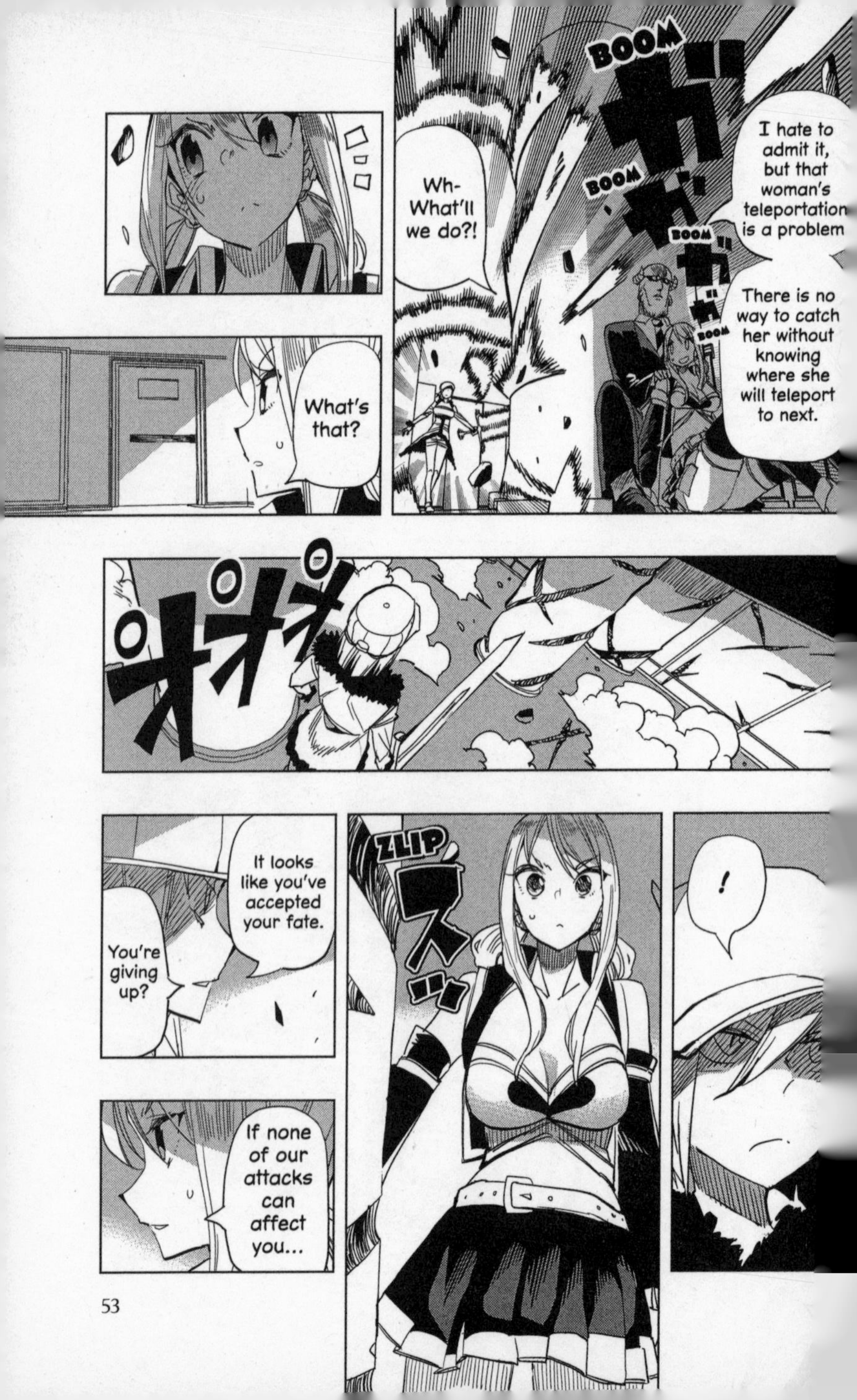
BOOM
BOOM
BOOM
BOOM
I hate to admit it, but that woman's teleportation is a problem
There is no way to catch her without knowing where she will teleport to next.
Wh- What'll we do?!
What's that?
!
ZLIP
It looks like you've accepted your fate.
You're giving up?
If none of our attacks can affect you...

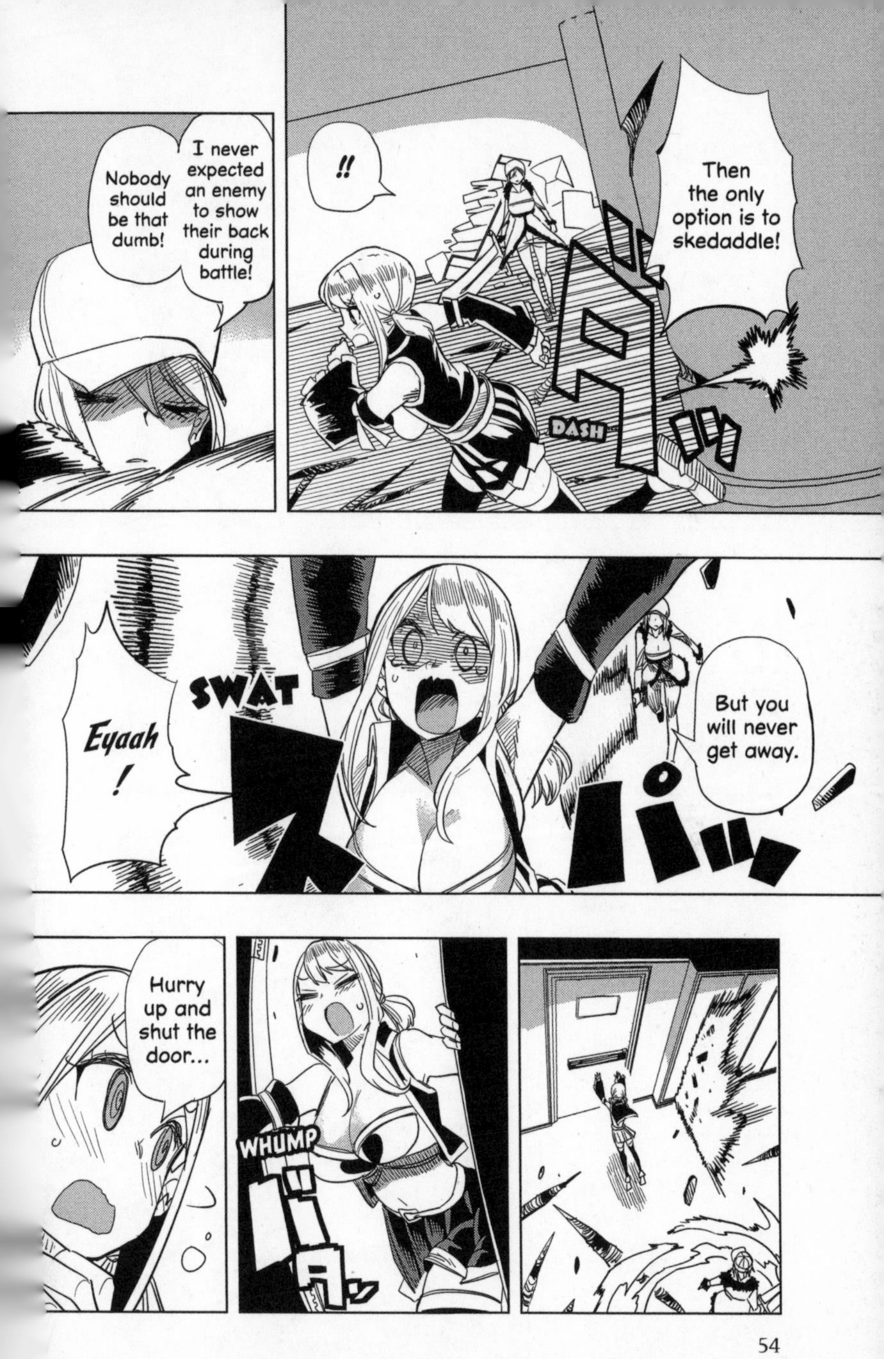
Then the only option is to skedaddle!
!!
DASH
I never expected an enemy to show their back during battle!
Nobody should be that dumb!
But you will never get away.
SWAT
Eyaah!
WHUMP
Hurry up and shut the door...

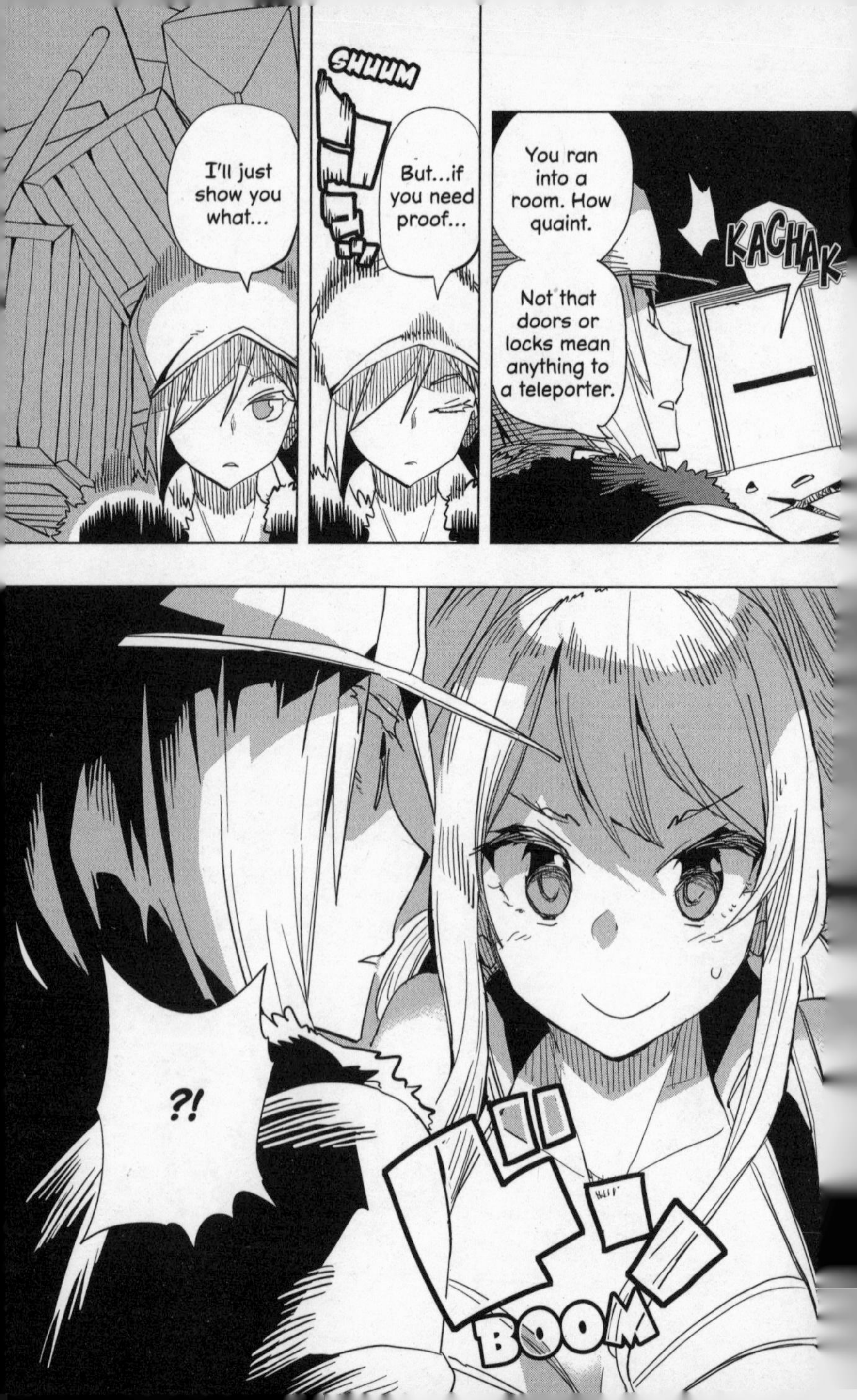
You ran into a room. How quaint.
Not that doors or locks mean anything to a teleporter.
KACHAK
SHUUM
But...if you need proof...
I'll just show you what...
BOOM
?!

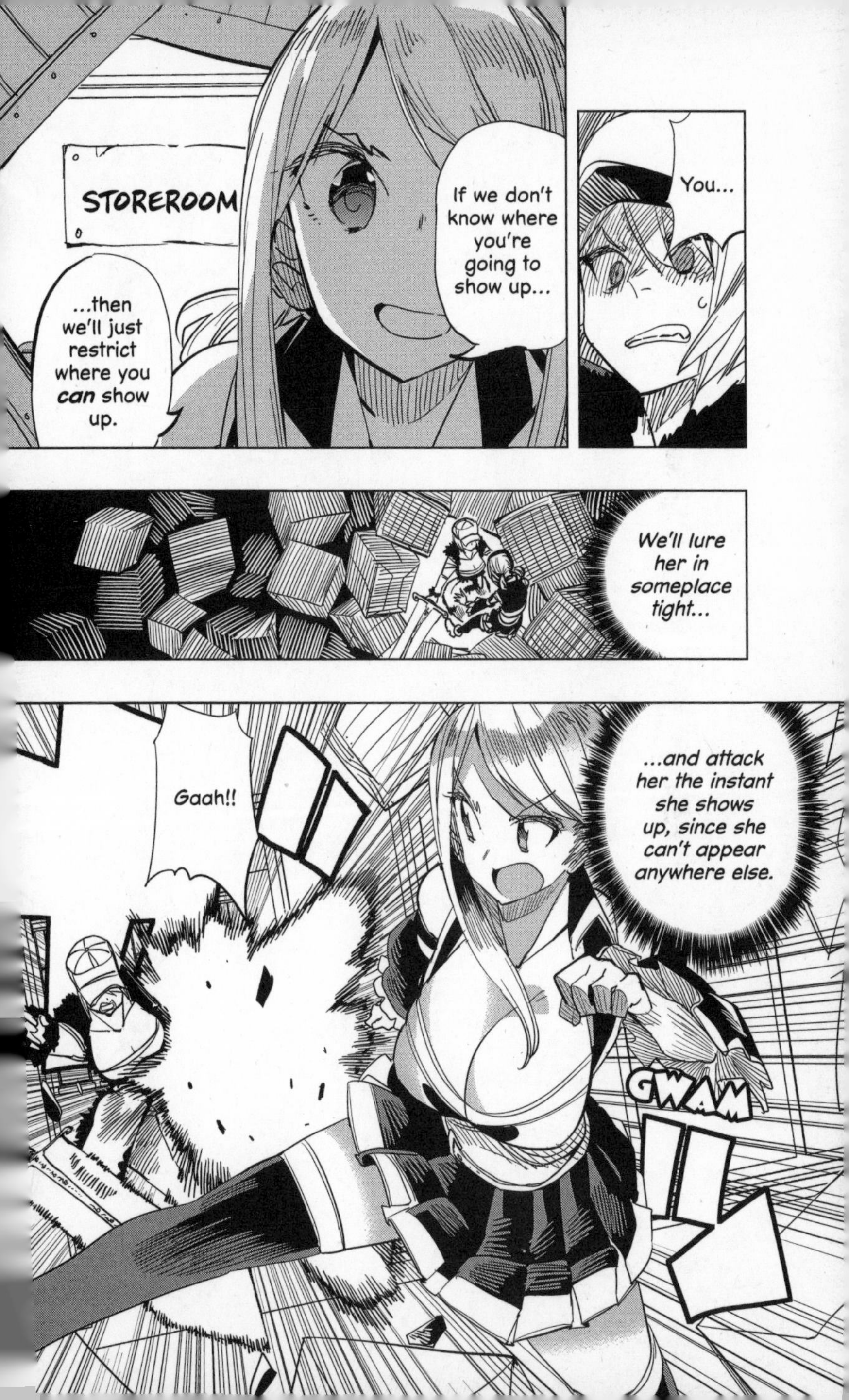
You...
If we don't know where you're going to show up...
STOREROOM
...then we'll just restrict where you *can* show up.
We'll lure her in someplace tight...
...and attack her the instant she shows up, since she can't appear anywhere else.
Gaah!!
GWAM

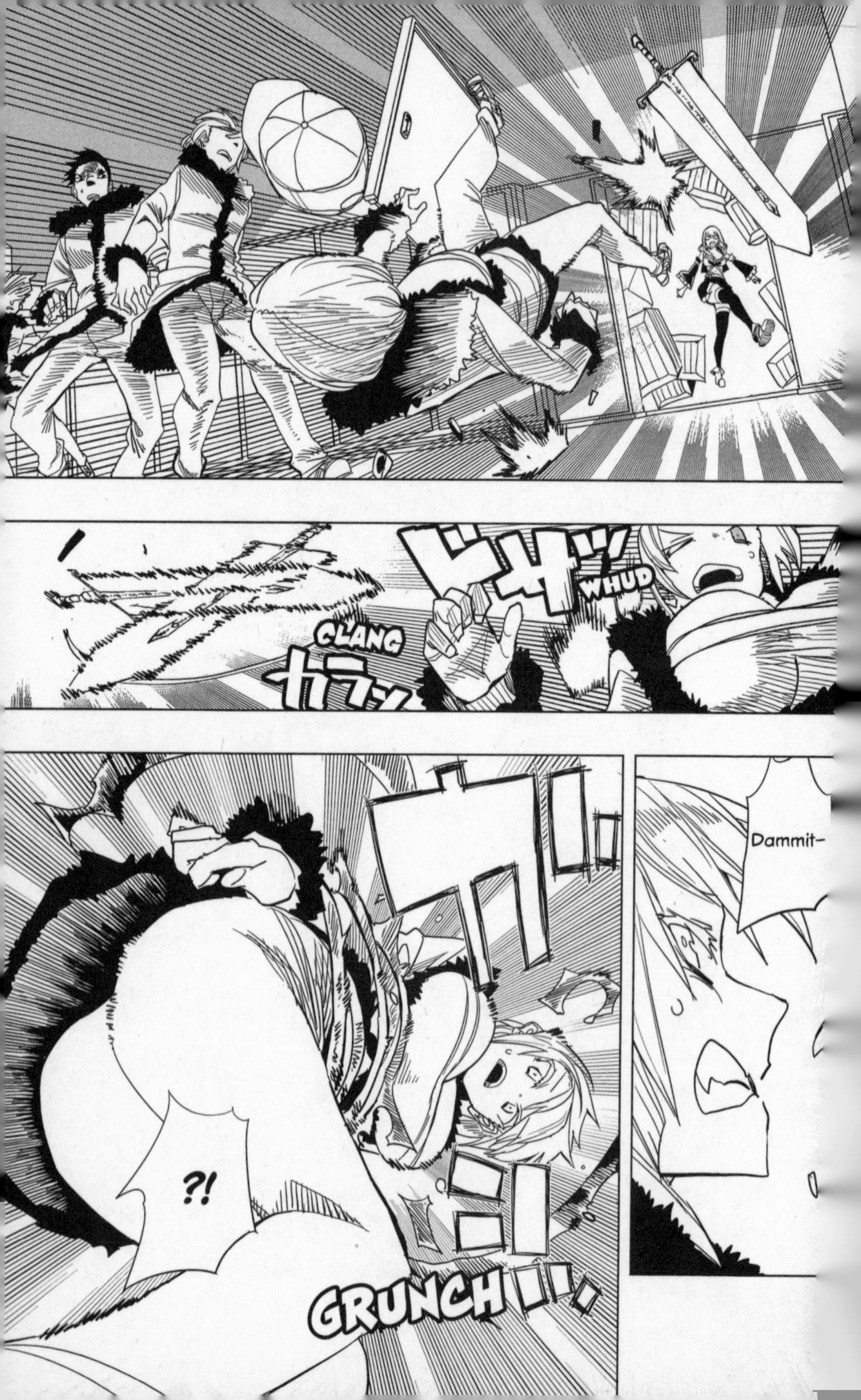
ドサッ WHUD
CLANG カラン
Dammit-
?!
GRUNCH

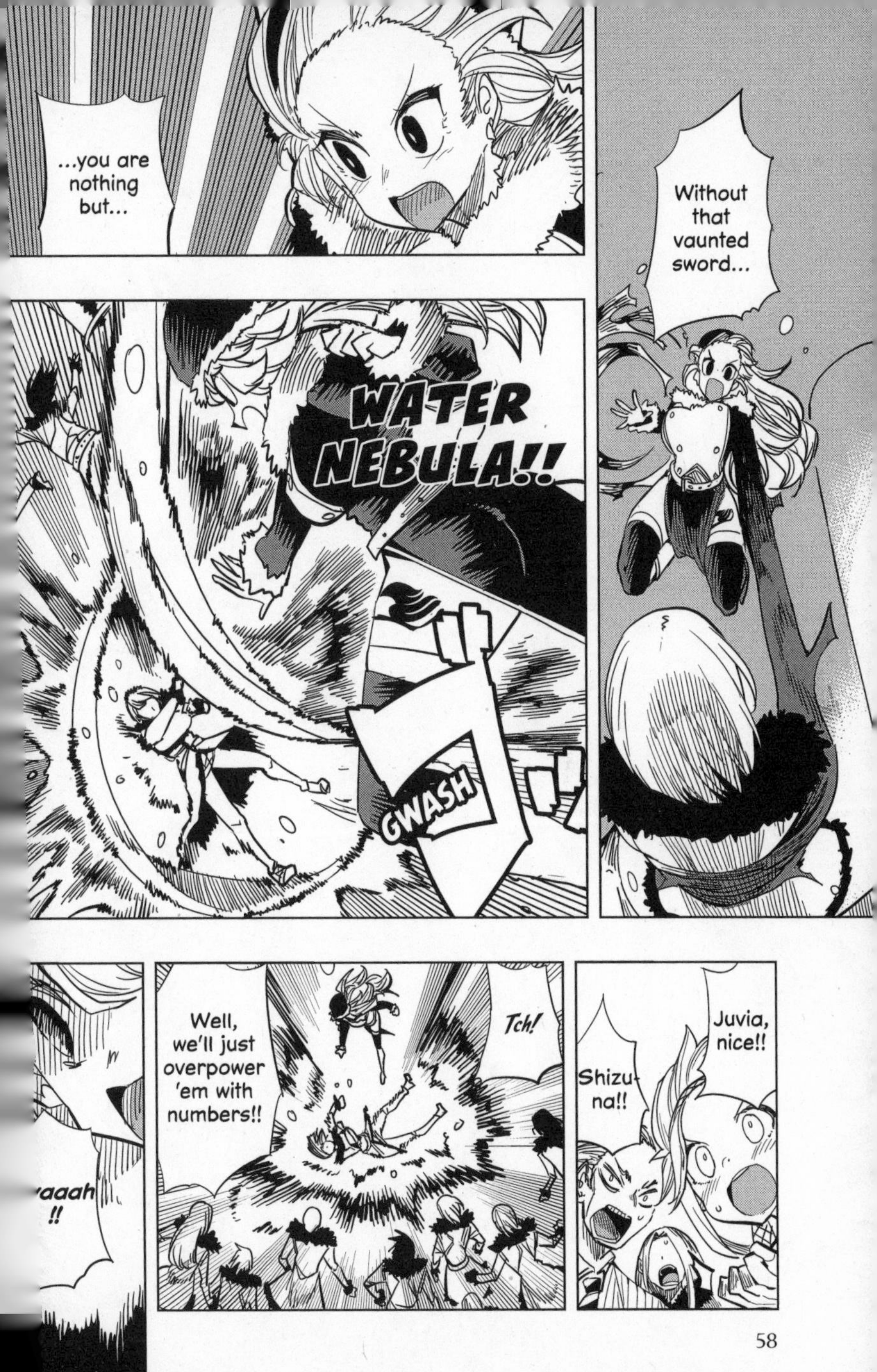

Without that vaunted sword...
...you are nothing but...
WATER NEBULA!!
GWASH
Juvia, nice!!
Shizu-na!!
Tch!
Well, we'll just overpower 'em with numbers!!
aaah !!

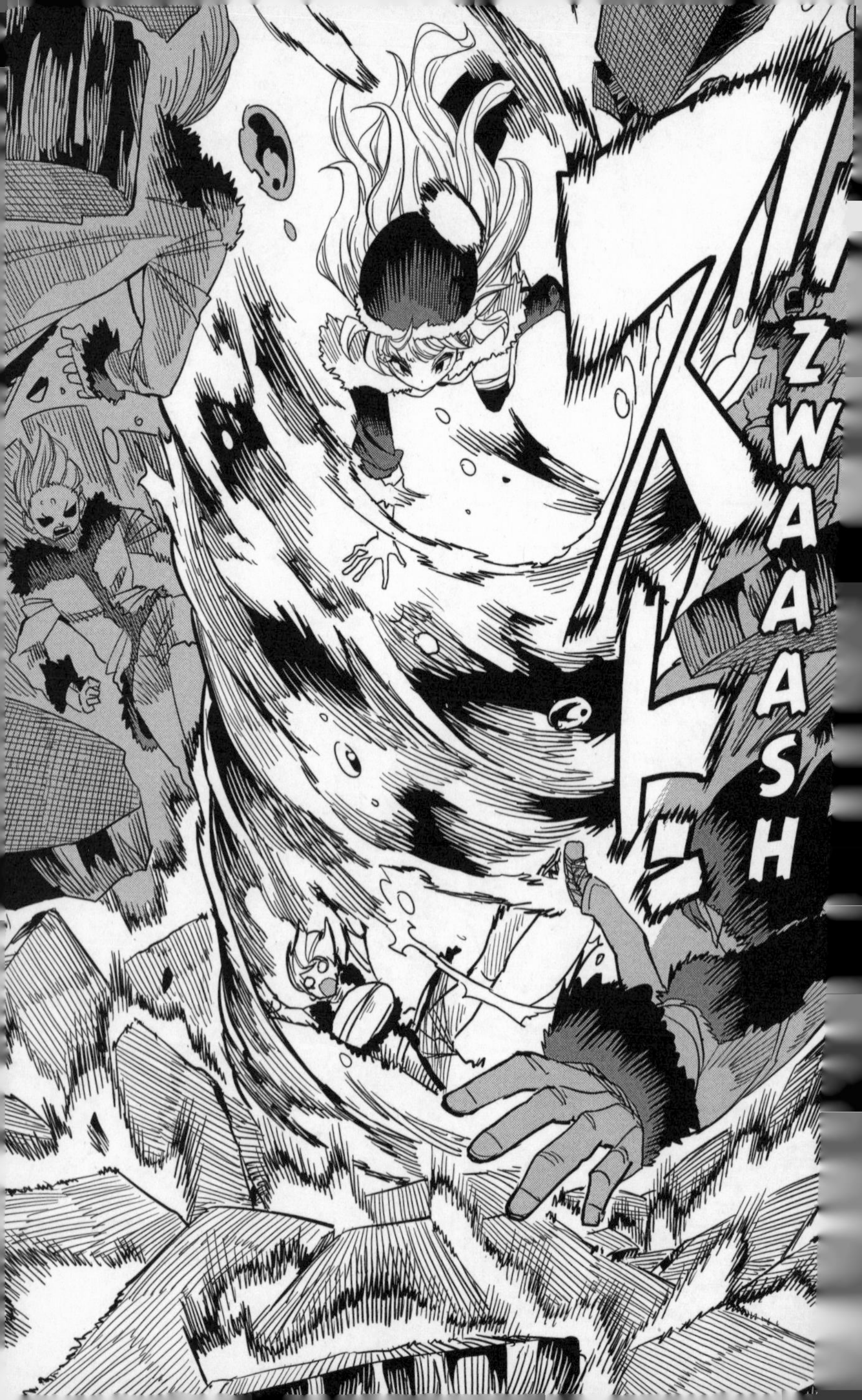
ZWAAAASH

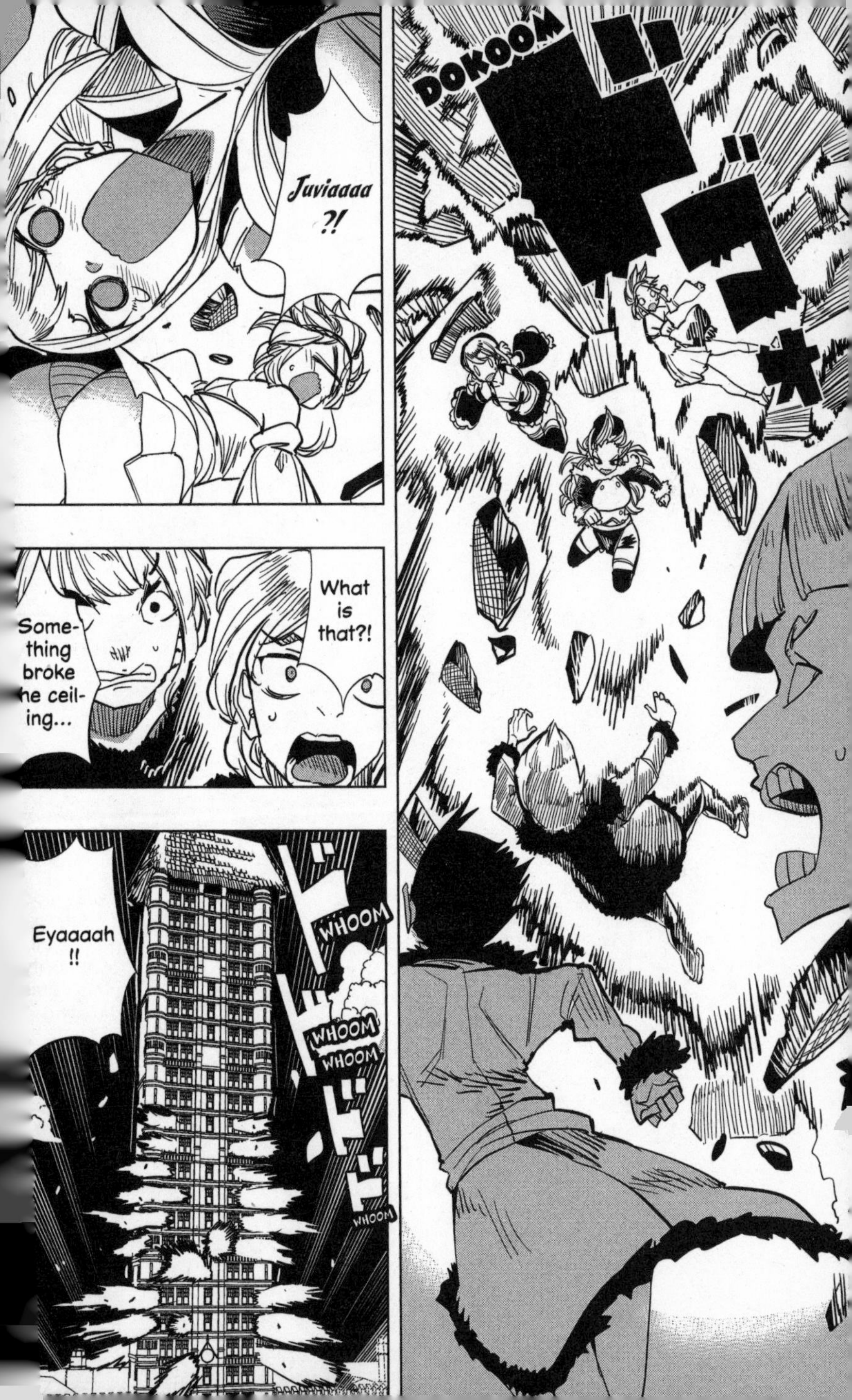
DOKOOM
Juviaaaa ?!
What is that?!
Some-thing broke he ceil-ing...
WHOOM
Eyaaaah !!
WHOOM
WHOOM
WHOOM

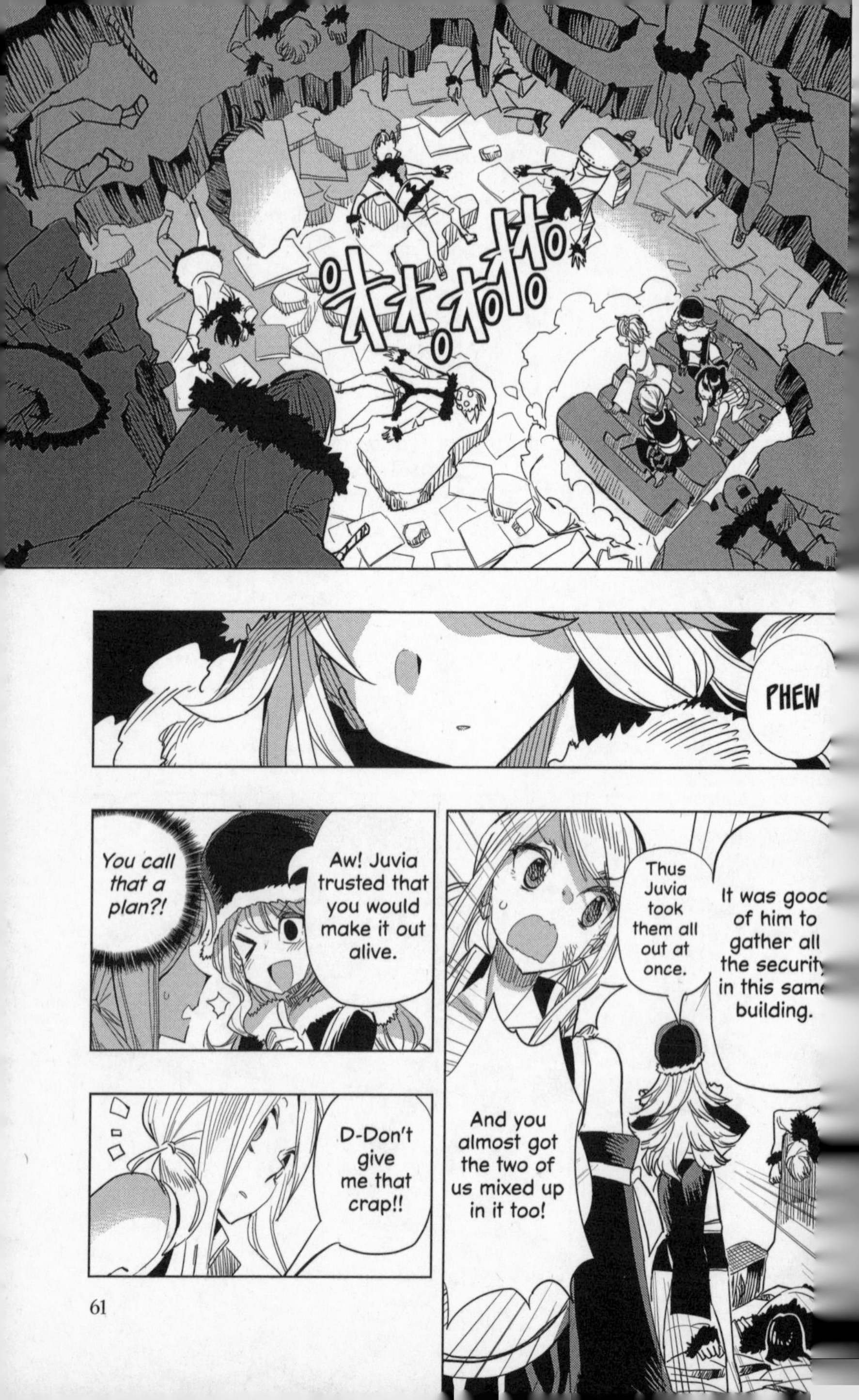
PHEW
It was good of him to gather all the security in this same building.
Thus Juvia took them all out at once.
And you almost got the two of us mixed up in it too!
Aw! Juvia trusted that you would make it out alive.
You call that a plan?!
D-Don't give me that crap!!

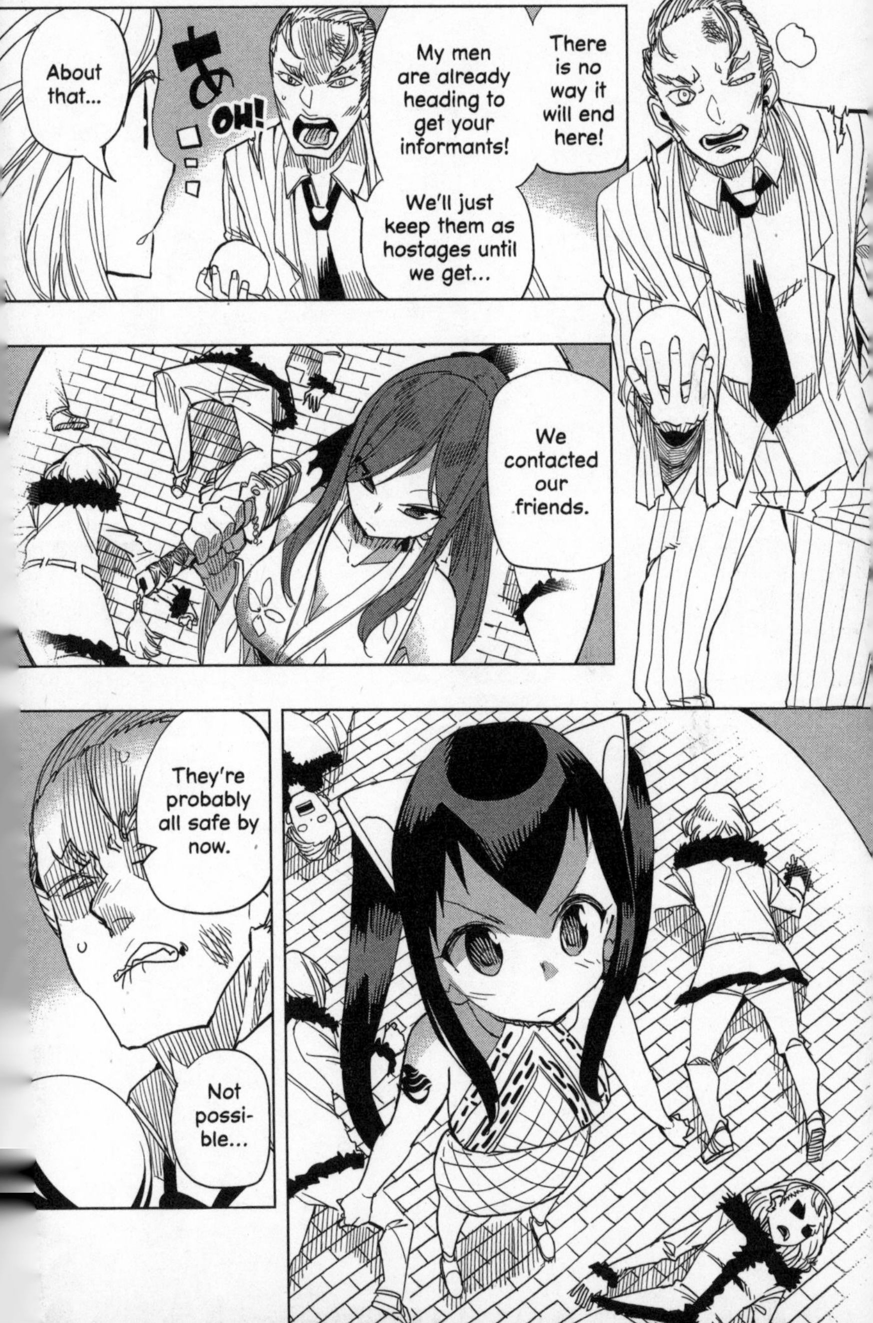
There is no way it will end here!
My men are already heading to get your informants!
We'll just keep them as hostages until we get...
あ OH!
About that...
We contacted our friends.
They're probably all safe by now.
Not possible...

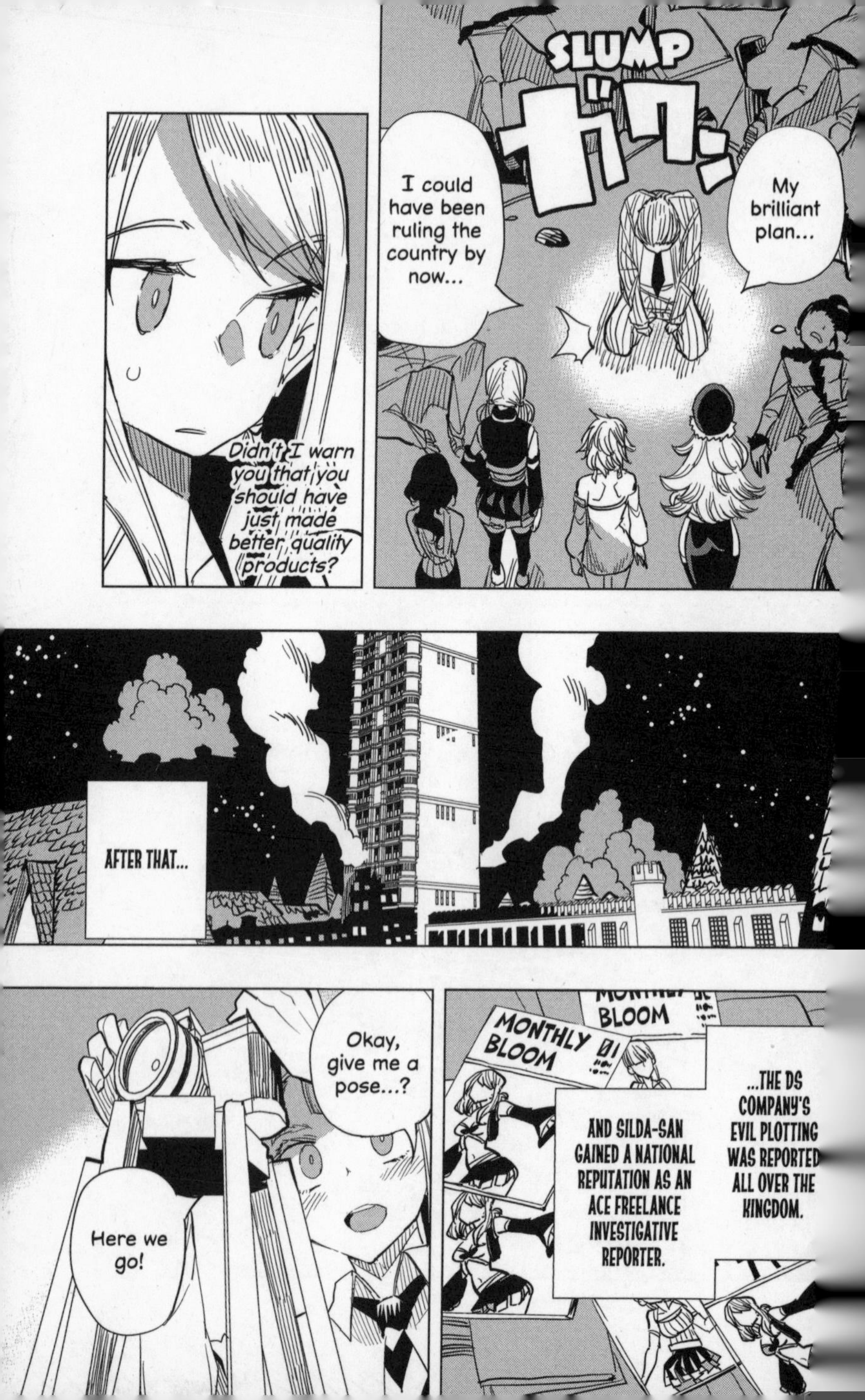
SLUMP
ガクッ
My brilliant plan...
I could have been ruling the country by now...
Didn't I warn you that you should have just made better quality products?
AFTER THAT...
MONTHLY BLOOM
MONTHLY BLOOM
...THE DS COMPANY'S EVIL PLOTTING WAS REPORTED ALL OVER THE KINGDOM.
AND SILDA-SAN GAINED A NATIONAL REPUTATION AS AN ACE FREELANCE INVESTIGATIVE REPORTER.
Okay, give me a pose...?
Here we go!

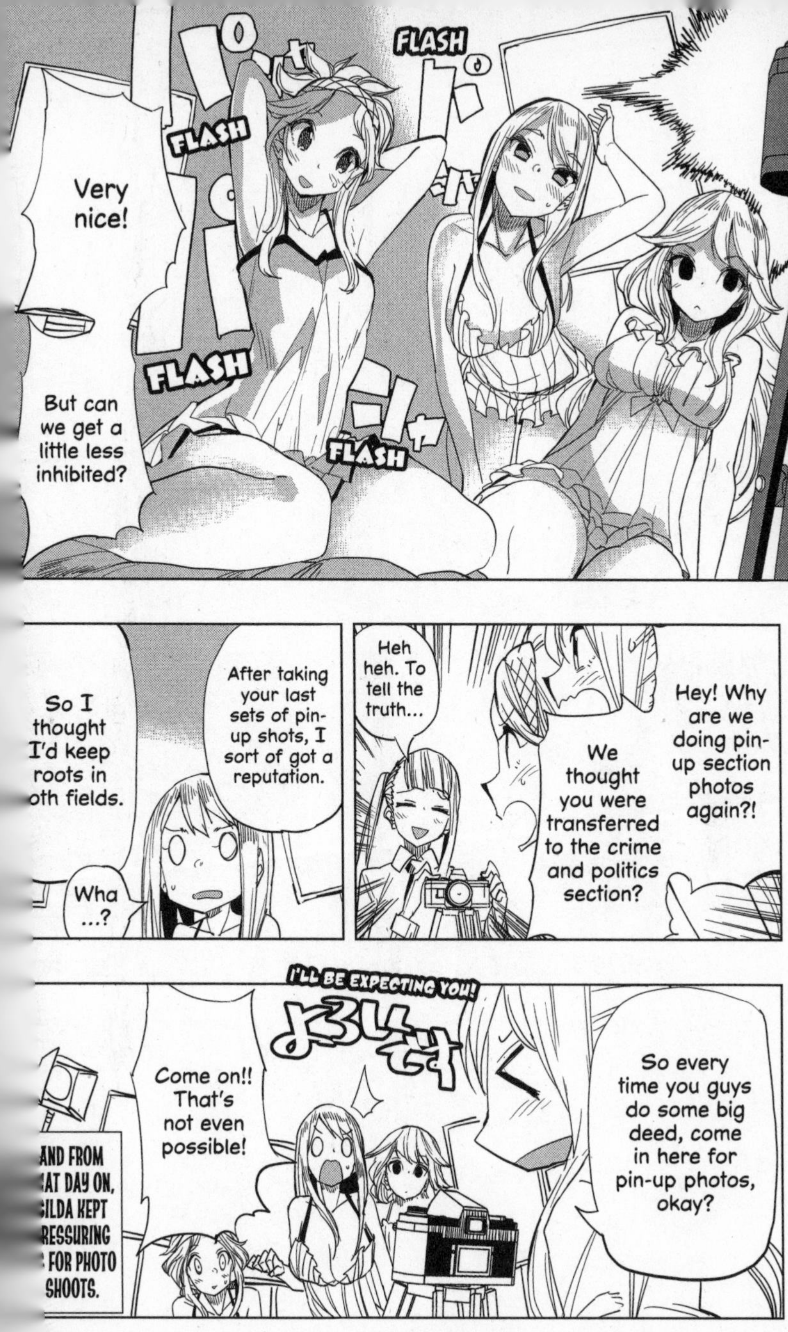
FLASH
FLASH
Very nice!
FLASH
FLASH
But can we get a little less inhibited?
Hey! Why are we doing pin-up section photos again?!
We thought you were transferred to the crime and politics section?
Heh heh. To tell the truth...
After taking your last sets of pin-up shots, I sort of got a reputation.
So I thought I'd keep roots in oth fields.
Wha ...?
So every time you guys do some big deed, come in here for pin-up photos, okay?
I'LL BE EXPECTING YOU!
Come on!! That's not even possible!
AND FROM AT DAY ON, ILDA KEPT RESSURING FOR PHOTO SHOOTS.

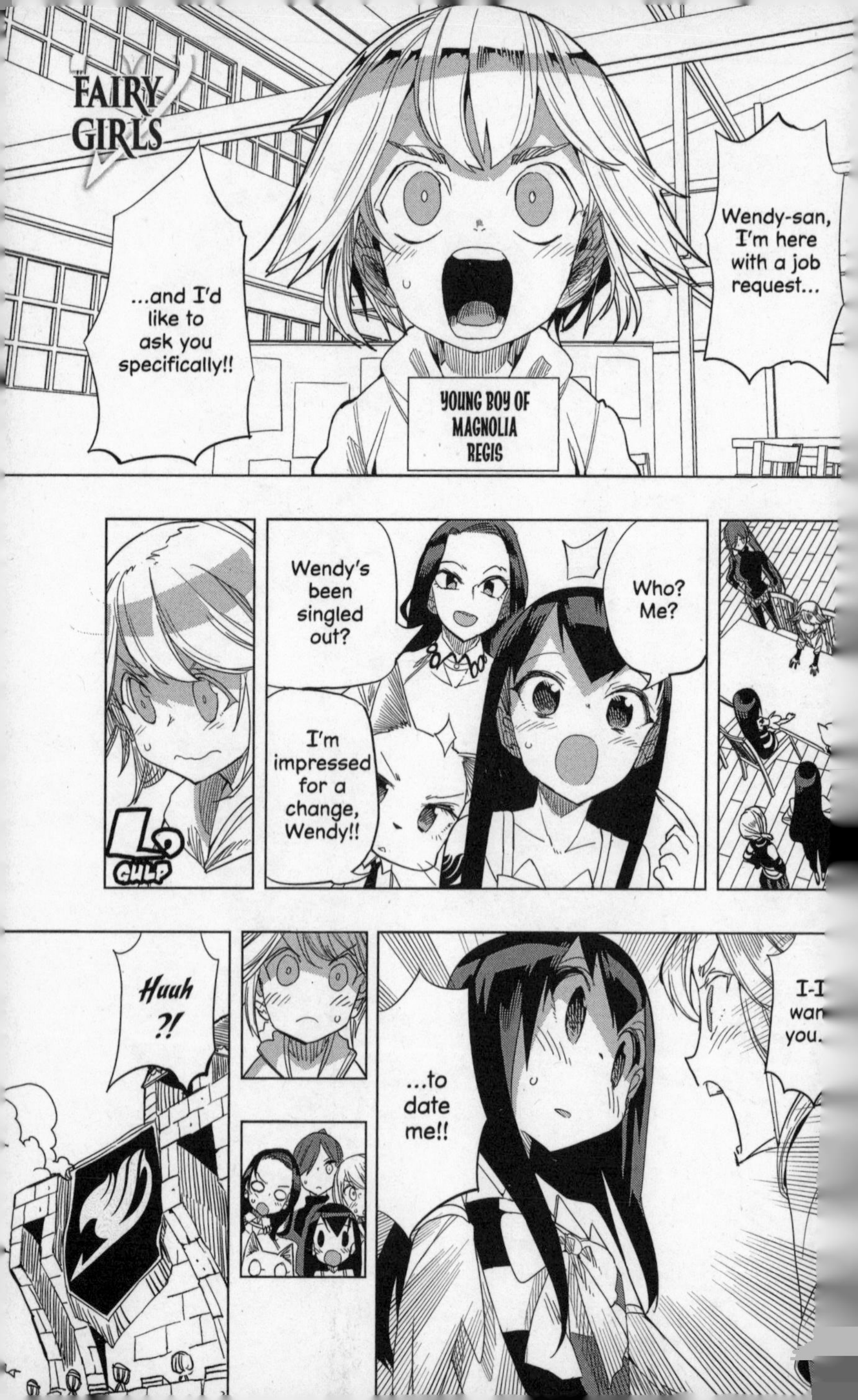
FAIRY GIRLS
Wendy-san, I'm here with a job request...
...and I'd like to ask you specifically!!
YOUNG BOY OF MAGNOLIA REGIS
Who? Me?
Wendy's been singled out?
I'm impressed for a change, Wendy!!
GULP
I-I wan you.
...to date me!!
Huuh ?!

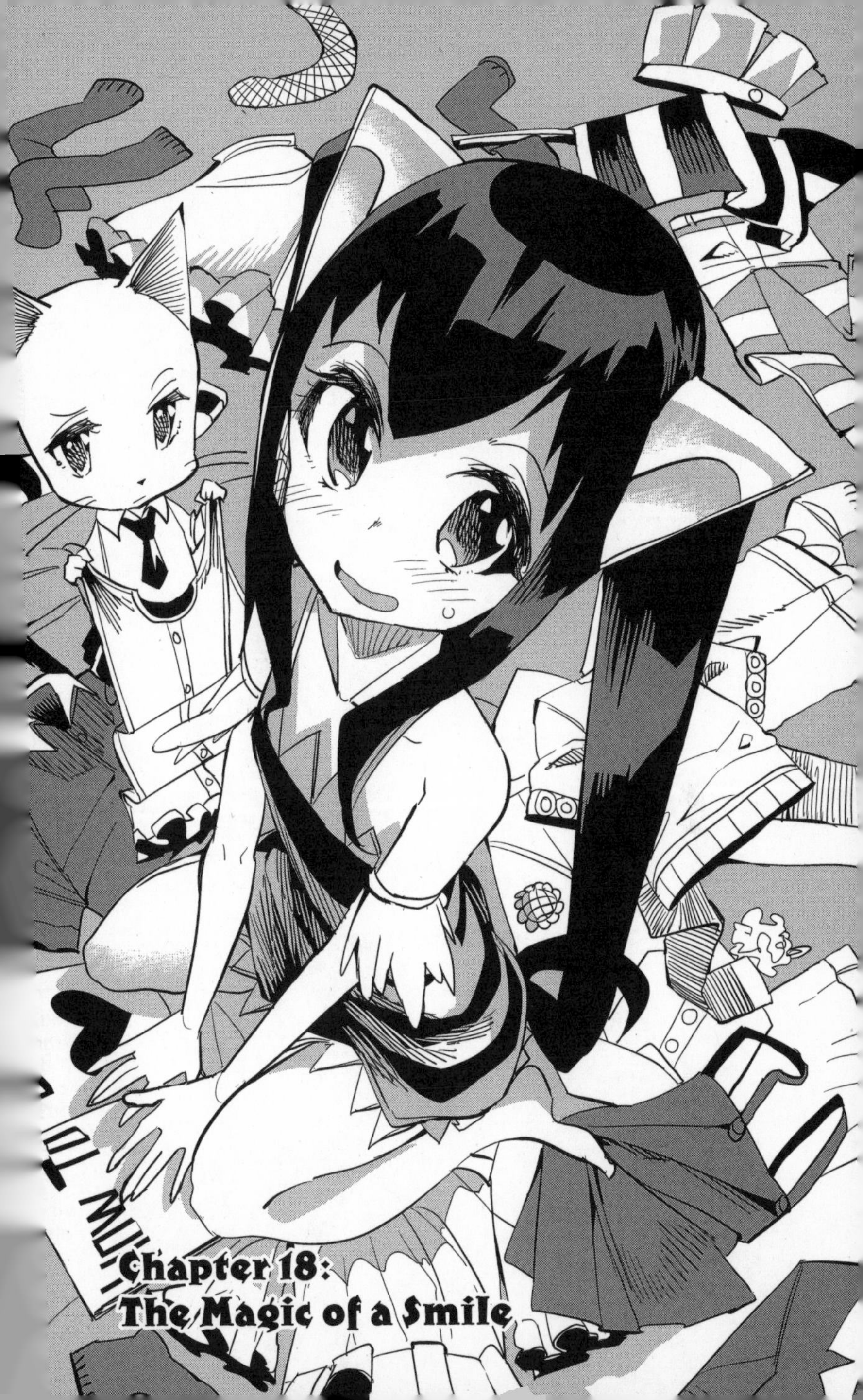
Chapter 18:
The Magic of a Smile

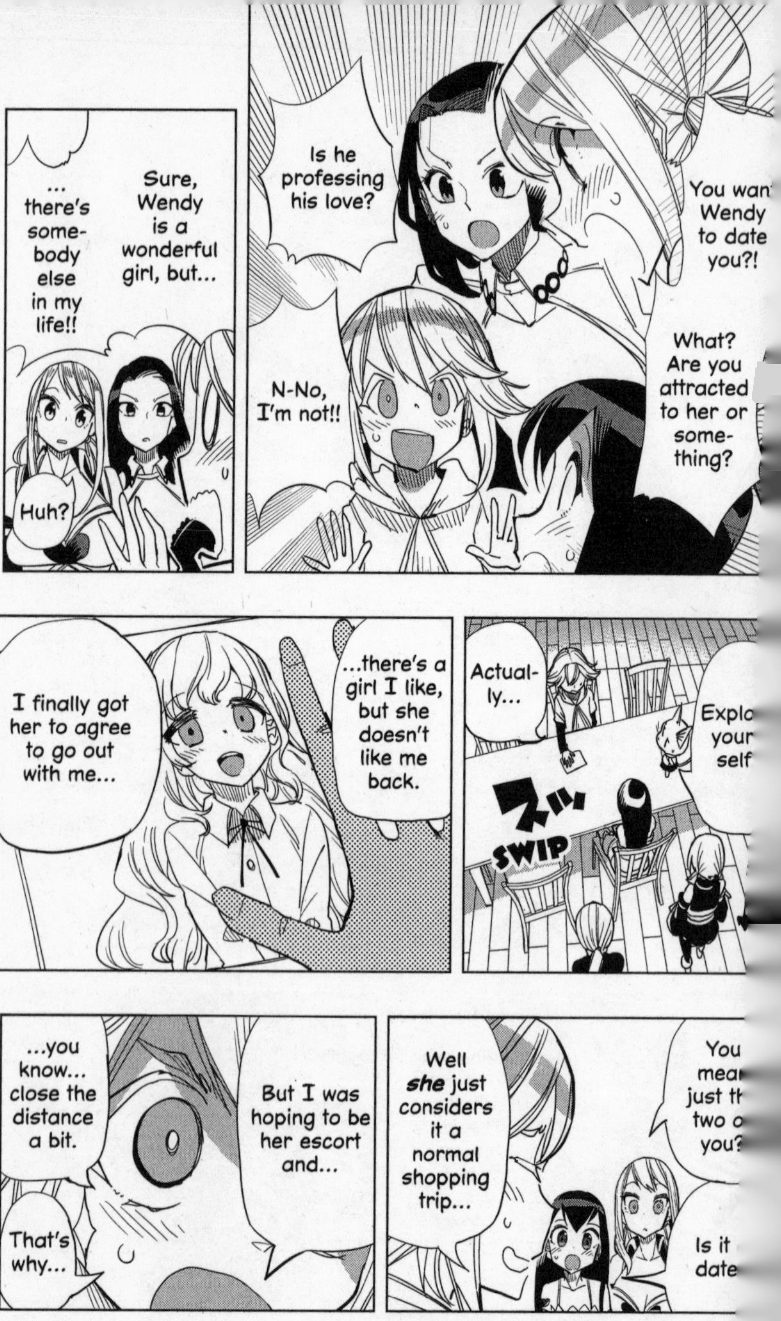
You wan Wendy to date you?!
Is he professing his love?
What? Are you attracted to her or something?
N-No, I'm not!!
Sure, Wendy is a wonderful girl, but...
... there's somebody else in my life!!
Huh?
Expla your self
Actually...
SWIP
...there's a girl I like, but she doesn't like me back.
I finally got her to agree to go out with me...
You mea just t two o you?
Is it date
Well *she* just considers it a normal shopping trip...
But I was hoping to be her escort and...
...you know... close the distance a bit.
That's why...

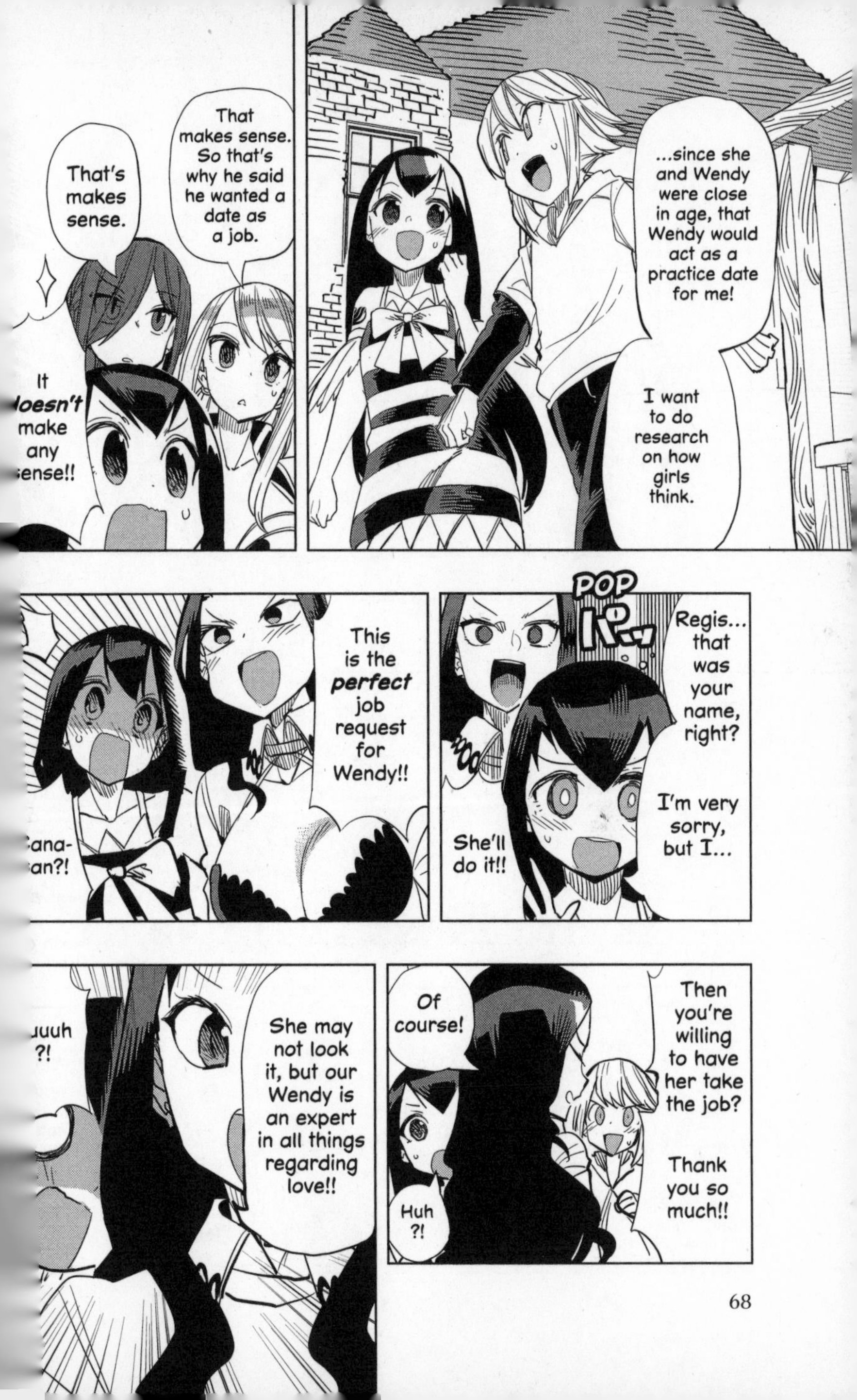

...since she and Wendy were close in age, that Wendy would act as a practice date for me!
I want to do research on how girls think.
That makes sense. So that's why he said he wanted a date as a job.
That's makes sense.
It oesn't make any ense!!
POP
Regis... that was your name, right?
I'm very sorry, but I...
She'll do it!!
This is the perfect job request for Wendy!!
ana- an?!
Then you're willing to have her take the job?
Of course!
Thank you so much!!
Huh?!
She may not look it, but our Wendy is an expert in all things regarding love!!
uuuh?!

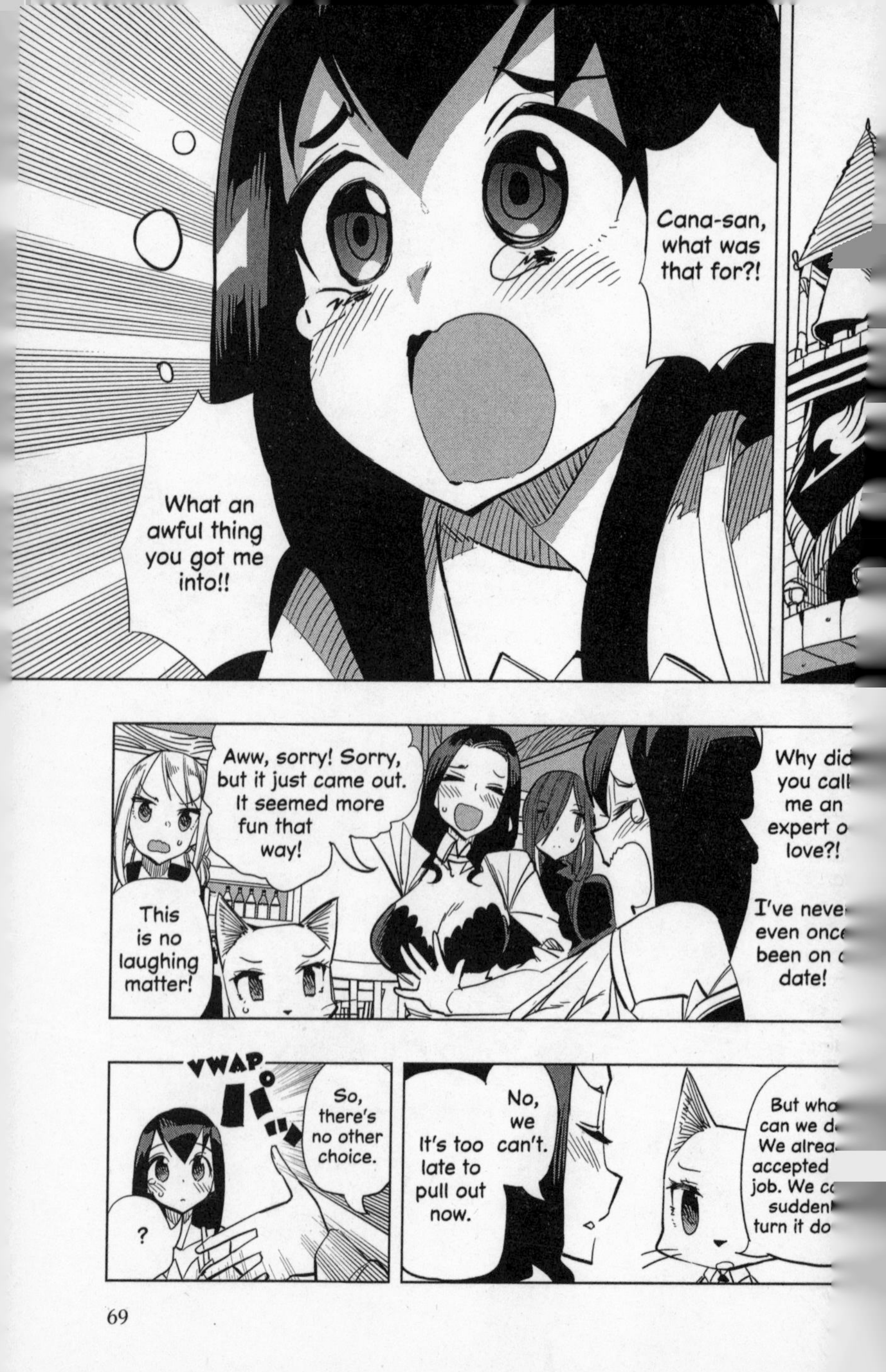
Cana-san, what was that for?!
What an awful thing you got me into!!
Why dic you call me an expert o love?!
I've neve even once been on c date!
Aww, sorry! Sorry, but it just came out. It seemed more fun that way!
This is no laughing matter!
But wha can we d We alrea accepted job. We c sudden turn it do
No, we can't.
It's too late to pull out now.
VWAP
So, there's no other choice.
?

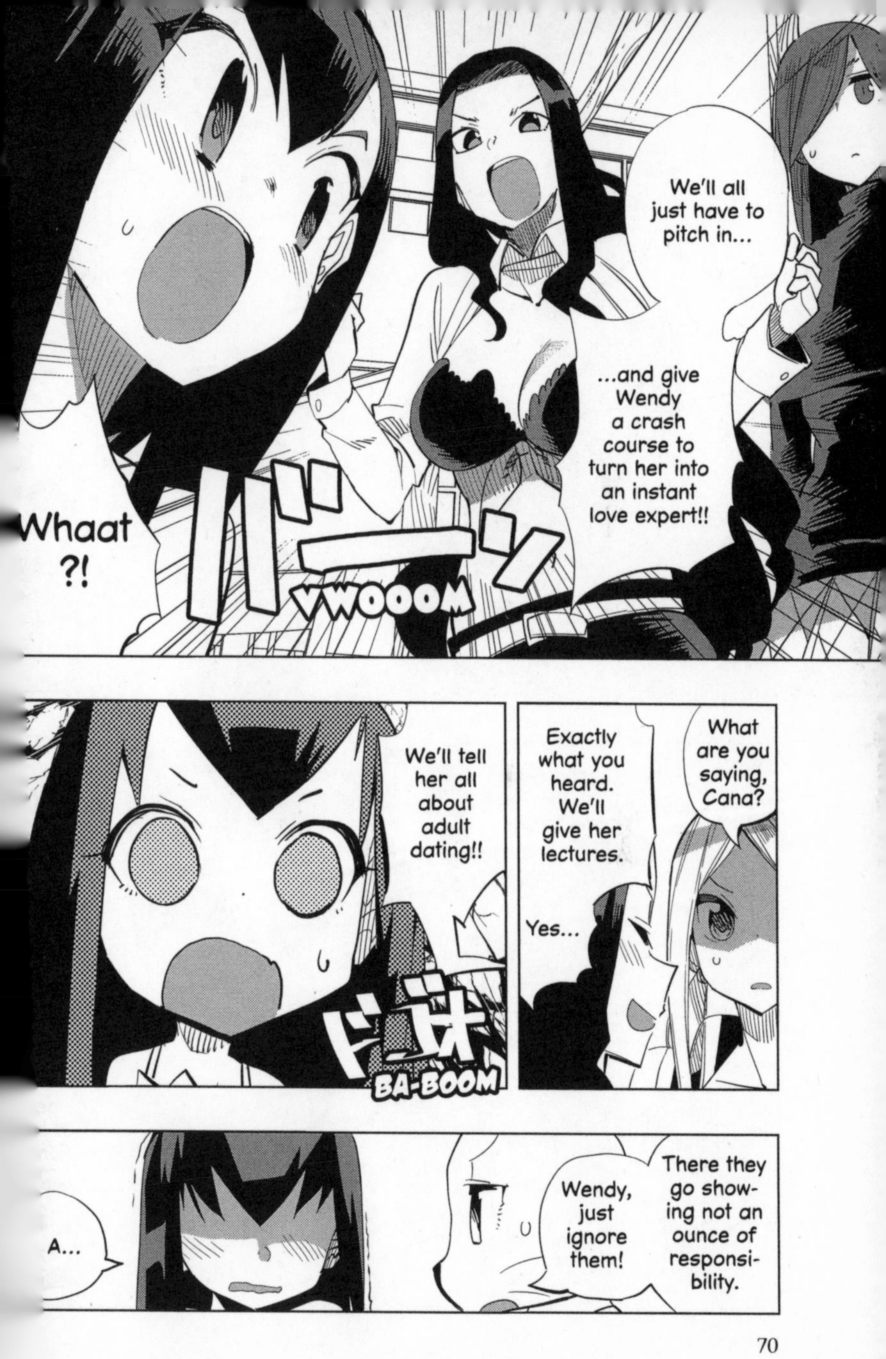
We'll all just have to pitch in...
...and give Wendy a crash course to turn her into an instant love expert!!
VWOOOM
Whaat ?!
What are you saying, Cana?
Exactly what you heard. We'll give her lectures.
Yes...
We'll tell her all about adult dating!!
BA-BOOM
There they go show-ing not an ounce of responsi-bility.
Wendy, just ignore them!
A...

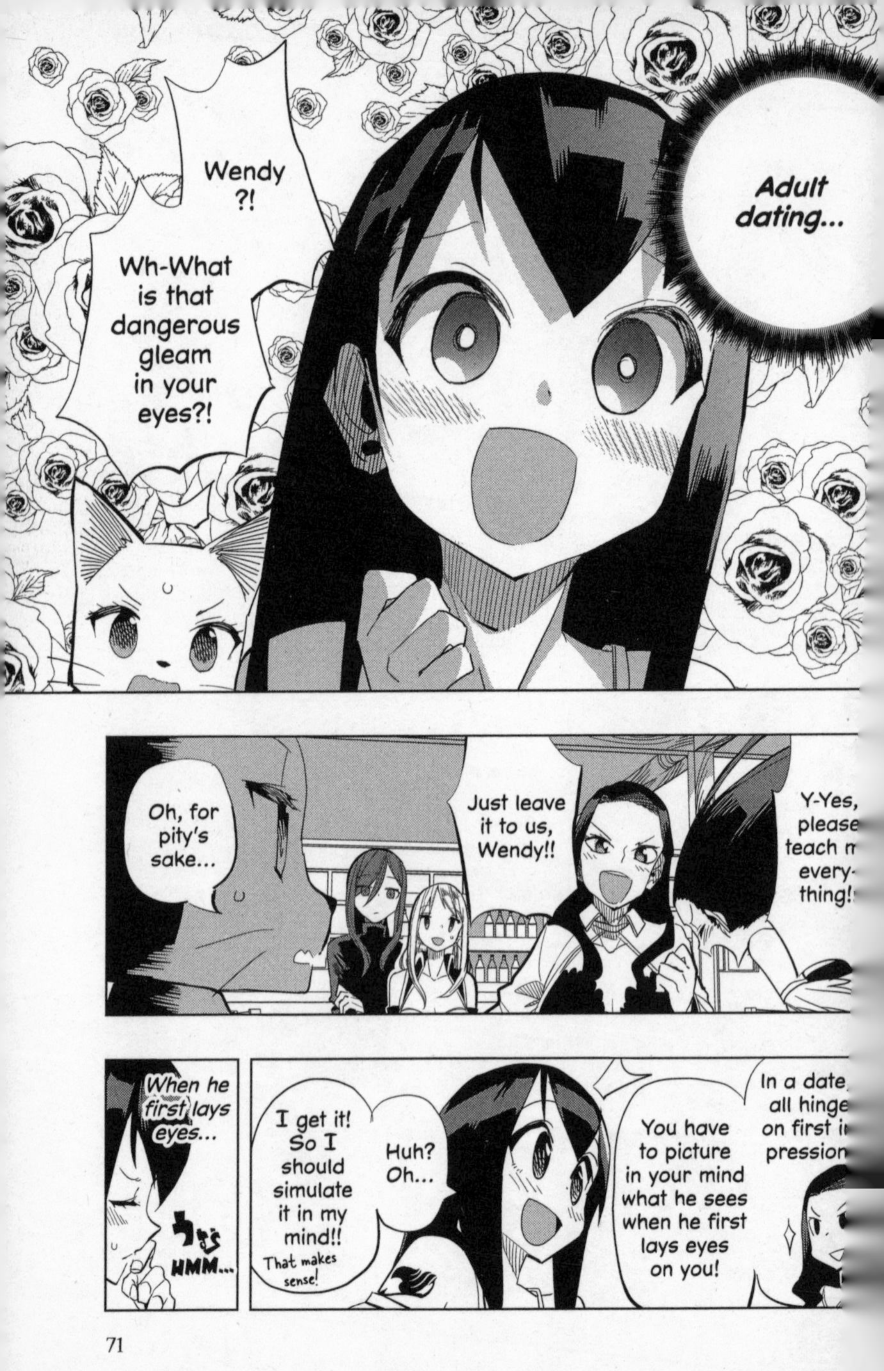

Adult dating...
Wendy ?!
Wh-What is that dangerous gleam in your eyes?!
Y-Yes, please teach m every- thing!
Just leave it to us, Wendy!!
Oh, for pity's sake...
In a date all hinge on first i pression
You have to picture in your mind what he sees when he first lays eyes on you!
Huh? Oh...
I get it! So I should simulate it in my mind!!
That makes sense!
When he first lays eyes...
HMM...

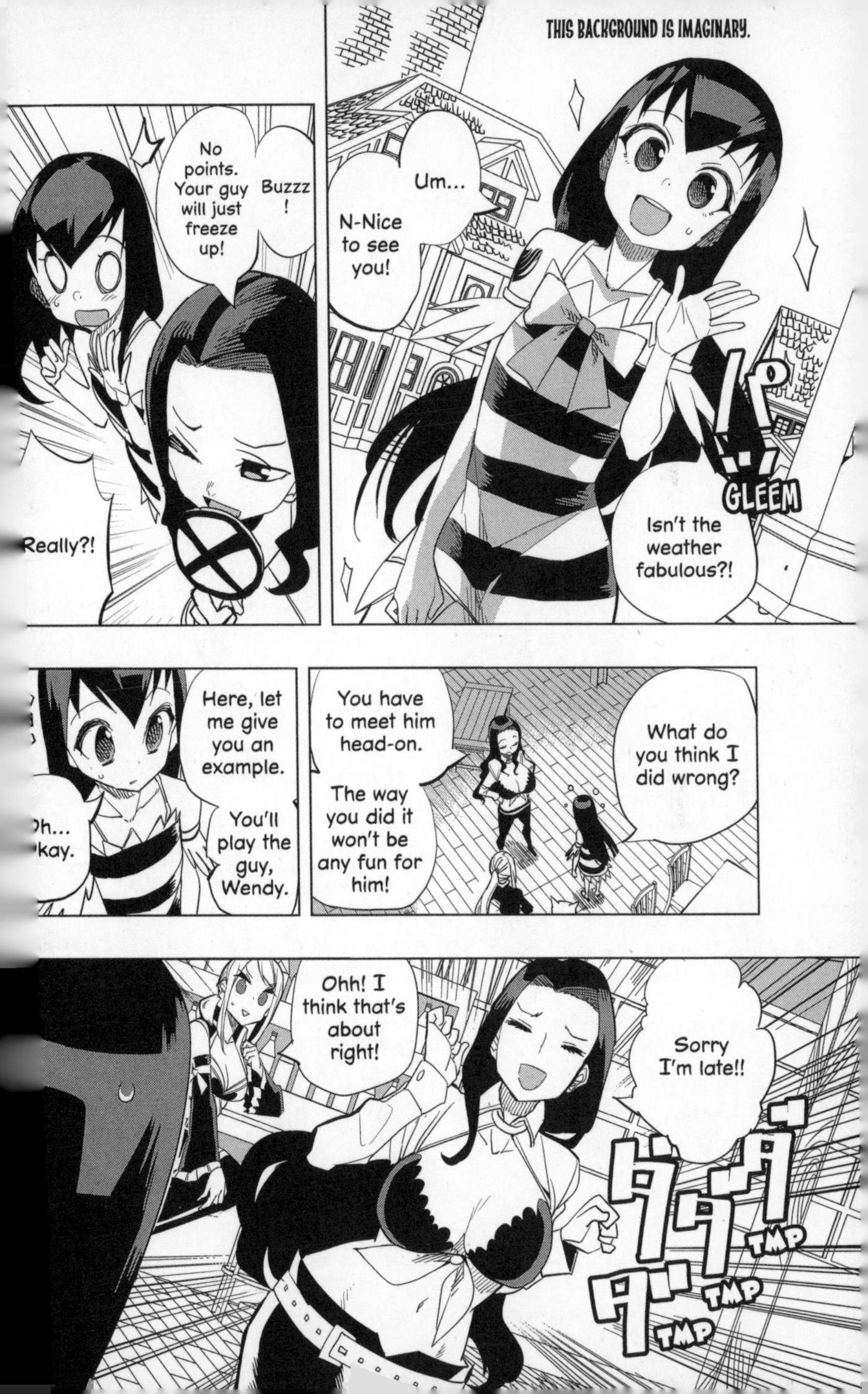
THIS BACKGROUND IS IMAGINARY.
Um...
N-Nice to see you!
GLEEM
Isn't the weather fabulous?!
Buzzz!
No points. Your guy will just freeze up!
Really?!
What do you think I did wrong?
You have to meet him head-on.
The way you did it won't be any fun for him!
Here, let me give you an example.
You'll play the guy, Wendy.
h... kay.
TMP TMP TMP
Sorry I'm late!!
Ohh! I think that's about right!

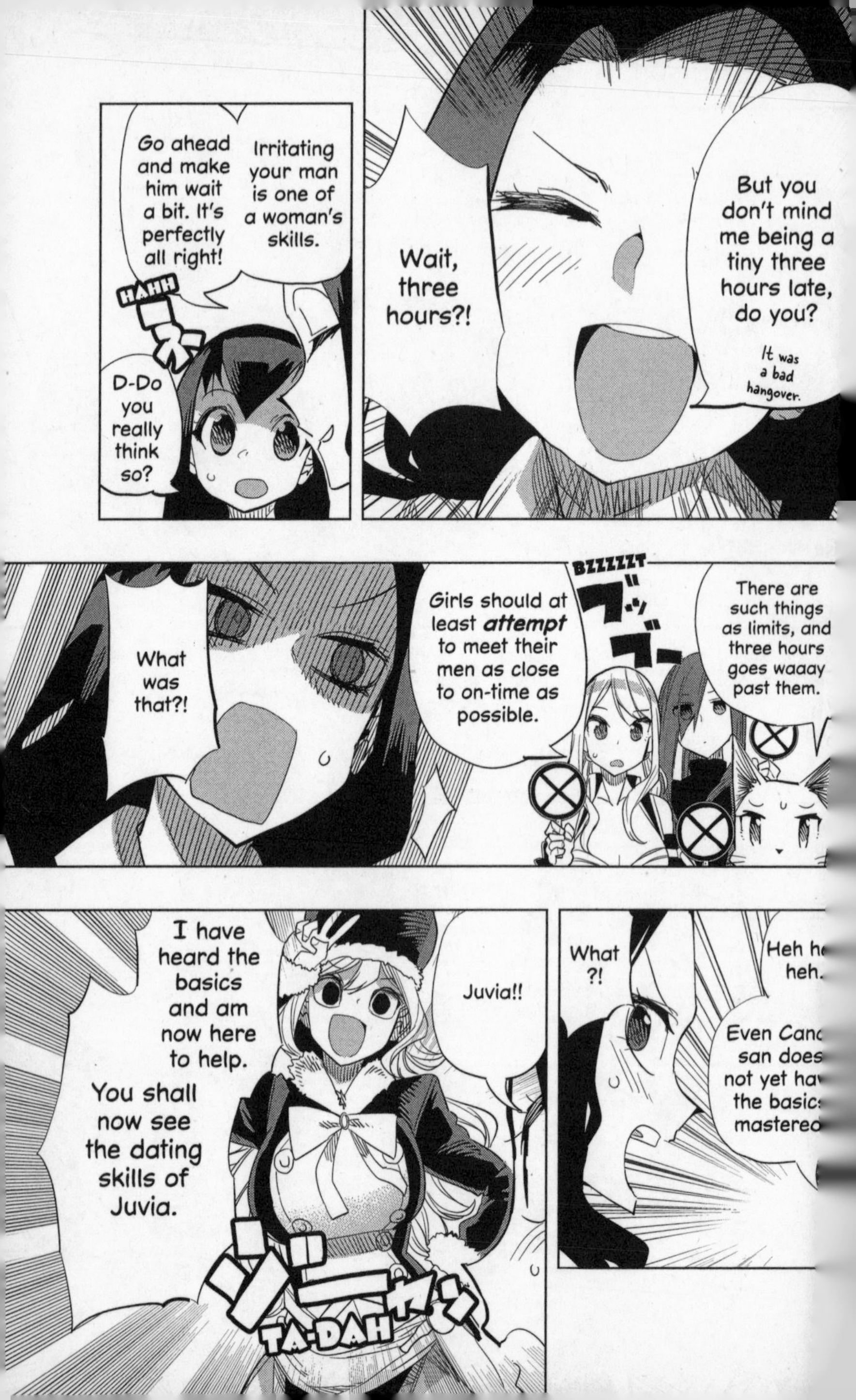

But you don't mind me being a tiny three hours late, do you?
It was a bad hangover.
Wait, three hours?!
Irritating your man is one of a woman's skills.
Go ahead and make him wait a bit. It's perfectly all right!
HAHH
D-Do you really think so?
There are such things as limits, and three hours goes waaay past them.
BZZZZZT
Girls should at least *attempt* to meet their men as close to on-time as possible.
What was that?!
Heh h heh.
Even Canc san does not yet hav the basics mastered
What ?!
Juvia!!
I have heard the basics and am now here to help.
You shall now see the dating skills of Juvia.
TA-DAH

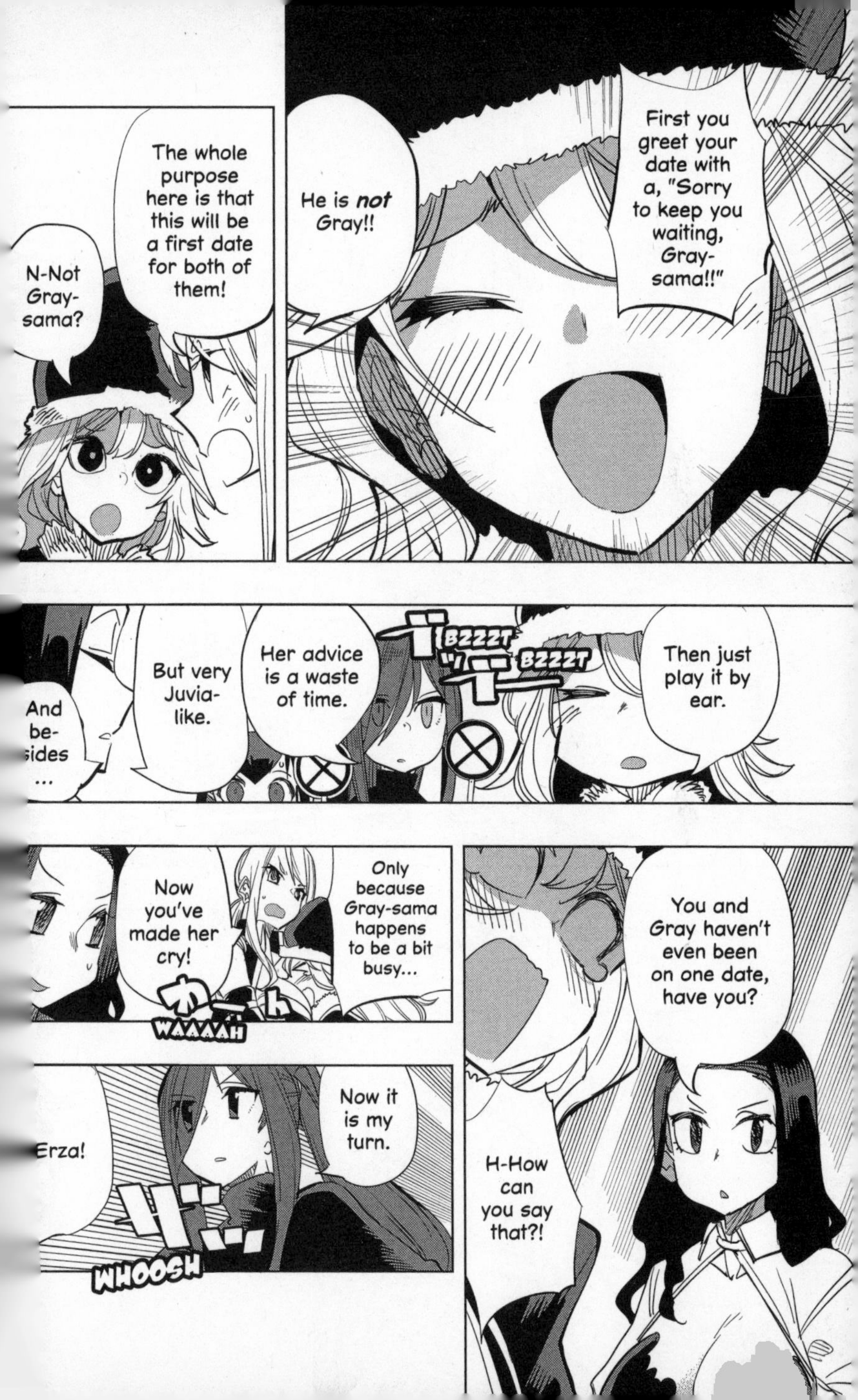
First you greet your date with a, "Sorry to keep you waiting, Gray-sama!!"
He is *not* Gray!!
The whole purpose here is that this will be a first date for both of them!
N-Not Gray-sama?
Then just play it by ear.
BZZZT
BZZZT
Her advice is a waste of time.
But very Juvia-like.
And besides …
You and Gray haven't even been on one date, have you?
H-How can you say that?!
Only because Gray-sama happens to be a bit busy...
Now you've made her cry!
WAAAAH
Now it is my turn.
WHOOSH
Erza!

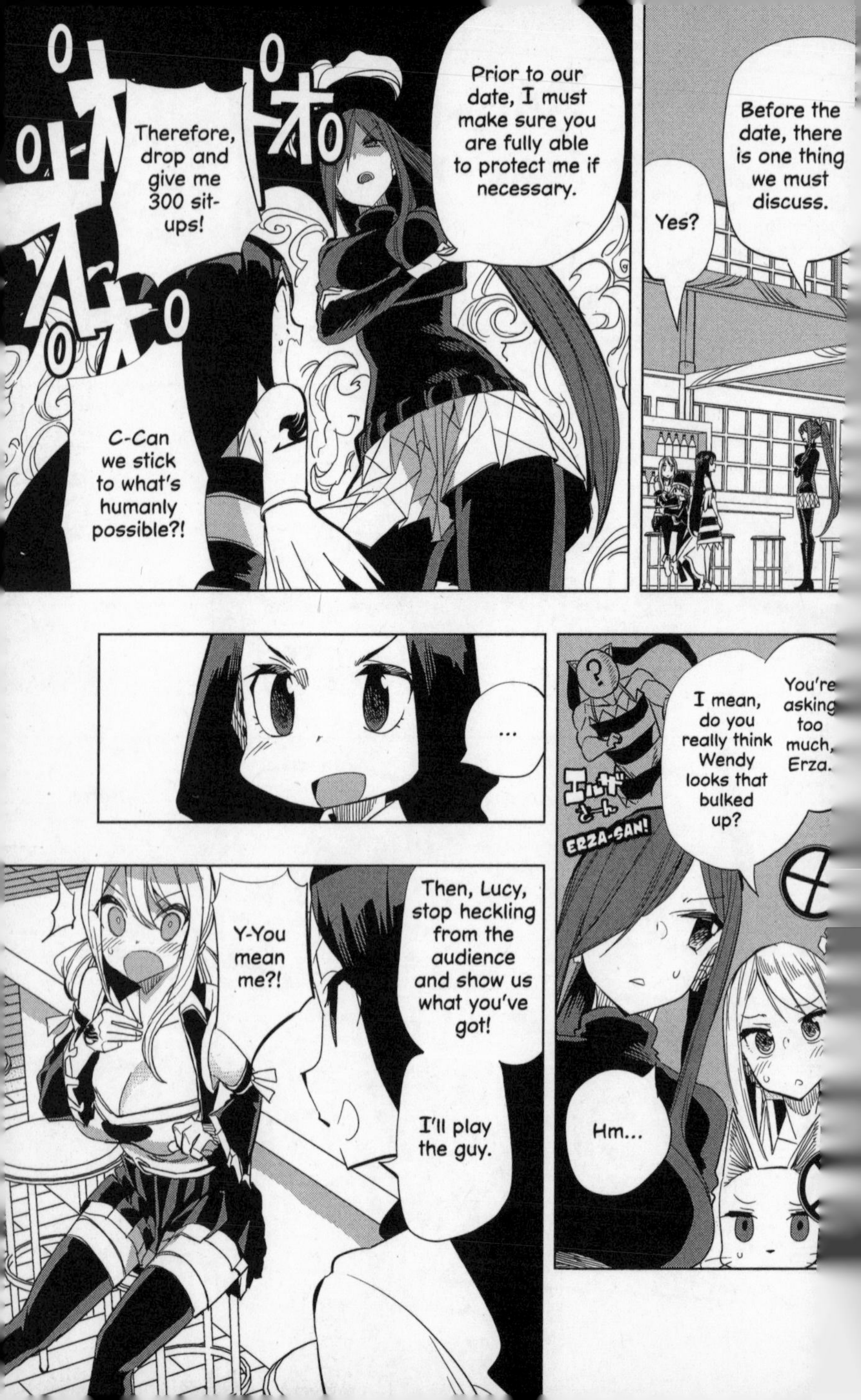
Before the date, there is one thing we must discuss.
Yes?
Prior to our date, I must make sure you are fully able to protect me if necessary.
Therefore, drop and give me 300 sit-ups!
C-Can we stick to what's humanly possible?!
You're asking too much, Erza.
I mean, do you really think Wendy looks that bulked up?
ERZA-SAN!
Hm...
...
Then, Lucy, stop heckling from the audience and show us what you've got!
Y-You mean me?!
I'll play the guy.

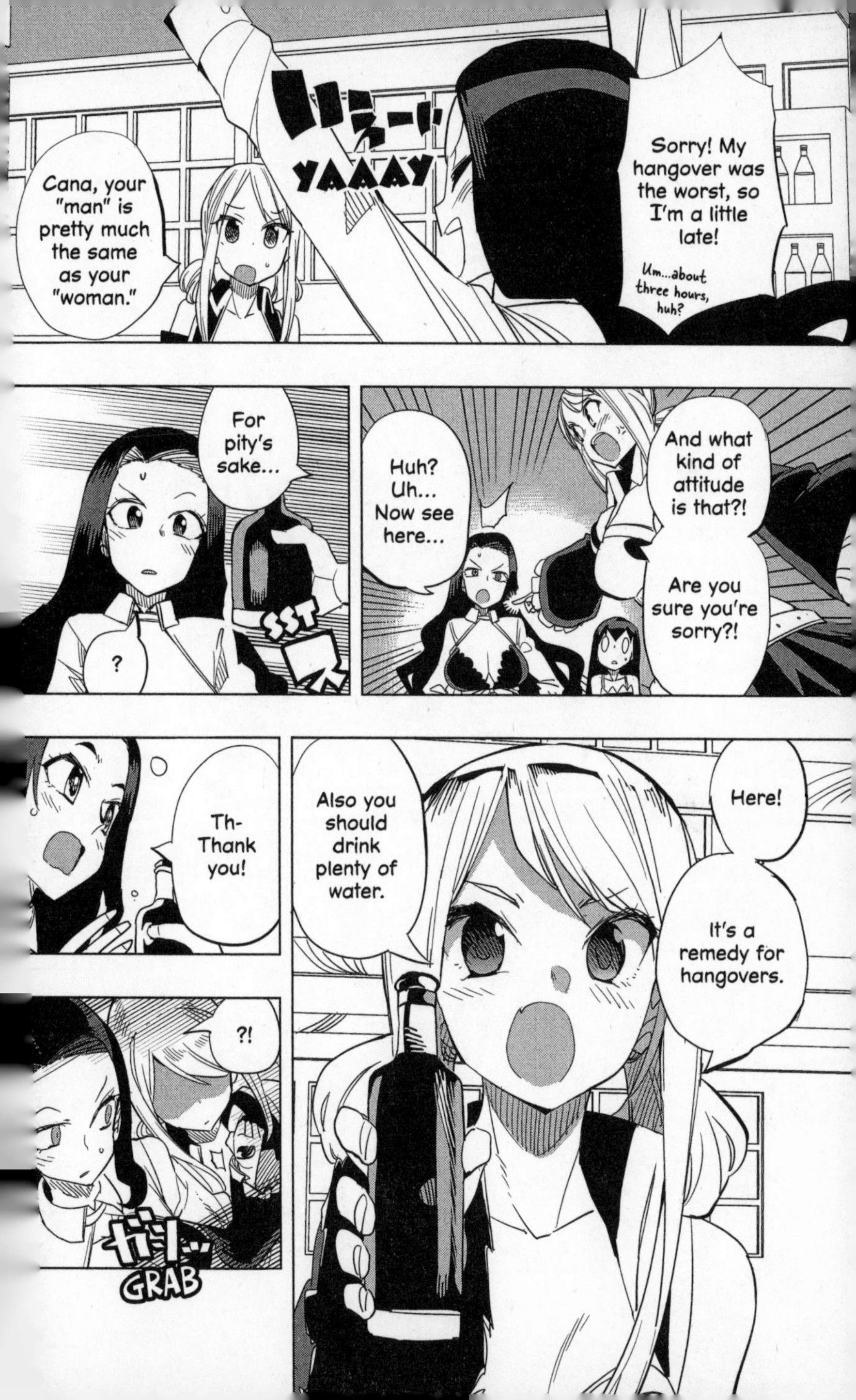
Sorry! My hangover was the worst, so I'm a little late!
Um...about three hours, huh?
YAAAY
Cana, your "man" is pretty much the same as your "woman."
And what kind of attitude is that?!
Are you sure you're sorry?!
Huh? Uh... Now see here...
For pity's sake...
SST
?
Here!
It's a remedy for hangovers.
Also you should drink plenty of water.
Th- Thank you!
?!
GRAB

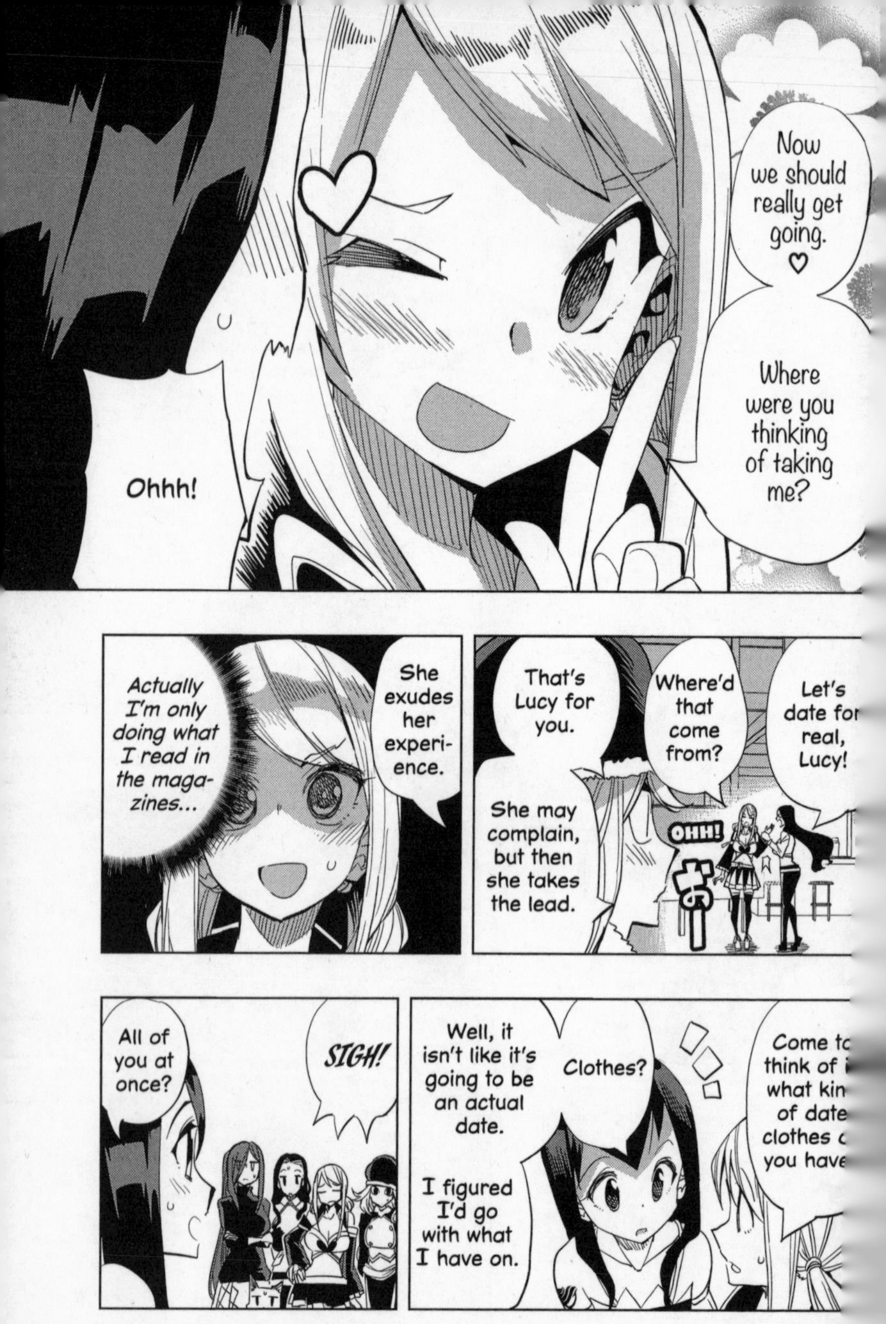
Now we should really get going. ♡
Where were you thinking of taking me?
Ohhh!
Let's date fo real, Lucy!
Where'd that come from?
That's Lucy for you.
She may complain, but then she takes the lead.
OHH!
She exudes her experience.
Actually I'm only doing what I read in the magazines...
Come t think of what kin of date clothes you have
Clothes?
Well, it isn't like it's going to be an actual date.
I figured I'd go with what I have on.
SIGH!
All of you at once?

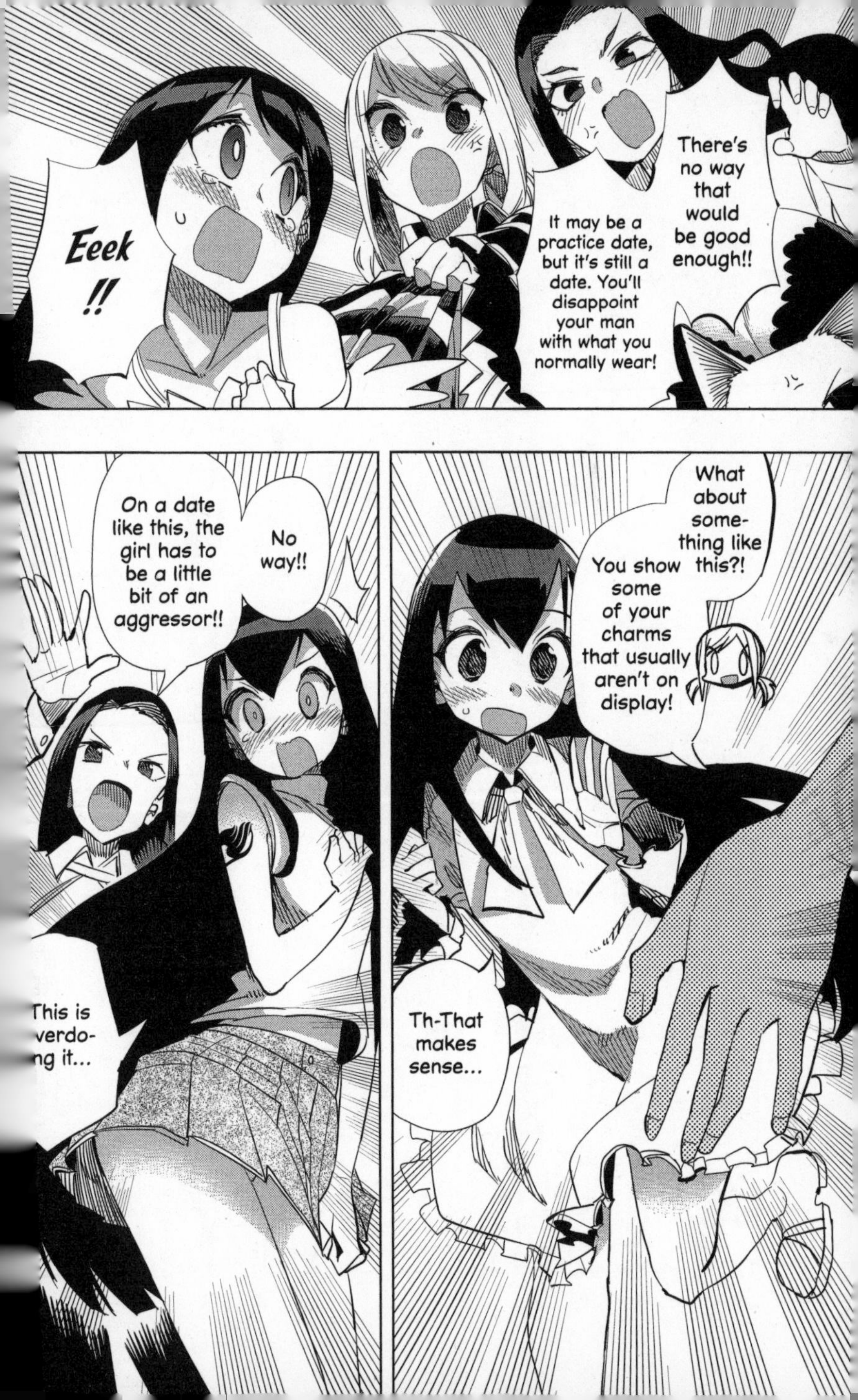
There's no way that would be good enough!!
It may be a practice date, but it's still a date. You'll disappoint your man with what you normally wear!
Eeek!!
What about some-thing like this?!
You show some of your charms that usually aren't on display!
Th-That makes sense...
No way!!
On a date like this, the girl has to be a little bit of an aggressor!!
This is verdo-ng it...

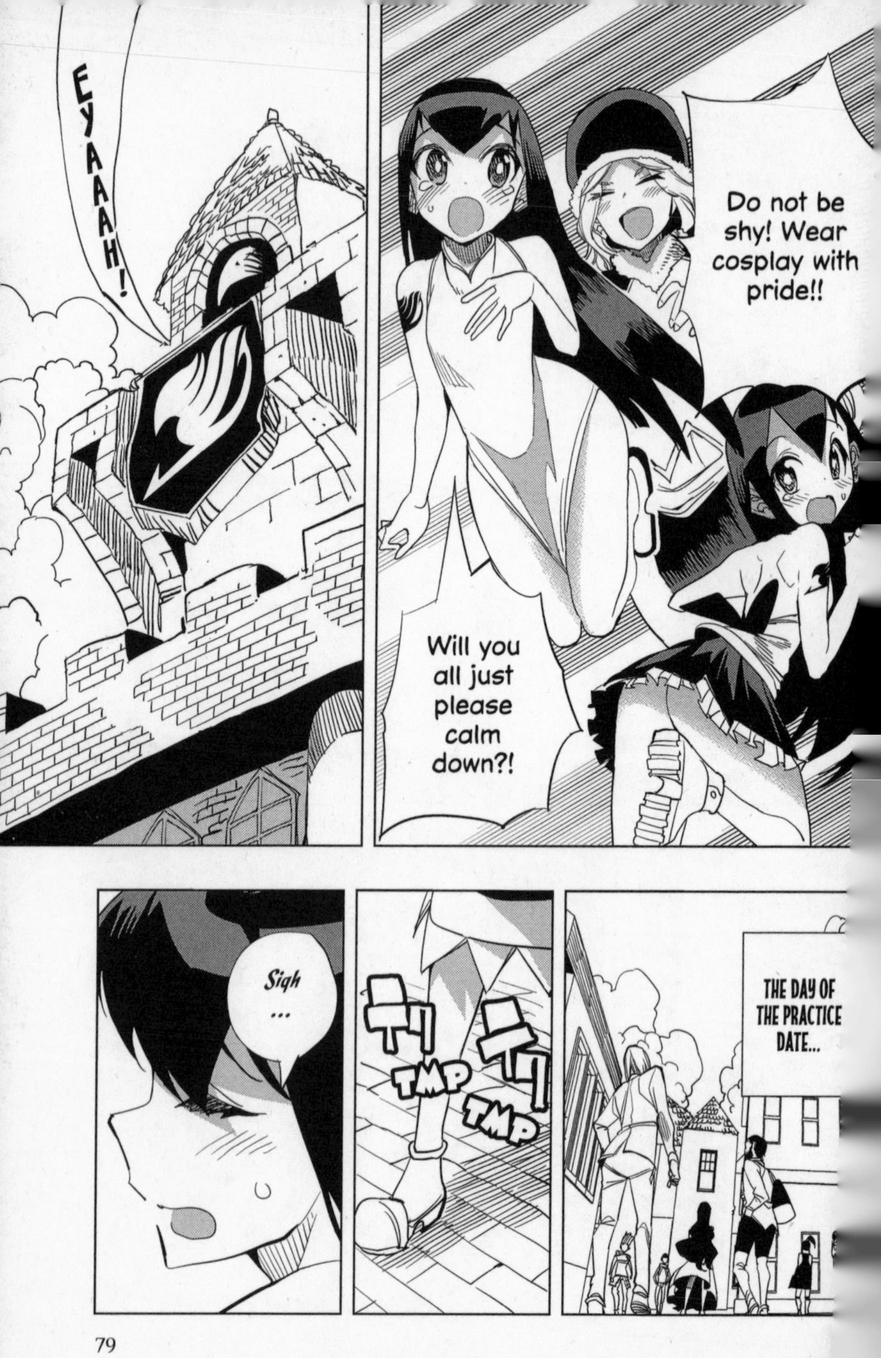
Do not be shy! Wear cosplay with pride!!
Will you all just please calm down?!
EYAAAH!
THE DAY OF THE PRACTICE DATE...
TMP
TMP
Sigh ...

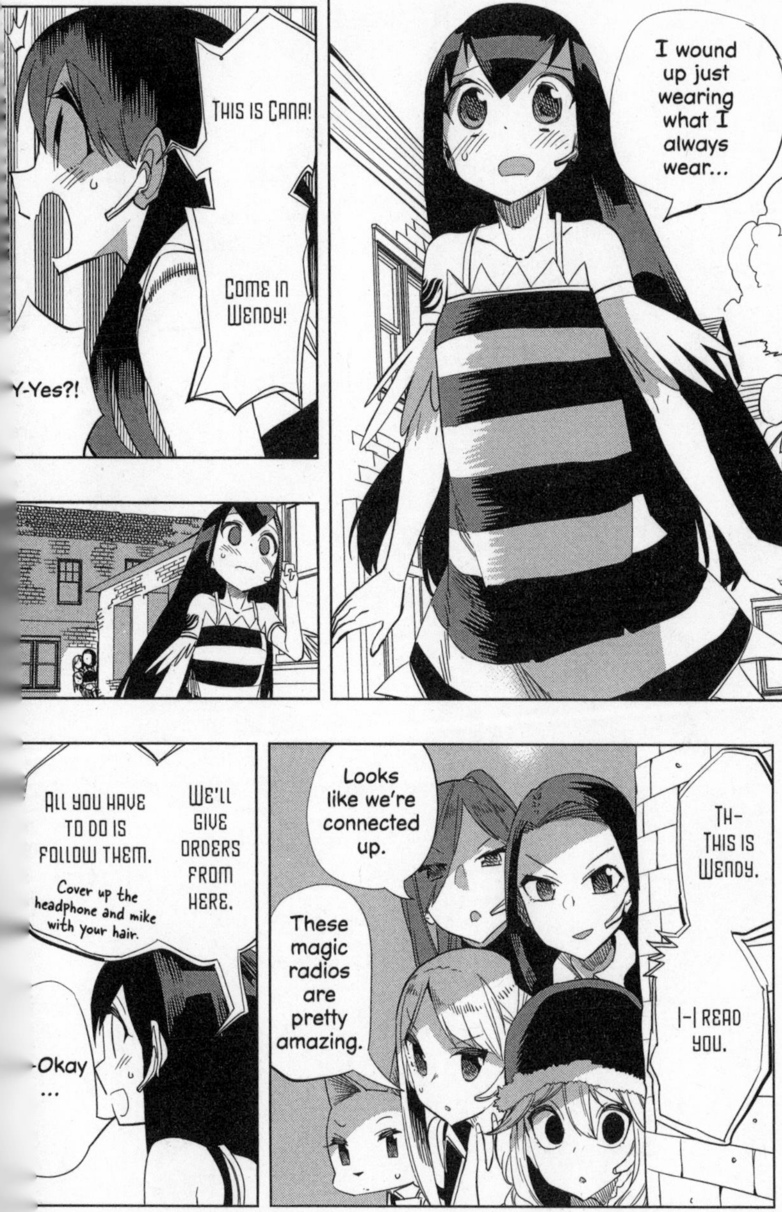
I wound up just wearing what I always wear...
THIS IS CANA!
COME IN WENDY!
Y-Yes?!
TH-THIS IS WENDY.
I-I READ YOU.
Looks like we're connected up.
These magic radios are pretty amazing.
WE'LL GIVE ORDERS FROM HERE.
ALL YOU HAVE TO DO IS FOLLOW THEM.
Cover up the headphone and mike with your hair.
-Okay ...

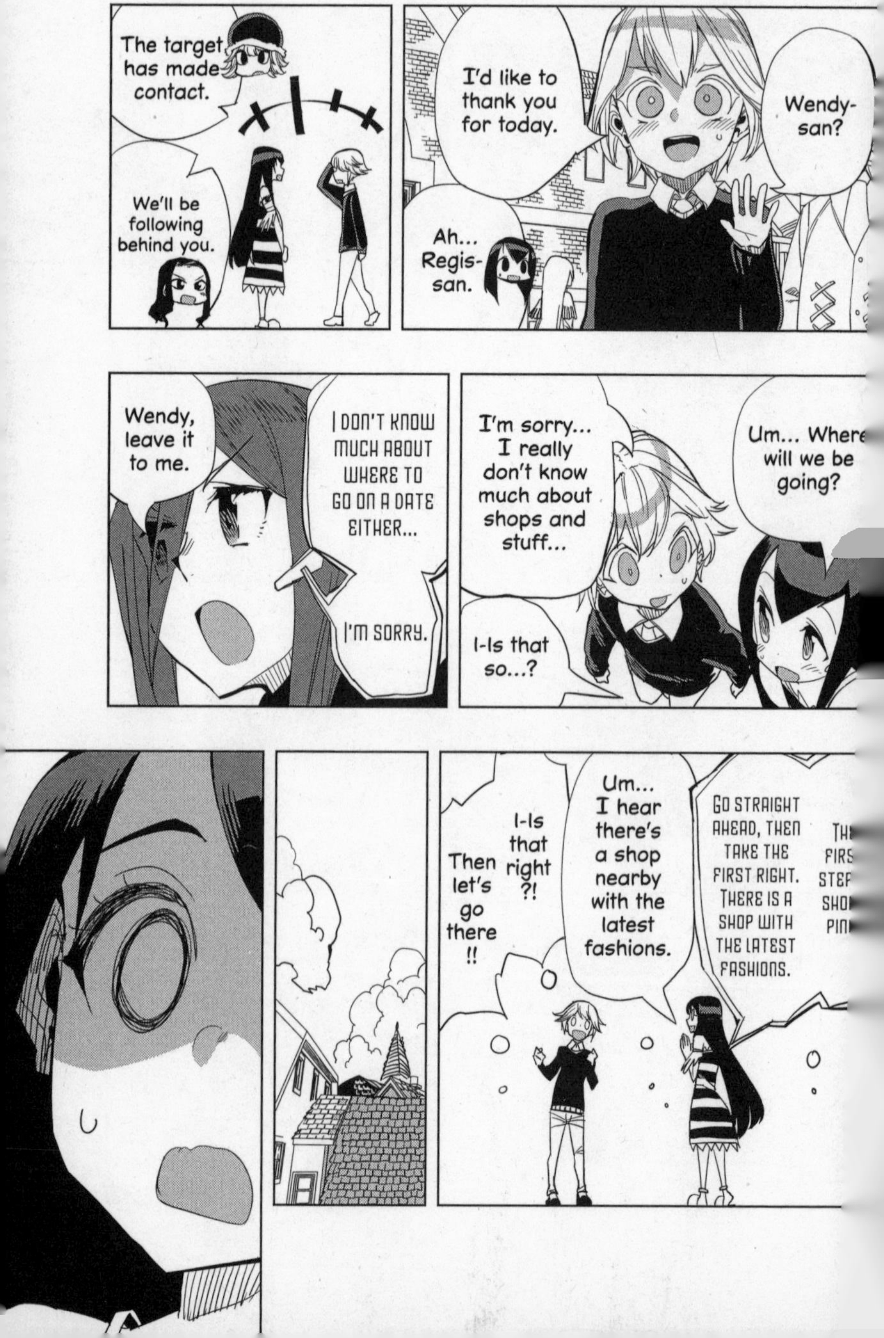
Wendy-san?
I'd like to thank you for today.
Ah... Regis-san.
The target has made contact.
We'll be following behind you.
Um... Where will we be going?
I'm sorry... I really don't know much about shops and stuff...
I-Is that so...?
I DON'T KNOW MUCH ABOUT WHERE TO GO ON A DATE EITHER...
I'M SORRY.
Wendy, leave it to me.
GO STRAIGHT AHEAD, THEN TAKE THE FIRST RIGHT. THERE IS A SHOP WITH THE LATEST FASHIONS.
Um... I hear there's a shop nearby with the latest fashions.
I-Is that right?!
Then let's go there!!

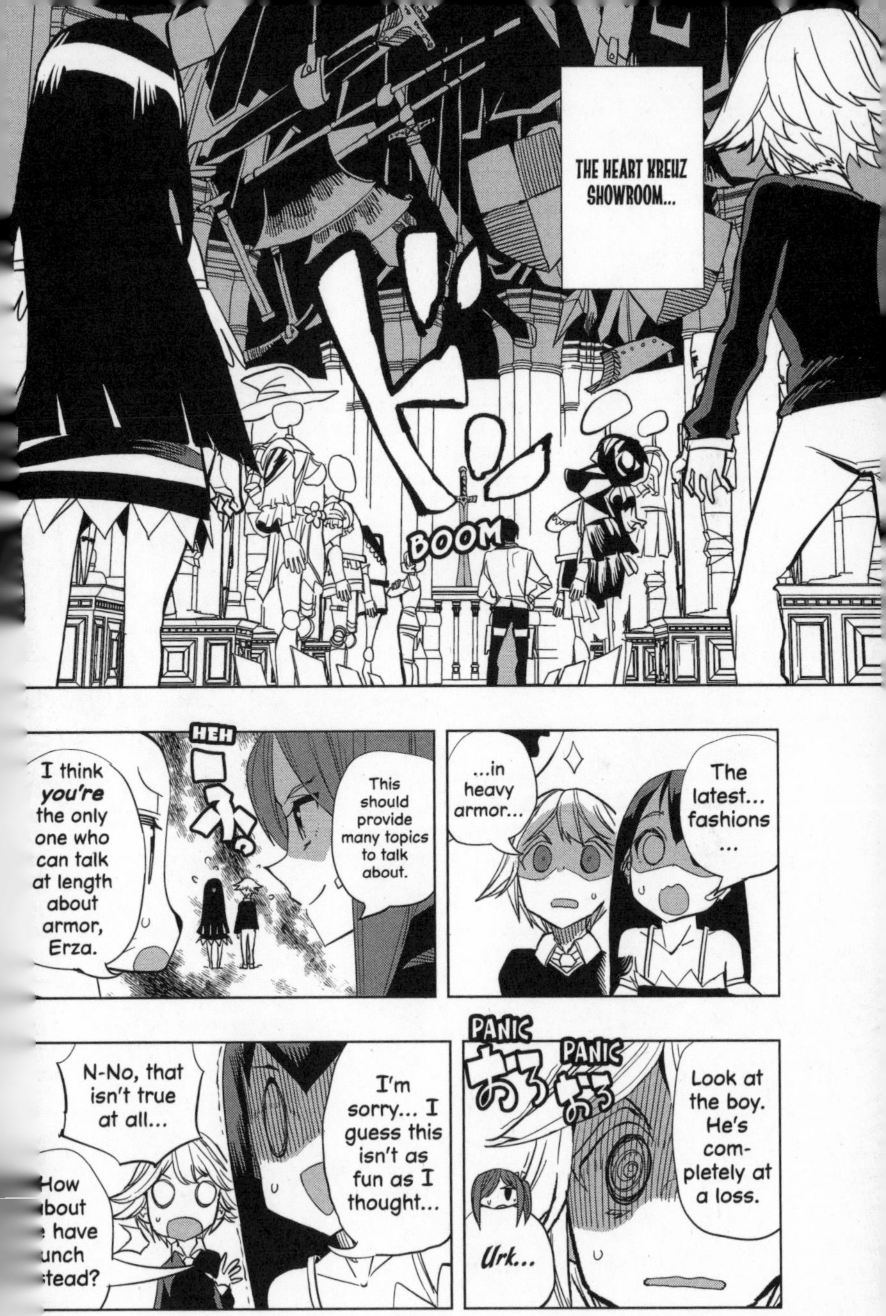
THE HEART KREUZ SHOWROOM...
BOOM
The latest... fashions ...
...in heavy armor...
This should provide many topics to talk about.
HEH
I think *you're* the only one who can talk at length about armor, Erza.
PANIC
PANIC
Look at the boy. He's com-pletely at a loss.
Urk...
I'm sorry... I guess this isn't as fun as I thought...
N-No, that isn't true at all...
How bout e have unch stead?

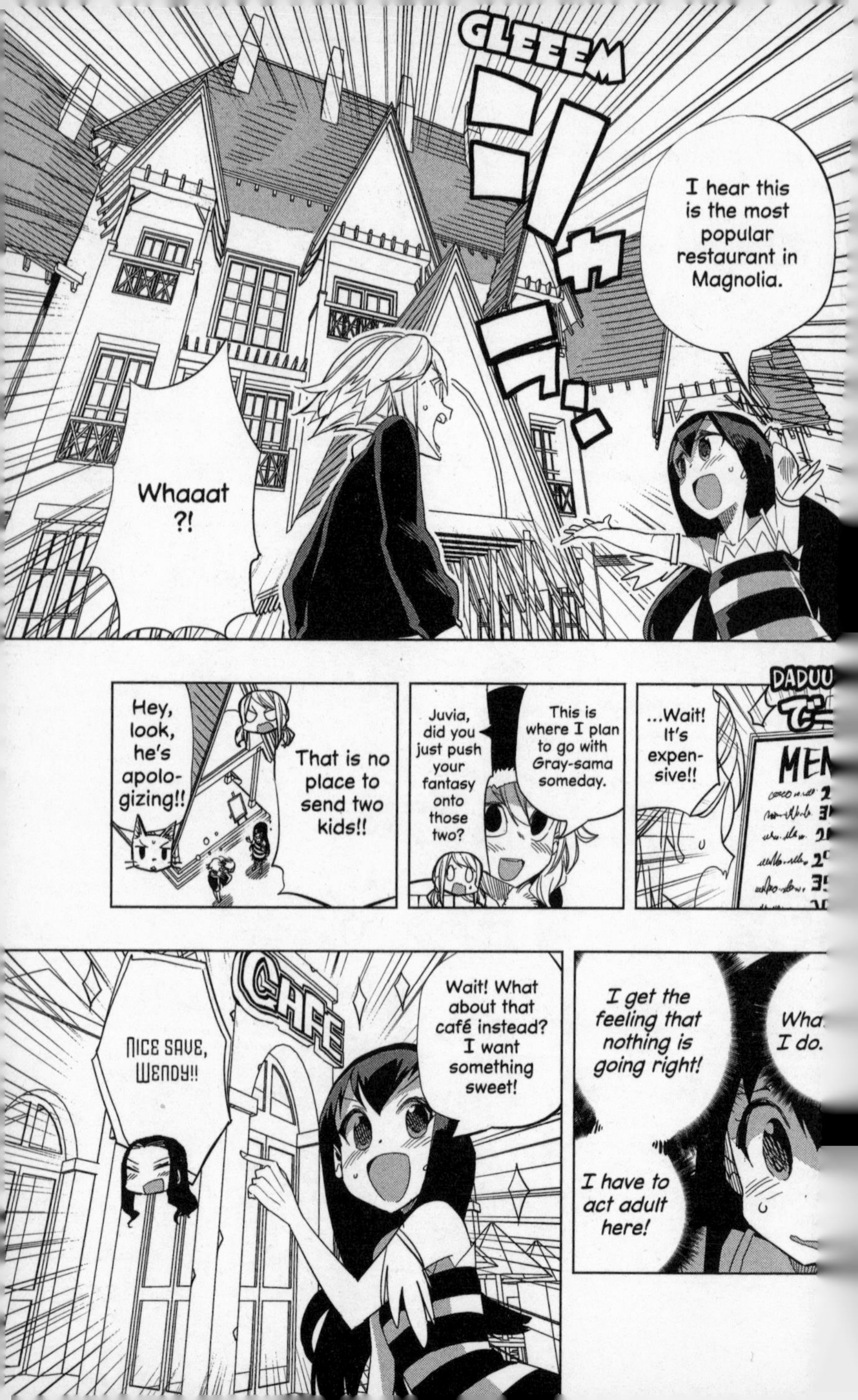
GLEEEM
I hear this is the most popular restaurant in Magnolia.
Whaaat?!
DADUU
...Wait! It's expen-sive!!
This is where I plan to go with Gray-sama someday.
Juvia, did you just push your fantasy onto those two?
That is no place to send two kids!!
Hey, look, he's apolo-gizing!!
I get the feeling that nothing is going right!
I have to act adult here!
Wait! What about that café instead? I want something sweet!
CAFE
NICE SAVE, WENDY!!

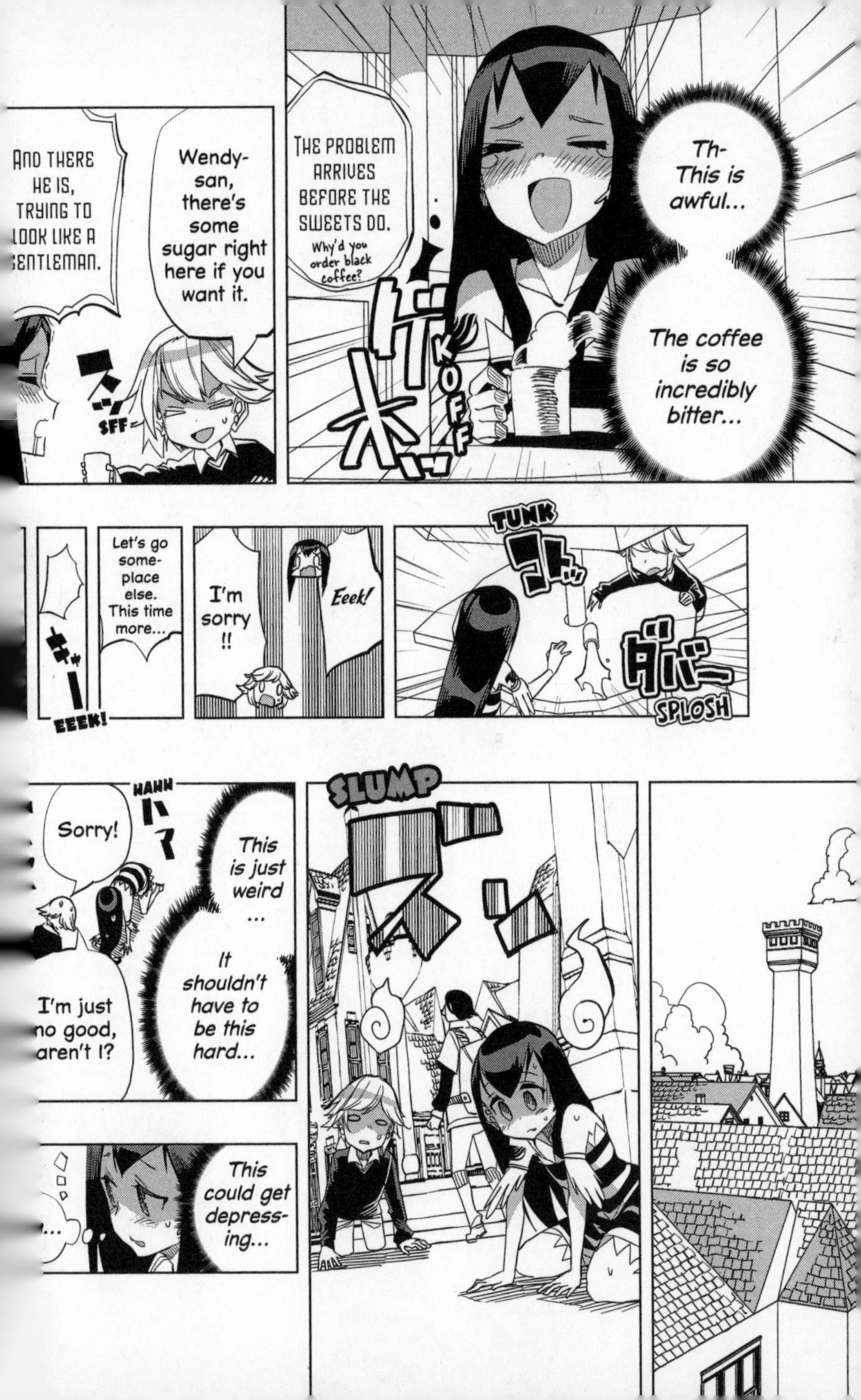
Th- This is awful...
The coffee is so incredibly bitter...
THE PROBLEM ARRIVES BEFORE THE SWEETS DO.
Why'd you order black coffee?
KOFF
Wendy-san, there's some sugar right here if you want it.
AND THERE HE IS, TRYING TO LOOK LIKE A ENTLEMAN.
SFF
TUNK
SPLOSH
Eeek!
I'm sorry !!
Let's go some-place else. This time more...
EEEK!
SLUMP
This is just weird ...
It shouldn't have to be this hard...
HAHH
Sorry!
I'm just no good, aren't I?
This could get depress-ing...
...

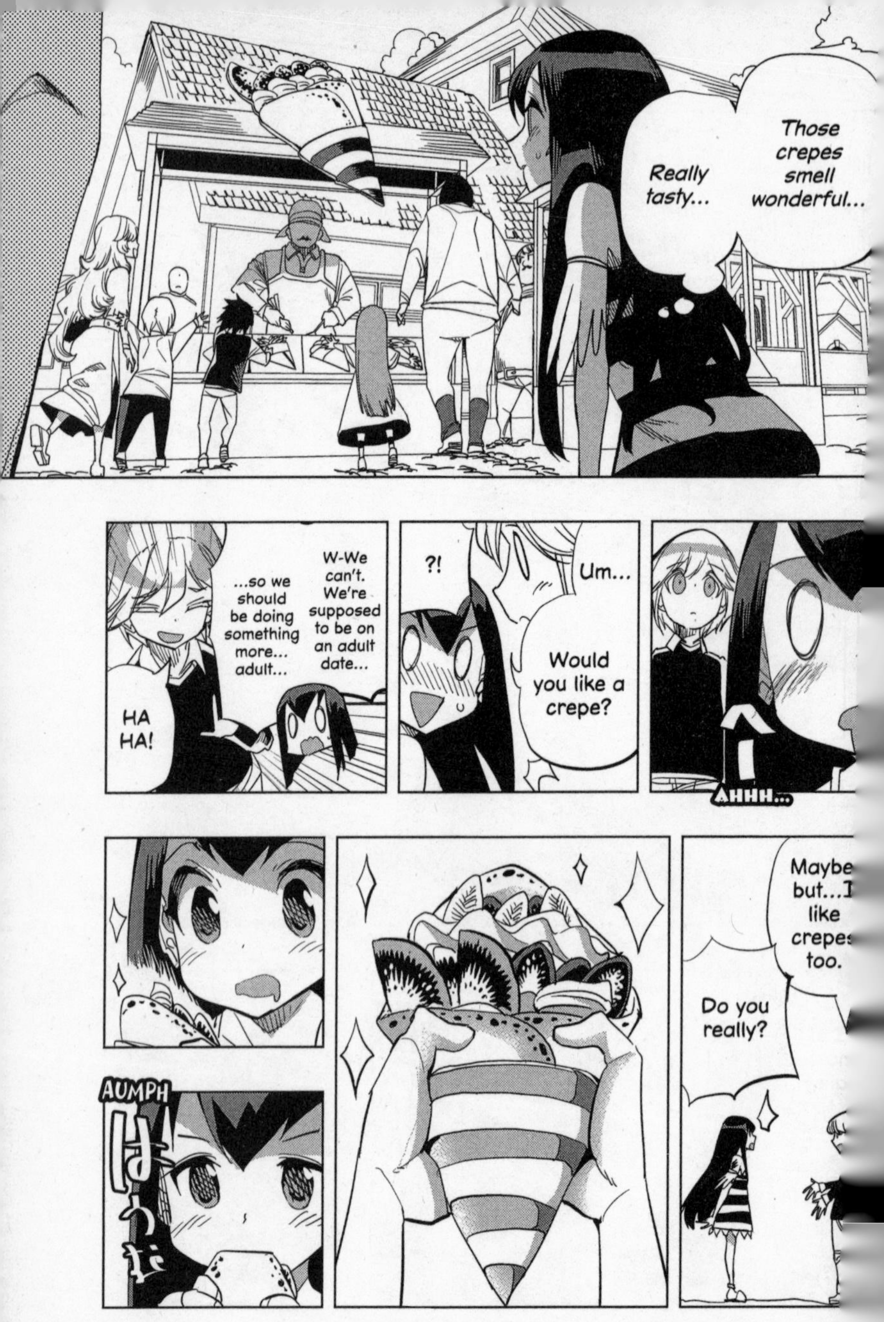

Those crepes smell wonderful...
Really tasty...
AHHH...
Um...
Would you like a crepe?
?!
W-We can't. We're supposed to be on an adult date...
...so we should be doing something more... adult...
HA HA!
Maybe but...I like crepes too.
Do you really?
AUMPH

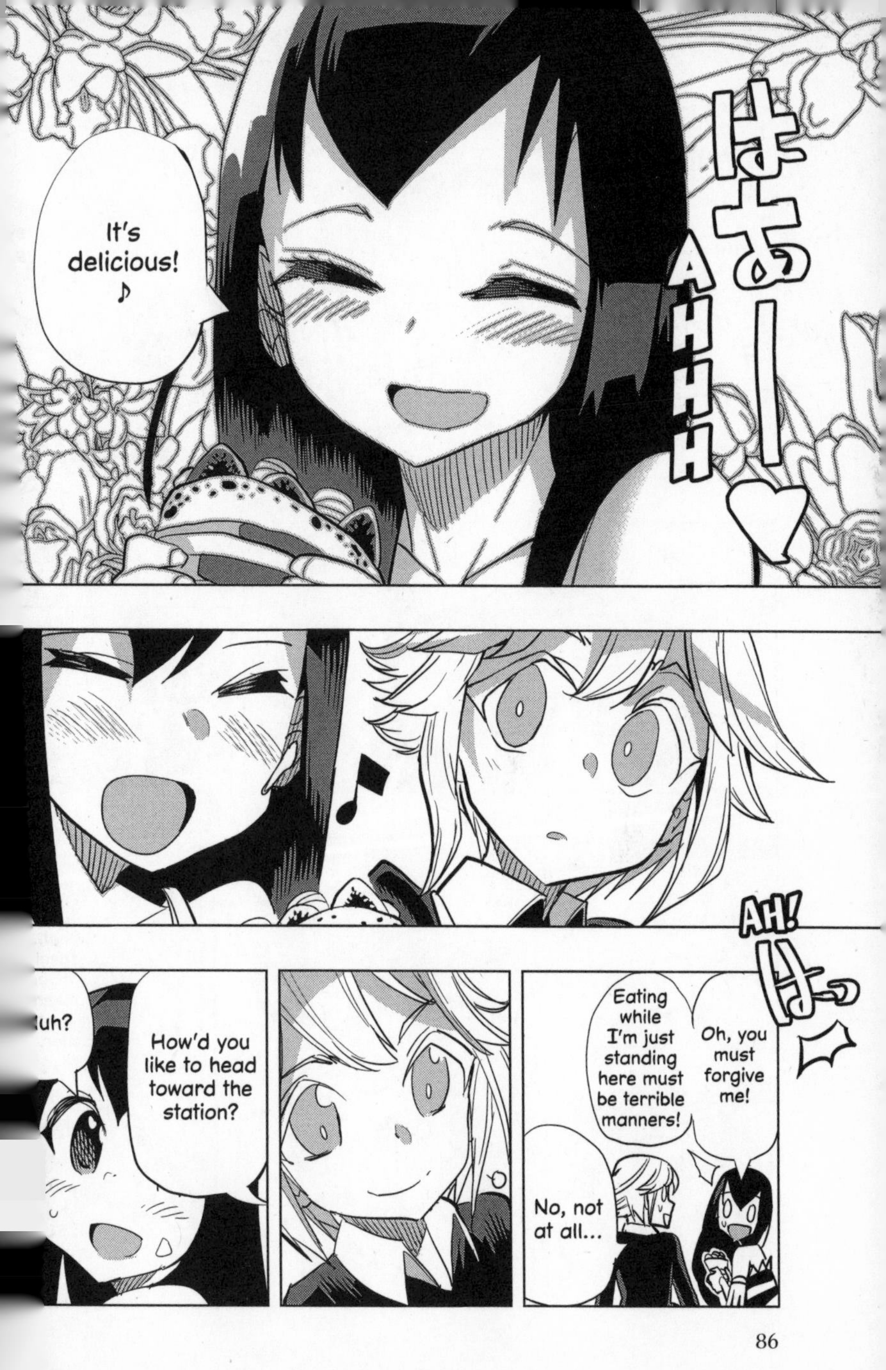
はぁー♥
AHHHH
It's delicious! ♪
AH!
はっ
Oh, you must forgive me!
Eating while I'm just standing here must be terrible manners!
No, not at all...
How'd you like to head toward the station?
uh?

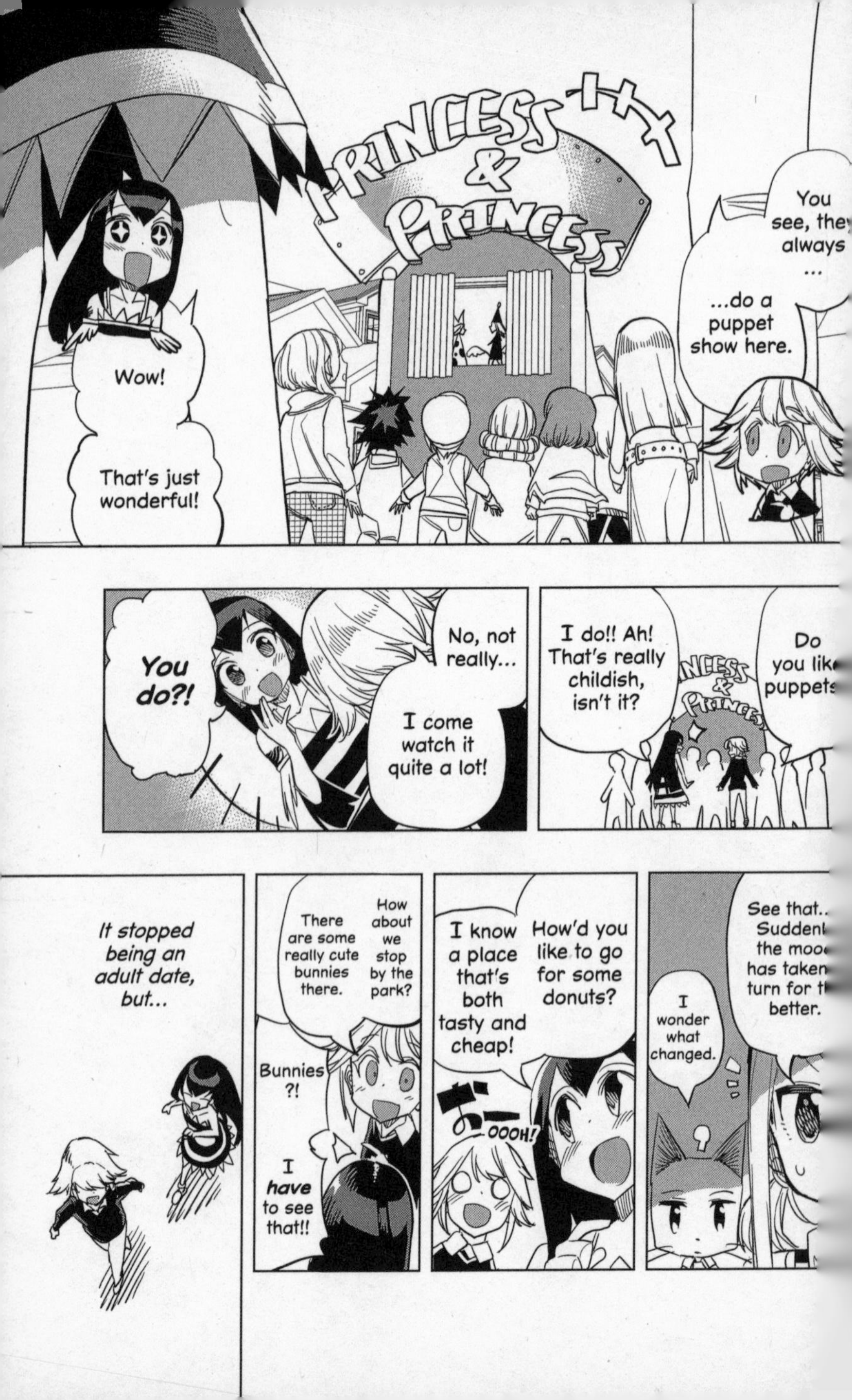
PRINCESS & PRINCESS
You see, the always ...
...do a puppet show here.
Wow!
That's just wonderful!
Do you lik puppets
I do!! Ah! That's really childish, isn't it?
No, not really...
I come watch it quite a lot!
You do?!
See that.. Suddenl the moo has taken turn for t better.
I wonder what changed.
How'd you like to go for some donuts?
I know a place that's both tasty and cheap!
OOOH!
How about we stop by the park?
There are some really cute bunnies there.
Bunnies?!
I *have* to see that!!
It stopped being an adult date, but...

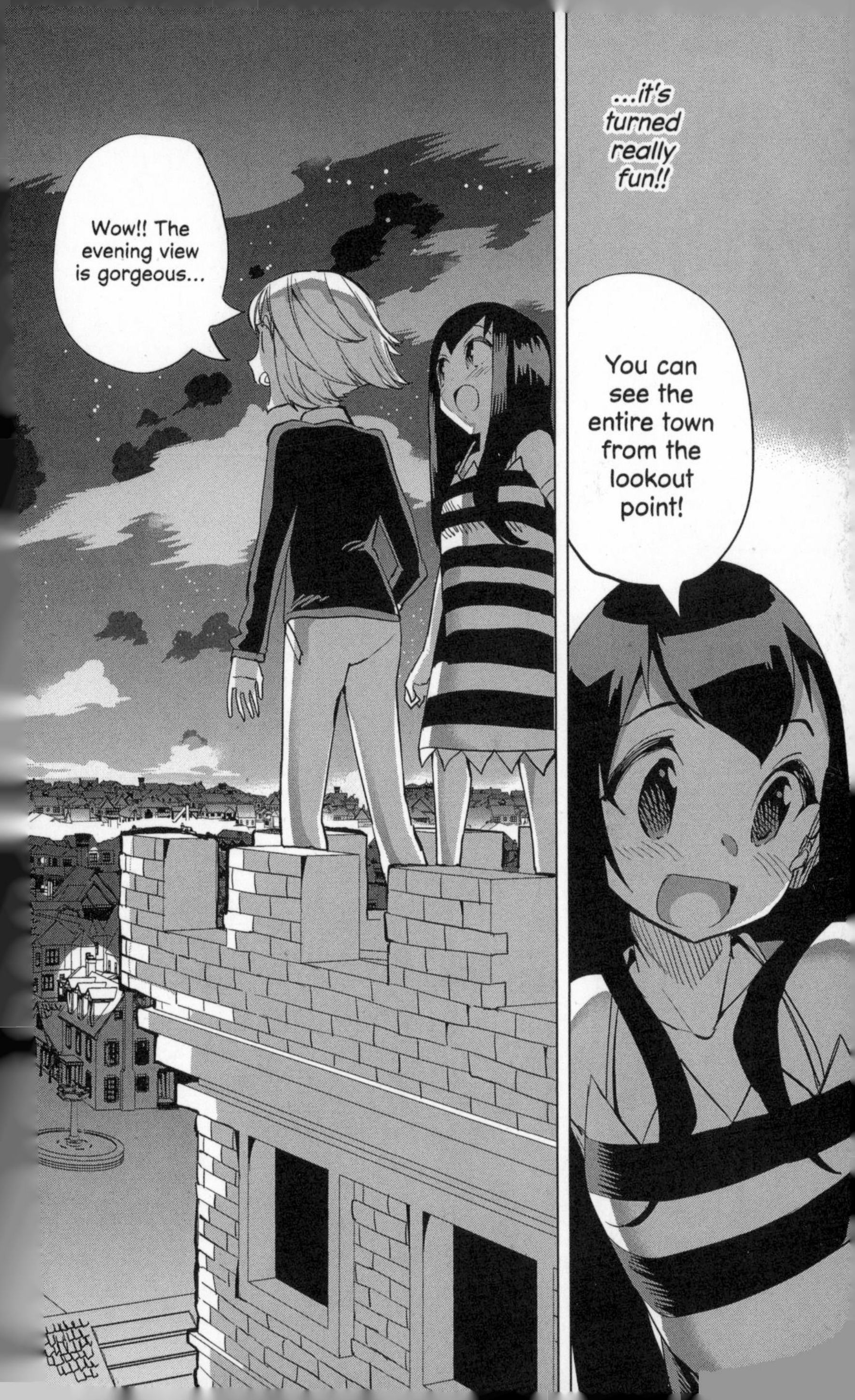
...it's turned really fun!!
You can see the entire town from the lookout point!
Wow!! The evening view is gorgeous...

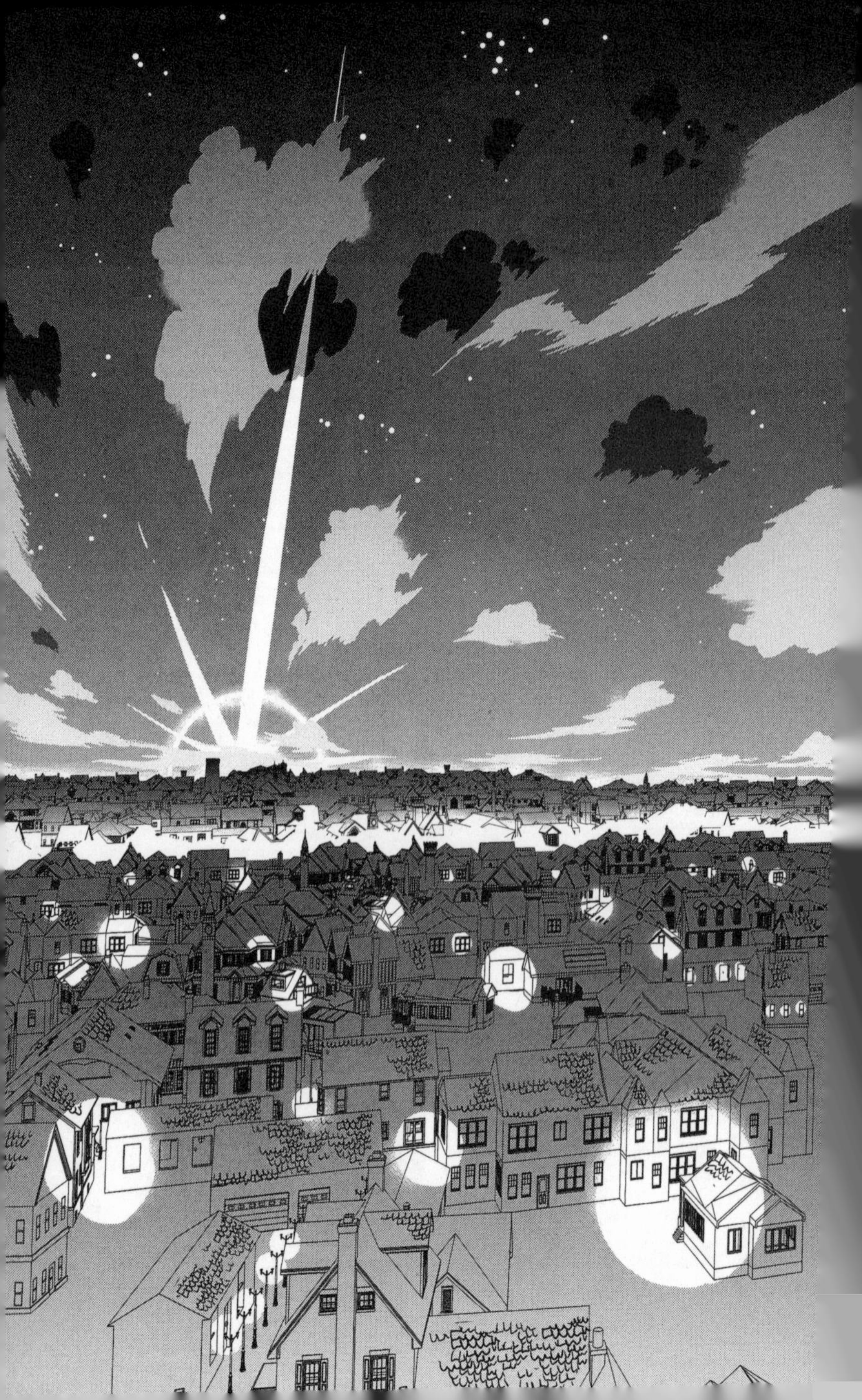

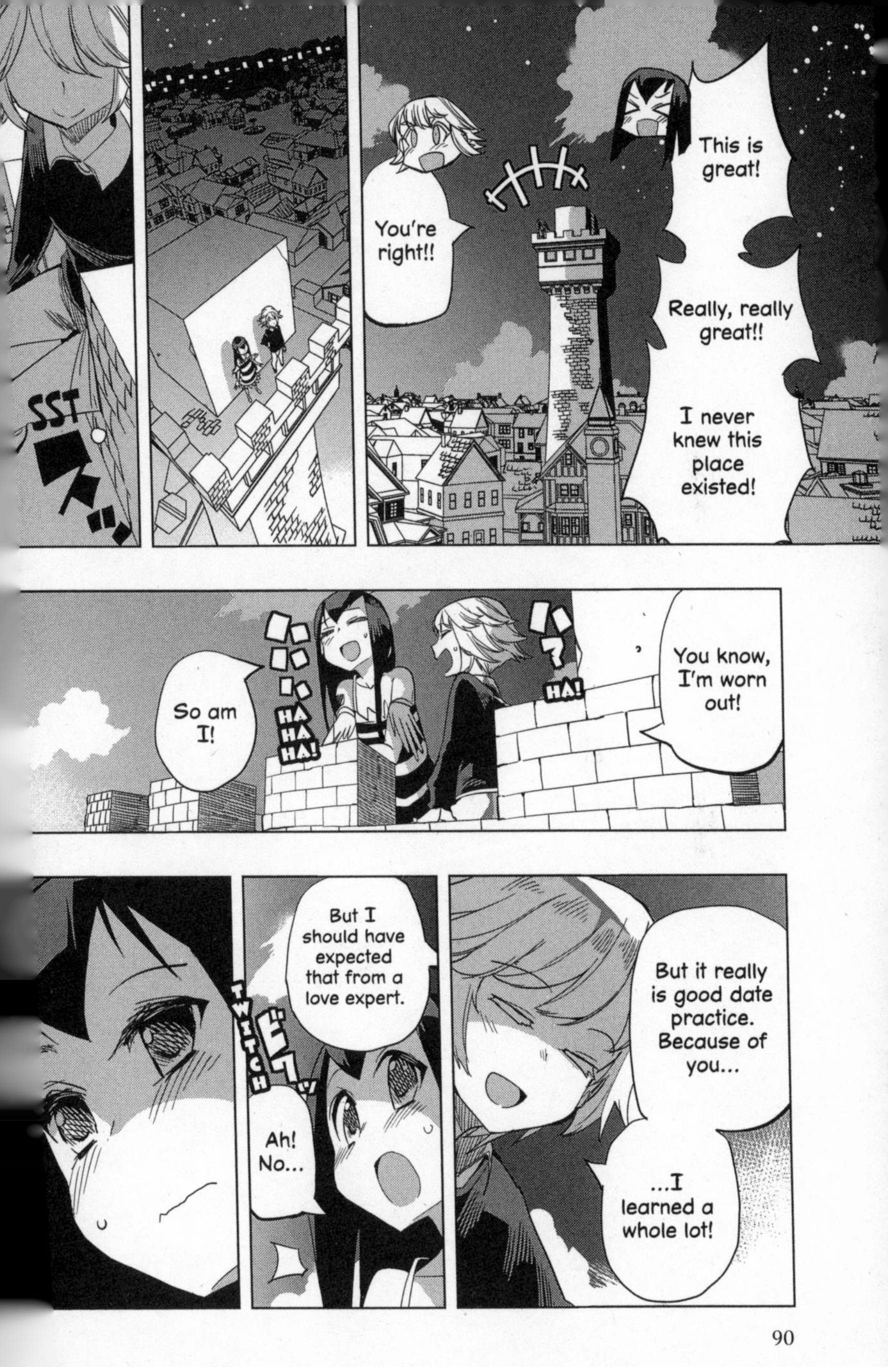
This is great!
Really, really great!!
I never knew this place existed!
You're right!!
SST
You know, I'm worn out!
?
HA!
HA HA HA!
So am I!
But it really is good date practice. Because of you...
...I learned a whole lot!
But I should have expected that from a love expert.
TWITCH
Ah! No...

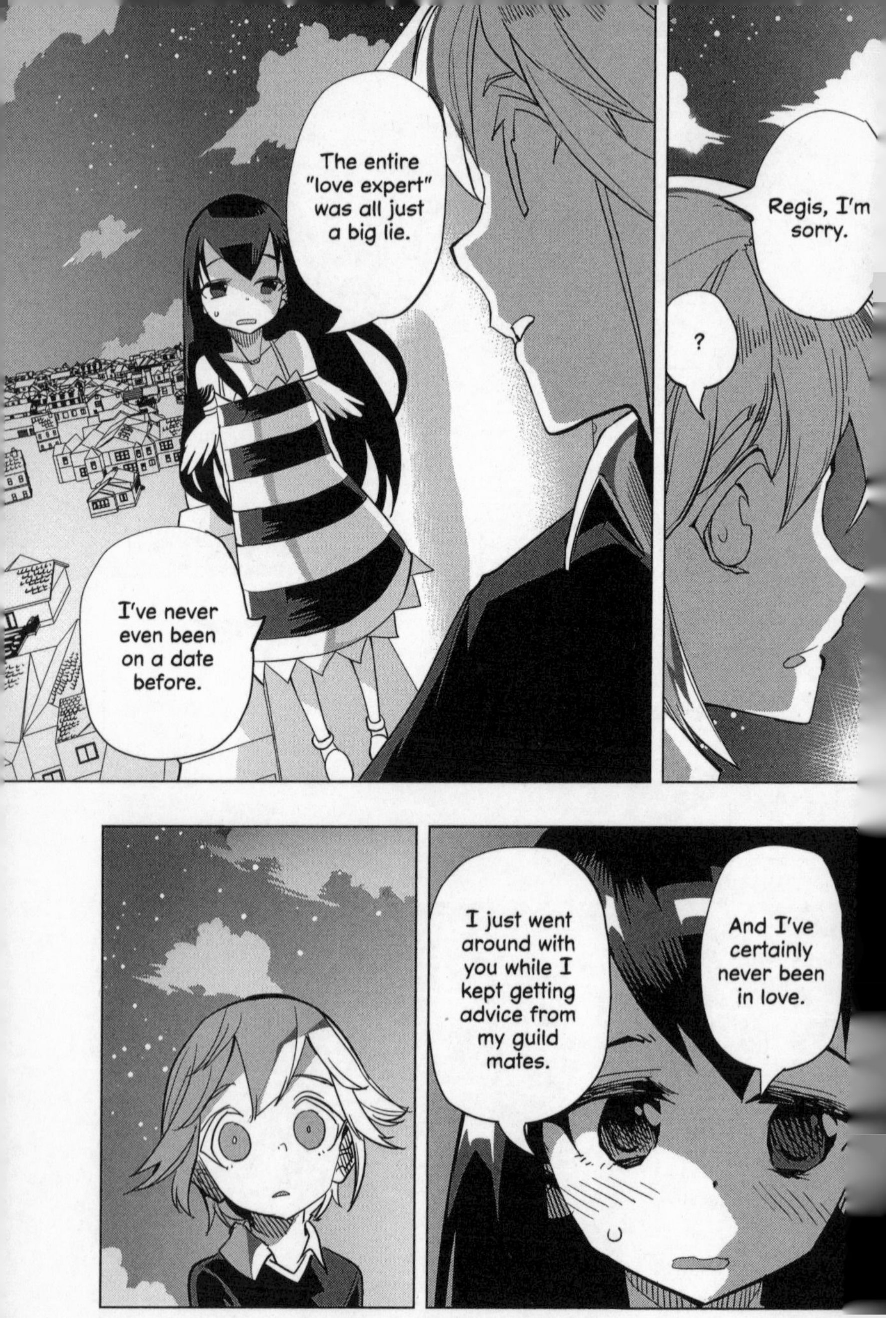

Regis, I'm sorry.
?
The entire "love expert" was all just a big lie.
I've never even been on a date before.
And I've certainly never been in love.
I just went around with you while I kept getting advice from my guild mates.

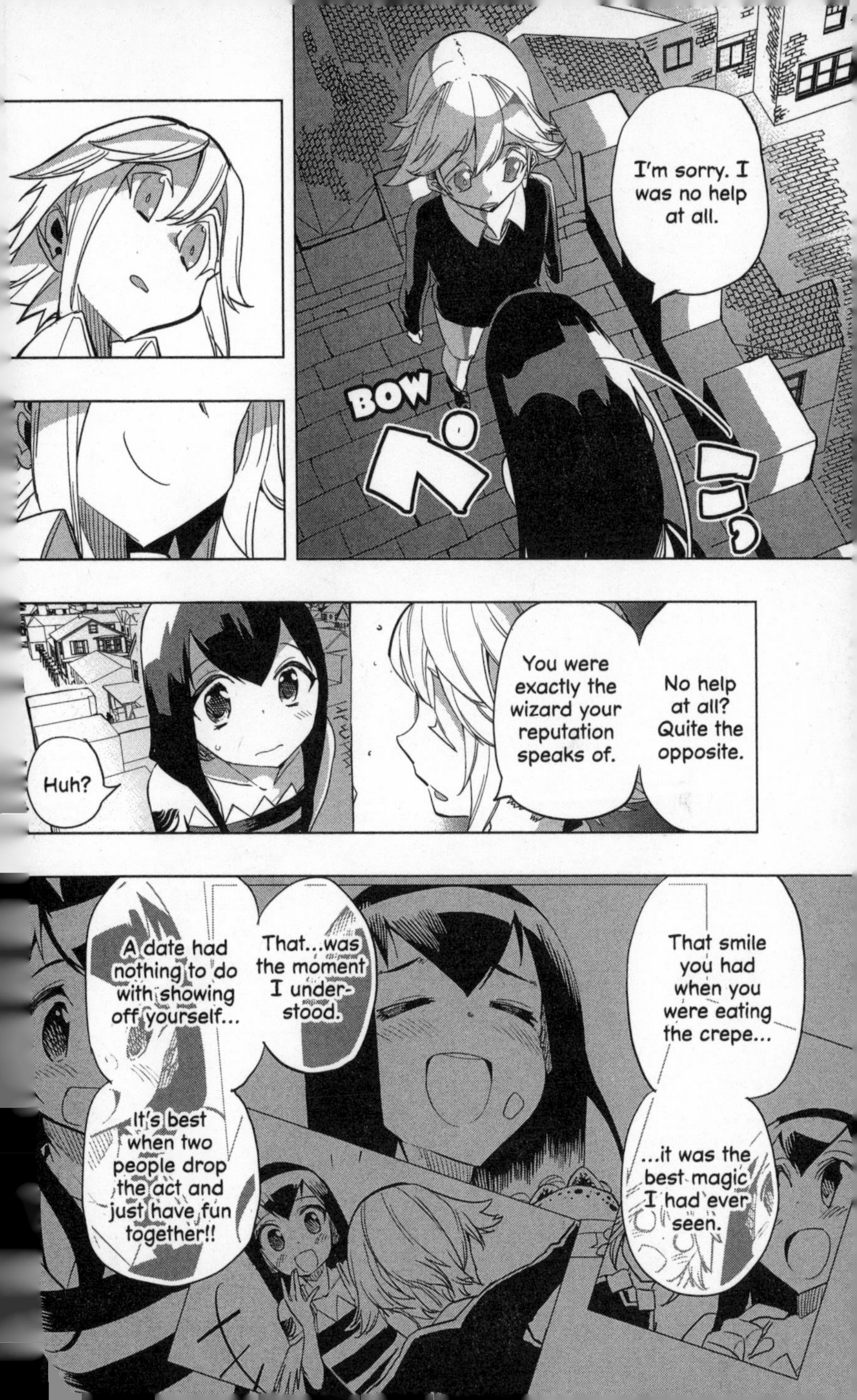
I'm sorry. I was no help at all.
BOW
No help at all? Quite the opposite.
You were exactly the wizard your reputation speaks of.
Huh?
That smile you had when you were eating the crepe...
...it was the best magic I had ever seen.
That...was the moment I understood.
A date had nothing to do with showing off yourself...
It's best when two people drop the act and just have fun together!!

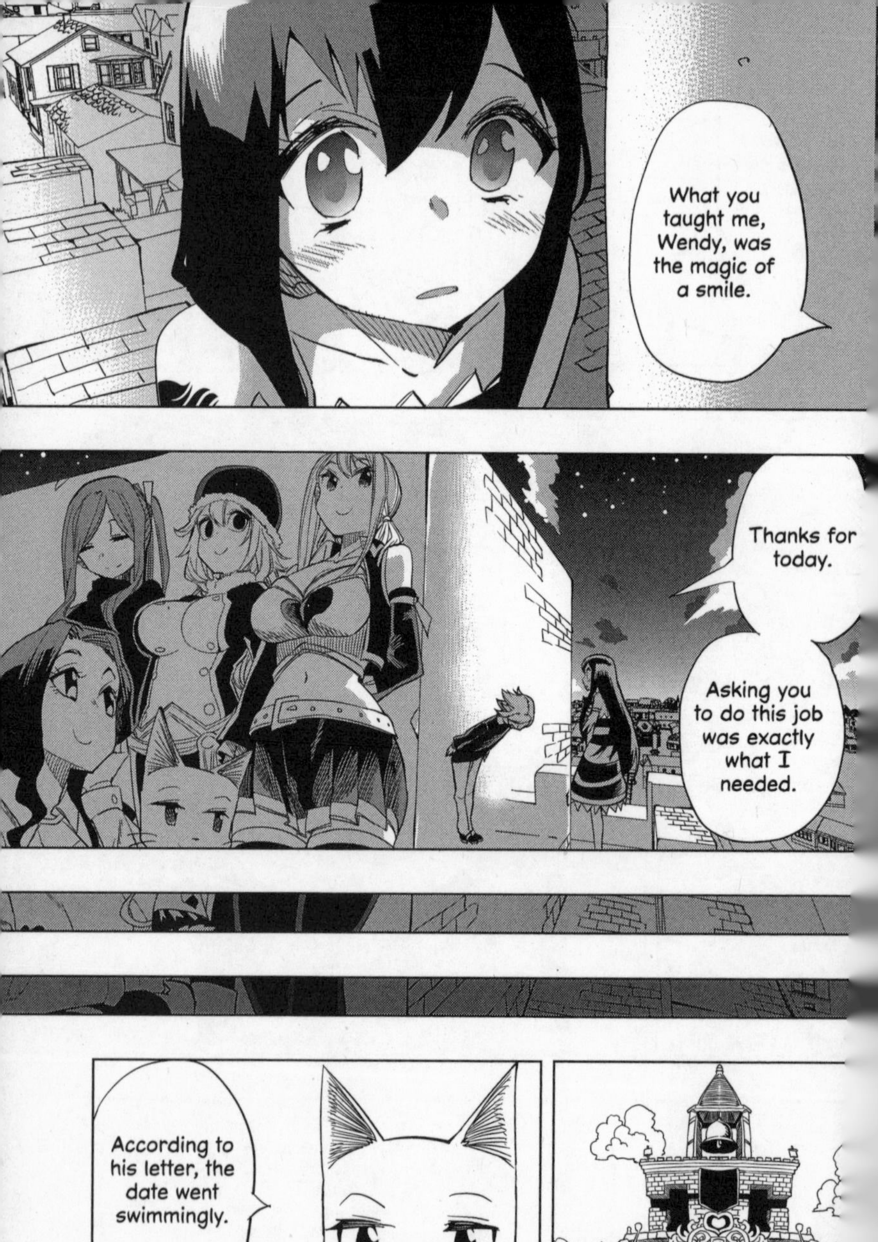
What you taught me, Wendy, was the magic of a smile.
Thanks for today.
Asking you to do this job was exactly what I needed.
According to his letter, the date went swimmingly.

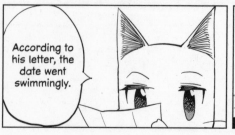

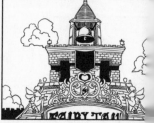

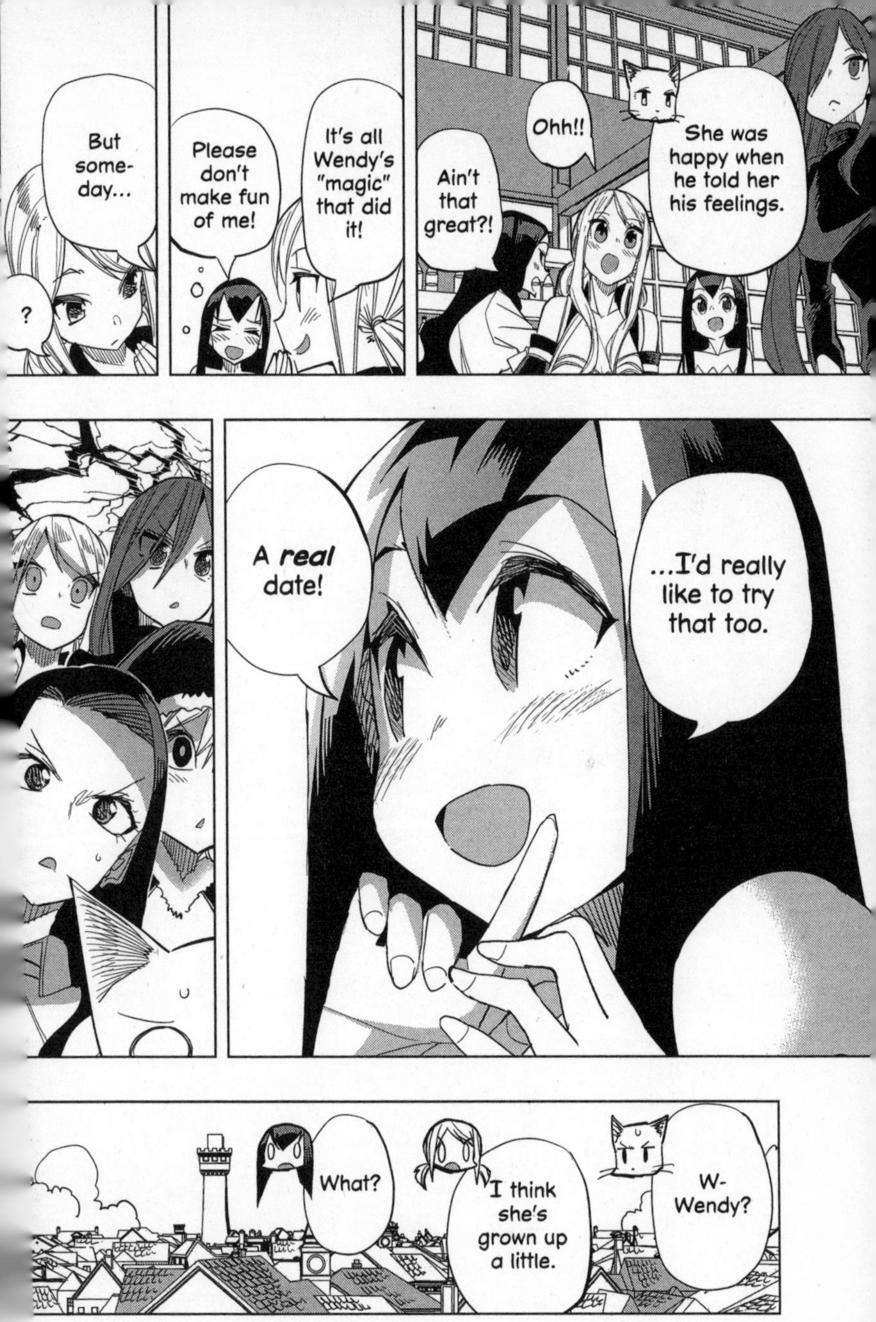
She was happy when he told her his feelings.
Ohh!!
Ain't that great?!
It's all Wendy's "magic" that did it!
Please don't make fun of me!
But someday...
?
...I'd really like to try that too.
A ***real*** date!
W- Wendy?
I think she's grown up a little.
What?

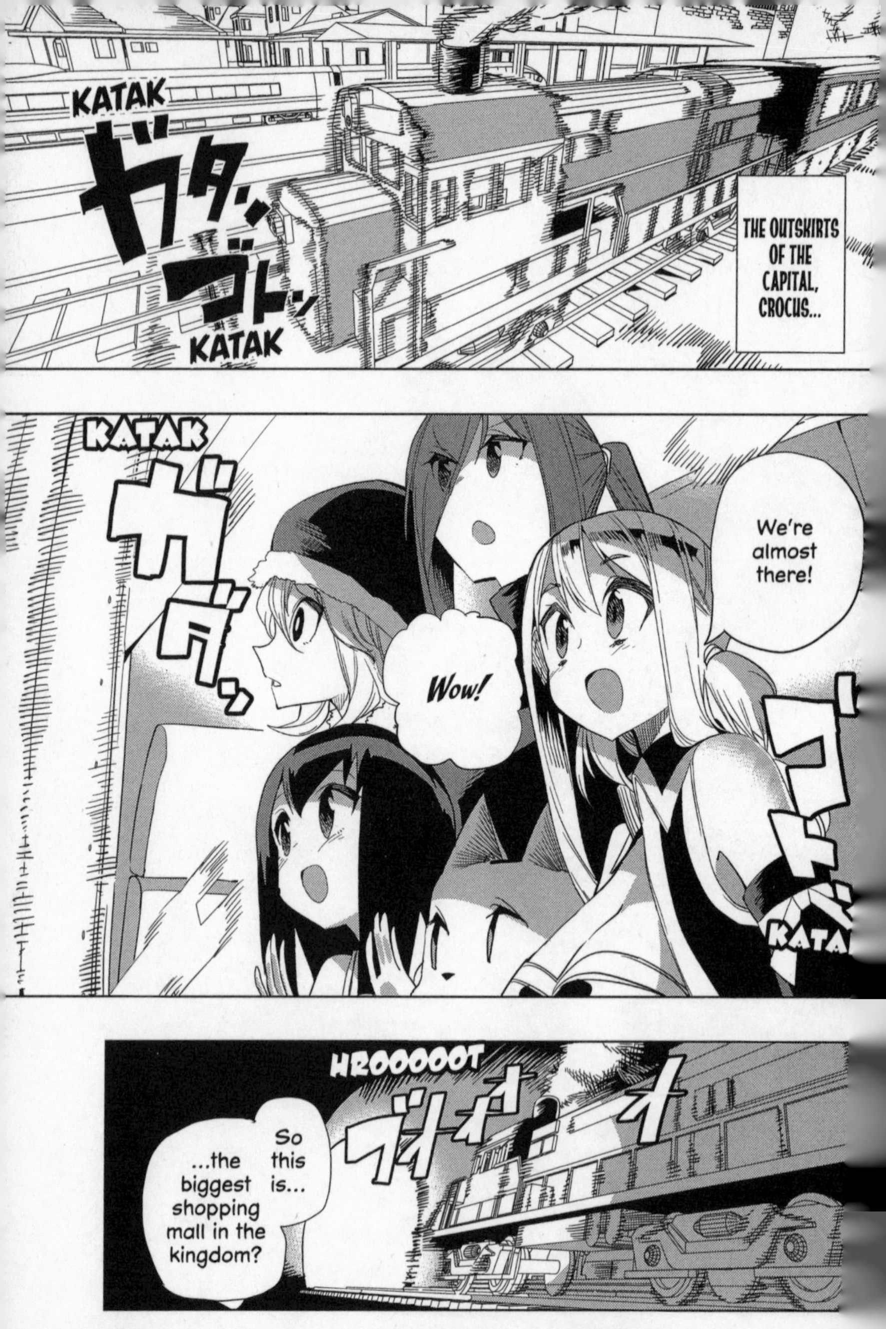
THE OUTSKIRTS OF THE CAPITAL, CROCUS...
KATAK
ガタッ
ゴトッ
KATAK
We're almost there!
ゴトッ
KATA
Wow!
KATAK
ガタッ
HROOOOOT
ブオォーオ
So this is...
...the biggest shopping mall in the kingdom?

Chapter 19: Invisible Crime

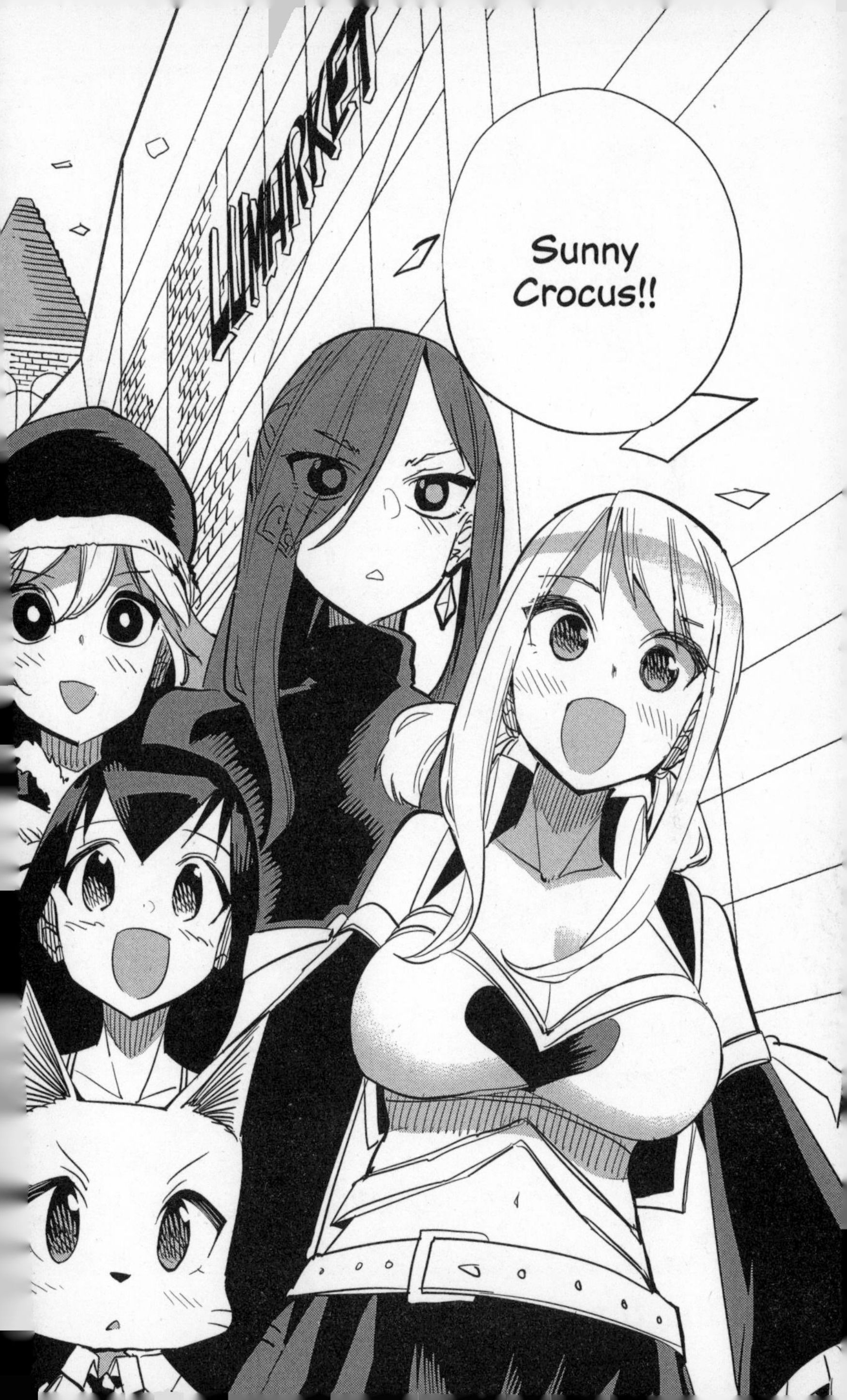
Sunny Crocus!!

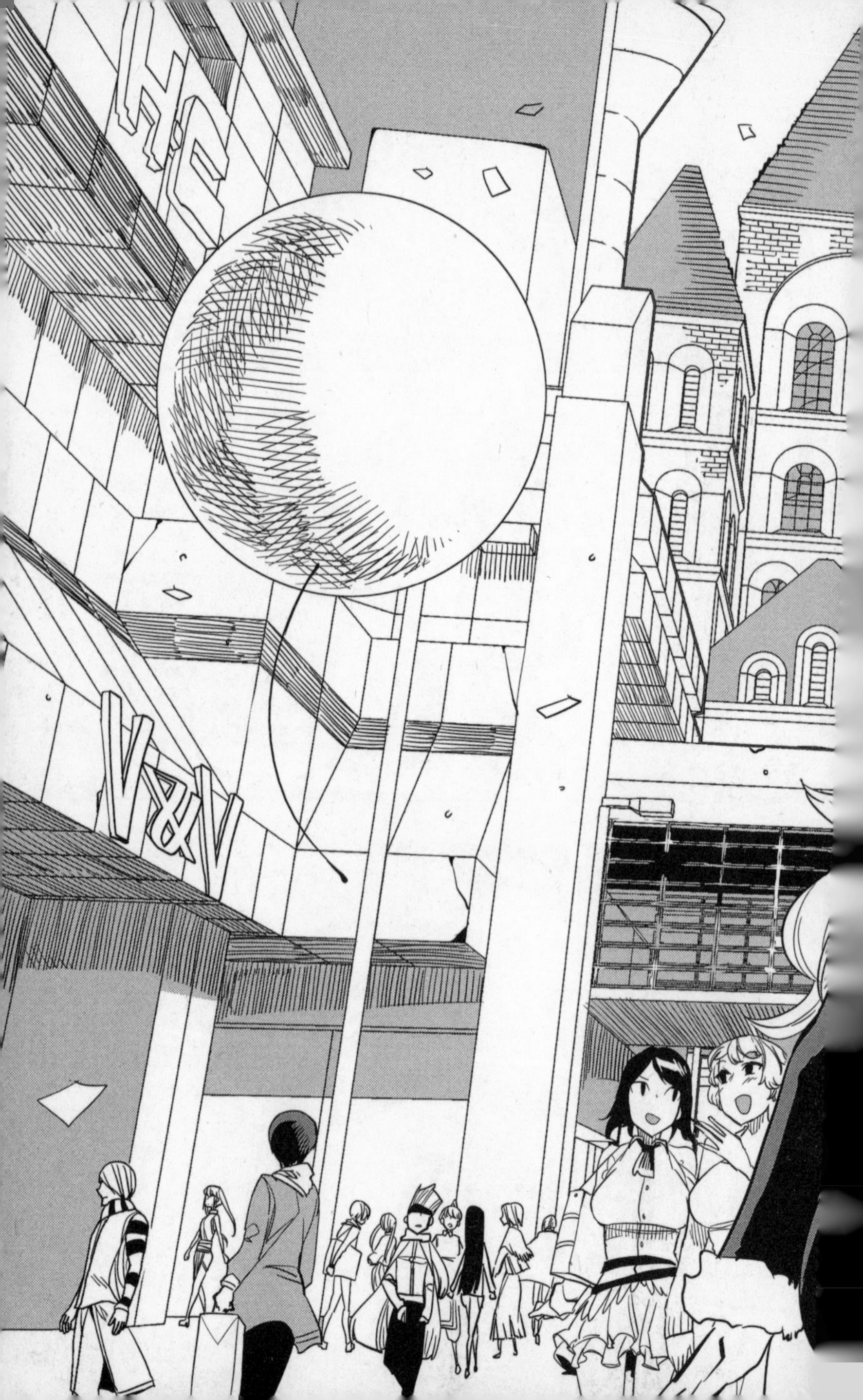
V&V

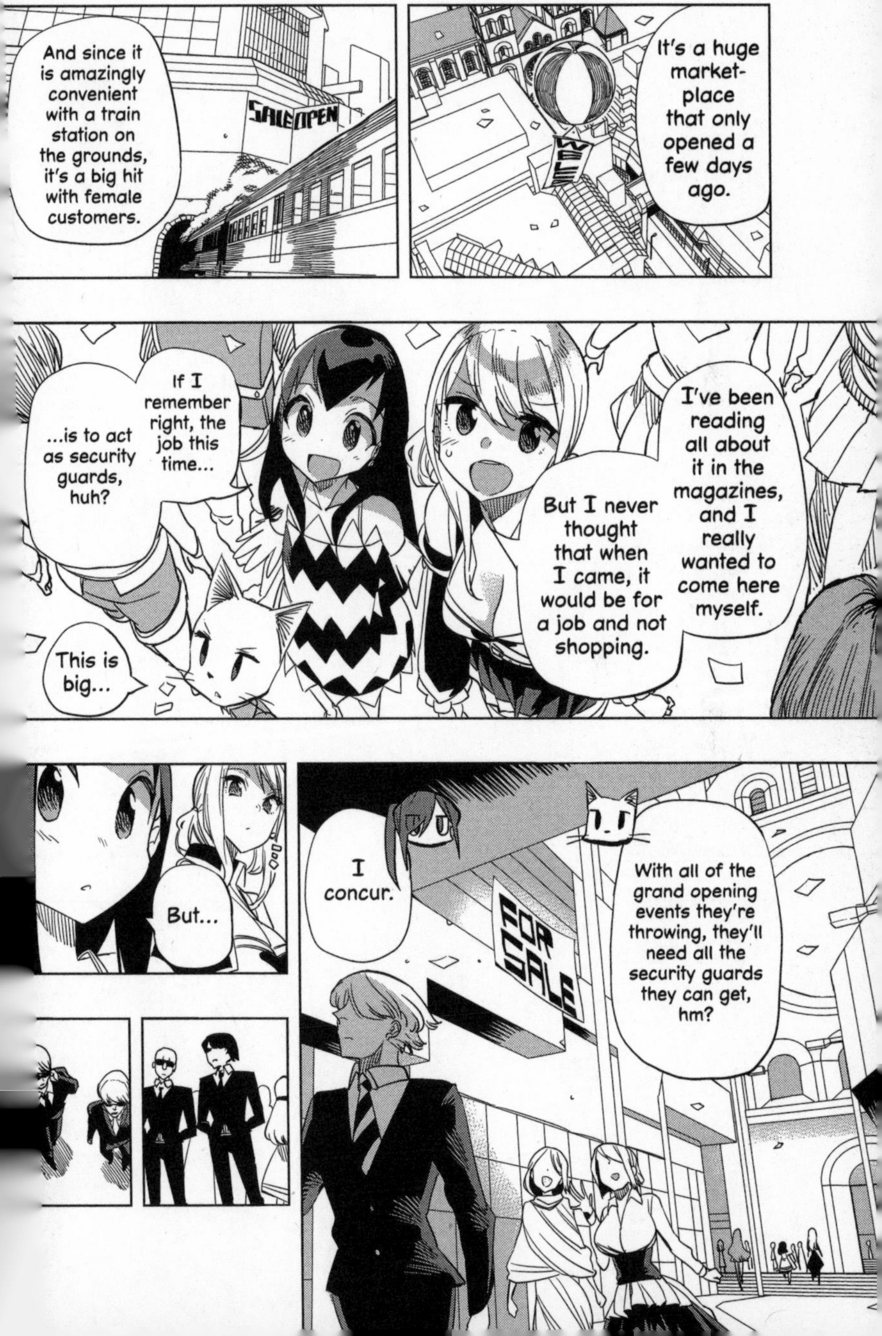
It's a huge market-place that only opened a few days ago.
And since it is amazingly convenient with a train station on the grounds, it's a big hit with female customers.
SALE OPEN
I've been reading all about it in the magazines, and I really wanted to come here myself.
But I never thought that when I came, it would be for a job and not shopping.
If I remember right, the job this time...
...is to act as security guards, huh?
This is big...
With all of the grand opening events they're throwing, they'll need all the security guards they can get, hm?
I concur.
FOR SALE
But...

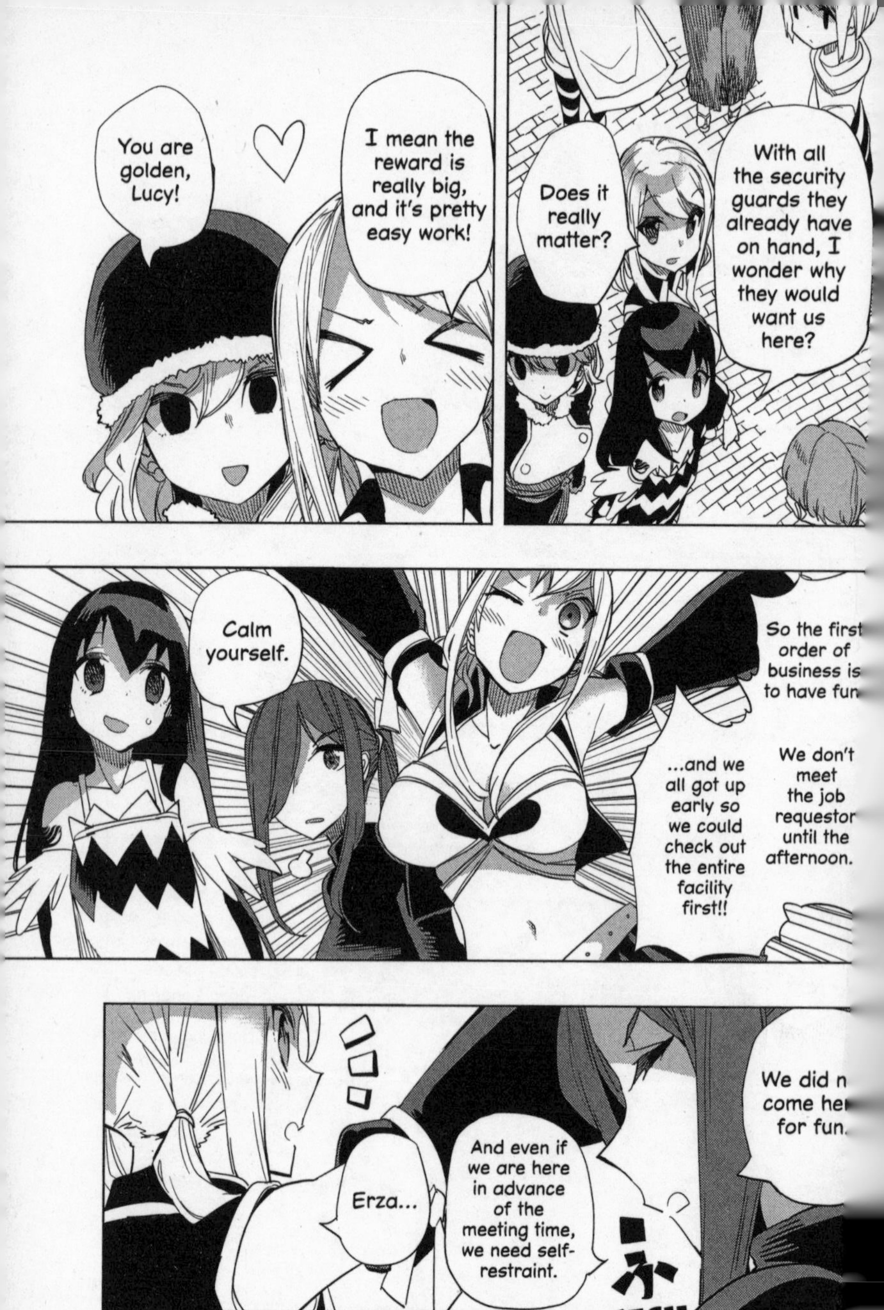
With all the security guards they already have on hand, I wonder why they would want us here?
Does it really matter?
I mean the reward is really big, and it's pretty easy work!
You are golden, Lucy!
So the first order of business is to have fun
We don't meet the job requestor until the afternoon.
...and we all got up early so we could check out the entire facility first!!
Calm yourself.
We did n
come he
for fun.
And even if we are here in advance of the meeting time, we need self-restraint.
Erza...
SIGH

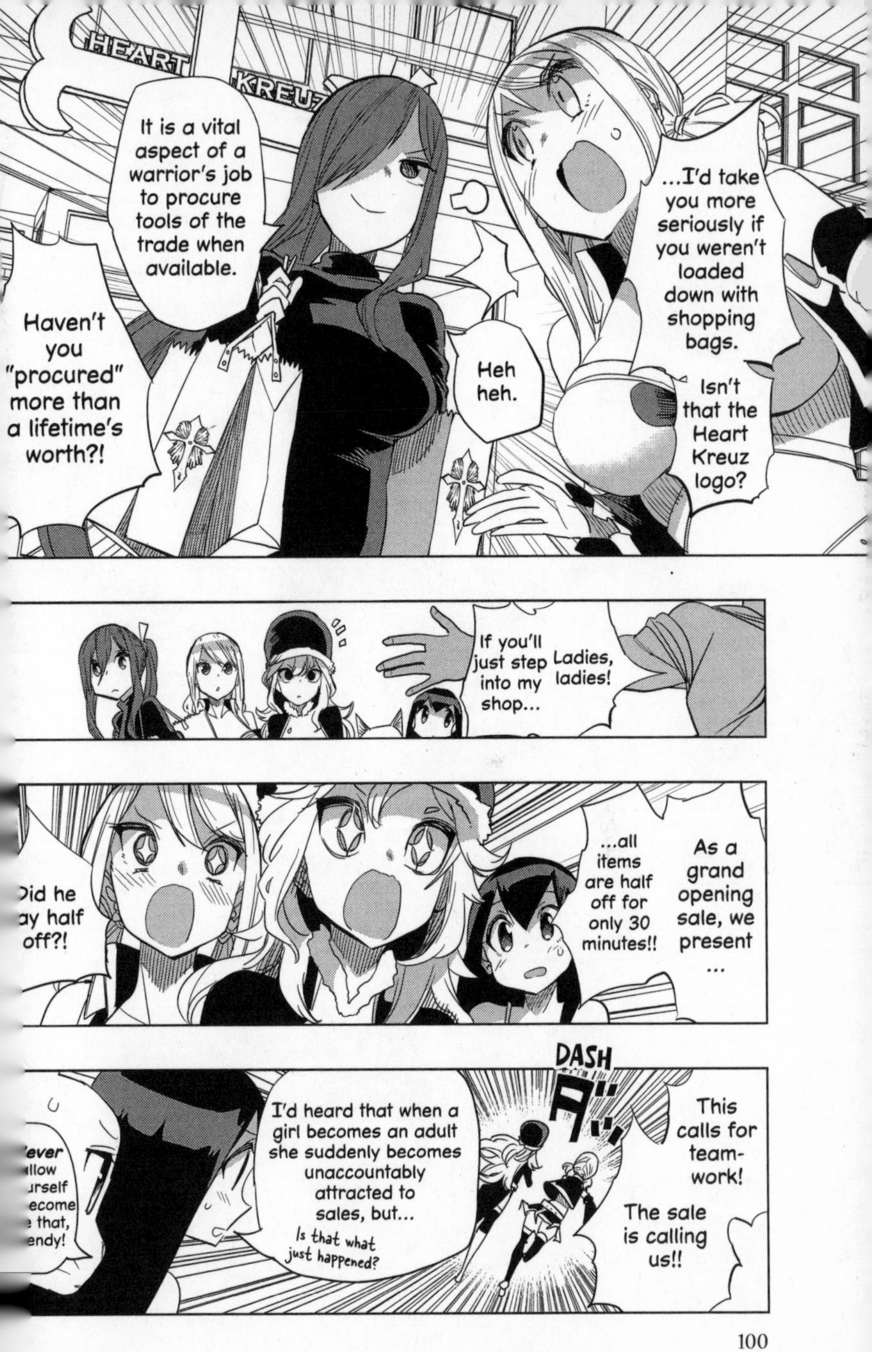
HEART KREUZ
...I'd take you more seriously if you weren't loaded down with shopping bags.
Isn't that the Heart Kreuz logo?
Heh heh.
It is a vital aspect of a warrior's job to procure tools of the trade when available.
Haven't you "procured" more than a lifetime's worth?!
Ladies, ladies!
If you'll just step into my shop...
As a grand opening sale, we present ...
...all items are half off for only 30 minutes!!
Did he ay half off?!
This calls for team-work!
The sale is calling us!!
DASH
I'd heard that when a girl becomes an adult she suddenly becomes unaccountably attracted to sales, but...
Is that what just happened?

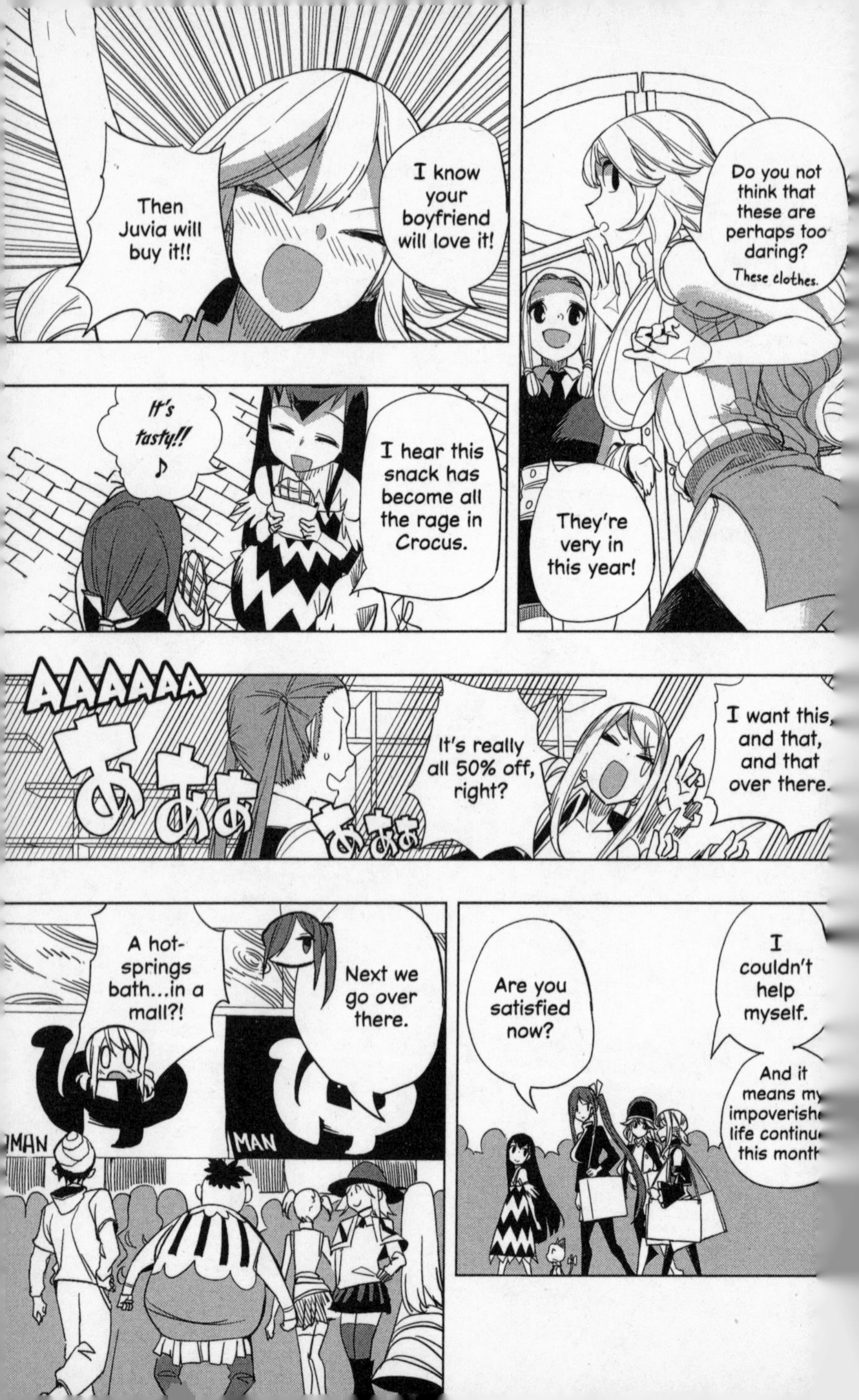
Do you not think that these are perhaps too daring? These clothes.
They're very in this year!
I know your boyfriend will love it!
Then Juvia will buy it!!
I hear this snack has become all the rage in Crocus.
It's tasty!! ♪
I want this, and that, and that over there.
It's really all 50% off, right?
AAAAAA
あああ
あああ
I couldn't help myself.
And it means my impoverishe life continu this month
Are you satisfied now?
Next we go over there.
A hot-springs bath...in a mall?!
MAN
MAN

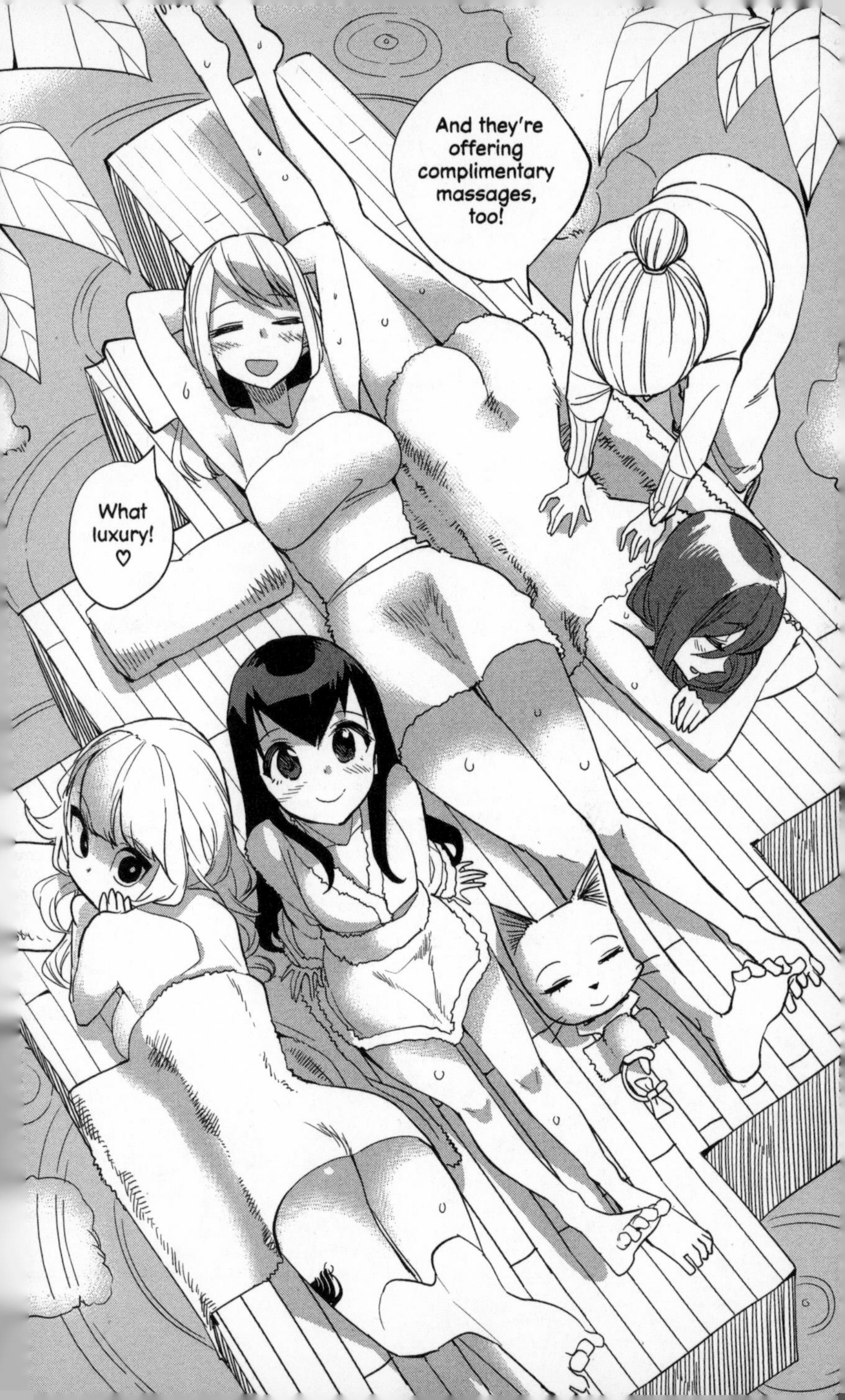
And they're offering complimentary massages, too!
What luxury! ♡

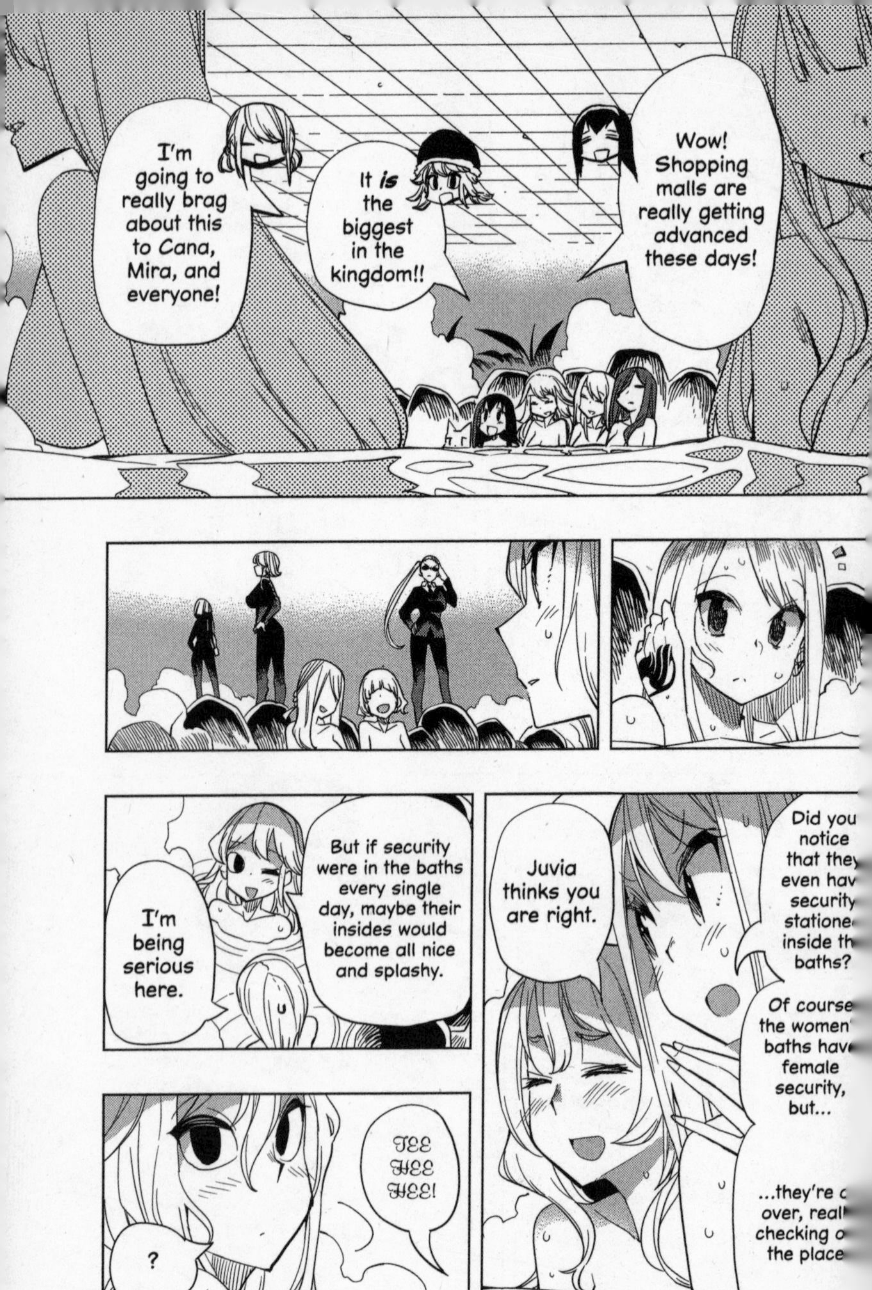
Wow! Shopping malls are really getting advanced these days!
It *is* the biggest in the kingdom!!
I'm going to really brag about this to Cana, Mira, and everyone!
Did you notice that they even hav security statione inside th baths?
Juvia thinks you are right.
Of course the women' baths hav female security, but...
...they're c over, real checking o the place
But if security were in the baths every single day, maybe their insides would become all nice and splashy.
I'm being serious here.
TEE HEE HEE!
?

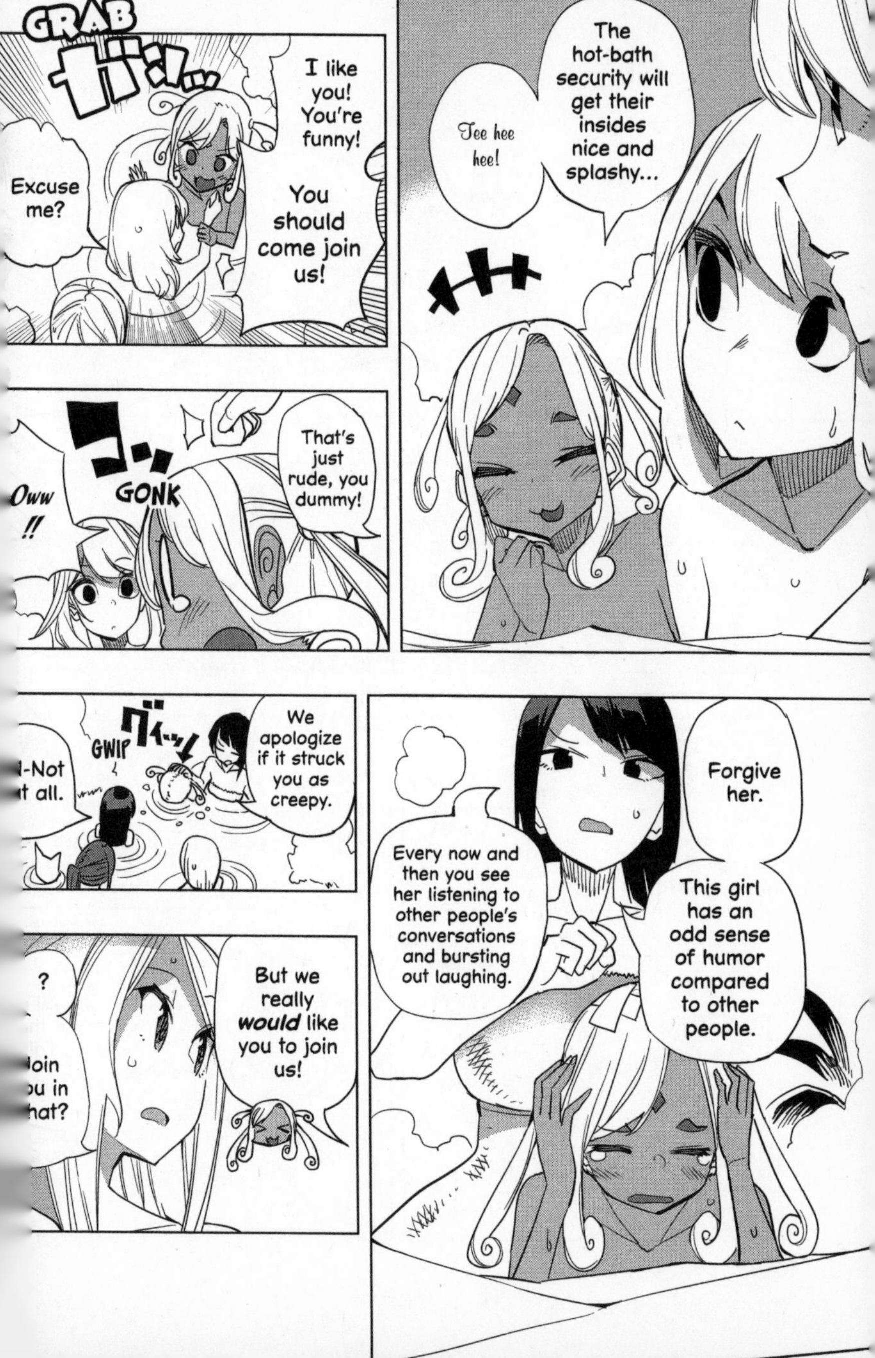
The hot-bath security will get their insides nice and splashy...
Tee hee hee!
GRAB
I like you! You're funny!
You should come join us!
Excuse me?
That's just rude, you dummy!
GONK
Oww !!
Forgive her.
This girl has an odd sense of humor compared to other people.
Every now and then you see her listening to other people's conversations and bursting out laughing.
We apologize if it struck you as creepy.
GWIP
-Not t all.
But we really *would* like you to join us!
?
Join ou in hat?

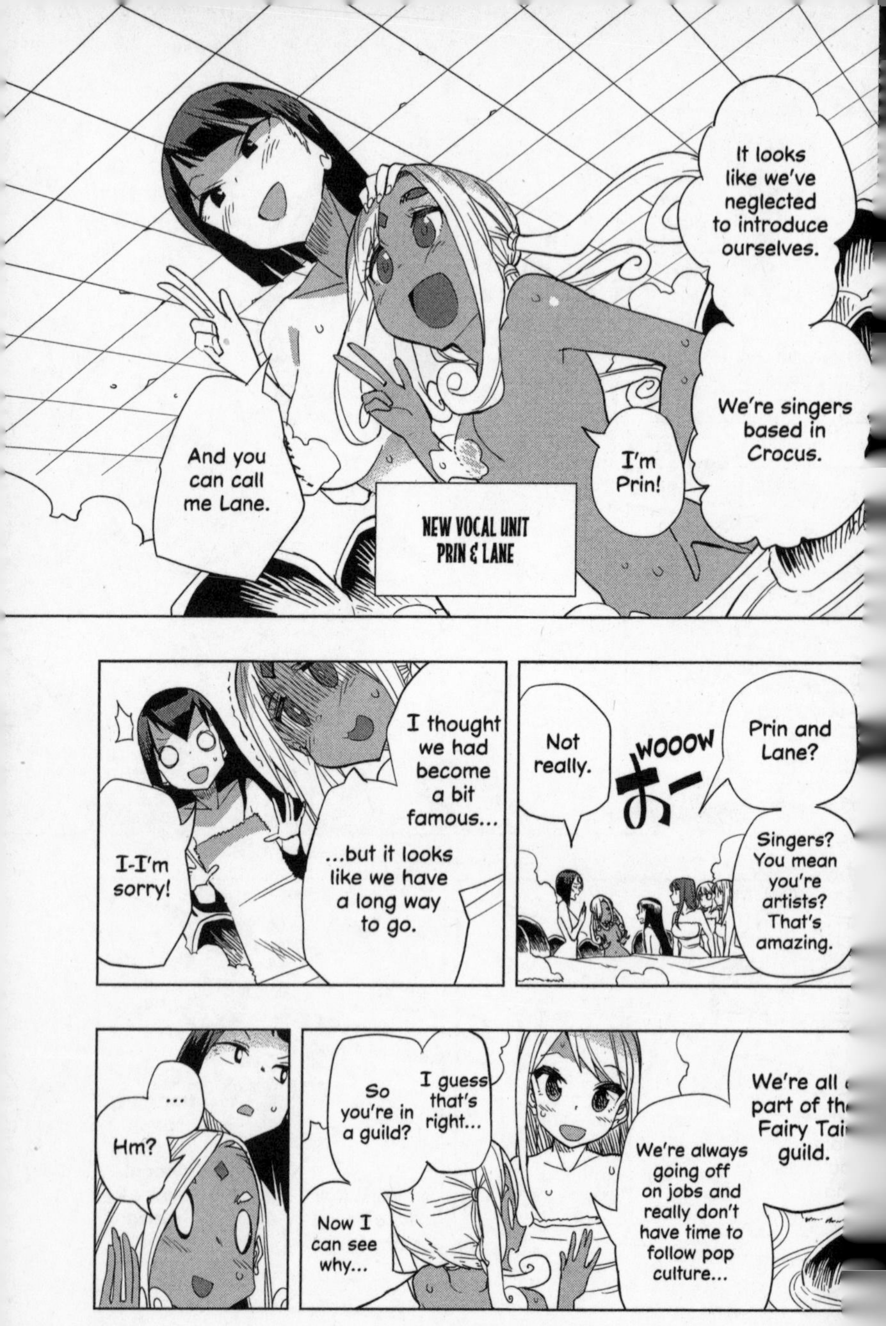
It looks like we've neglected to introduce ourselves.
We're singers based in Crocus.
I'm Prin!
And you can call me Lane.
NEW VOCAL UNIT PRIN & LANE
Prin and Lane?
WOOOW
おー
Singers? You mean you're artists? That's amazing.
Not really.
I thought we had become a bit famous...
...but it looks like we have a long way to go.
I-I'm sorry!
We're all part of th Fairy Tai guild.
We're always going off on jobs and really don't have time to follow pop culture...
I guess that's right...
So you're in a guild?
Now I can see why...
...
Hm?

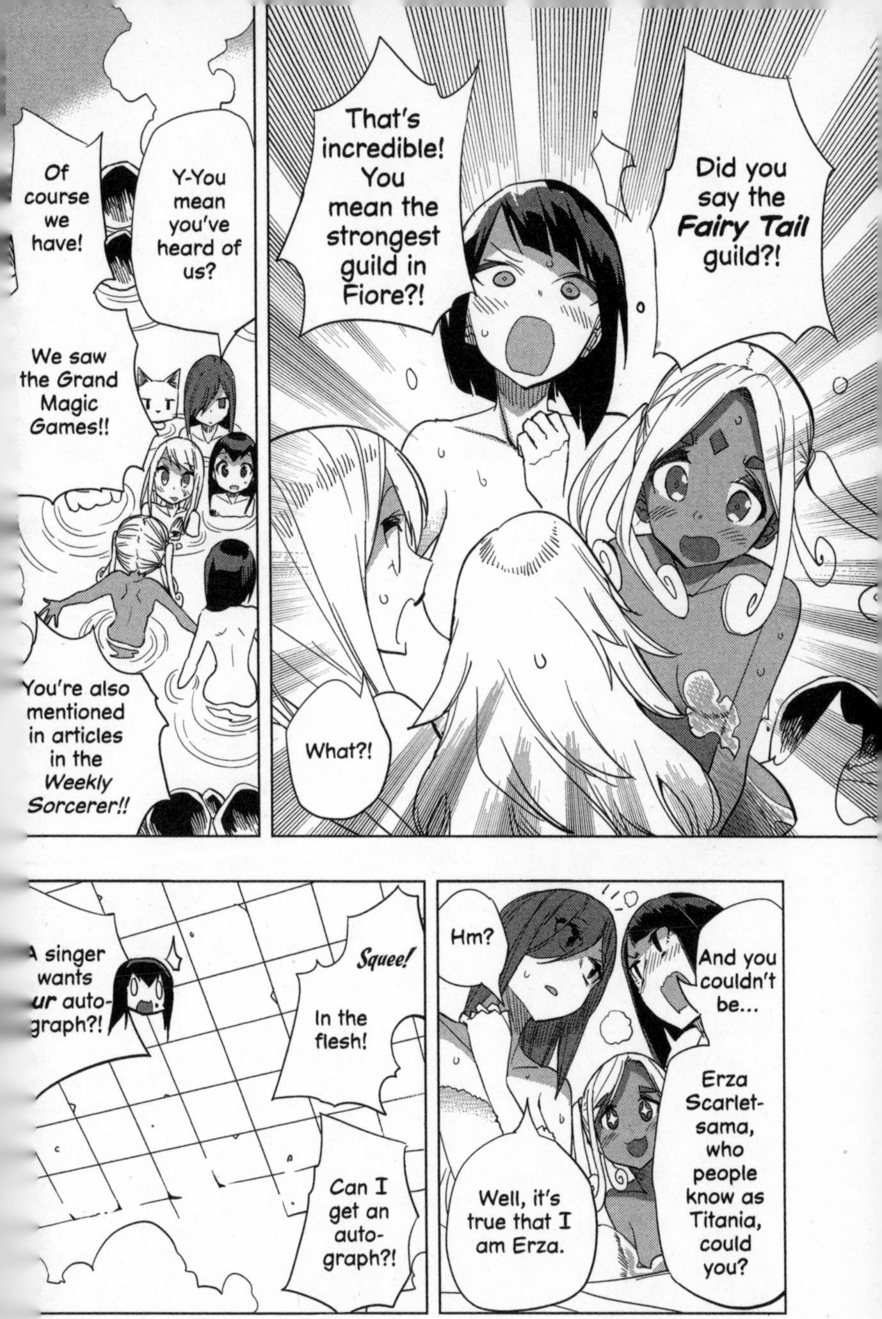
Did you say the Fairy Tail guild?!
That's incredible! You mean the strongest guild in Fiore?!
What?!
Y-You mean you've heard of us?
Of course we have!
We saw the Grand Magic Games!!
You're also mentioned in articles in the Weekly Sorcerer!!
Hm?
And you couldn't be...
Erza Scarlet-sama, who people know as Titania, could you?
Well, it's true that I am Erza.
Squee!
In the flesh!
Can I get an autograph?!
A singer wants ur autograph?!

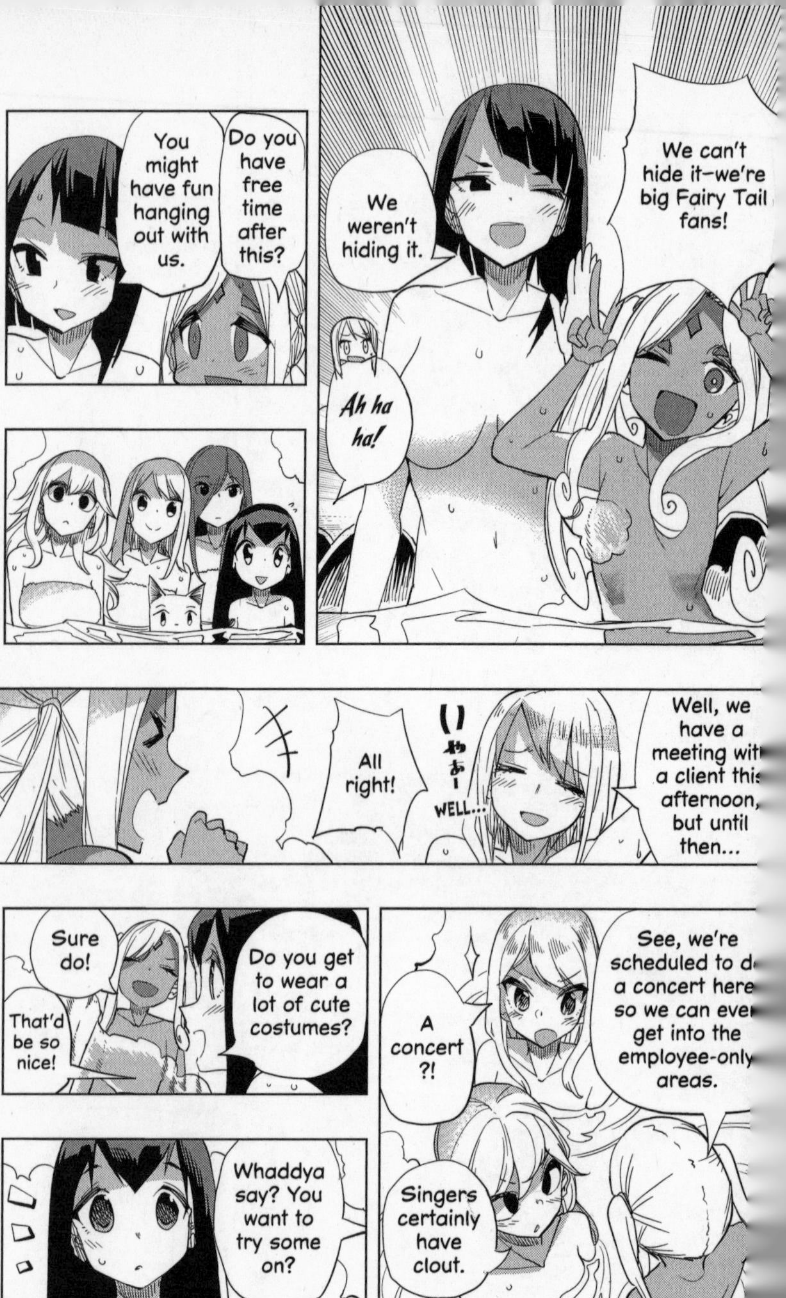

We can't hide it—we're big Fairy Tail fans!
We weren't hiding it.
Ah ha ha!
Do you have free time after this?
You might have fun hanging out with us.
Well, we have a meeting wit a client thi afternoon, but until then...
WELL...
All right!
See, we're scheduled to d a concert here so we can eve get into the employee-onl areas.
A concert?!
Singers certainly have clout.
Do you get to wear a lot of cute costumes?
Sure do!
That'd be so nice!
Whaddya say? You want to try some on?

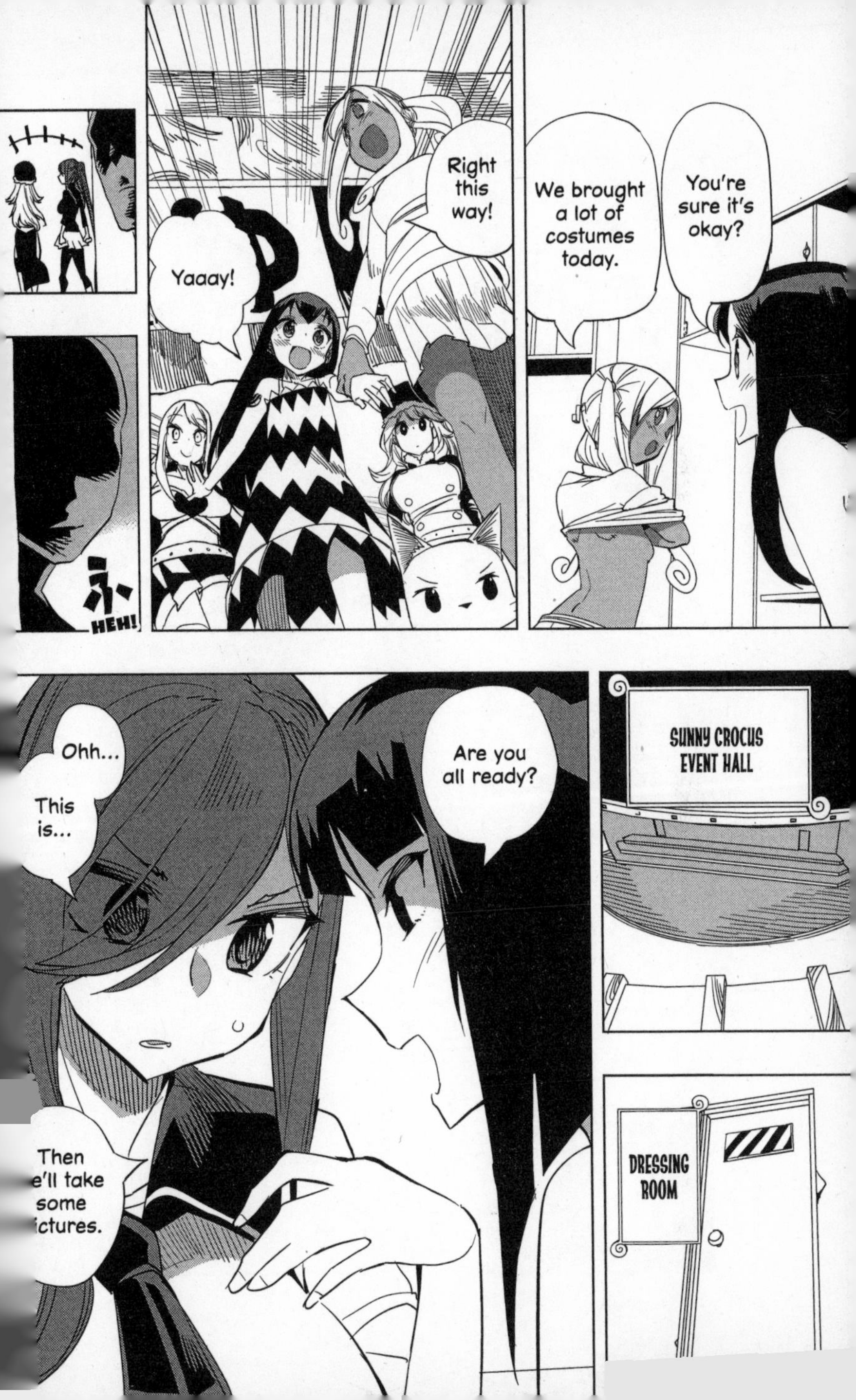
You're sure it's okay?
We brought a lot of costumes today.
Right this way!
Yaaay!
ふ
HEH!
SUNNY CROCUS EVENT HALL
DRESSING ROOM
Are you all ready?
Ohh... This is...
Then e'll take some ictures.

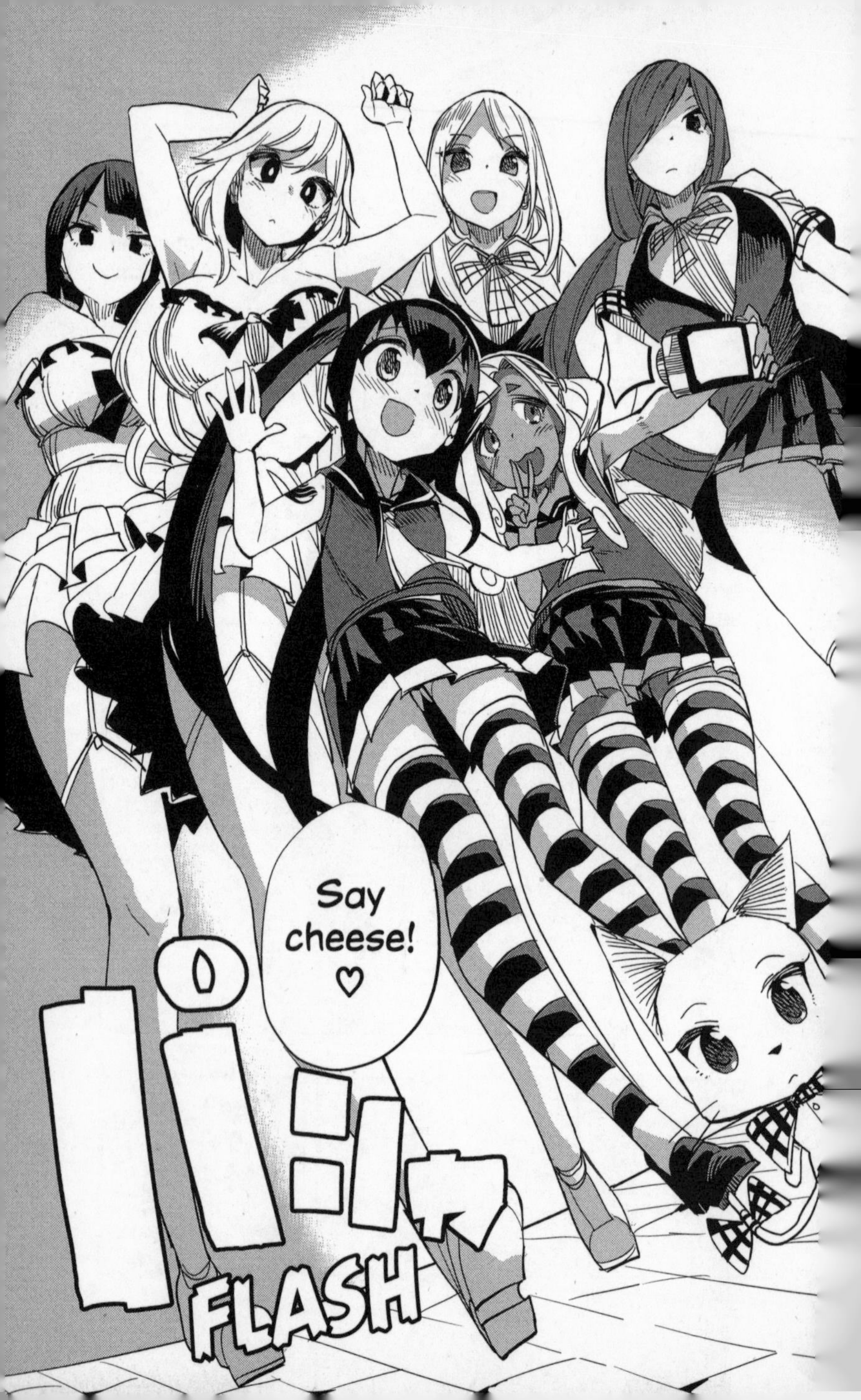
Say cheese! ♡
FLASH

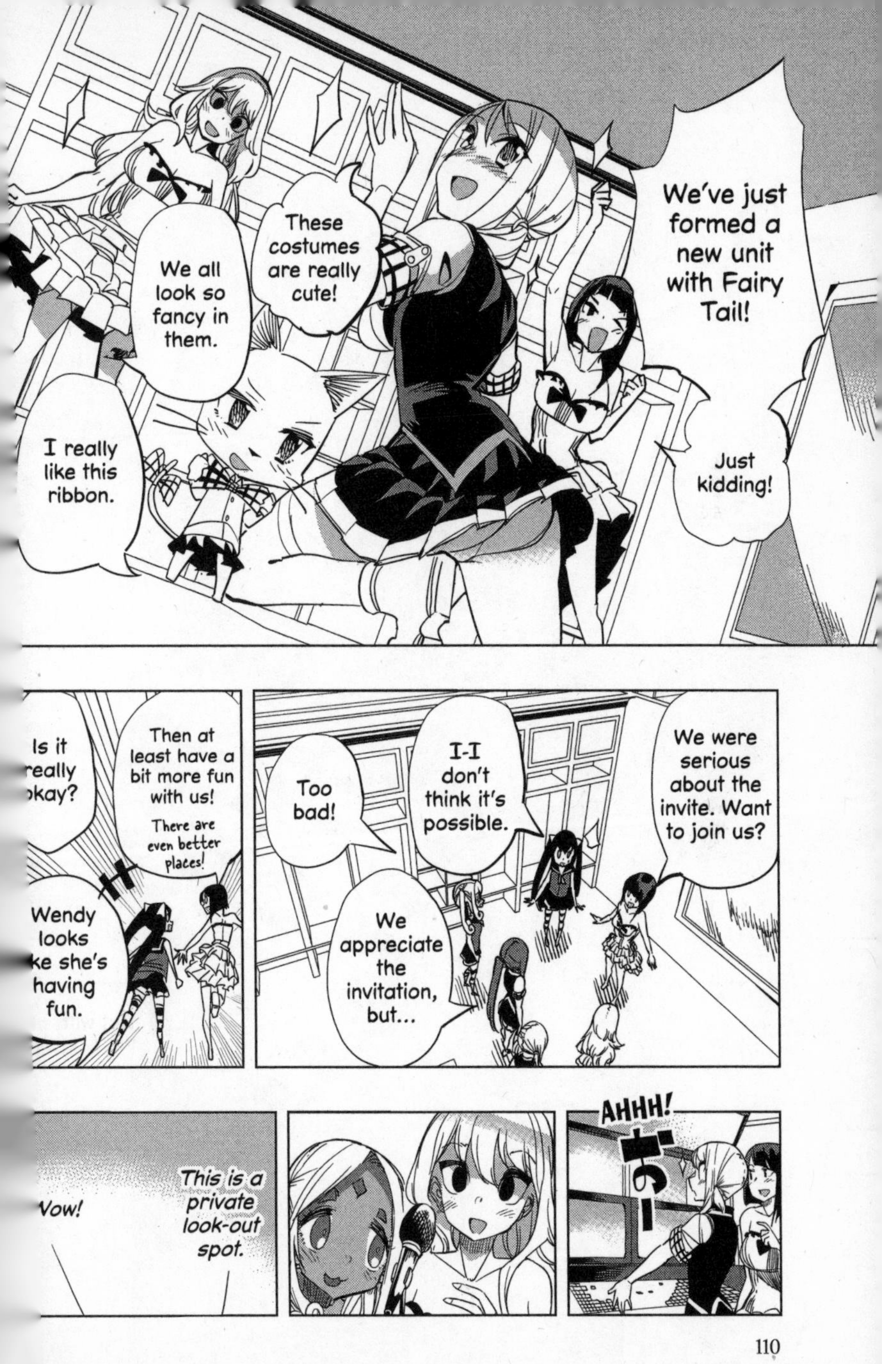
We've just formed a new unit with Fairy Tail!
Just kidding!
These costumes are really cute!
We all look so fancy in them.
I really like this ribbon.
We were serious about the invite. Want to join us?
I-I don't think it's possible.
Too bad!
We appreciate the invitation, but...
Then at least have a bit more fun with us!
There are even better places!
Is it eally kay?
Wendy looks ke she's having fun.
AHHH!
This is a private look-out spot.
ow!

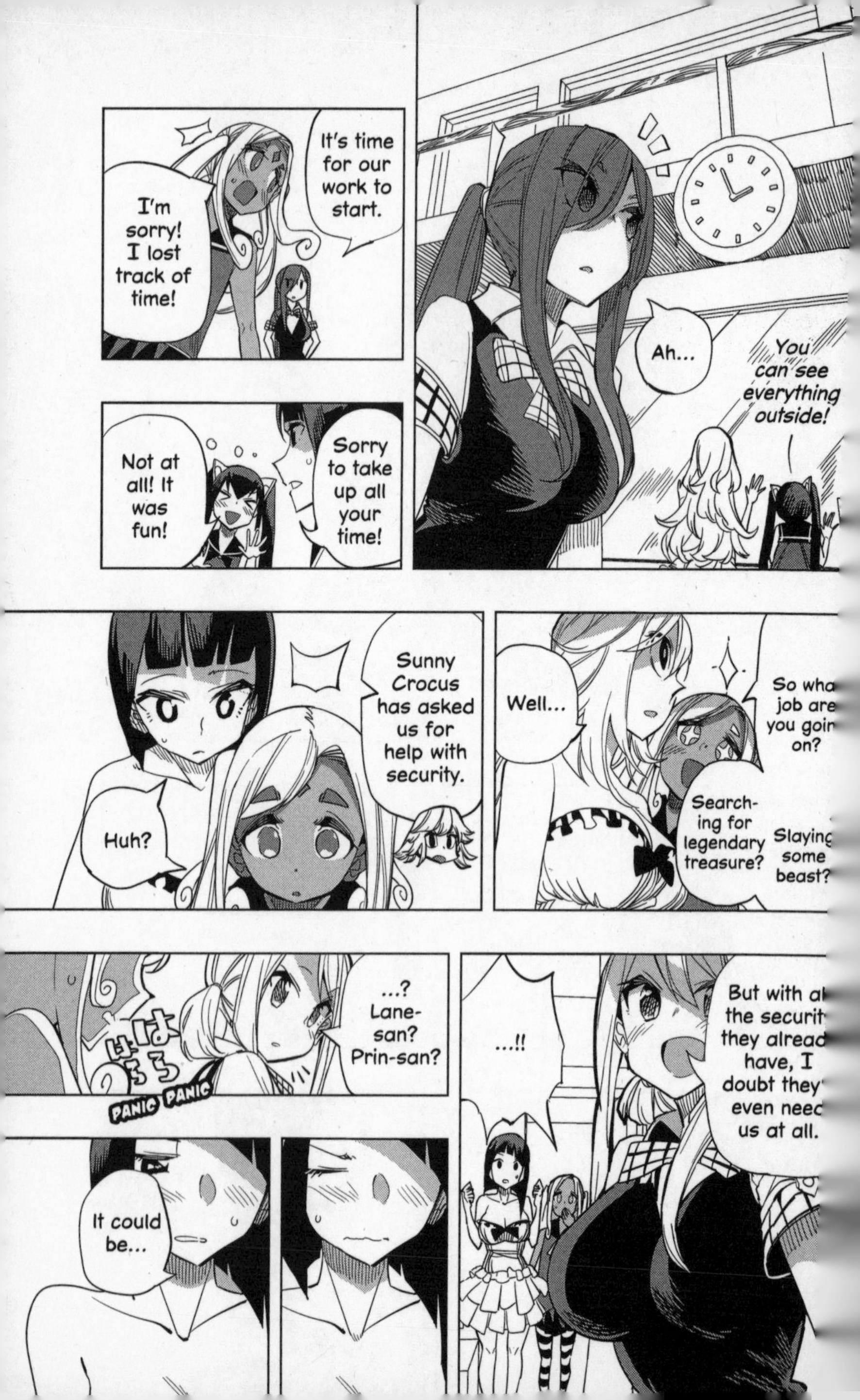
Ah...
You can see everything outside!
It's time for our work to start.
I'm sorry! I lost track of time!
Sorry to take up all your time!
Not at all! It was fun!
So wha job are you goin on?
Well...
Slaying some beast?
Searching-ing for legendary treasure?
Sunny Crocus has asked us for help with security.
Huh?
But with al the securit they alread have, I doubt they' even neec us at all.
...!!
...? Lane-san? Prin-san?
PANIC PANIC
It could be...

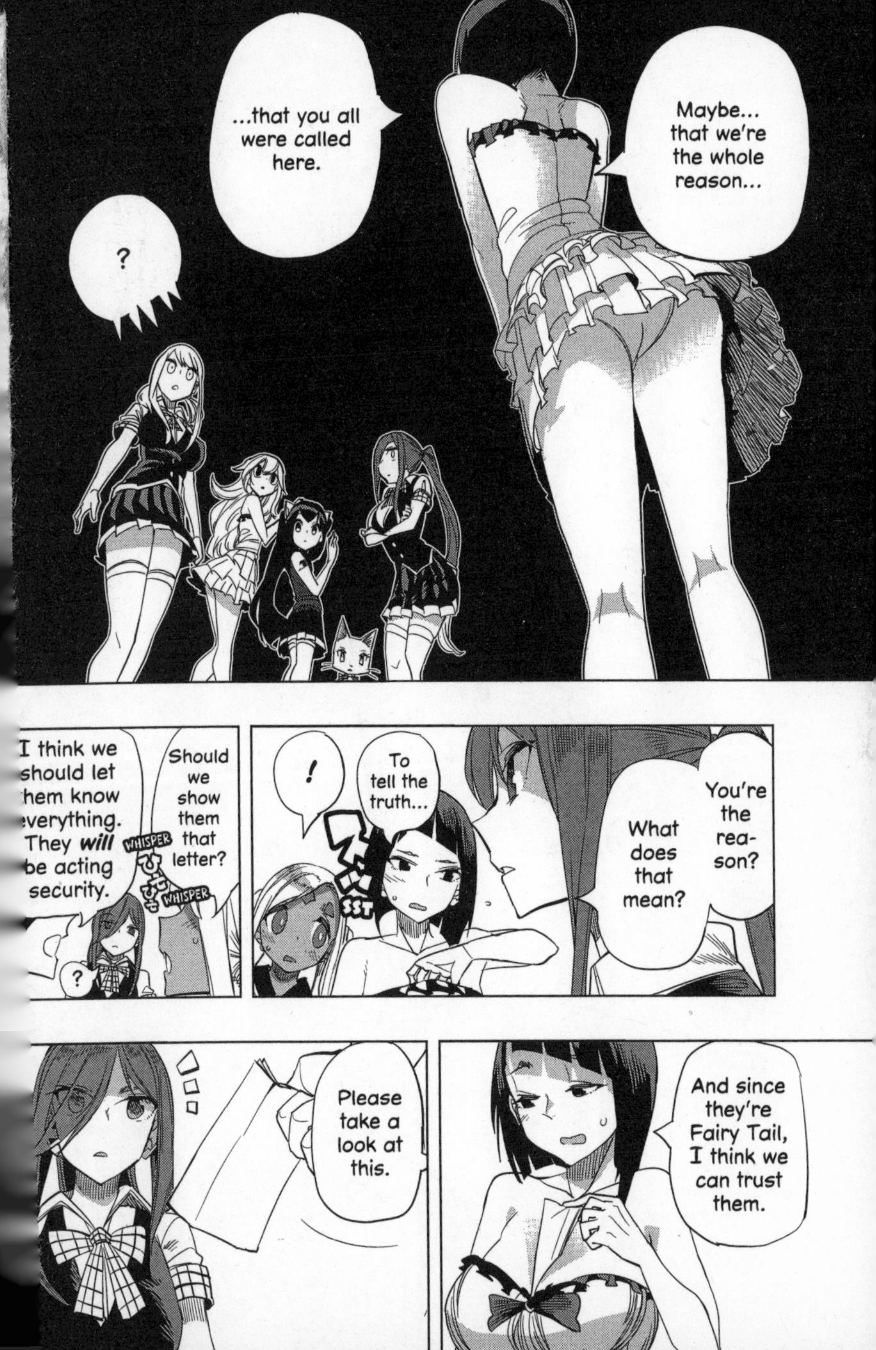

Maybe... that we're the whole reason...
...that you all were called here.
?
You're the rea-son?
What does that mean?
To tell the truth...
!
SST
Should we show them that letter?
WHISPER
WHISPER
I think we should let hem know verything. They *will* be acting security.
?
And since they're Fairy Tail, I think we can trust them.
Please take a look at this.

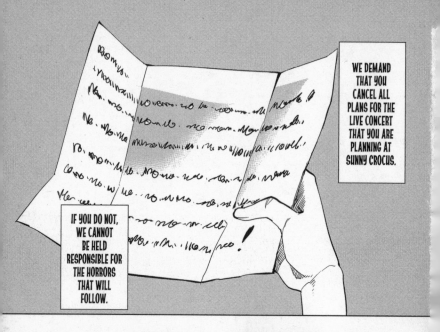

WE DEMAND THAT YOU CANCEL ALL PLANS FOR THE LIVE CONCERT THAT YOU ARE PLANNING AT SUNNY CROCUS.

IF YOU DO NOT, WE CANNOT BE HELD RESPONSIBLE FOR THE HORRORS THAT WILL FOLLOW.

Yes...

So is this...

...sup- posed to be an extortion letter?

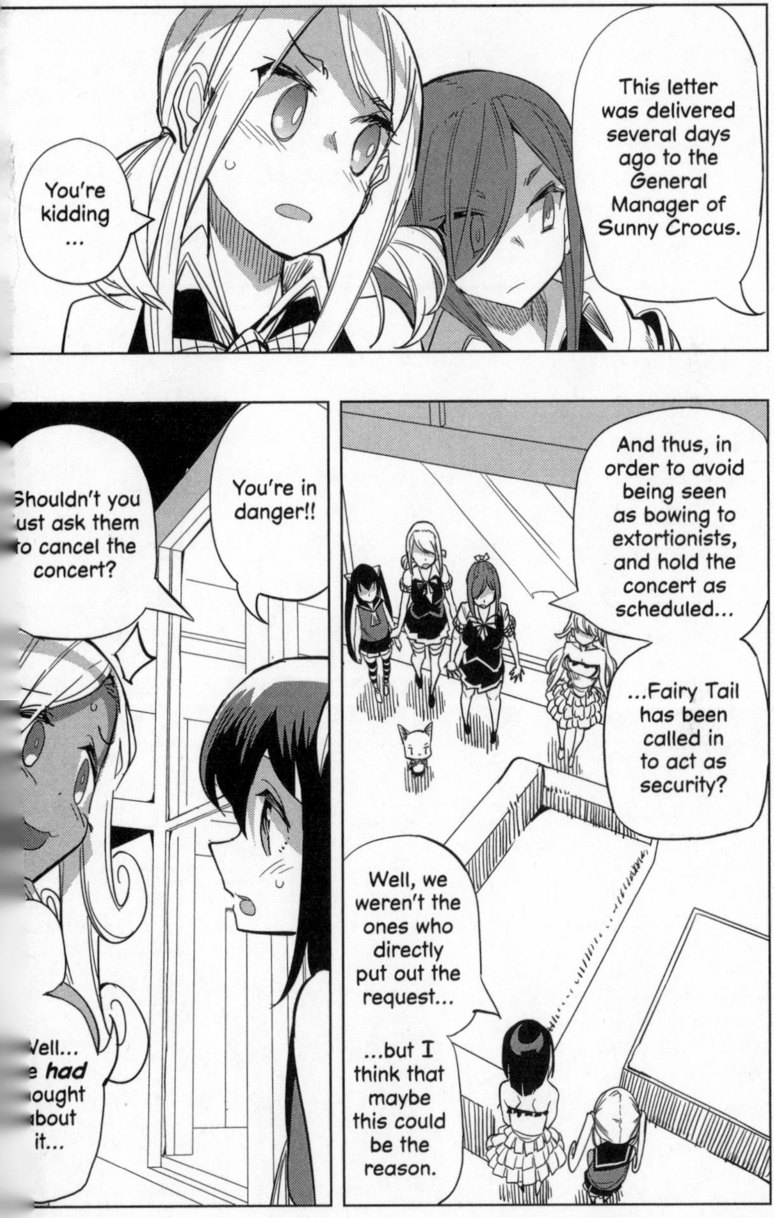

This letter was delivered several days ago to the General Manager of Sunny Crocus.
You're kidding ...
And thus, in order to avoid being seen as bowing to extortionists, and hold the concert as scheduled...
...Fairy Tail has been called in to act as security?
Well, we weren't the ones who directly put out the request...
...but I think that maybe this could be the reason.
You're in danger!!
Shouldn't you ust ask them o cancel the concert?
Vell... e *had* ought bout it...

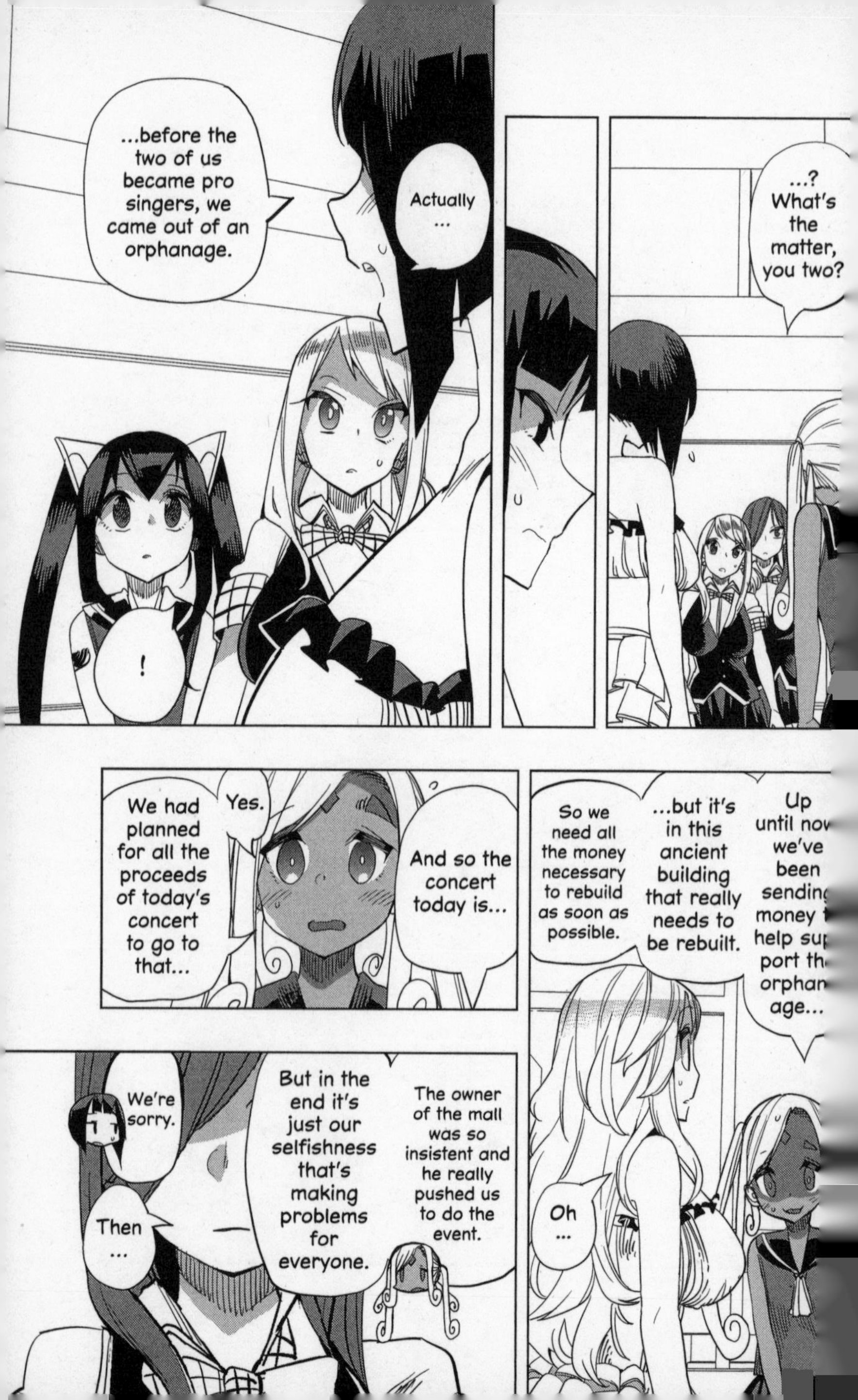
...? What's the matter, you two?
Actually ...
...before the two of us became pro singers, we came out of an orphanage.
!
Up until no we've been sendin money t help sup port th orphan age...
...but it's in this ancient building that really needs to be rebuilt.
So we need all the money necessary to rebuild as soon as possible.
And so the concert today is...
Yes.
We had planned for all the proceeds of today's concert to go to that...
Oh ...
The owner of the mall was so insistent and he really pushed us to do the event.
But in the end it's just our selfishness that's making problems for everyone.
We're sorry.
Then ...

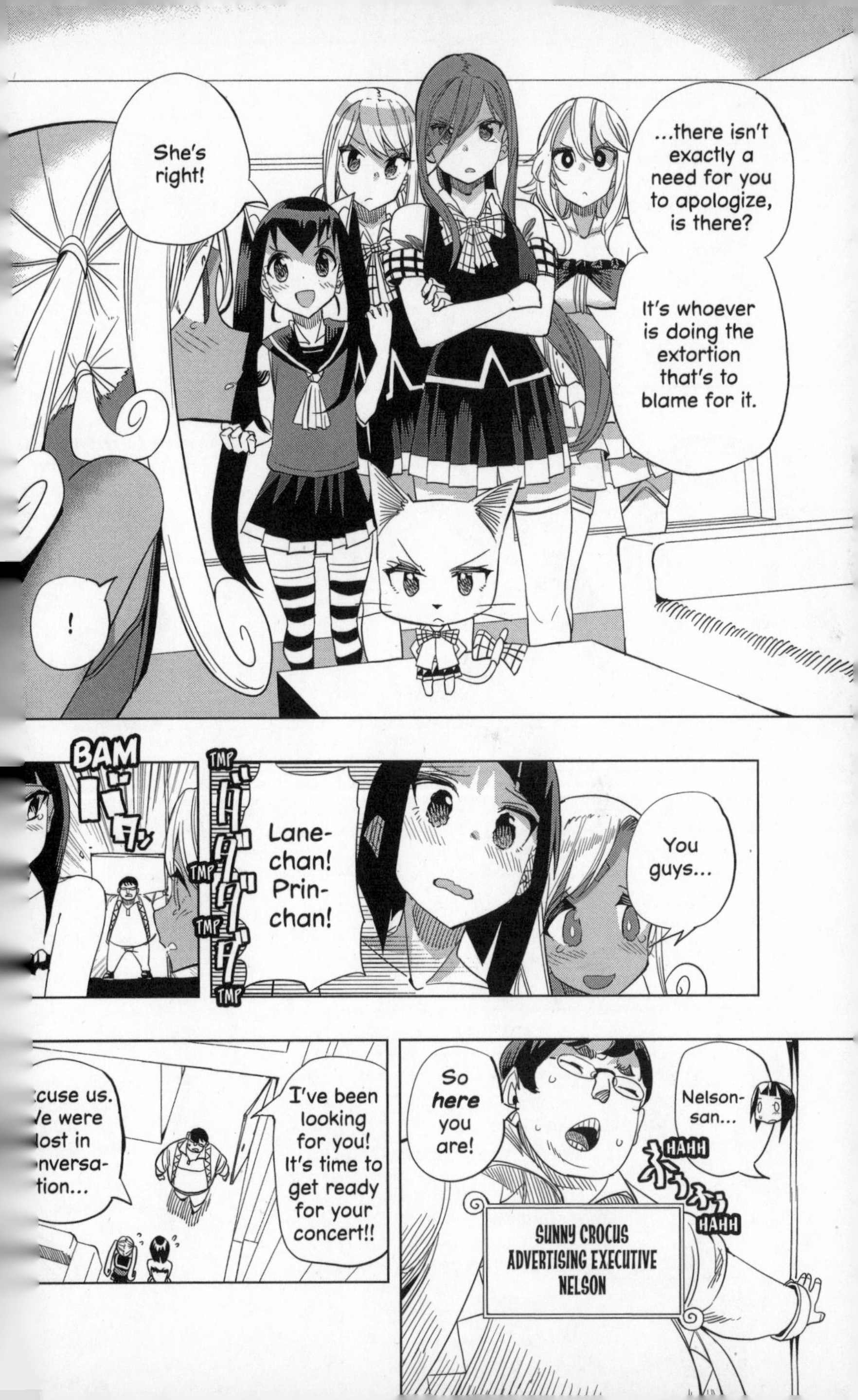

...there isn't exactly a need for you to apologize, is there?
It's whoever is doing the extortion that's to blame for it.
She's right!
!
You guys...
Lane-chan! Prin-chan!
TMP TMP TMP TMP
BAM
Nelson-san...
HAHH HAHH
So *here* you are!
SUNNY CROCUS ADVERTISING EXECUTIVE NELSON
I've been looking for you! It's time to get ready for your concert!!
cuse us. e were lost in nversa-tion...

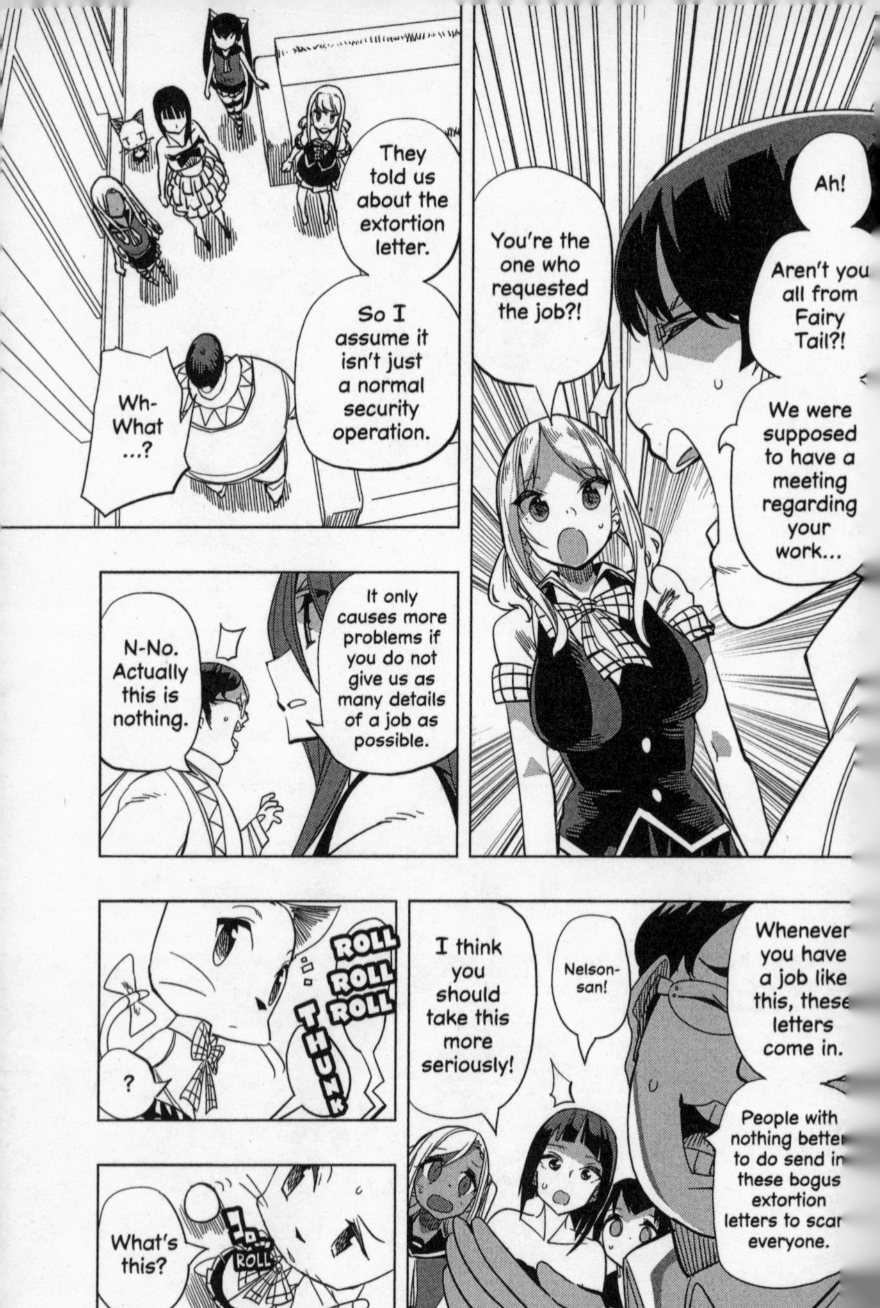
Ah!
Aren't you all from Fairy Tail?!
We were supposed to have a meeting regarding your work...
You're the one who requested the job?!
They told us about the extortion letter.
So I assume it isn't just a normal security operation.
Wh-What ...?
It only causes more problems if you do not give us as many details of a job as possible.
N-No. Actually this is nothing.
Whenever you have a job like this, these letters come in.
People with nothing bette to do send i these bogus extortion letters to scar everyone.
Nelson-san!
I think you should take this more seriously!
ROLL ROLL ROLL
THUNK
?
ROLL
What's this?

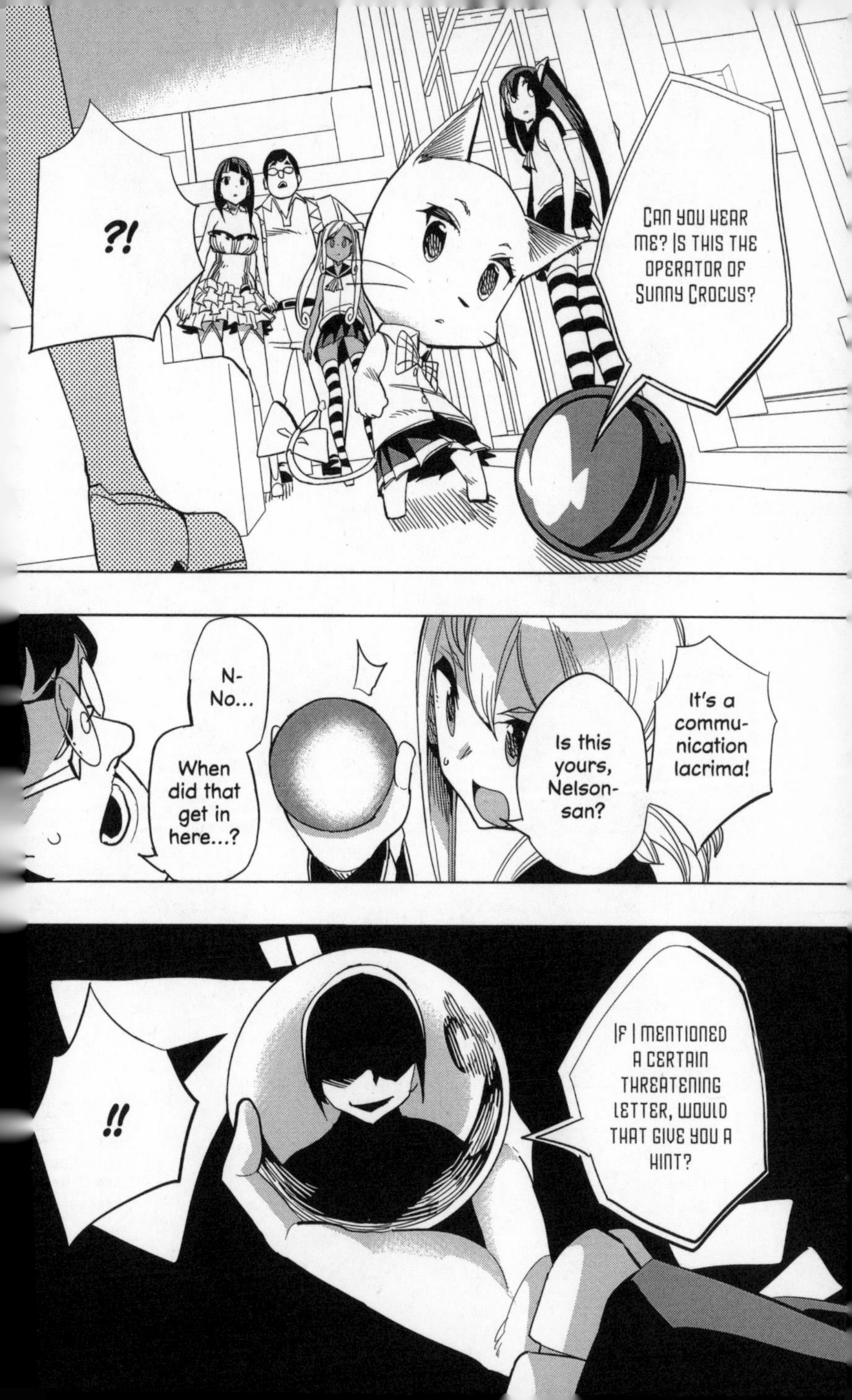
CAN YOU HEAR ME? IS THIS THE OPERATOR OF SUNNY CROCUS?
?!
It's a communication lacrima!
Is this yours, Nelson-san?
N- No...
When did that get in here...?
IF I MENTIONED A CERTAIN THREATENING LETTER, WOULD THAT GIVE YOU A HINT?
!!

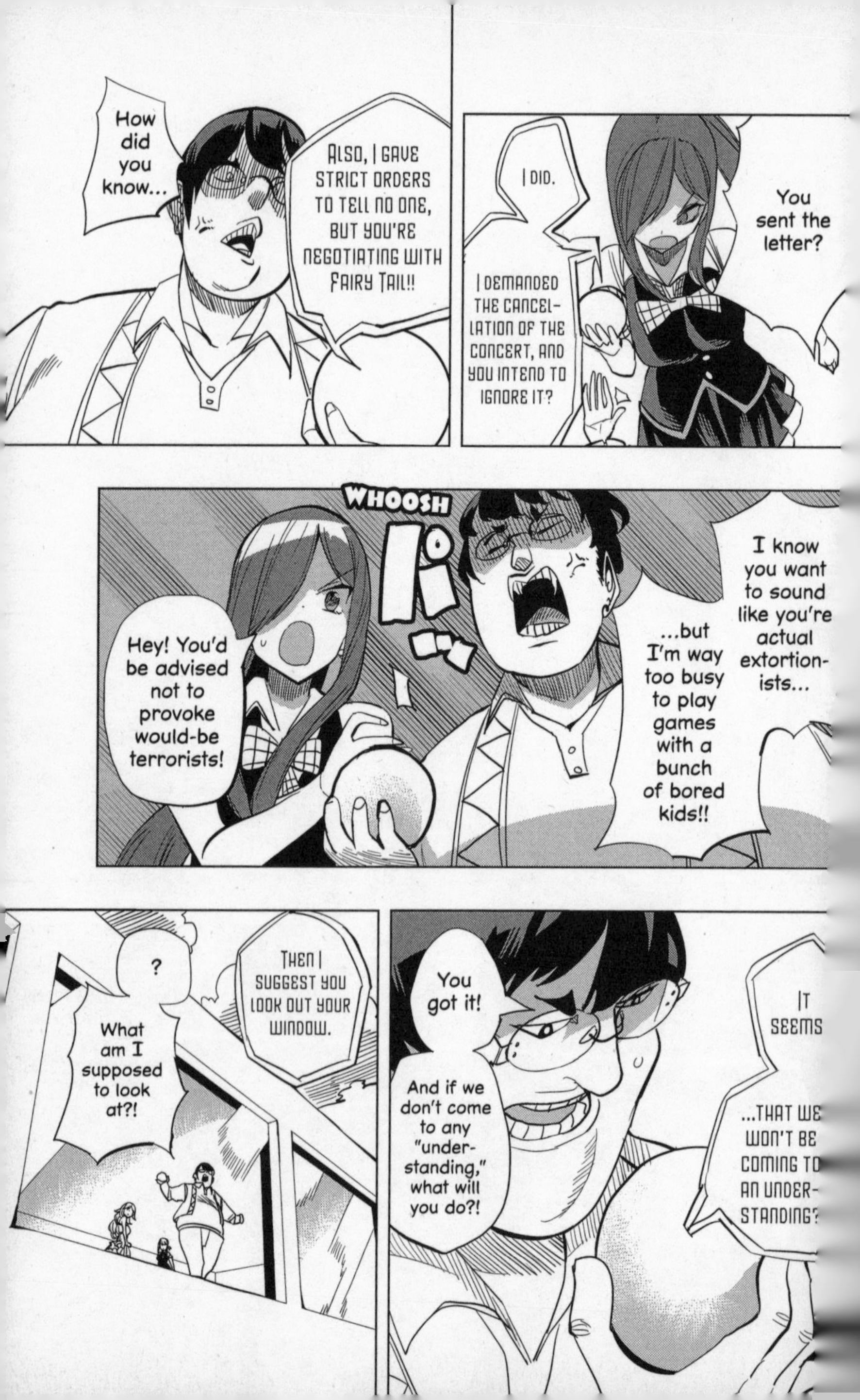
You sent the letter?
I did.
I DEMANDED THE CANCEL-LATION OF THE CONCERT, AND YOU INTEND TO IGNORE IT?
How did you know...
ALSO, I GAVE STRICT ORDERS TO TELL NO ONE, BUT YOU'RE NEGOTIATING WITH FAIRY TAIL!!
I know you want to sound like you're actual extortion-ists...
...but I'm way too busy to play games with a bunch of bored kids!!
WHOOSH
Hey! You'd be advised not to provoke would-be terrorists!
IT SEEMS
...THAT WE WON'T BE COMING TO AN UNDER-STANDING?
You got it!
And if we don't come to any "under-standing," what will you do?!
THEN I SUGGEST YOU LOOK OUT YOUR WINDOW.
?
What am I supposed to look at?!

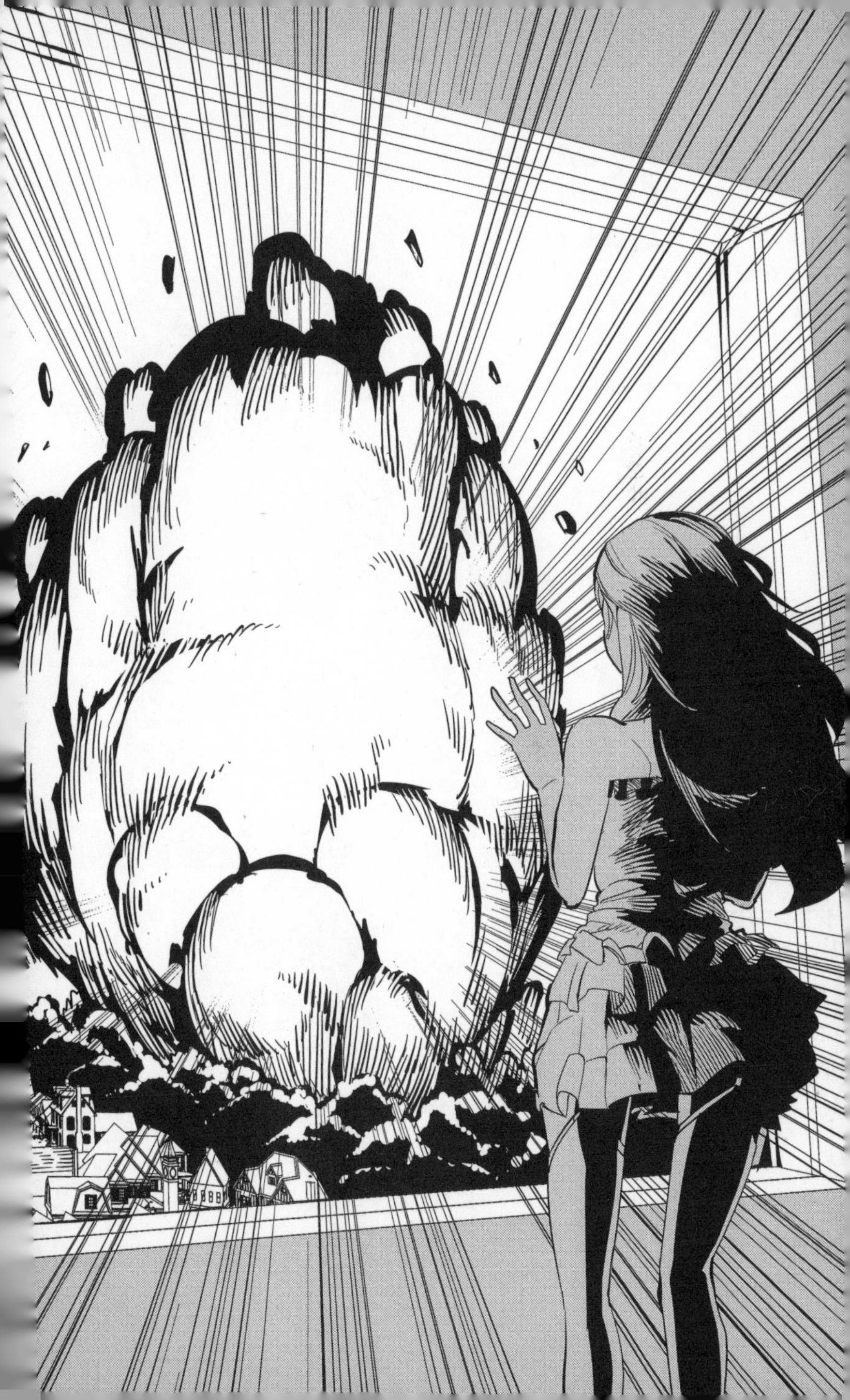

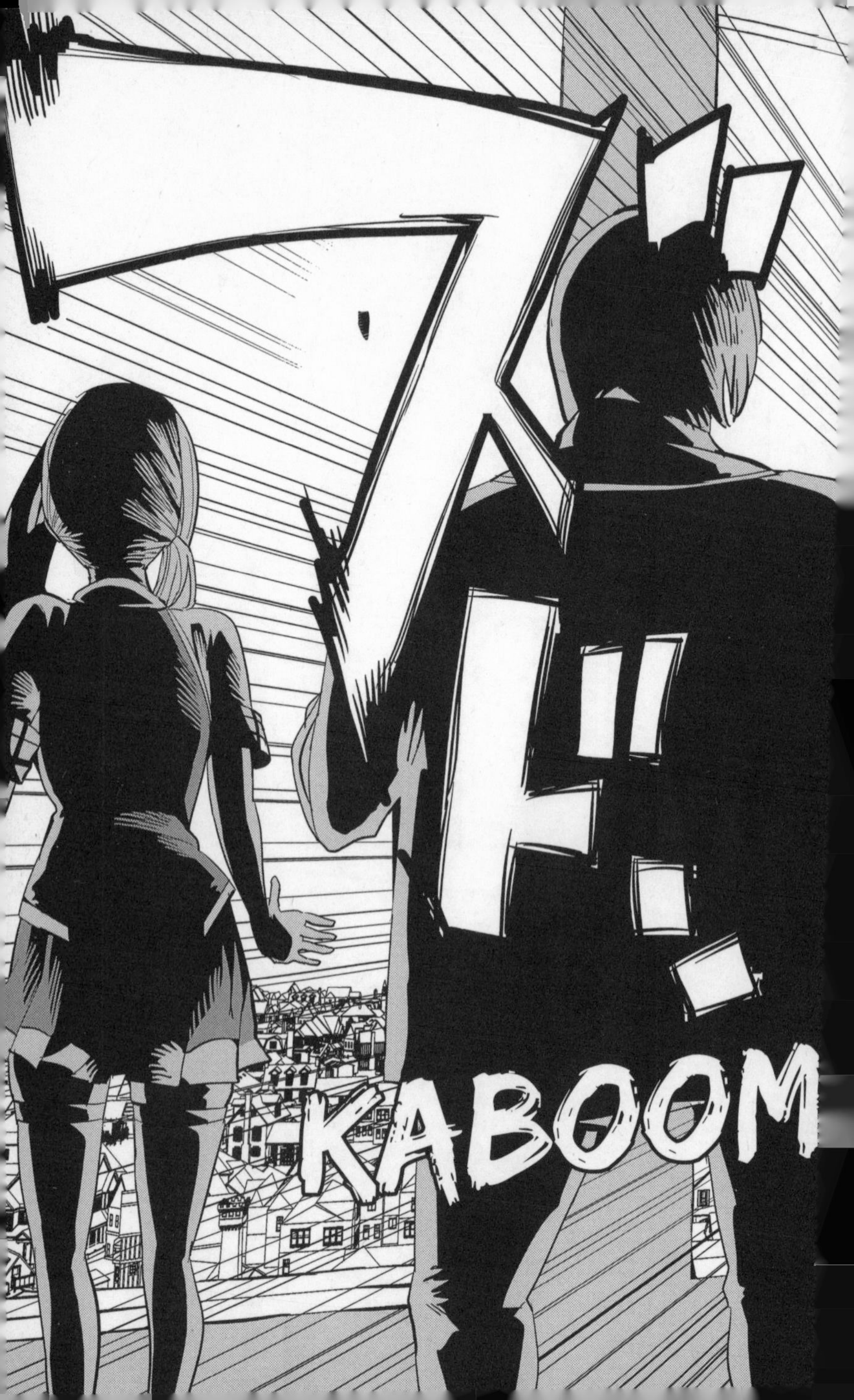
KABOOM

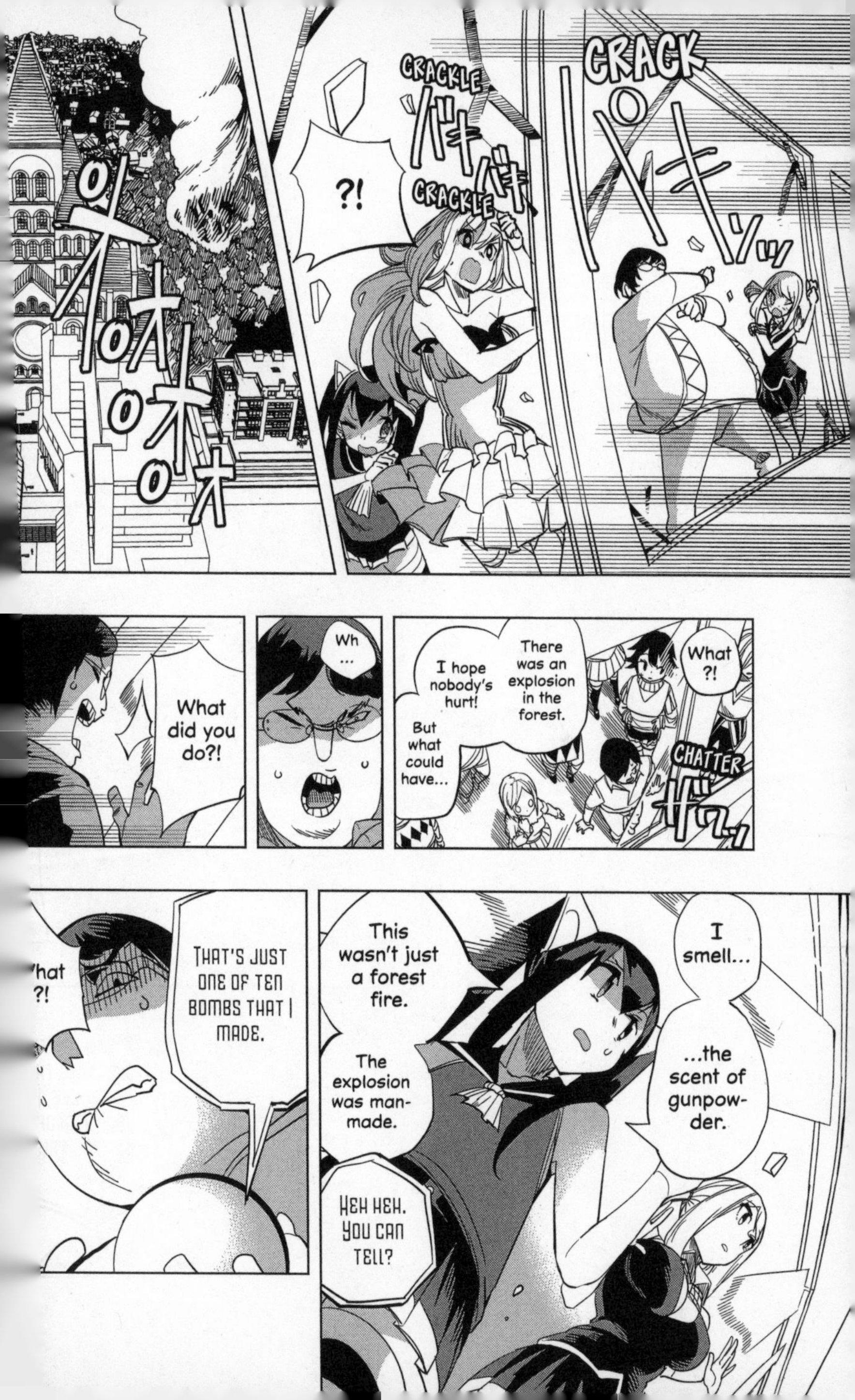
CRACK
CRACKLE
CRACKLE
?!
What ?!
CHATTER
There was an explosion in the forest.
I hope nobody's hurt!
But what could have...
Wh ...
What did you do?!
I smell...
...the scent of gunpowder.
This wasn't just a forest fire.
The explosion was man-made.
HEH HEH. YOU CAN TELL?
THAT'S JUST ONE OF TEN BOMBS THAT I MADE.

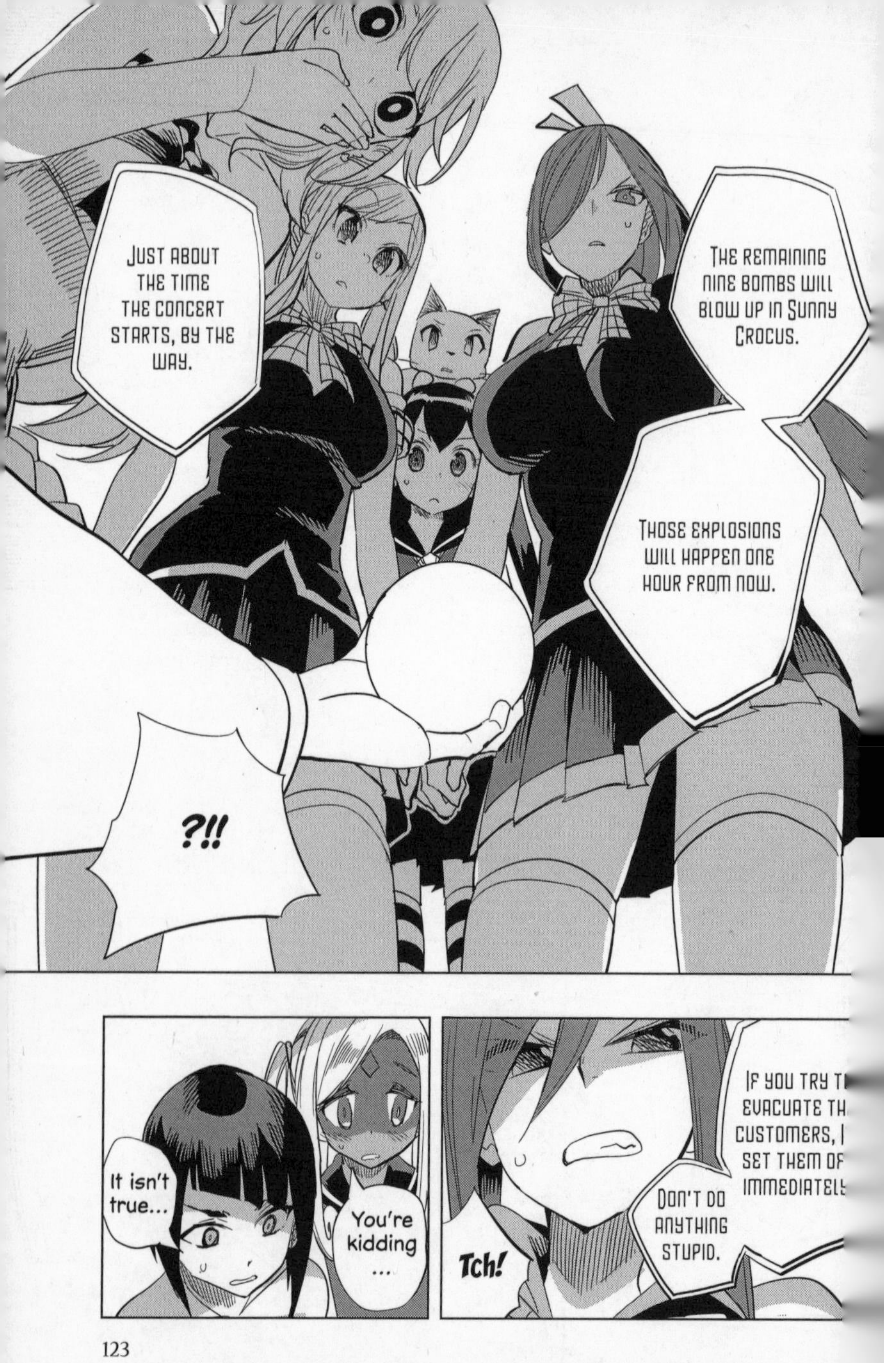
The remaining nine bombs will blow up in Sunny Crocus.
Those explosions will happen one hour from now.
Just about the time the concert starts, by the way.
?!!
If you try t
evacuate th
customers, I
set them of
immediatel
Don't do anything stupid.
Tch!
You're kidding ...
It isn't true...

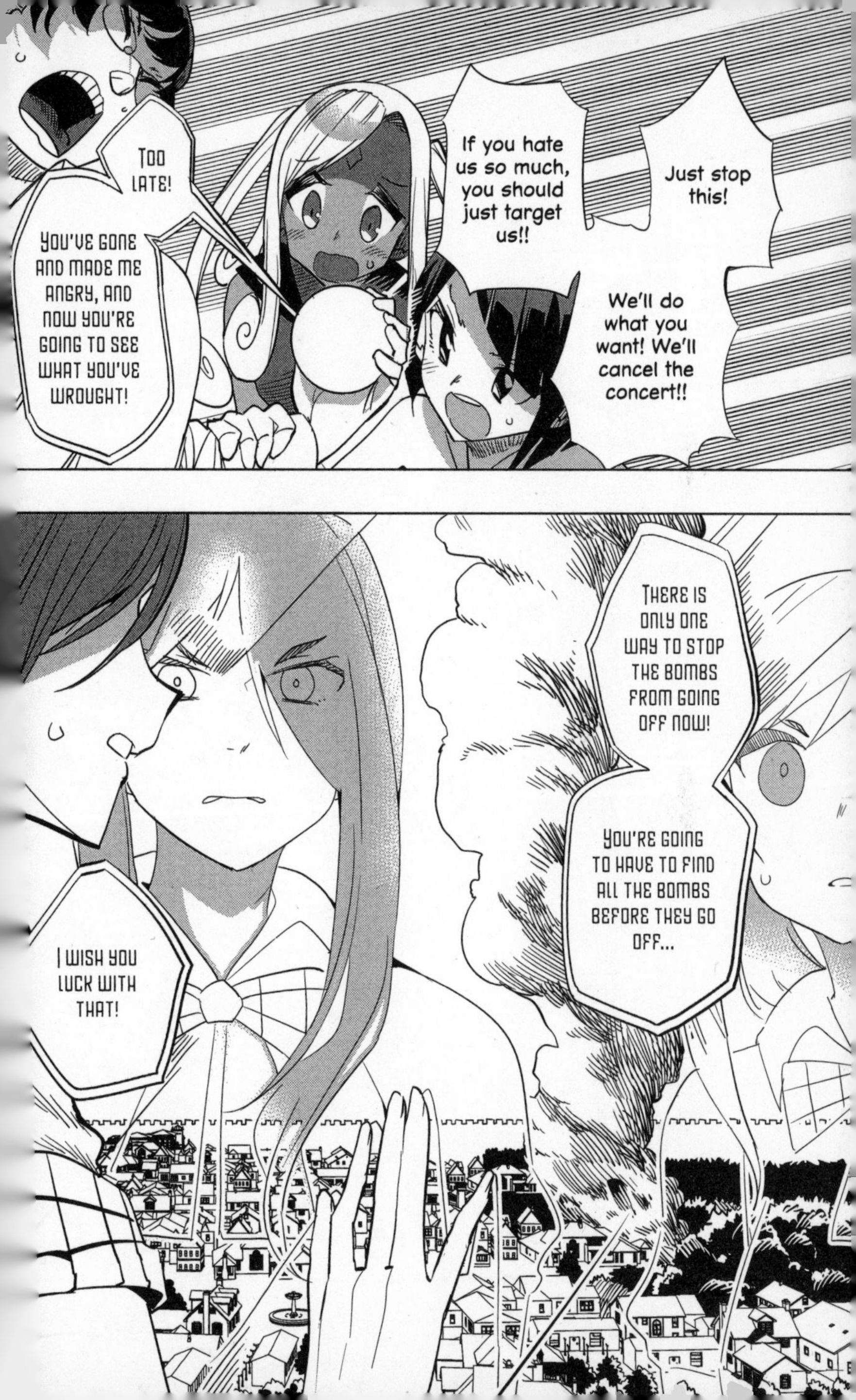
Just stop this!
If you hate us so much, you should just target us!!
We'll do what you want! We'll cancel the concert!!
TOO LATE!
YOU'VE GONE AND MADE ME ANGRY, AND NOW YOU'RE GOING TO SEE WHAT YOU'VE WROUGHT!
THERE IS ONLY ONE WAY TO STOP THE BOMBS FROM GOING OFF NOW!
YOU'RE GOING TO HAVE TO FIND ALL THE BOMBS BEFORE THEY GO OFF...
I WISH YOU LUCK WITH THAT!

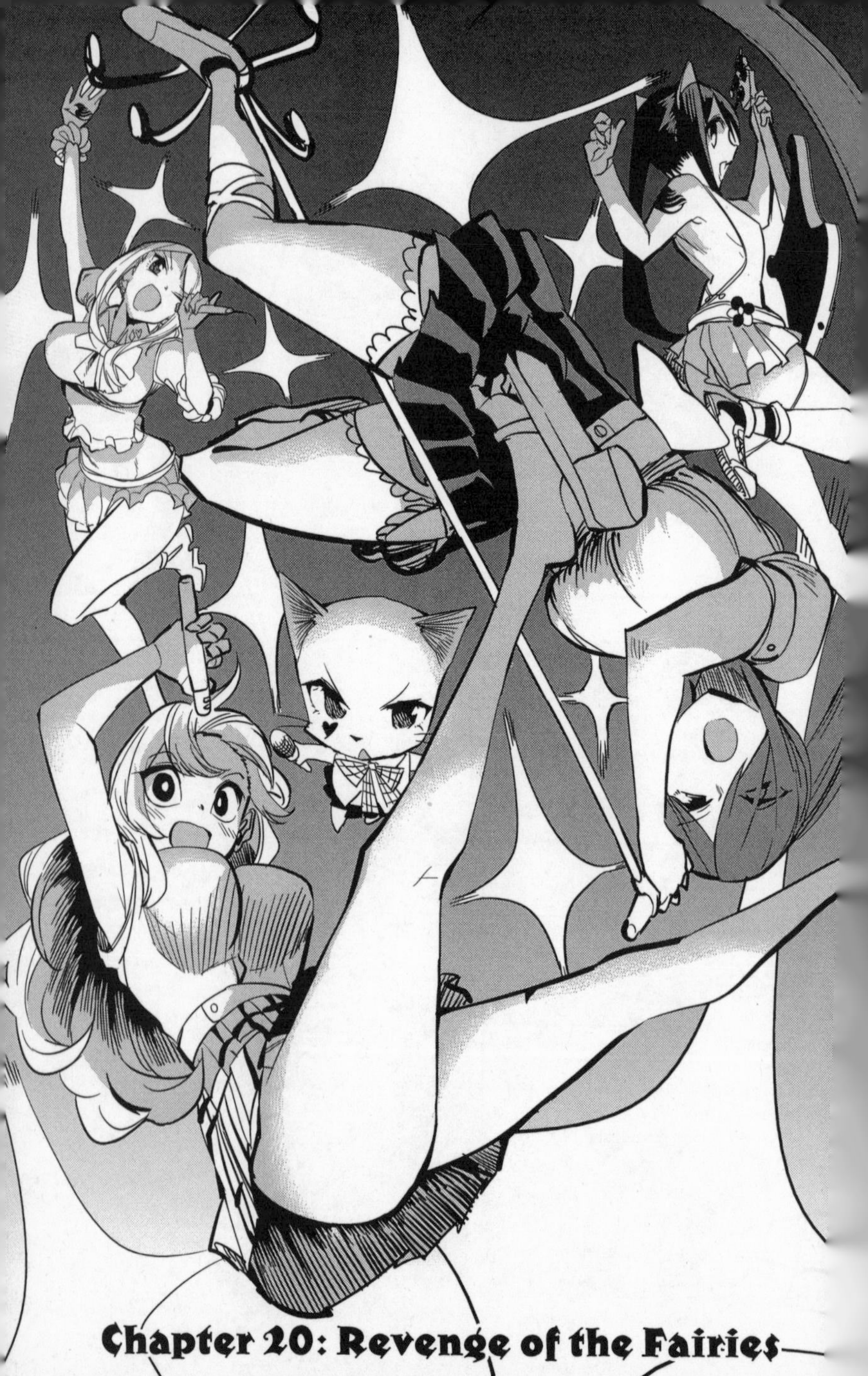

Chapter 20: Revenge of the Fairies

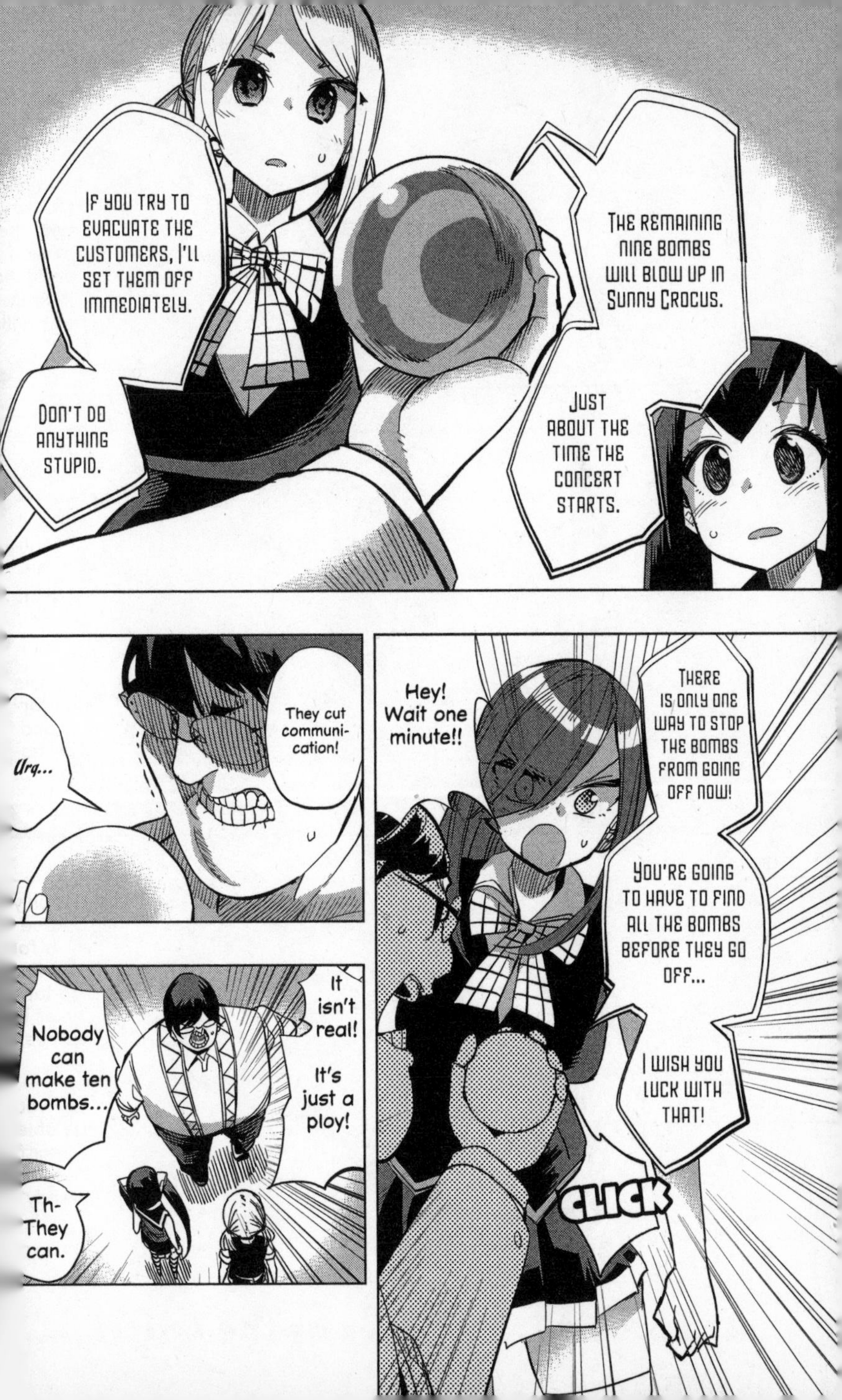

THE REMAINING NINE BOMBS WILL BLOW UP IN SUNNY CROCUS.
JUST ABOUT THE TIME THE CONCERT STARTS.
IF YOU TRY TO EVACUATE THE CUSTOMERS, I'LL SET THEM OFF IMMEDIATELY.
DON'T DO ANYTHING STUPID.
THERE IS ONLY ONE WAY TO STOP THE BOMBS FROM GOING OFF NOW!
Hey! Wait one minute!!
YOU'RE GOING TO HAVE TO FIND ALL THE BOMBS BEFORE THEY GO OFF...
I WISH YOU LUCK WITH THAT!
CLICK
They cut communi-cation!
Urg...
It isn't real!
It's just a ploy!
Nobody can make ten bombs...
Th- They can.

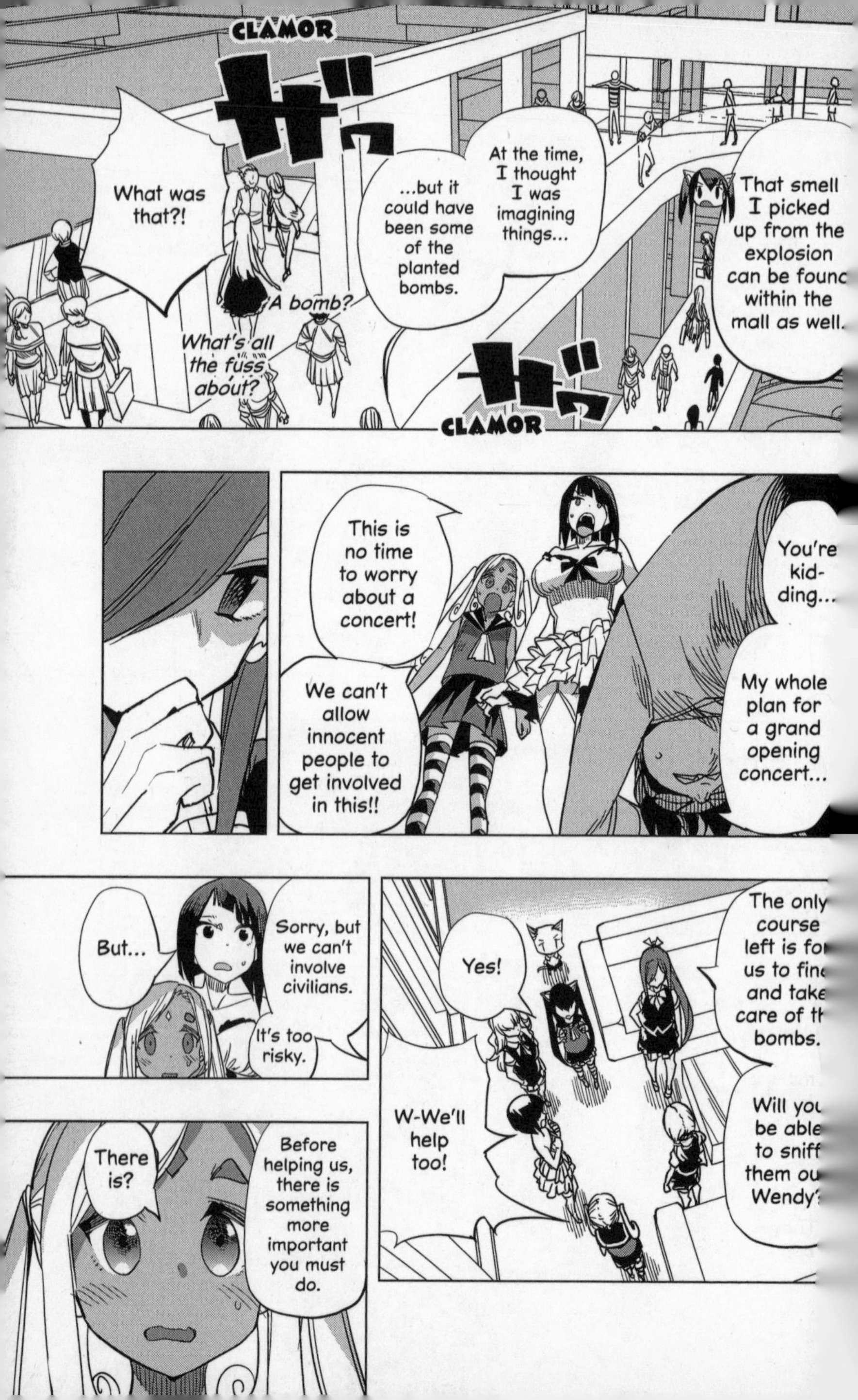
CLAMOR
That smell I picked up from the explosion can be found within the mall as well.
At the time, I thought I was imagining things...
...but it could have been some of the planted bombs.
CLAMOR
A bomb?
What was that?!
What's all the fuss about?
You're kid-ding...
My whole plan for a grand opening concert...
This is no time to worry about a concert!
We can't allow innocent people to get involved in this!!
The only course left is for us to find and take care of the bombs.
Will you be able to sniff them out, Wendy?
Yes!
W-We'll help too!
Sorry, but we can't involve civilians.
It's too risky.
But...
Before helping us, there is something more important you must do.
There is?

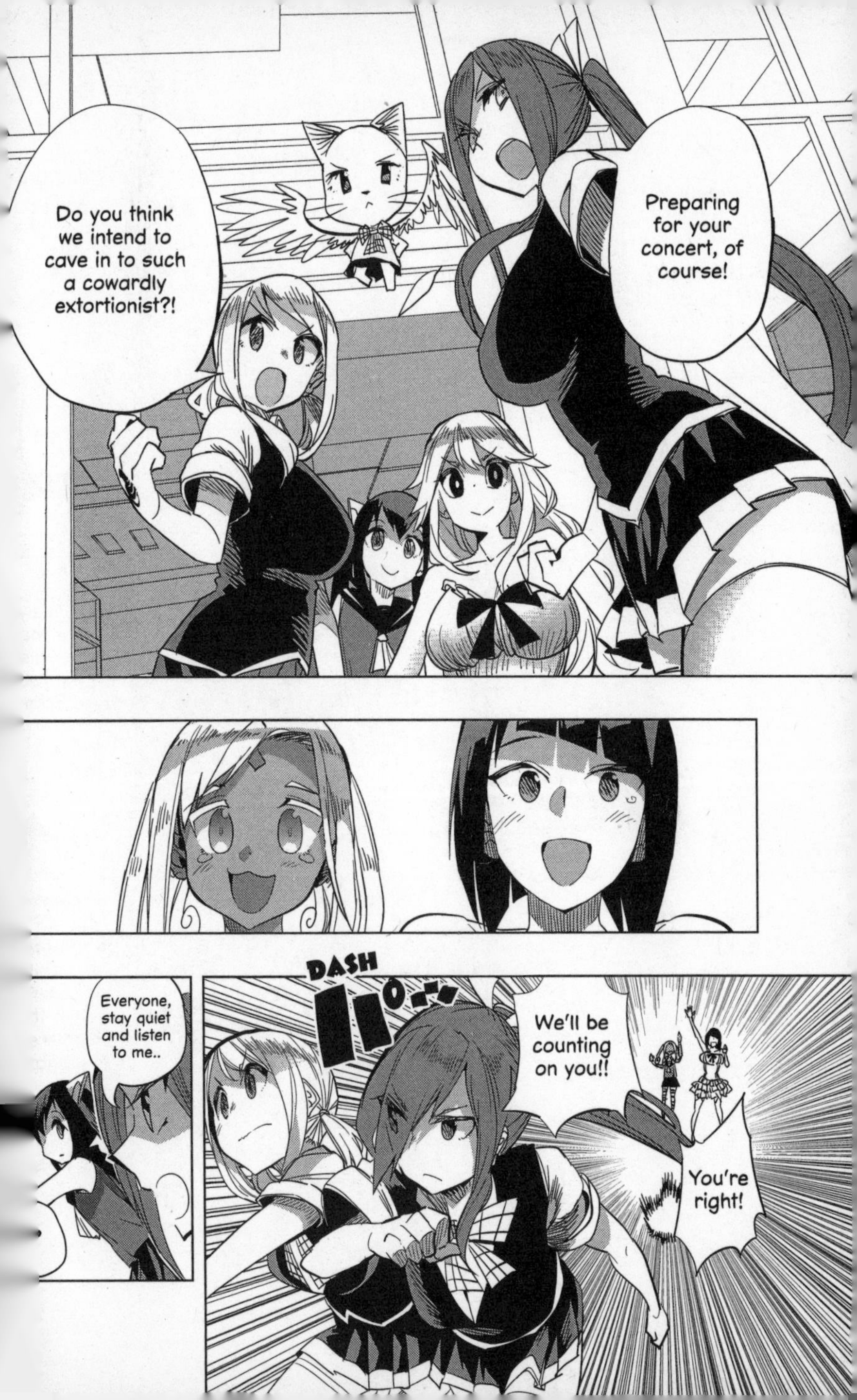
Preparing for your concert, of course!
Do you think we intend to cave in to such a cowardly extortionist?!
DASH
We'll be counting on you!!
You're right!
Everyone, stay quiet and listen to me..

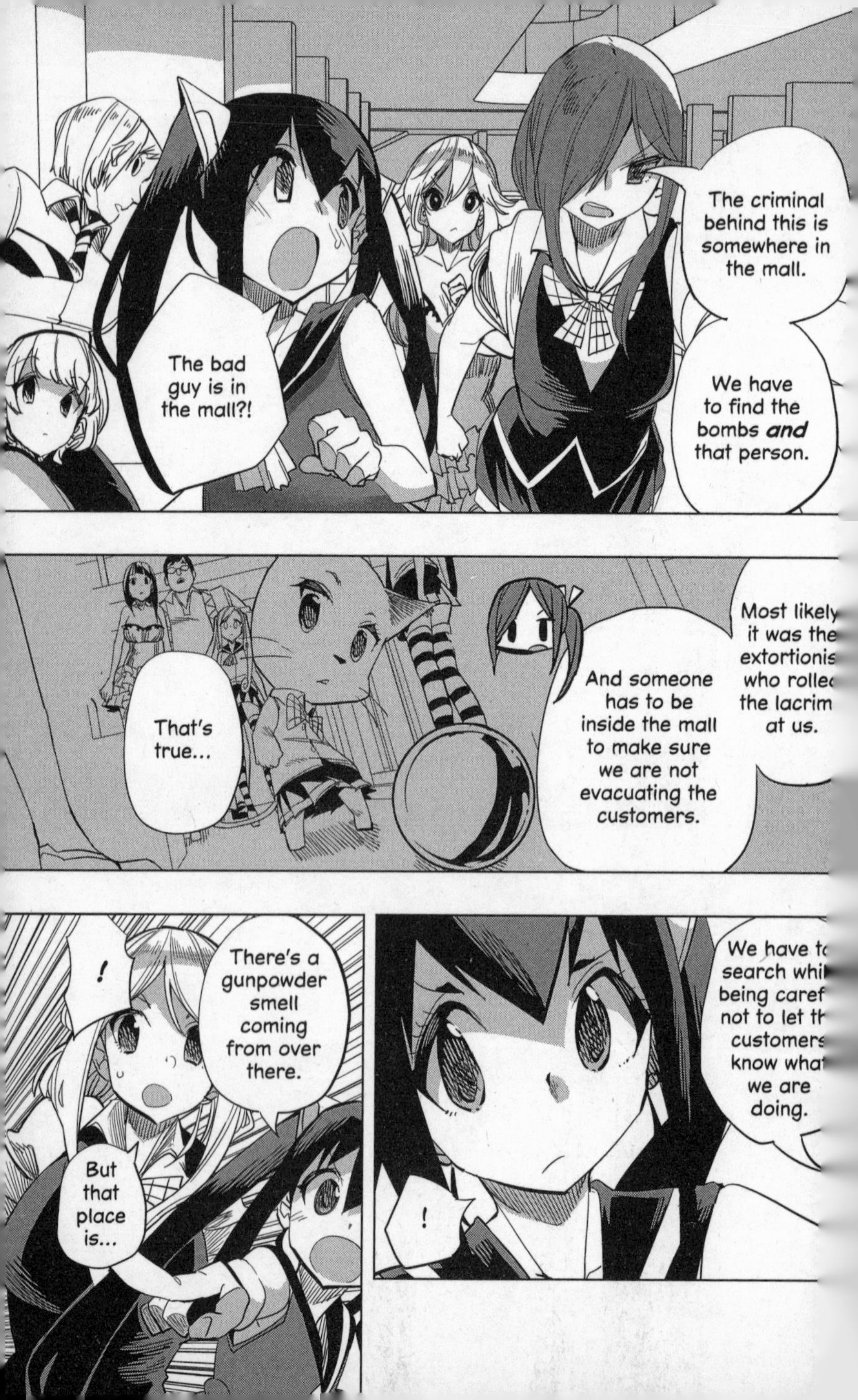
The criminal behind this is somewhere in the mall.
We have to find the bombs *and* that person.
The bad guy is in the mall?!
Most likely it was the extortionis who rollec the lacrim at us.
And someone has to be inside the mall to make sure we are not evacuating the customers.
That's true...
We have t search whi being caref not to let th customers know wha we are doing.
!
!
There's a gunpowder smell coming from over there.
But that place is...

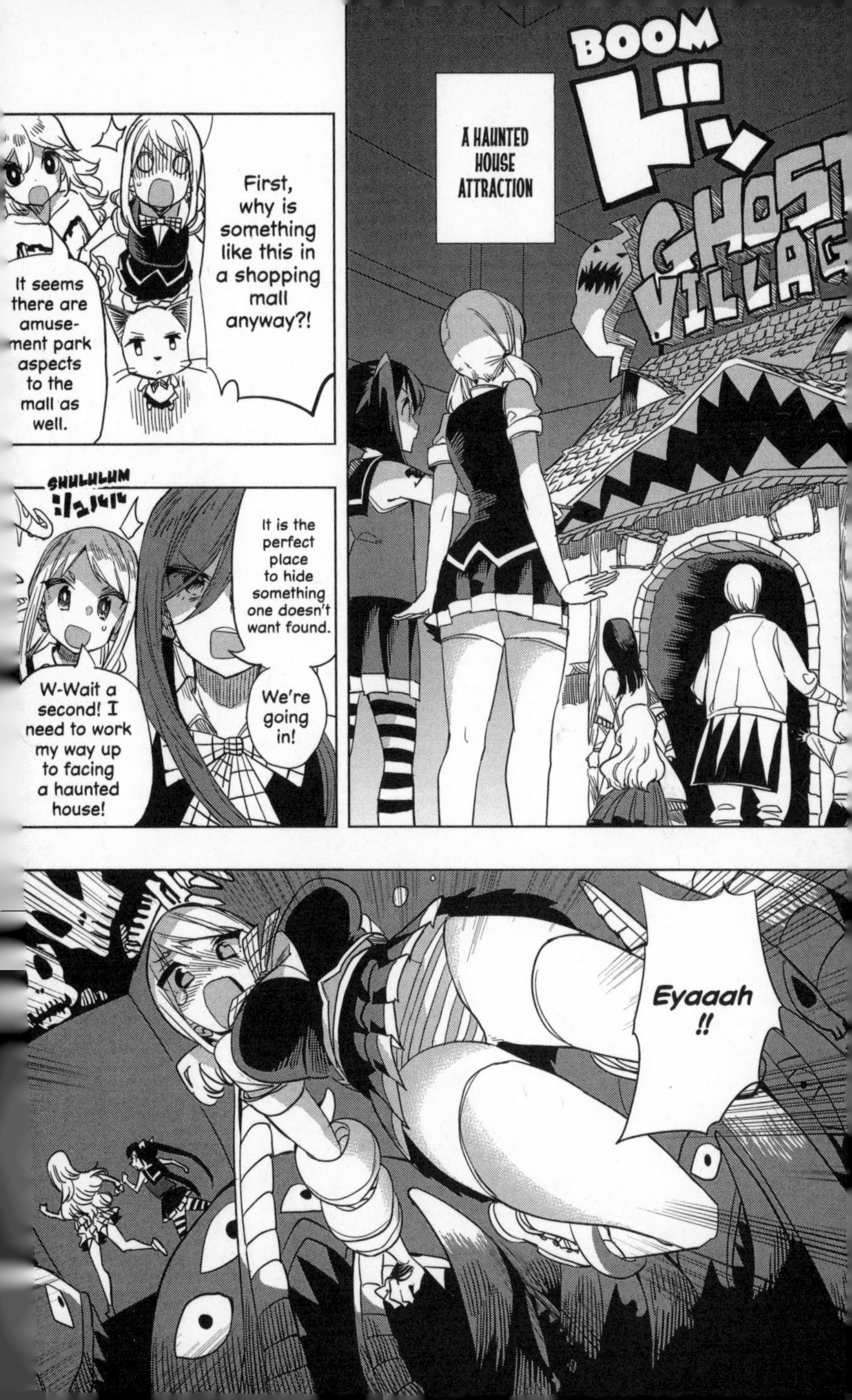
BOOM
A HAUNTED HOUSE ATTRACTION
First, why is something like this in a shopping mall anyway?!
It seems there are amusement park aspects to the mall as well.
It is the perfect place to hide something one doesn't want found.
We're going in!
SHULULUM
W-Wait a second! I need to work my way up to facing a haunted house!
Eyaaah!!

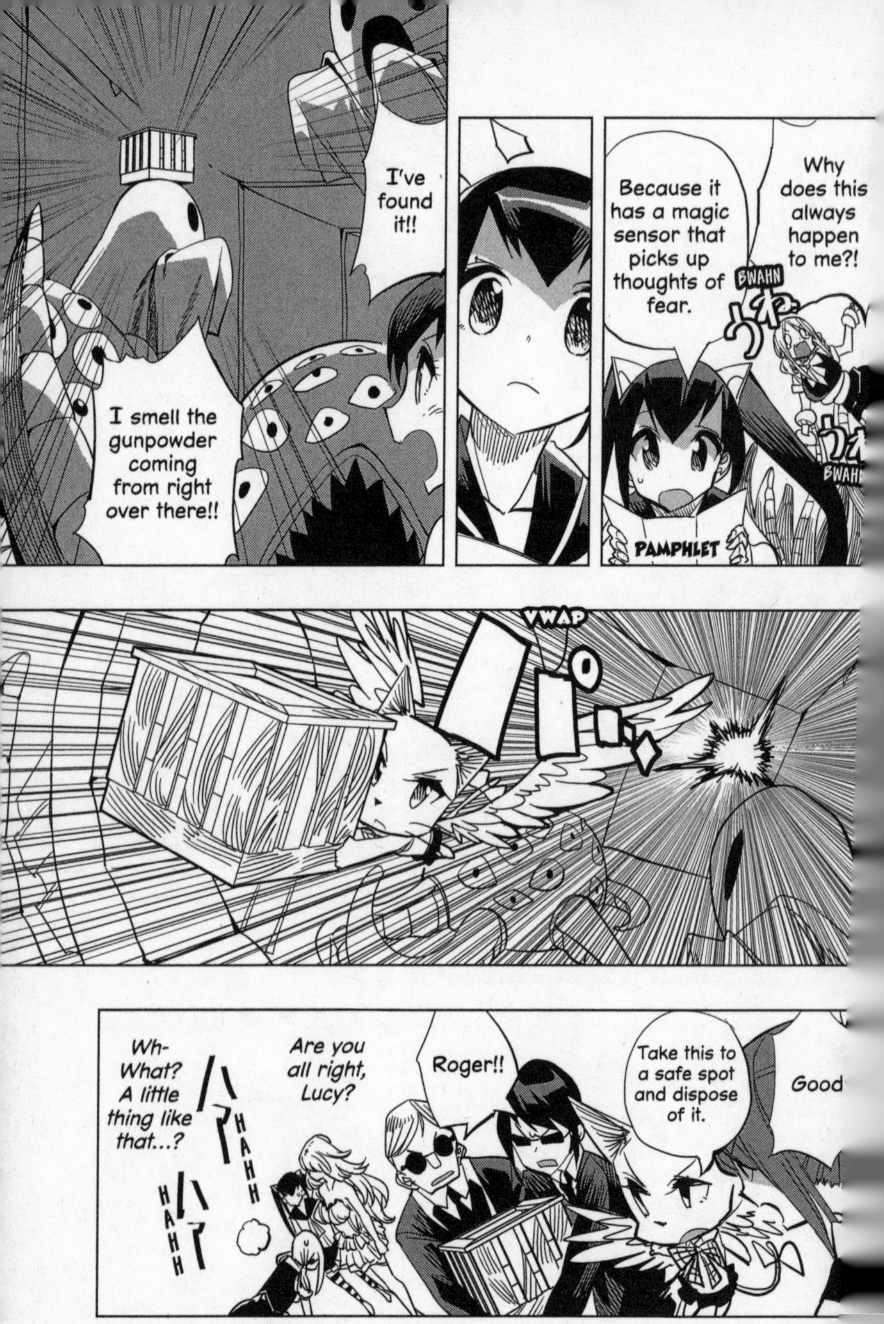
Why does this always happen to me?!
BWAHN
BWAHN
Because it has a magic sensor that picks up thoughts of fear.
PAMPHLET
I've found it!!
I smell the gunpowder coming from right over there!!
VWAP
Good
Take this to a safe spot and dispose of it.
Roger!!
Are you all right, Lucy?
Wh- What? A little thing like that...?
HAHH
HAHH

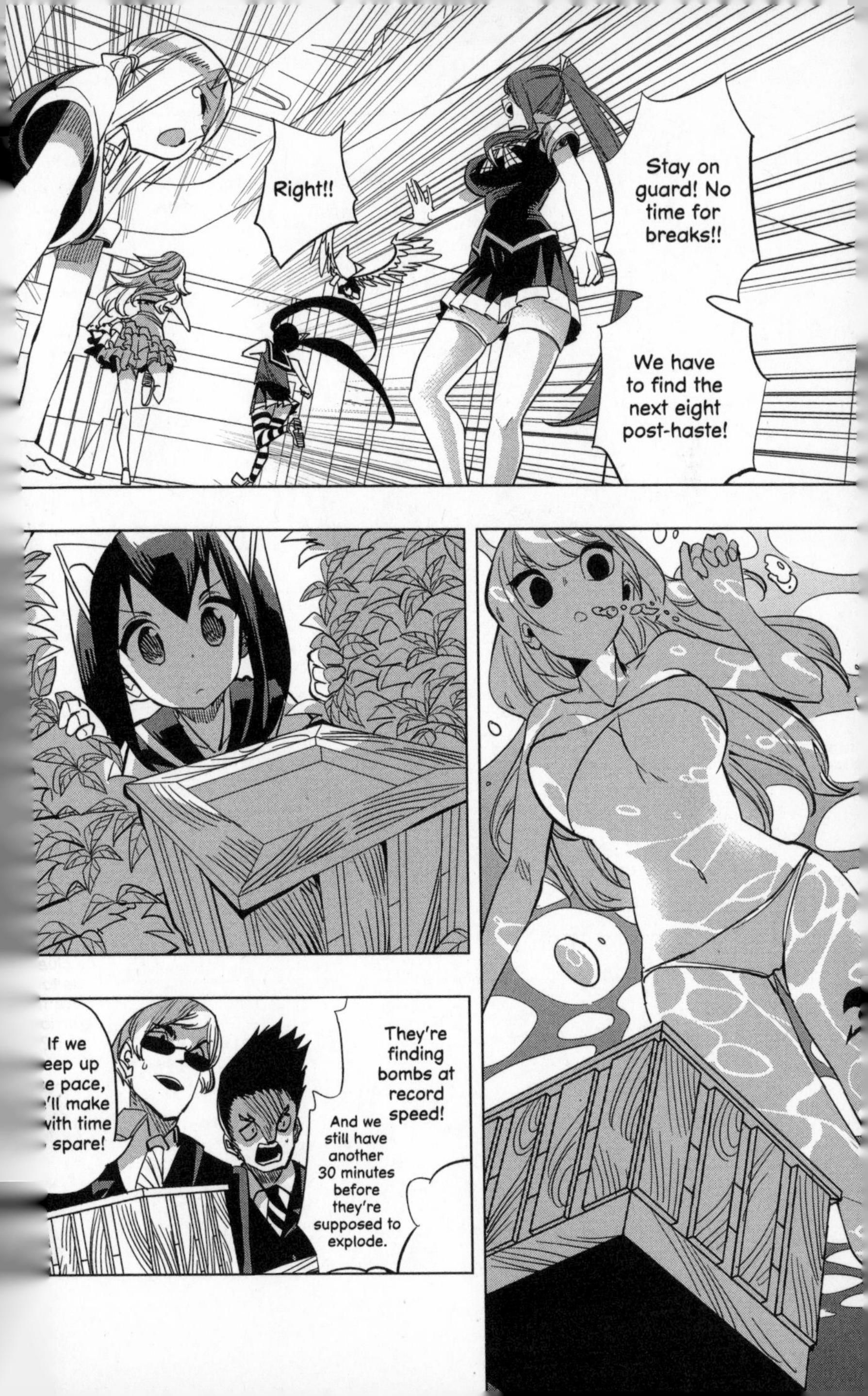
Stay on guard! No time for breaks!!
We have to find the next eight post-haste!
Right!!
They're finding bombs at record speed!
And we still have another 30 minutes before they're supposed to explode.
If we eep up e pace, 'll make with time spare!

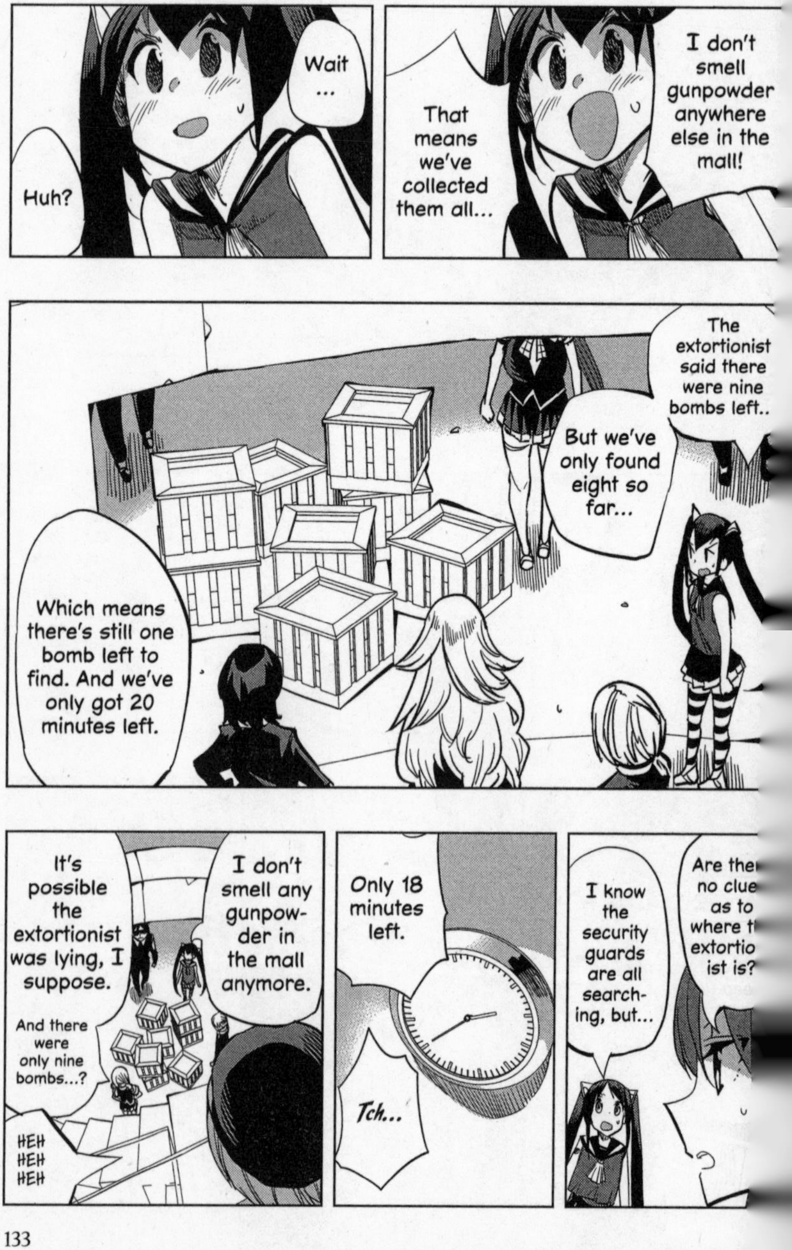
I don't smell gunpowder anywhere else in the mall!
That means we've collected them all...
Wait ...
Huh?
The extortionist said there were nine bombs left..
But we've only found eight so far...
Which means there's still one bomb left to find. And we've only got 20 minutes left.
Are the no clue as to where t extortio ist is?
I know the security guards are all search-ing, but...
Only 18 minutes left.
Tch...
I don't smell any gunpow-der in the mall anymore.
It's possible the extortionist was lying, I suppose.
And there were only nine bombs...?
HEH HEH HEH

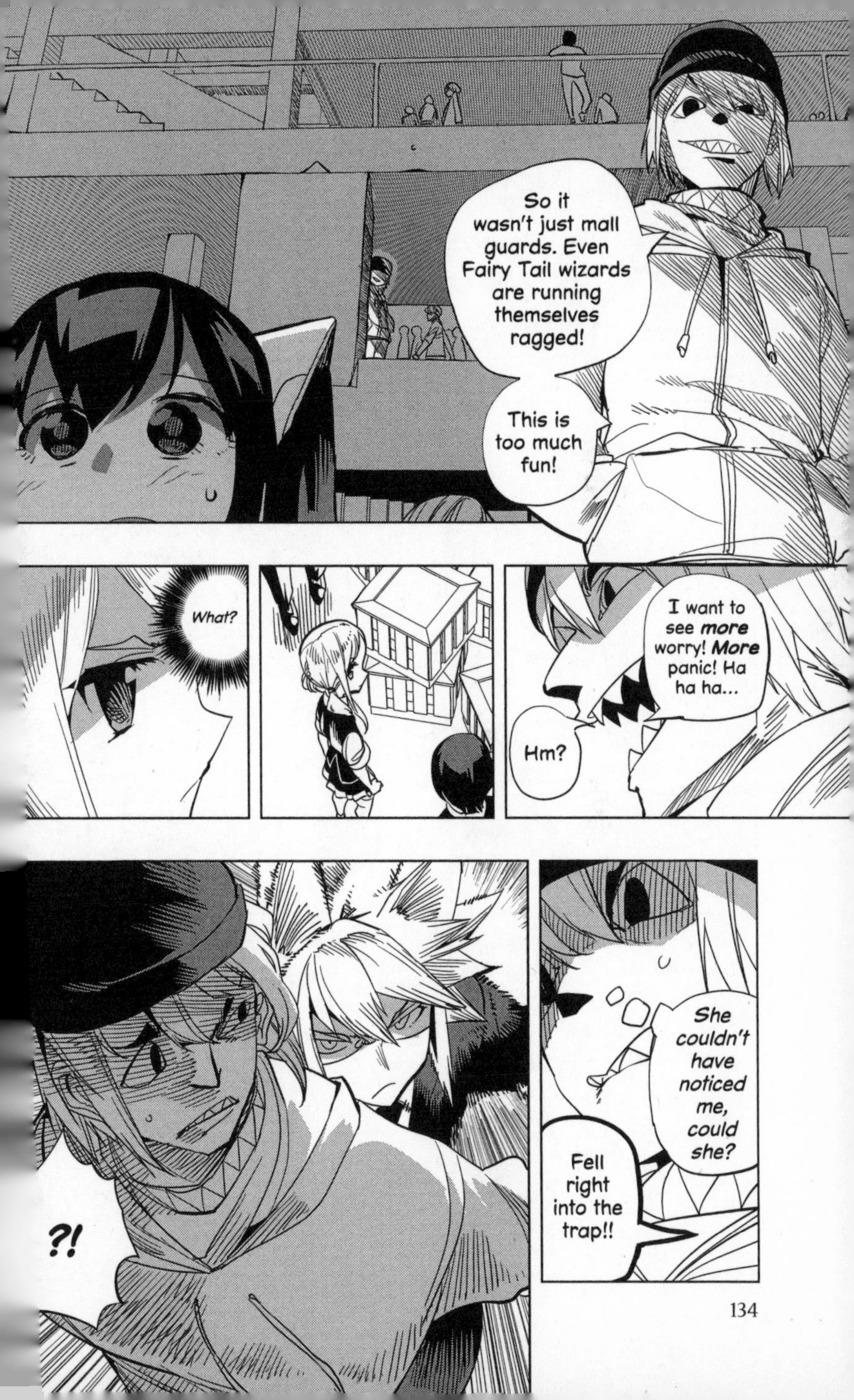
So it wasn't just mall guards. Even Fairy Tail wizards are running themselves ragged!
This is too much fun!
I want to see *more* worry! *More* panic! Ha ha ha...
Hm?
What?
She couldn't have noticed me, could she?
Fell right into the trap!!
?!

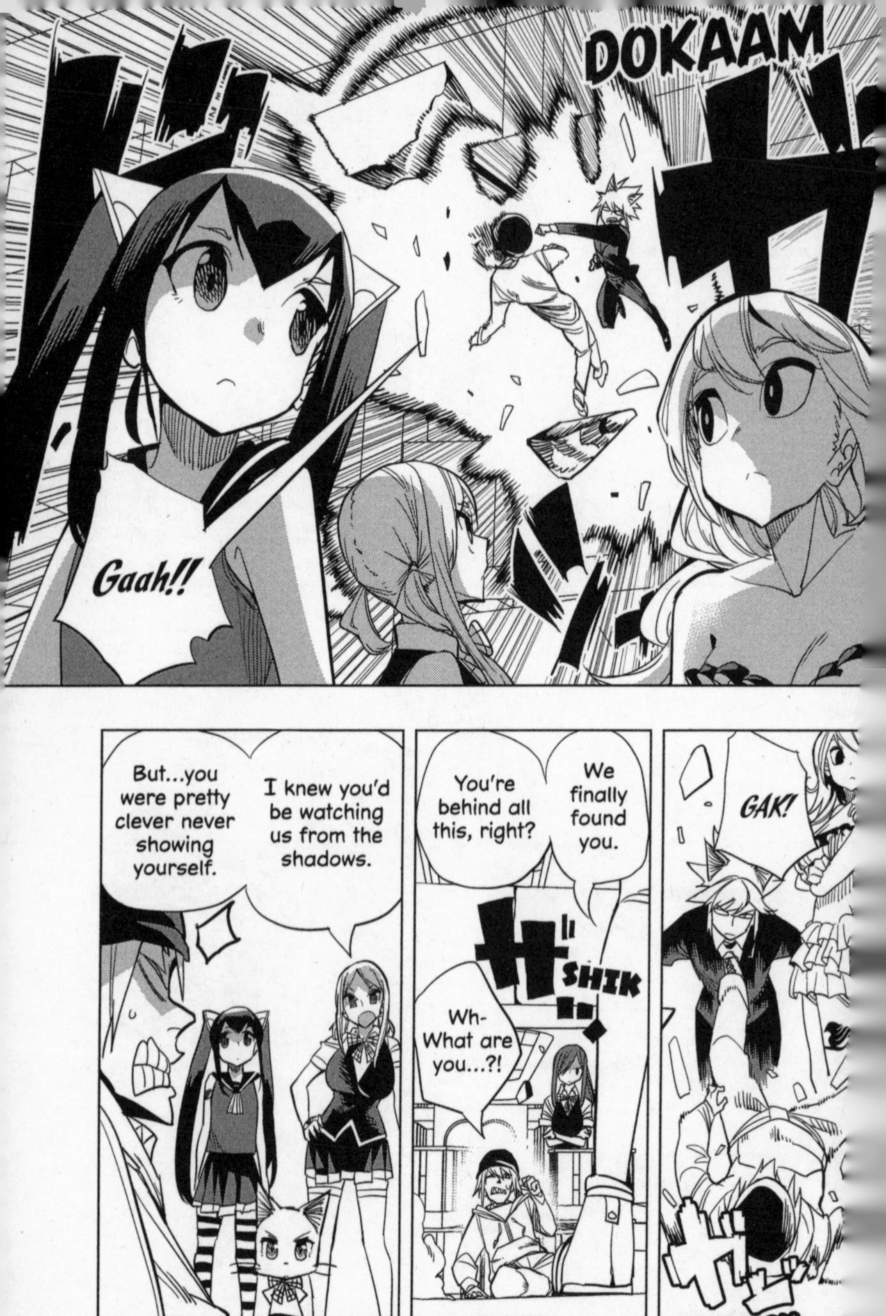
DOKAAM
Gaah!!
GAK!
GRUNCH
We finally found you.
You're behind all this, right?
SHIK
Wh- What are you...?!
I knew you'd be watching us from the shadows.
But...you were pretty clever never showing yourself.

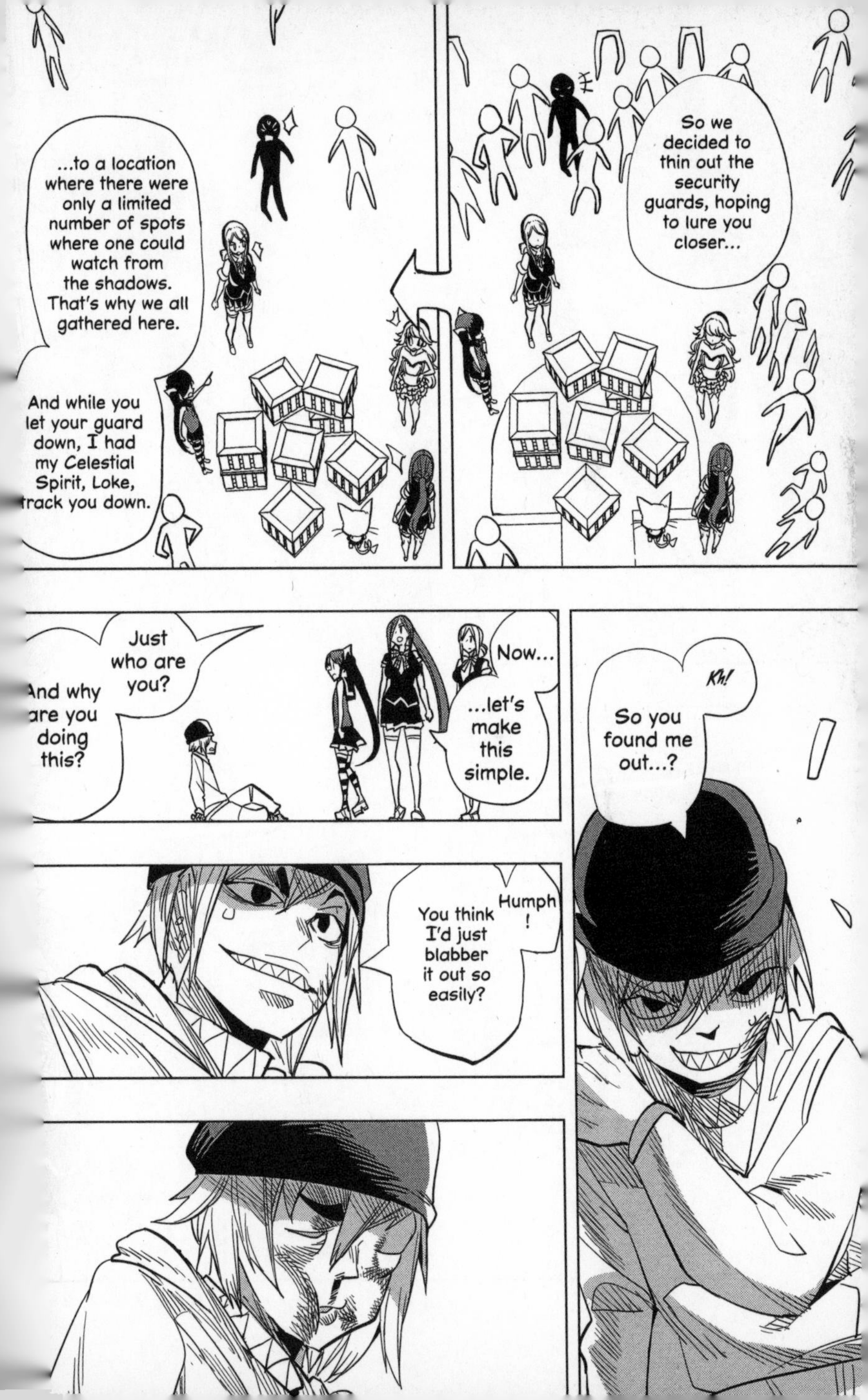
So we decided to thin out the security guards, hoping to lure you closer...
...to a location where there were only a limited number of spots where one could watch from the shadows. That's why we all gathered here.
And while you let your guard down, I had my Celestial Spirit, Loke, track you down.
Kh!
So you found me out...?
Now...
...let's make this simple.
Just who are you?
And why are you doing this?
Humph!
You think I'd just blabber it out so easily?

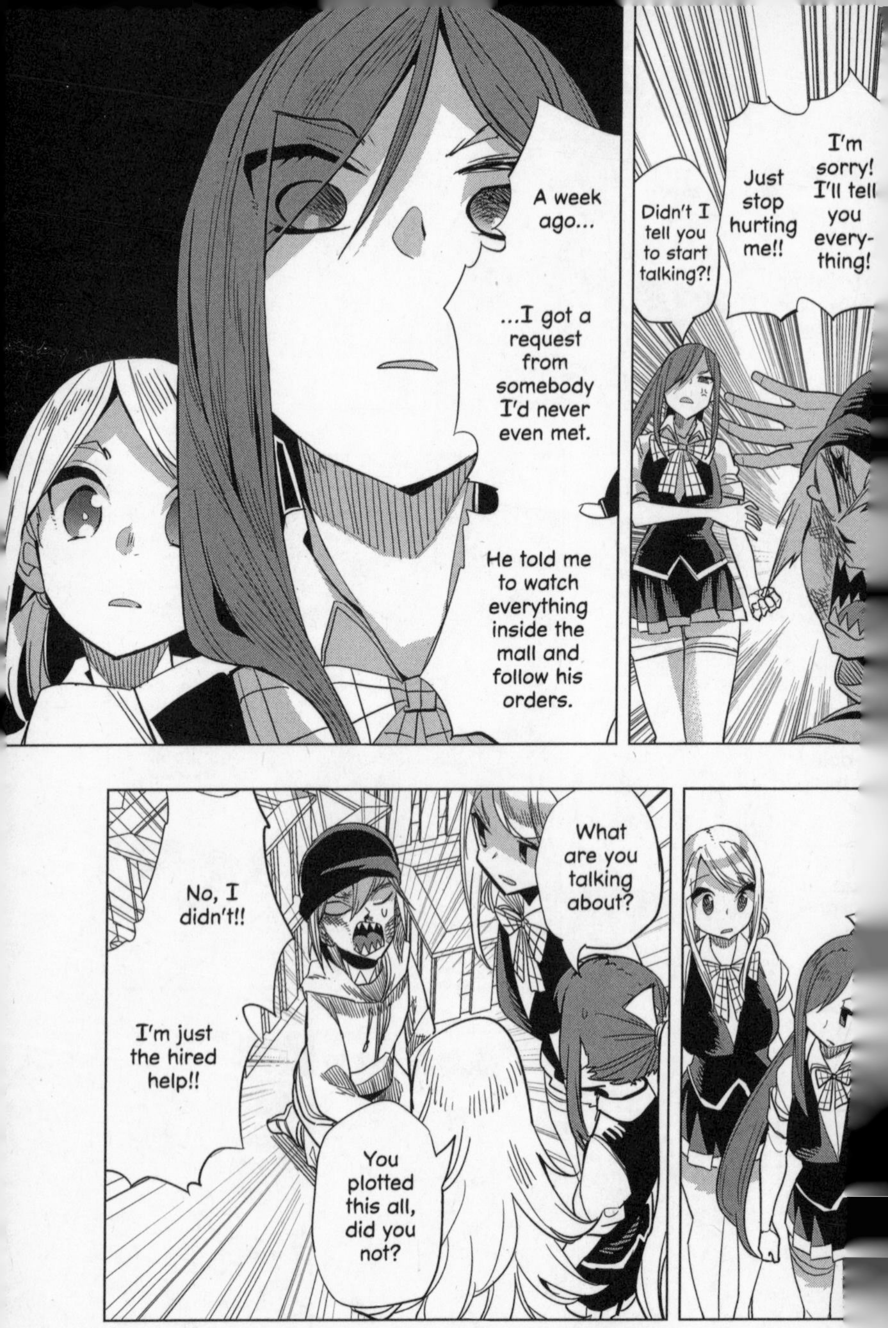
I'm sorry! I'll tell you every-thing!
Just stop hurting me!!
Didn't I tell you to start talking?!
A week ago...
...I got a request from somebody I'd never even met.
He told me to watch everything inside the mall and follow his orders.
What are you talking about?
No, I didn't!!
I'm just the hired help!!
You plotted this all, did you not?

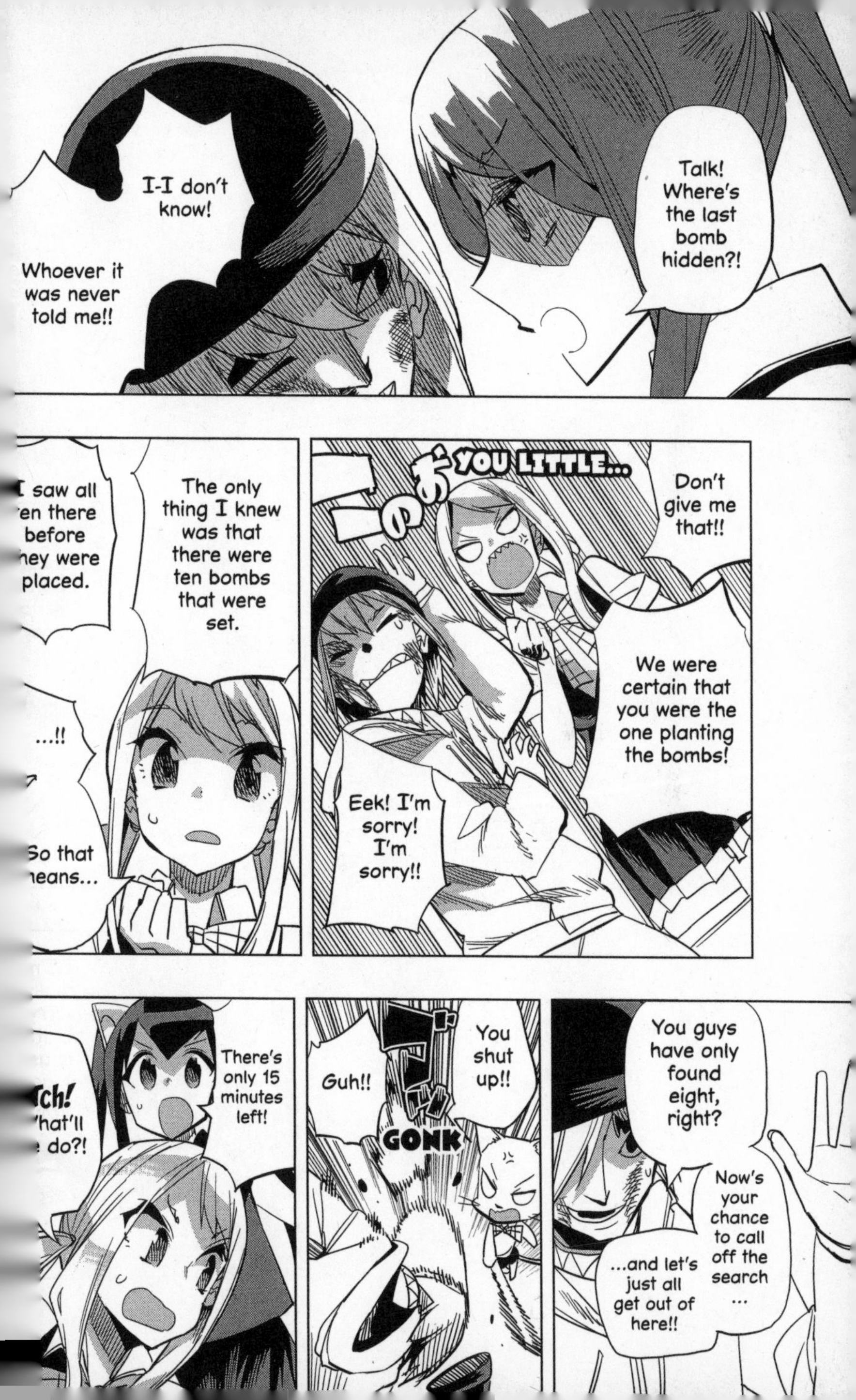

Talk! Where's the last bomb hidden?!
I-I don't know!
Whoever it was never told me!!
YOU LITTLE...
Don't give me that!!
We were certain that you were the one planting the bombs!
Eek! I'm sorry! I'm sorry!!
The only thing I knew was that there were ten bombs that were set.
I saw all en there before ney were placed.
...!!
So that neans...
You guys have only found eight, right?
Now's your chance to call off the search ...
...and let's just all get out of here!!
You shut up!!
GONK
Guh!!
There's only 15 minutes left!
Tch!
'hat'll do?!

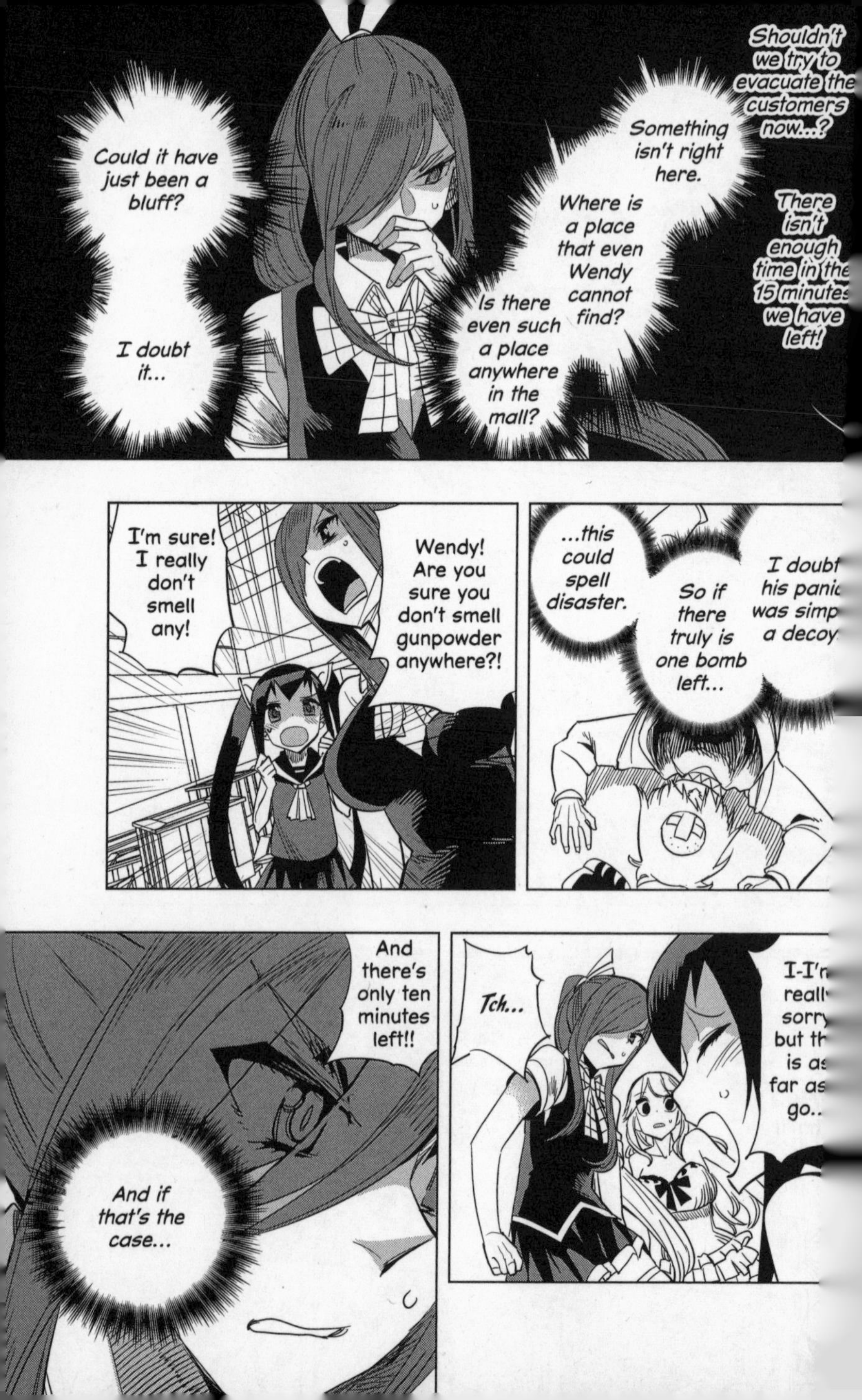

Shouldn't we try to evacuate the customers now...?
There isn't enough time in the 15 minutes we have left!
Something isn't right here.
Where is a place that even Wendy cannot find?
Is there even such a place anywhere in the mall?
Could it have just been a bluff?
I doubt it...
I doubt his panic was simp a decoy
So if there truly is one bomb left...
...this could spell disaster.
Wendy! Are you sure you don't smell gunpowder anywhere?!
I'm sure! I really don't smell any!
I-I'm really sorry but th is as far as go..
Tch...
And there's only ten minutes left!!
And if that's the case...

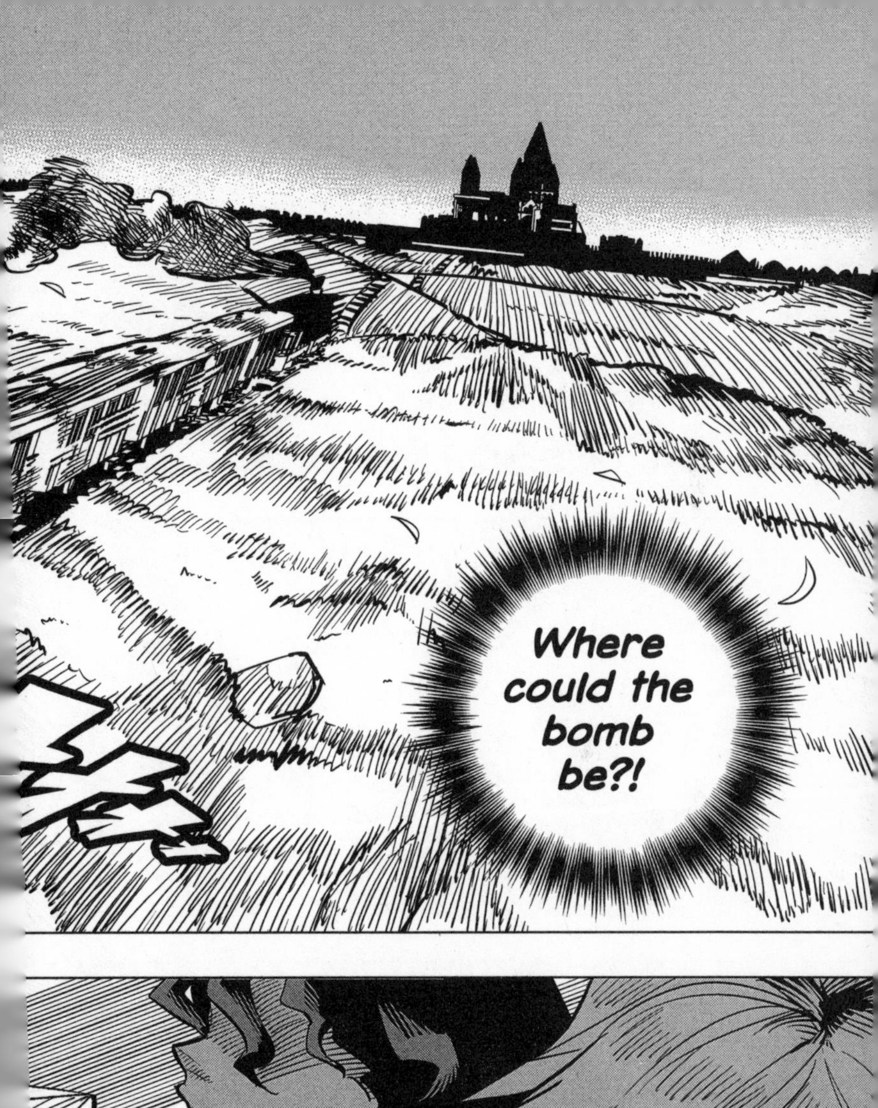
Where could the bomb be?!
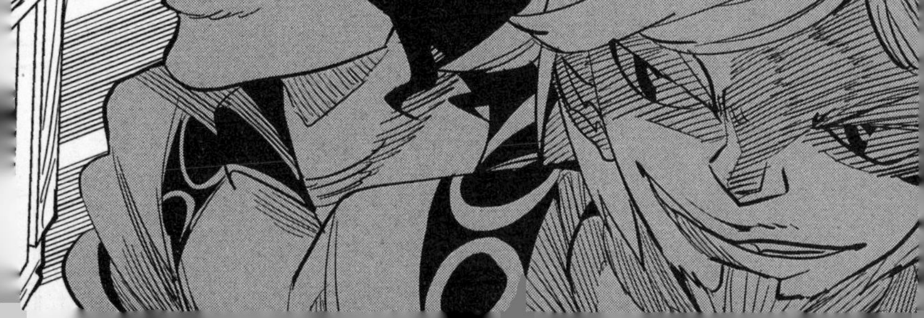

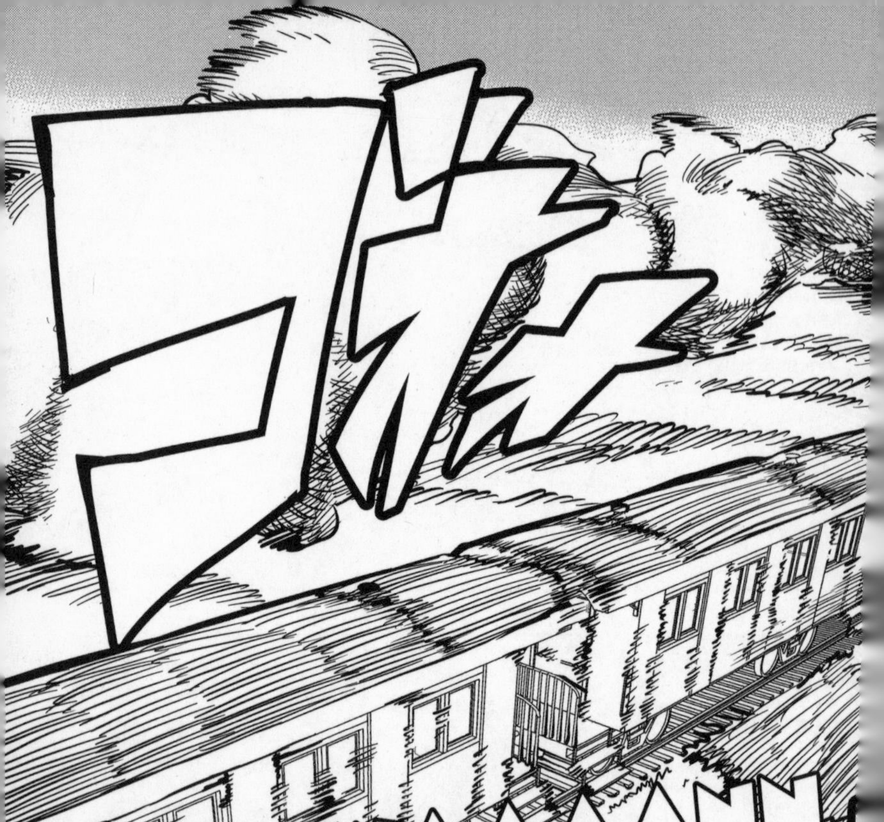
BWAAAANN
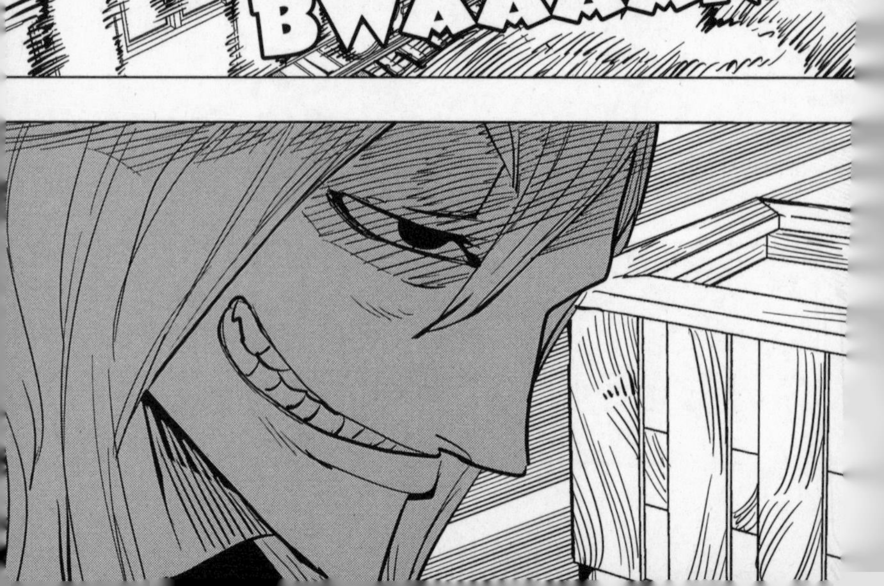

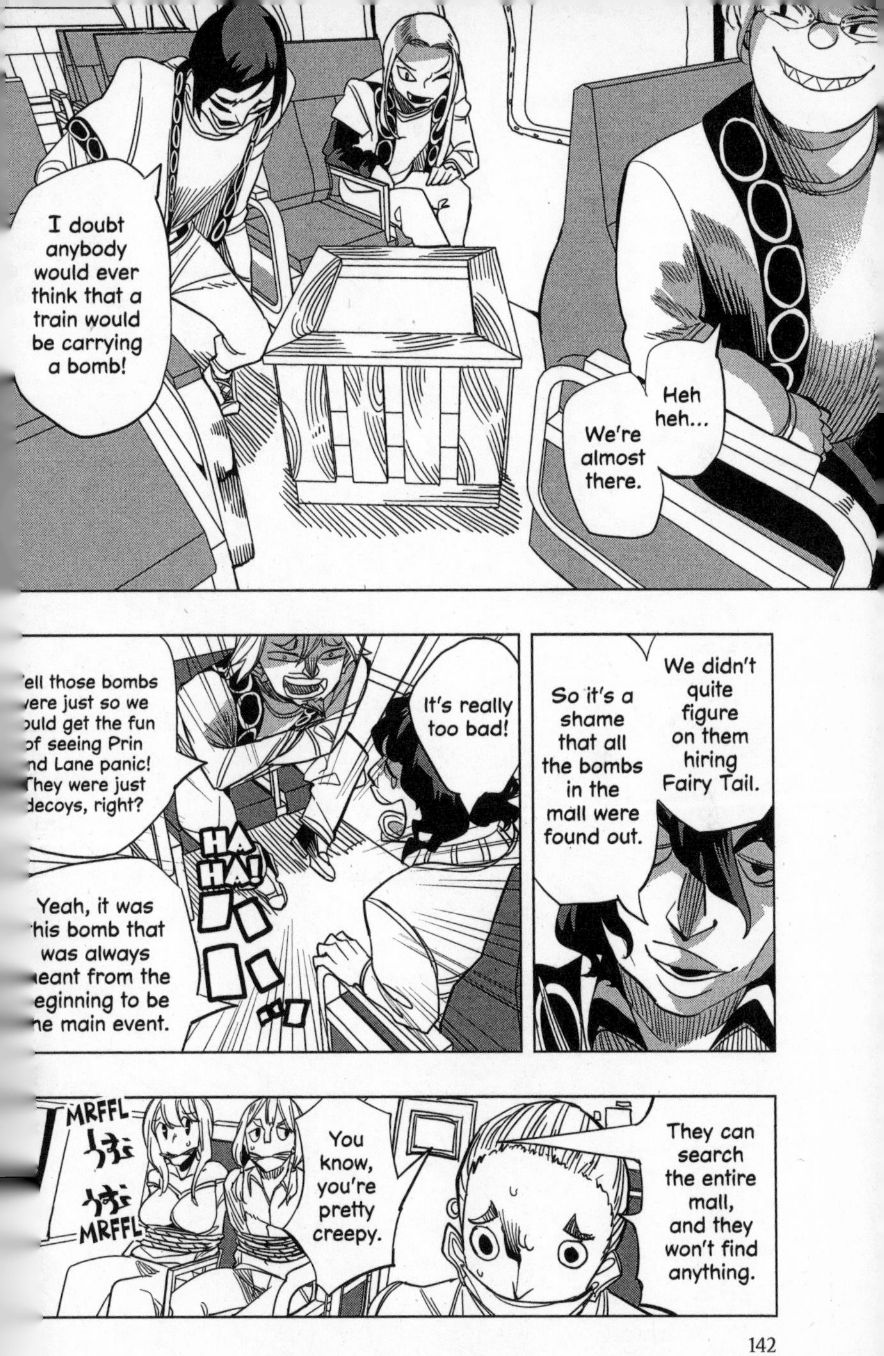
Heh heh... We're almost there.
I doubt anybody would ever think that a train would be carrying a bomb!
We didn't quite figure on them hiring Fairy Tail.
So it's a shame that all the bombs in the mall were found out.
It's really too bad!
ell those bombs vere just so we ould get the fun of seeing Prin nd Lane panic! They were just decoys, right?
HA HA!
Yeah, it was his bomb that was always eant from the eginning to be e main event.
They can search the entire mall, and they won't find anything.
You know, you're pretty creepy.
MRFFL
MRFFL

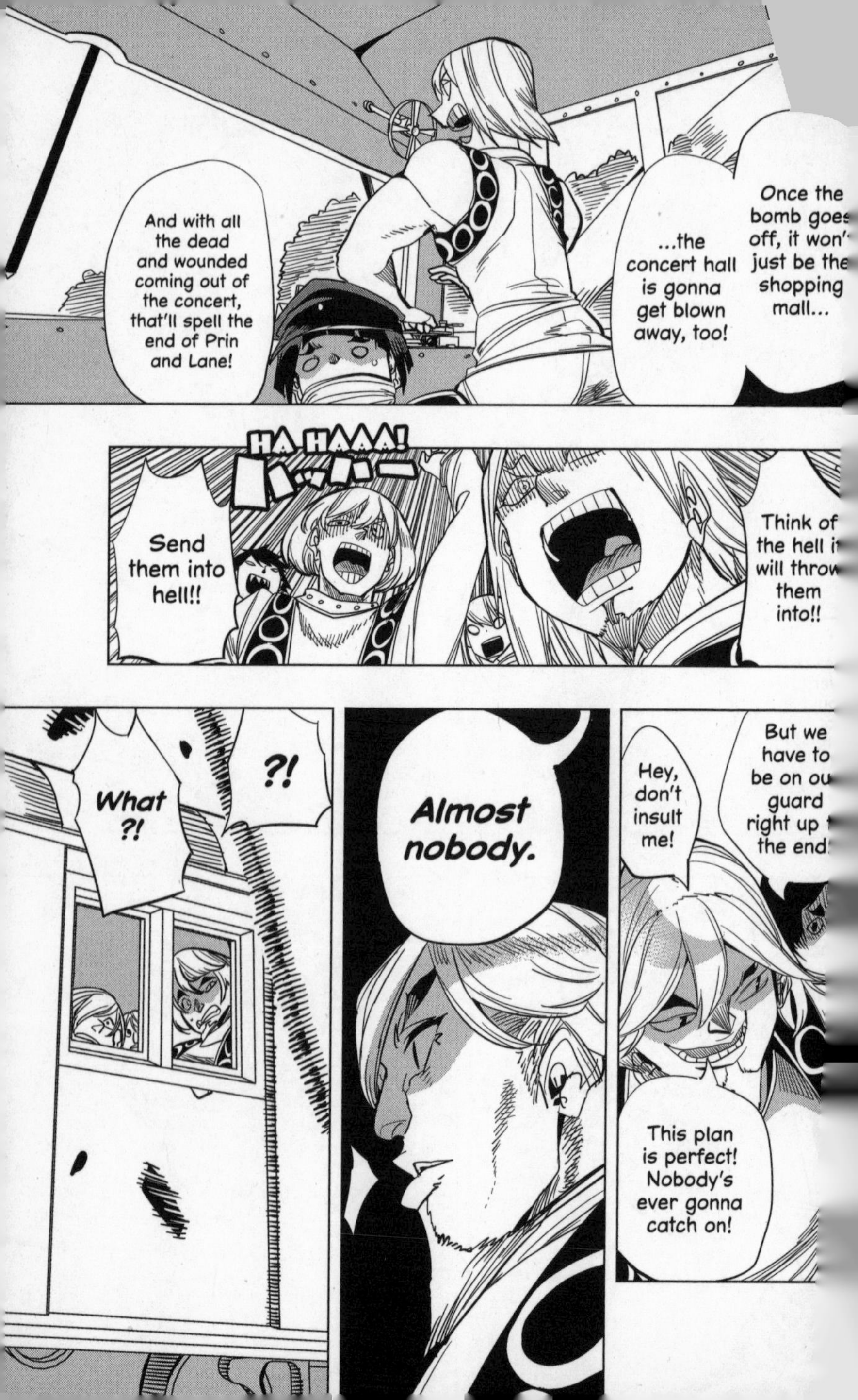
Once the bomb goes off, it won' just be the shopping mall...
...the concert hall is gonna get blown away, too!
And with all the dead and wounded coming out of the concert, that'll spell the end of Prin and Lane!
Think of the hell i will throw them into!!
HA HAAA!
Send them into hell!!
But we have to be on ou guard right up t the end
Hey, don't insult me!
This plan is perfect! Nobody's ever gonna catch on!
Almost nobody.
?!
What ?!

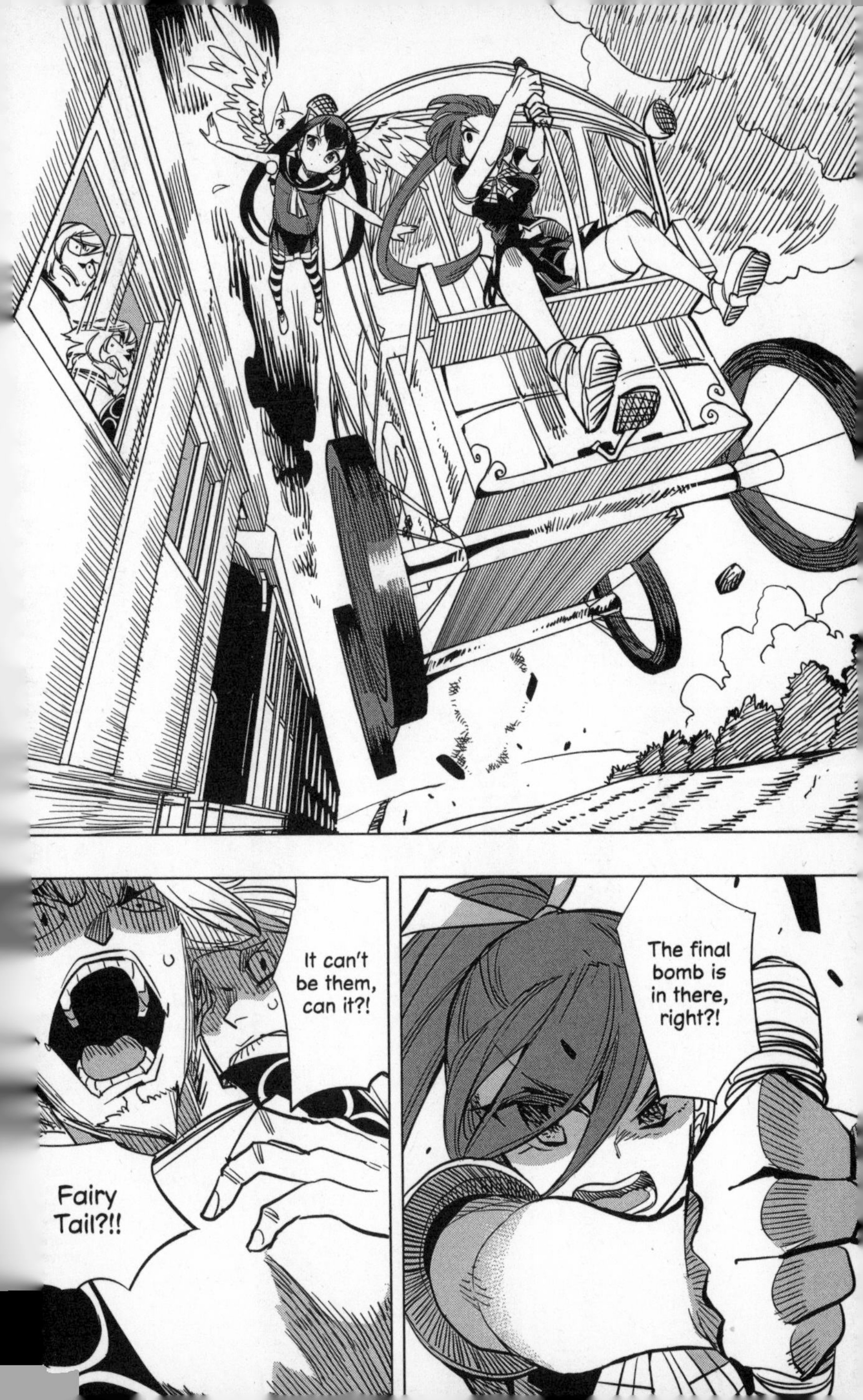
The final bomb is in there, right?!
It can't be them, can it?!
Fairy Tail?!!

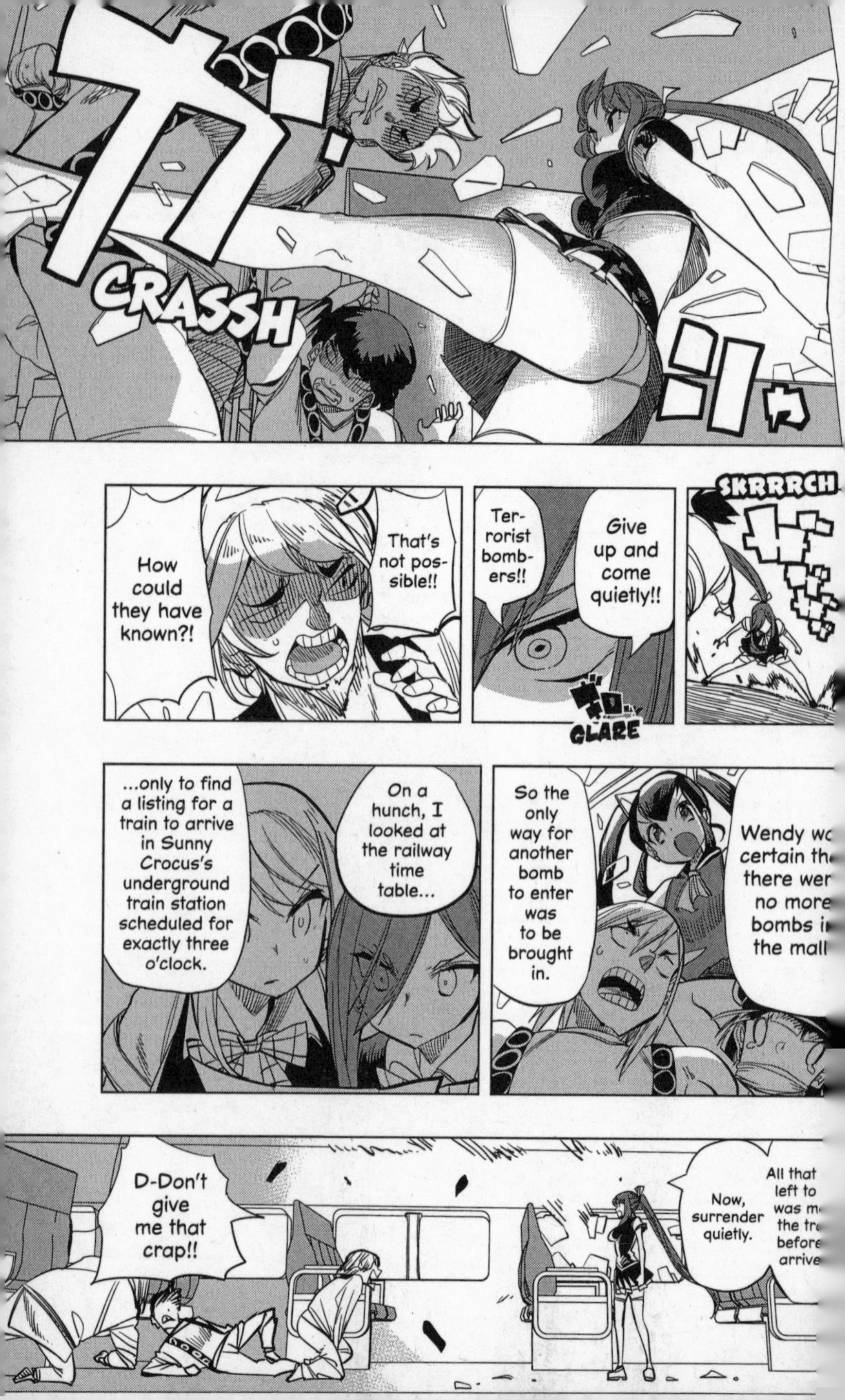
CRASSH
SKRRRCH
Give up and come quietly!!
Ter-rorist bomb-ers!!
GLARE
That's not pos-sible!!
How could they have known?!
Wendy wa certain th there wer no more bombs i the mall
So the only way for another bomb to enter was to be brought in.
On a hunch, I looked at the railway time table...
...only to find a listing for a train to arrive in Sunny Crocus's underground train station scheduled for exactly three o'clock.
All that left to was m the tr before arrive
Now, surrender quietly.
D-Don't give me that crap!!

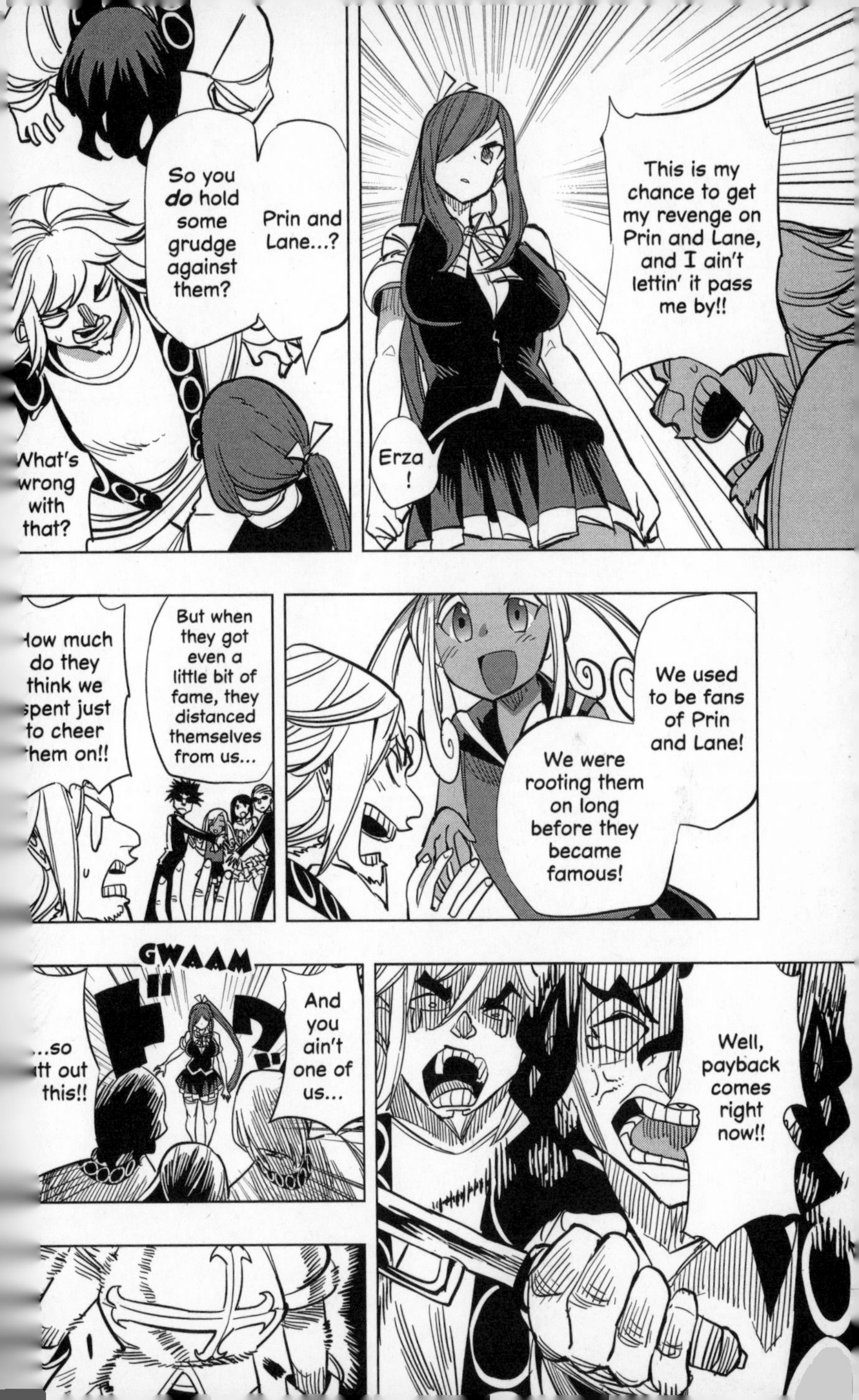
This is my chance to get my revenge on Prin and Lane, and I ain't lettin' it pass me by!!
Erza!
Prin and Lane...?
So you *do* hold some grudge against them?
What's wrong with that?
We used to be fans of Prin and Lane!
We were rooting them on long before they became famous!
But when they got even a little bit of fame, they distanced themselves from us...
How much do they think we spent just to cheer them on!!
Well, payback comes right now!!
And you ain't one of us...
GWAAM
...so tt out this!!

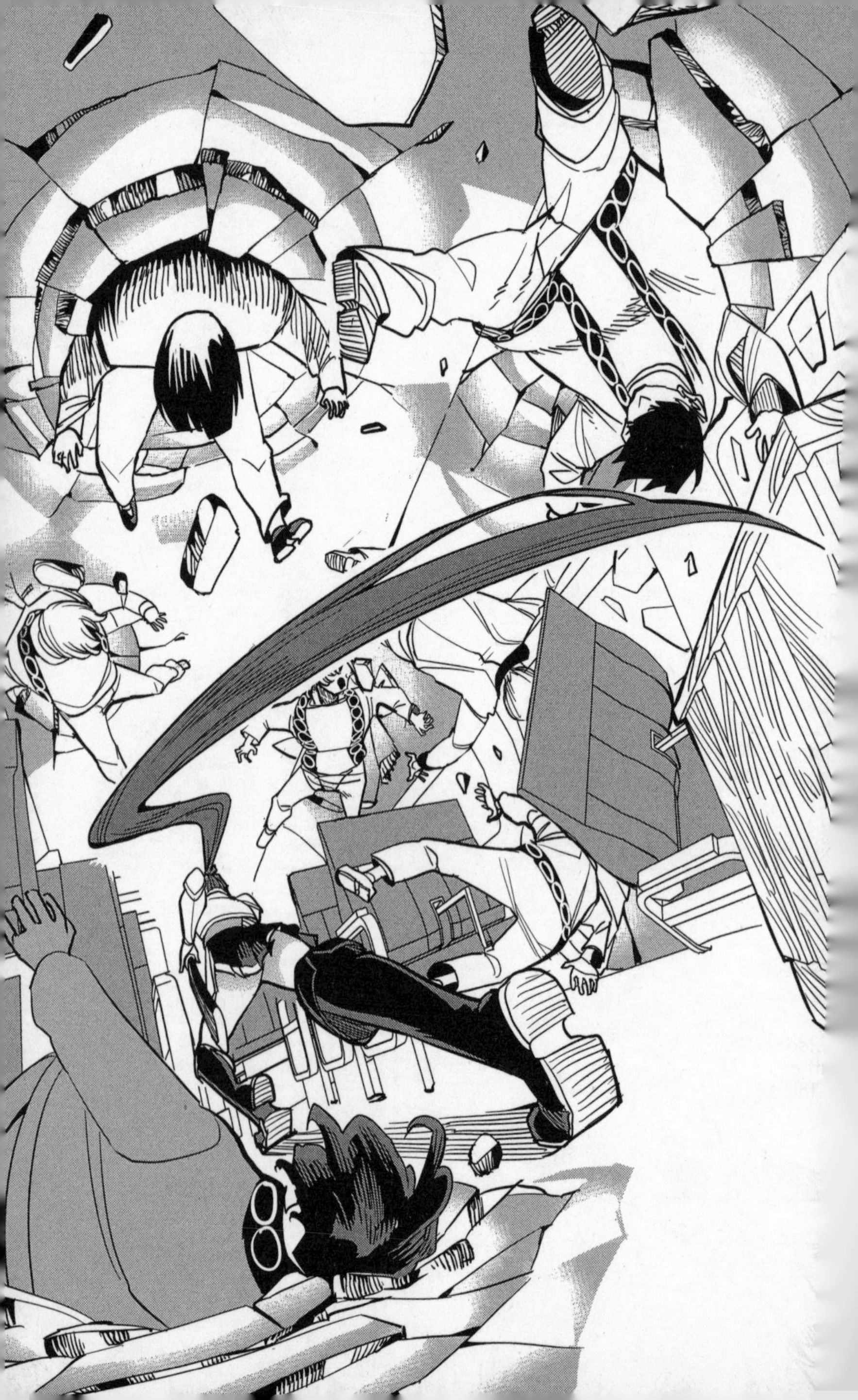

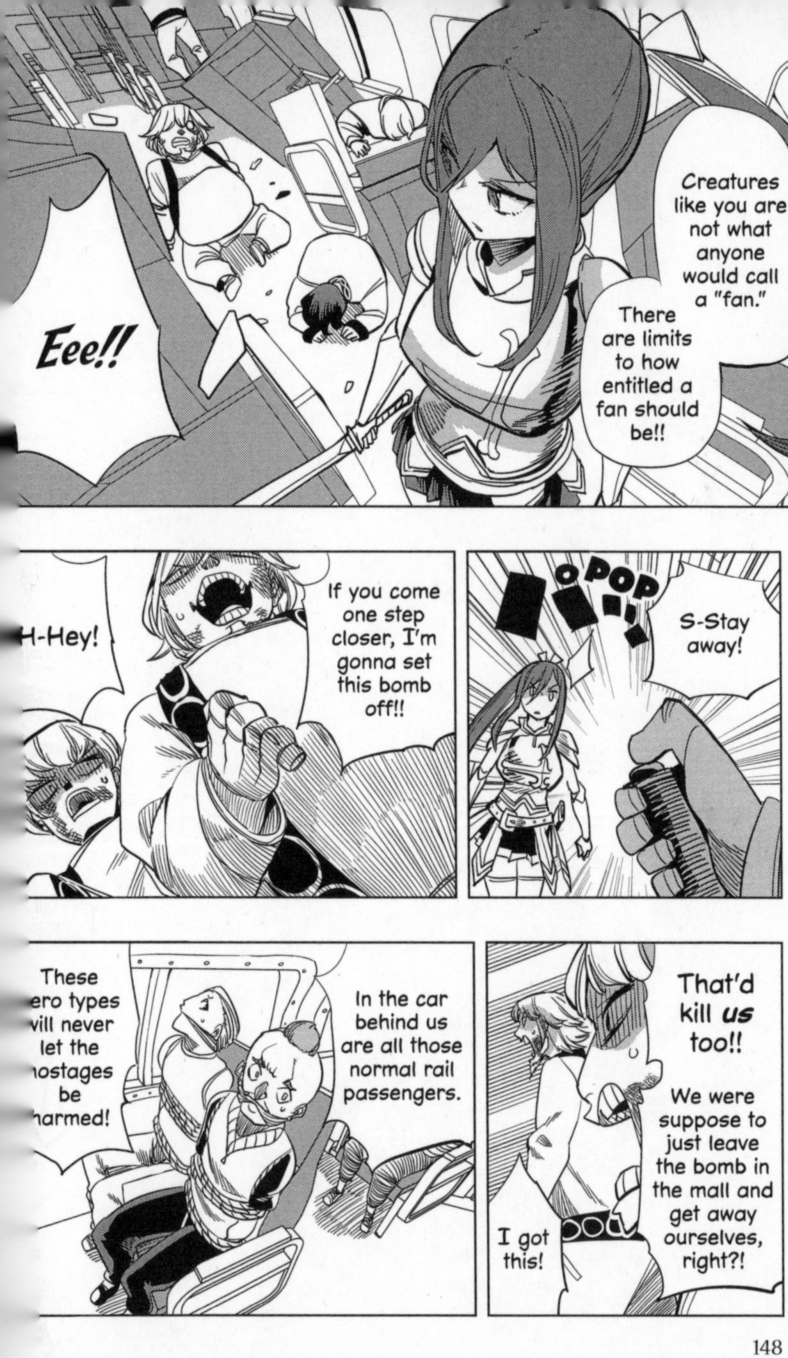

Creatures like you are not what anyone would call a "fan."
There are limits to how entitled a fan should be!!
Eee!!
POP
S-Stay away!
If you come one step closer, I'm gonna set this bomb off!!
H-Hey!
That'd kill *us* too!!
We were suppose to just leave the bomb in the mall and get away ourselves, right?!
I got this!
In the car behind us are all those normal rail passengers.
These ero types vill never let the iostages be iarmed!

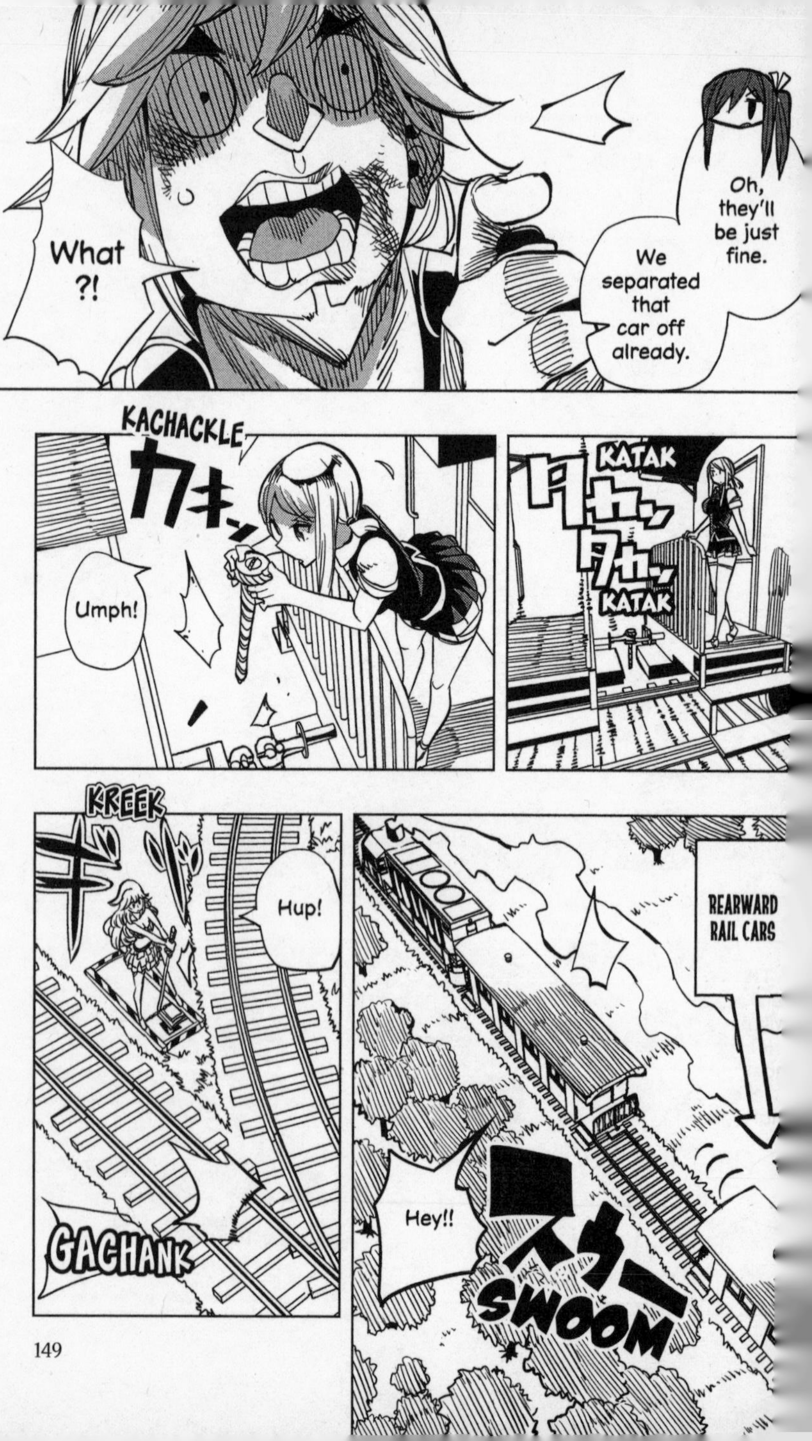
Oh, they'll be just fine.
We separated that car off already.
What ?!
KATAK
KATAK
KACHACKLE
Umph!
REARWARD RAIL CARS
Hey!!
SWOOM
KREEK
Hup!
GACHANK

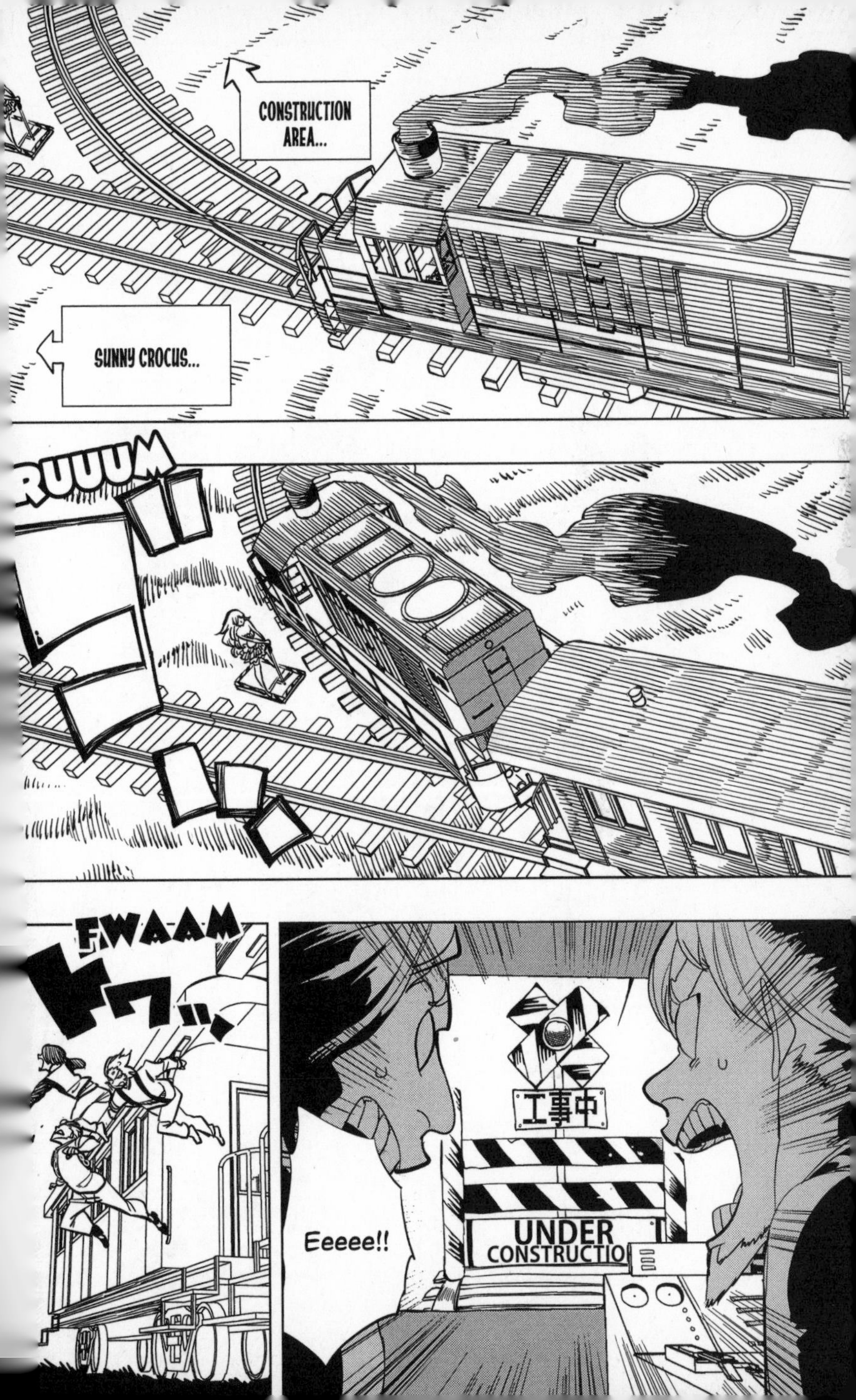
CONSTRUCTION AREA...
SUNNY CROCUS...
RUUUM
工事中
UNDER CONSTRUCTIO
Eeeee!!
FWAAM

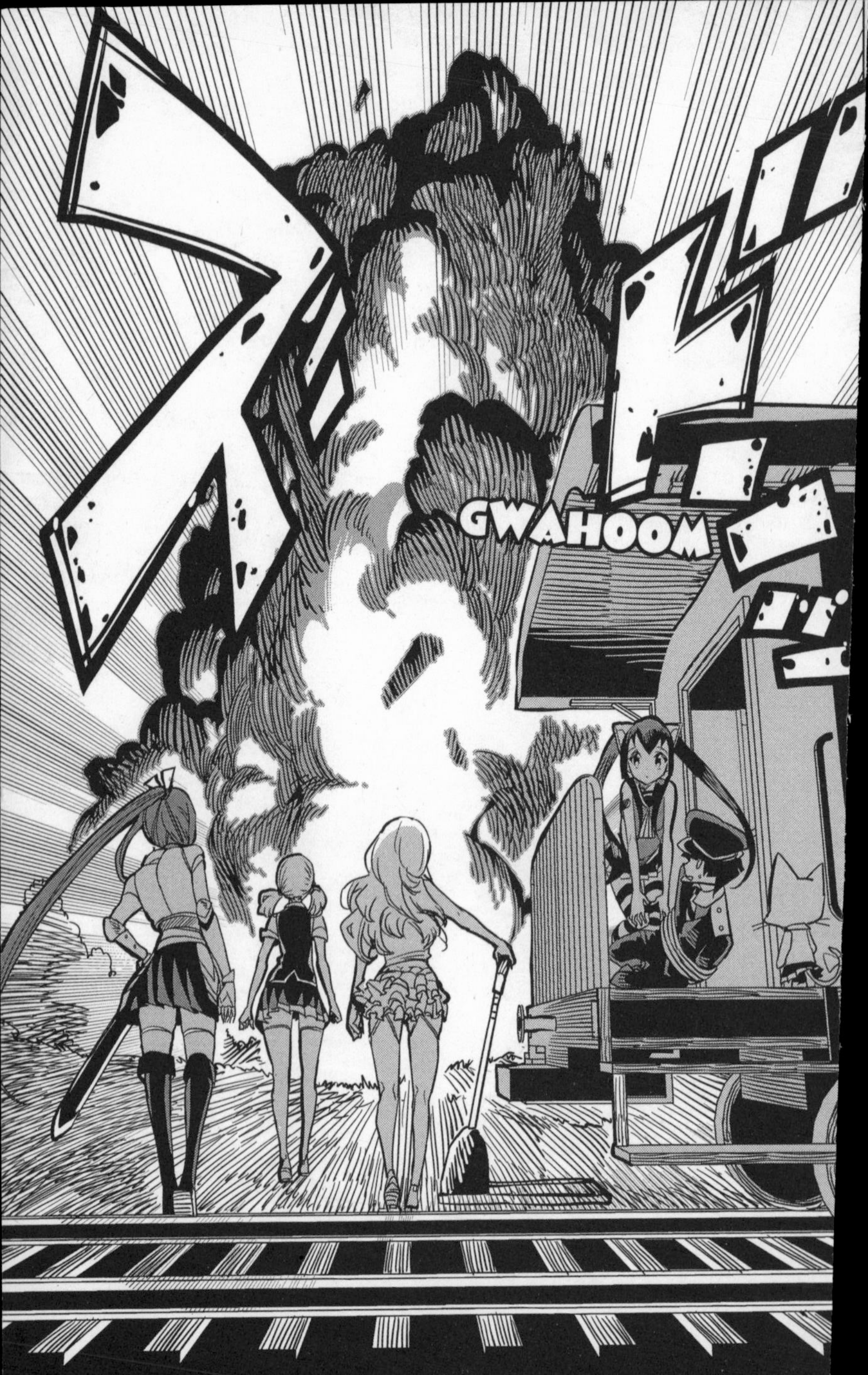
GWAHOOM

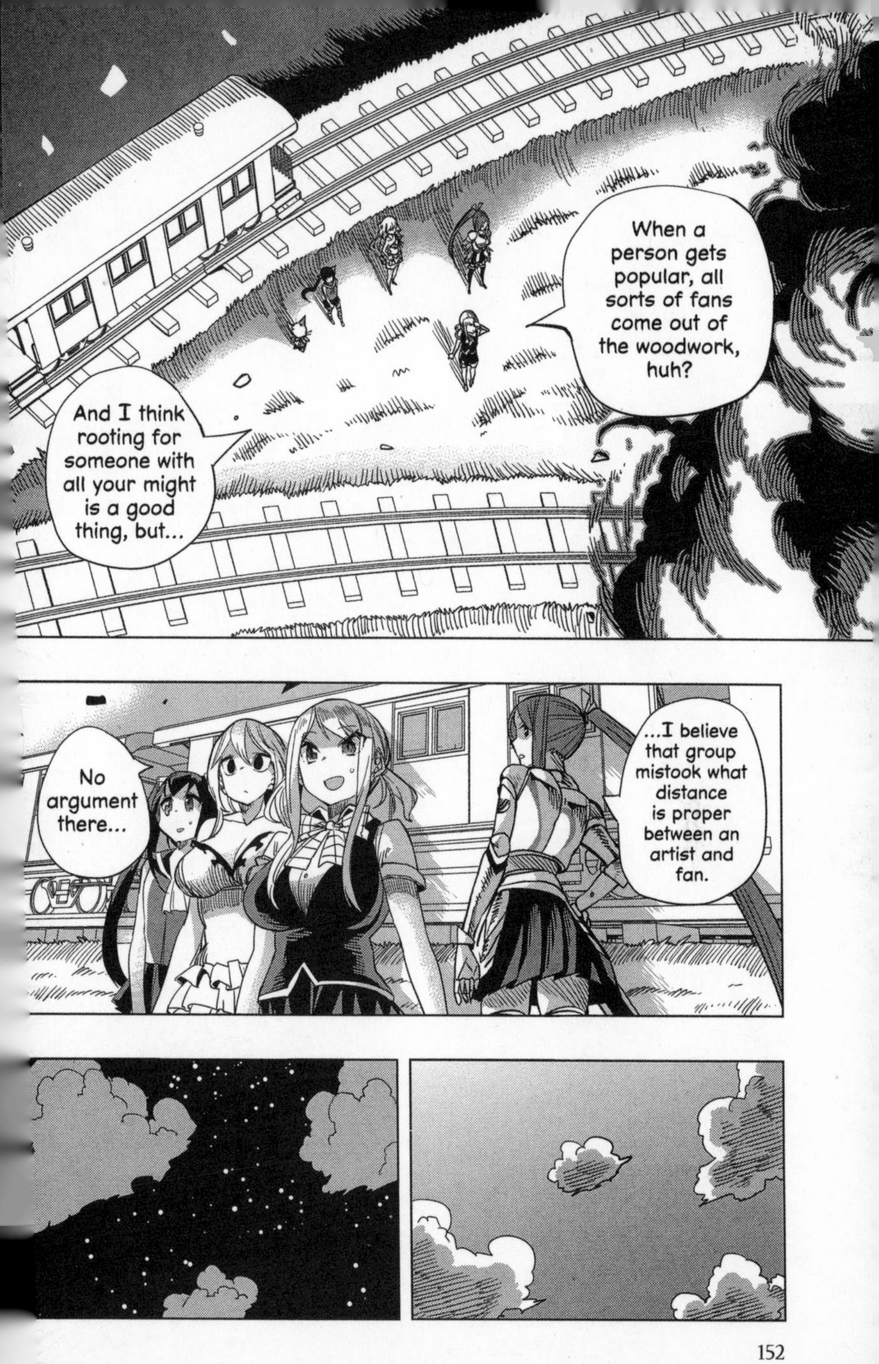
When a person gets popular, all sorts of fans come out of the woodwork, huh?
And I think rooting for someone with all your might is a good thing, but...
...I believe that group mistook what distance is proper between an artist and fan.
No argument there...

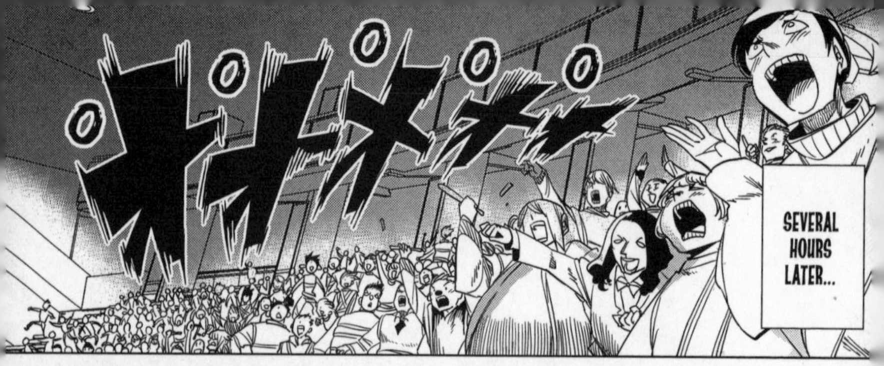
SEVERAL HOURS LATER...

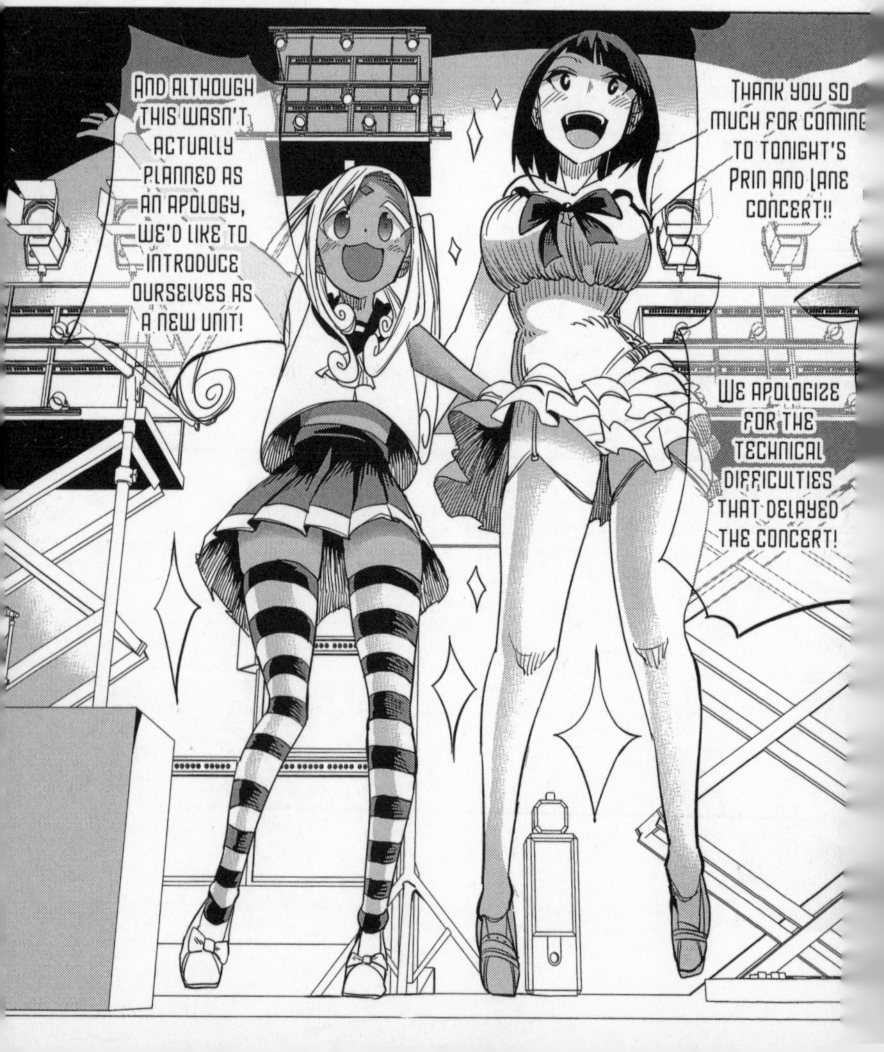
THANK YOU SO MUCH FOR COMING TO TONIGHT'S PRIN AND LANE CONCERT!!
WE APOLOGIZE FOR THE TECHNICAL DIFFICULTIES THAT DELAYED THE CONCERT!
AND ALTHOUGH THIS WASN'T ACTUALLY PLANNED AS AN APOLOGY, WE'D LIKE TO INTRODUCE OURSELVES AS A NEW UNIT!

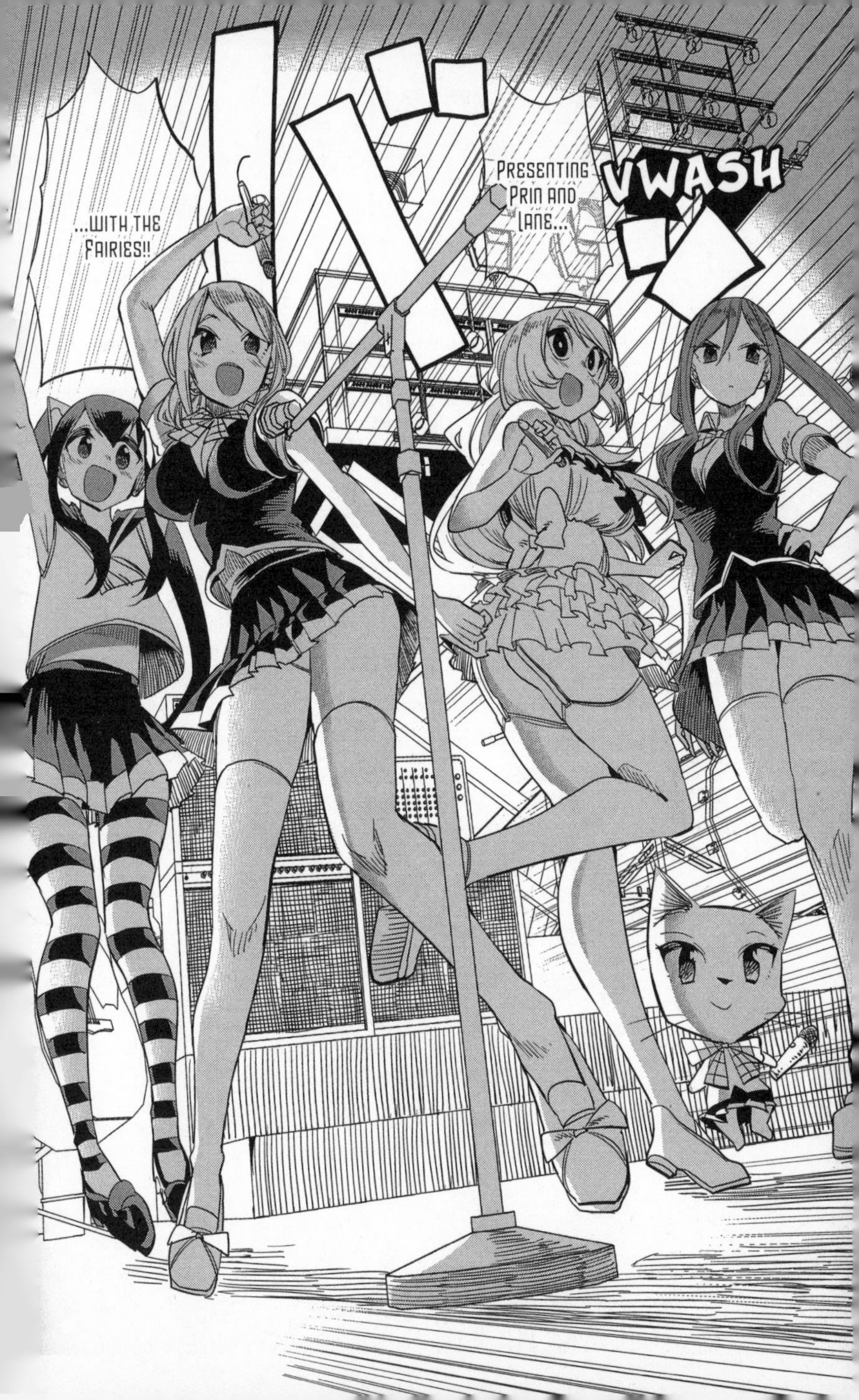
VWASH
PRESENTING PRIN AND LANE...
...WITH THE FAIRIES!!

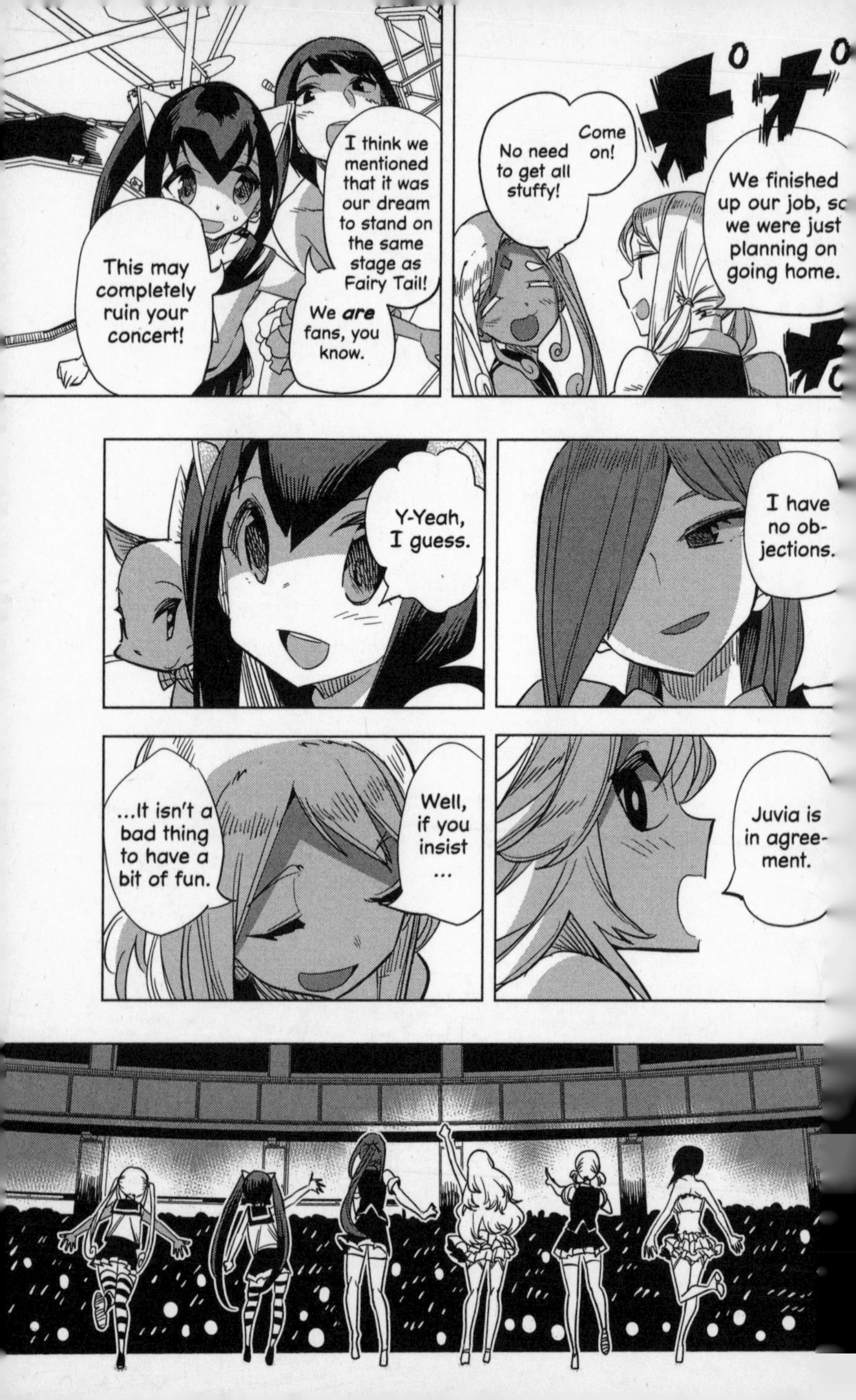
We finished up our job, so we were just planning on going home.
Come on! No need to get all stuffy!
I think we mentioned that it was our dream to stand on the same stage as Fairy Tail!
We *are* fans, you know.
This may completely ruin your concert!
I have no objections.
Y-Yeah, I guess.
Juvia is in agreement.
Well, if you insist ...
...It isn't a bad thing to have a bit of fun.

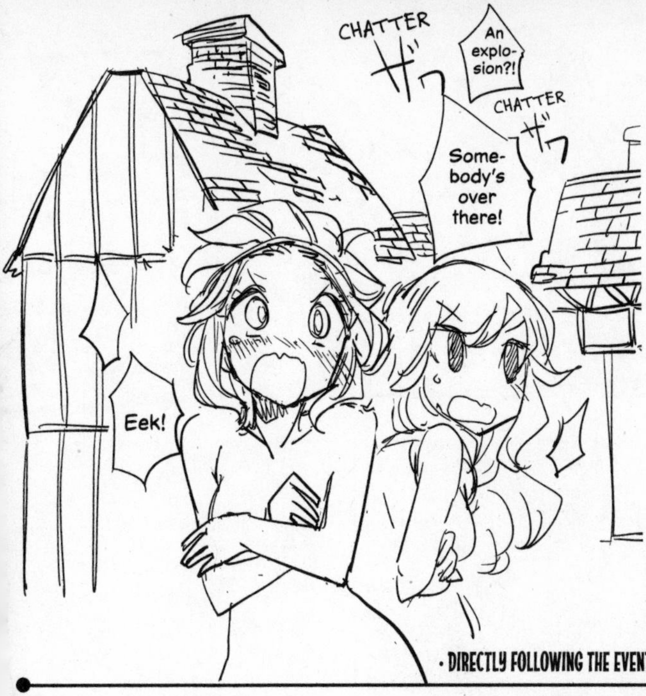
An explosion?!
CHATTER
CHATTER
Somebody's over there!
Eek!

• DIRECTLY FOLLOWING THE EVENTS OF PAGE 35.

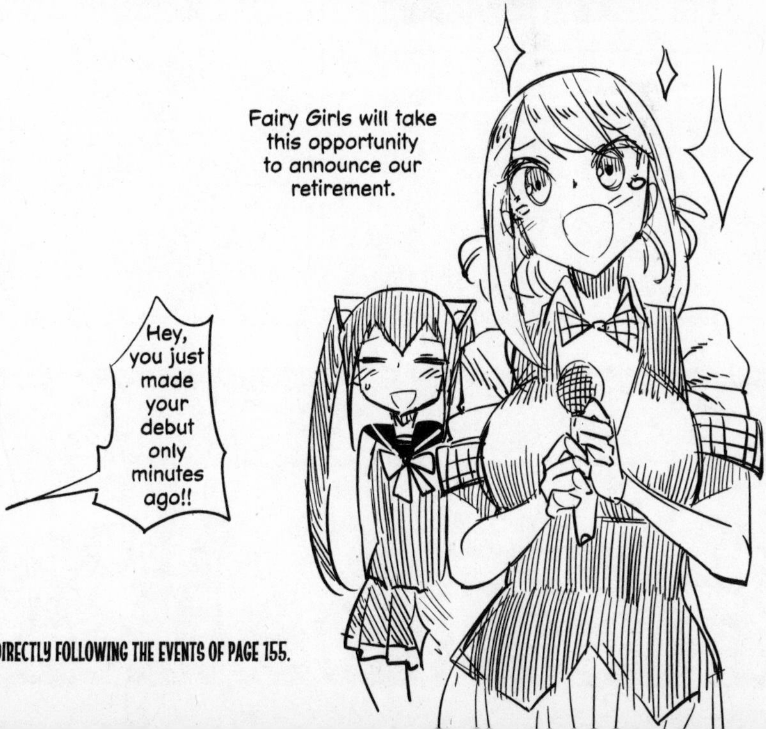
Fairy Girls will take this opportunity to announce our retirement.
Hey, you just made your debut only minutes ago!!

• DIRECTLY FOLLOWING THE EVENTS OF PAGE 155.

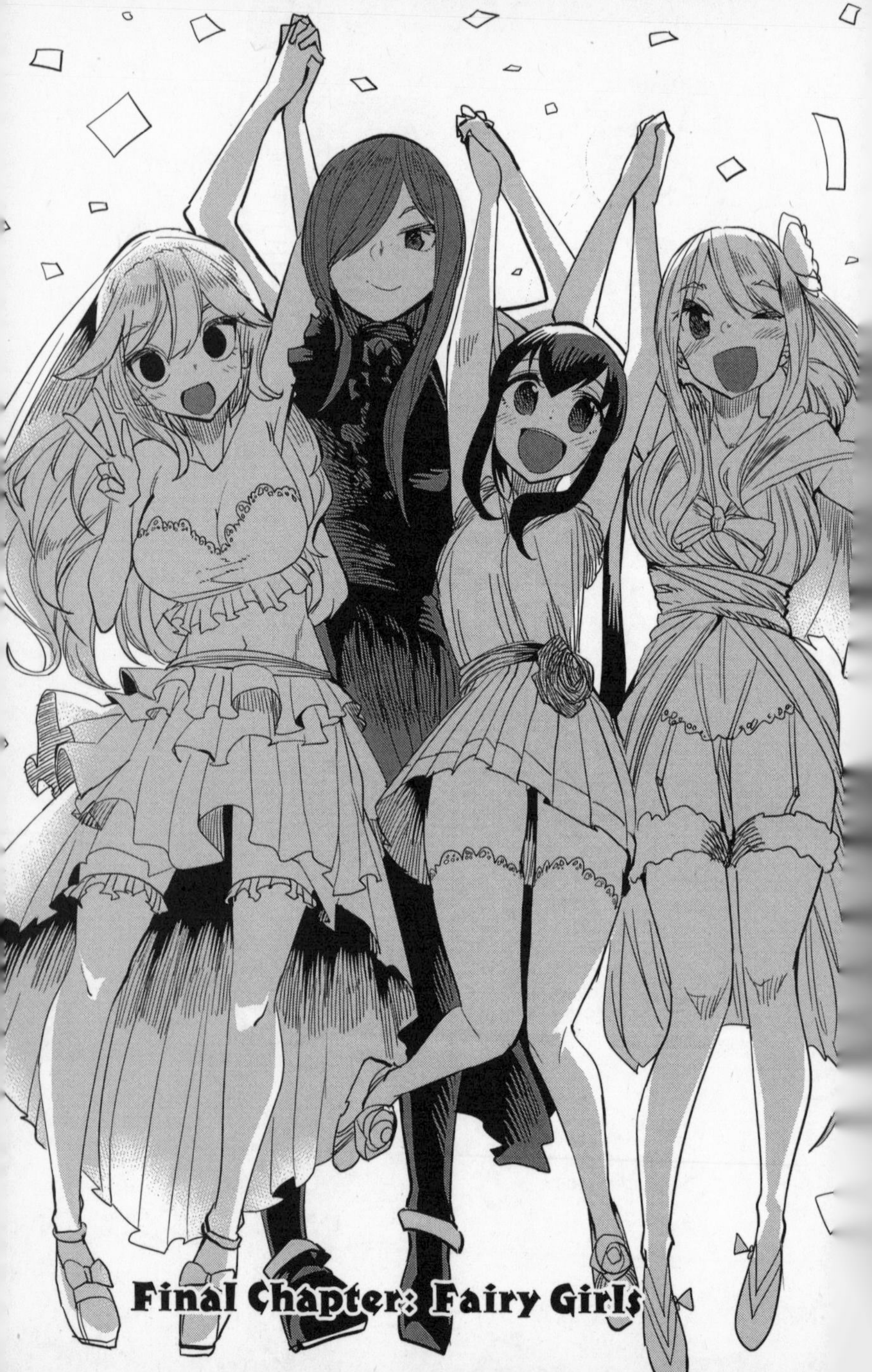

Final Chapter: Fairy Girls

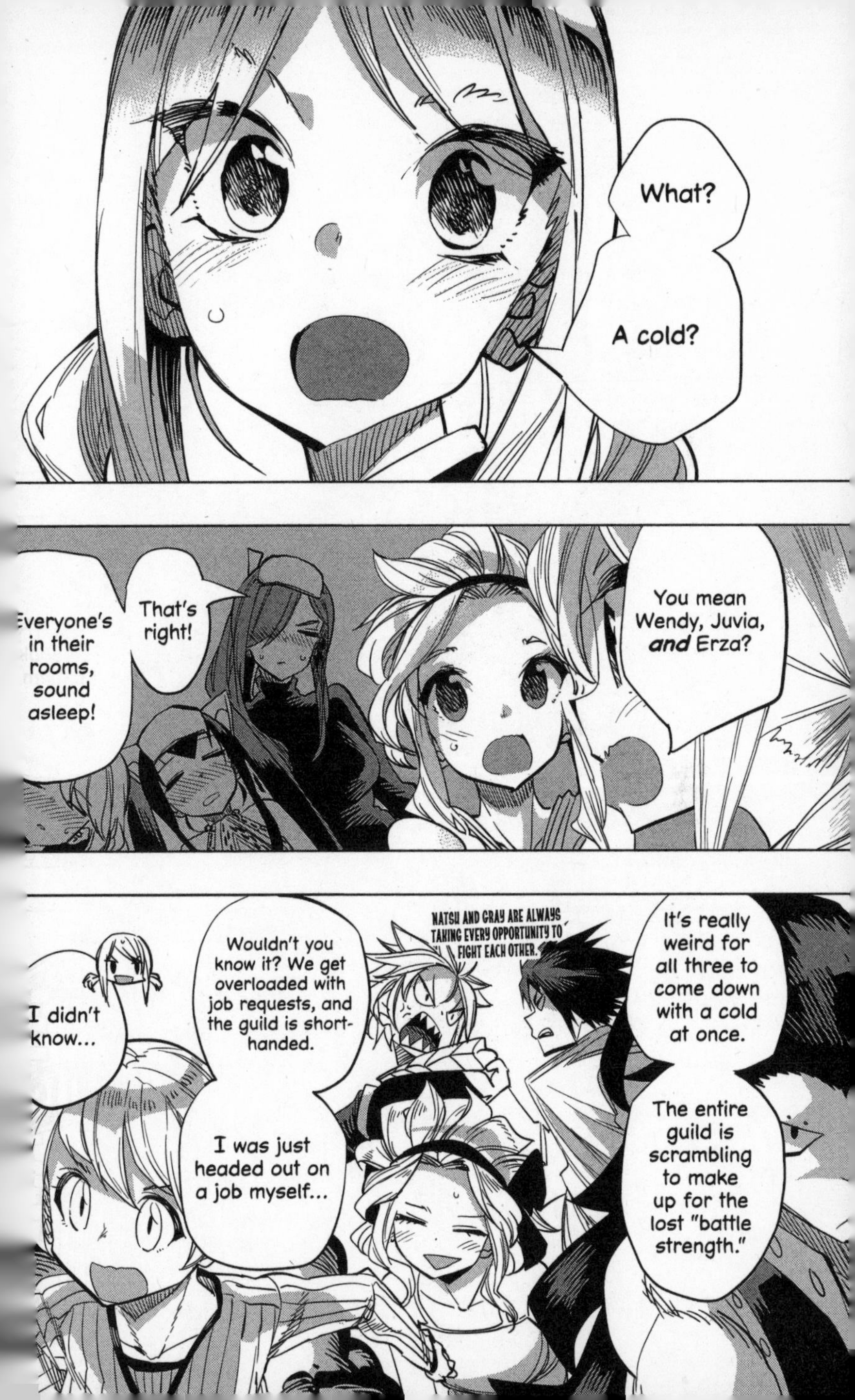
What?
A cold?
You mean Wendy, Juvia, ***and*** Erza?
That's right!
Everyone's in their rooms, sound asleep!
It's really weird for all three to come down with a cold at once.
The entire guild is scrambling to make up for the lost "battle strength."
NATSU AND GRAY ARE ALWAYS TAKING EVERY OPPORTUNITY TO FIGHT EACH OTHER.
Wouldn't you know it? We get overloaded with job requests, and the guild is short-handed.
I was just headed out on a job myself...
I didn't know...

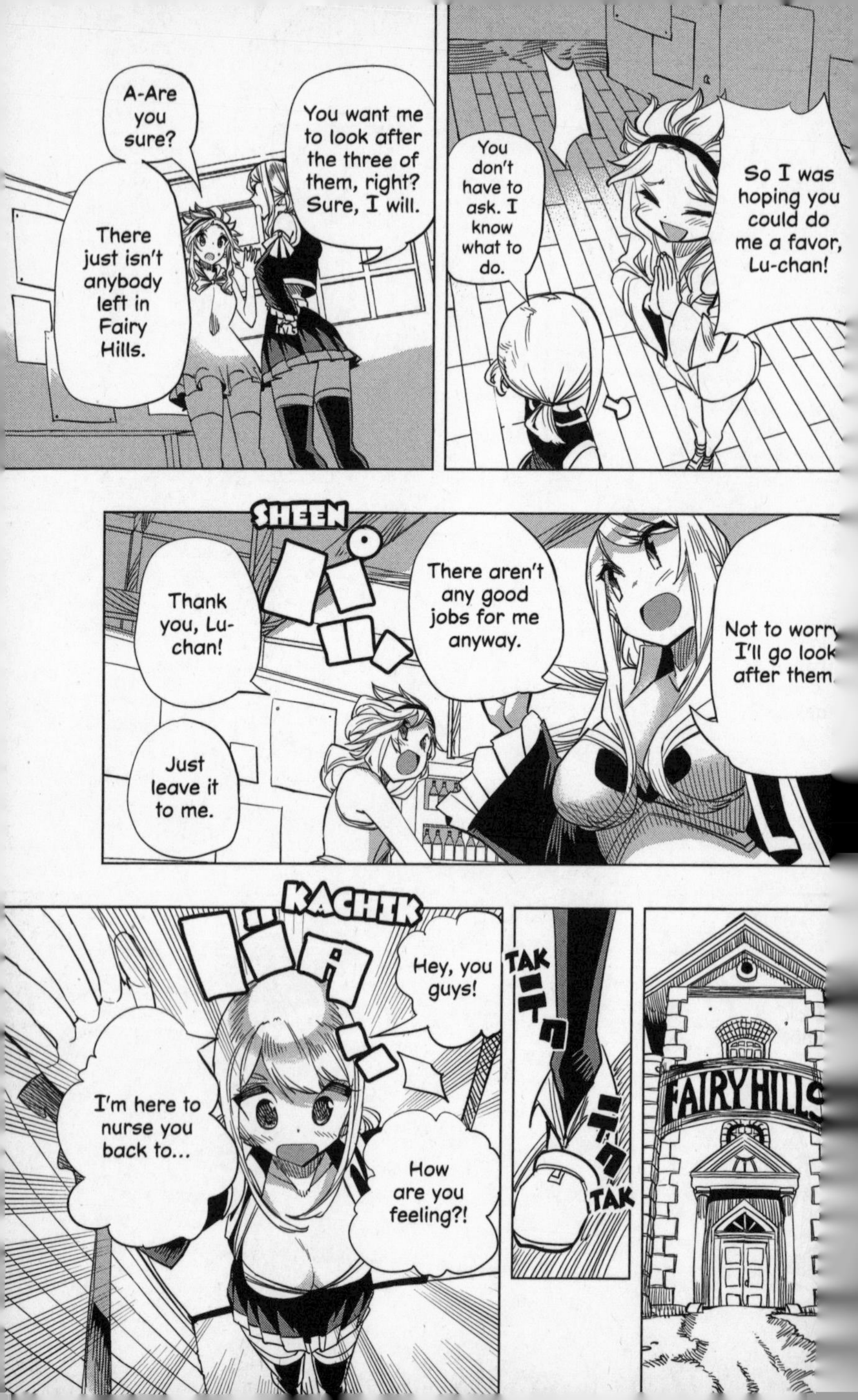
So I was hoping you could do me a favor, Lu-chan!
You don't have to ask. I know what to do.
You want me to look after the three of them, right? Sure, I will.
A-Are you sure?
There just isn't anybody left in Fairy Hills.
Not to worry I'll go look after them.
SHEEN
There aren't any good jobs for me anyway.
Thank you, Lu-chan!
Just leave it to me.
FAIRY HILLS
TAK
TAK
KACHIK
Hey, you guys!
How are you feeling?!
I'm here to nurse you back to...

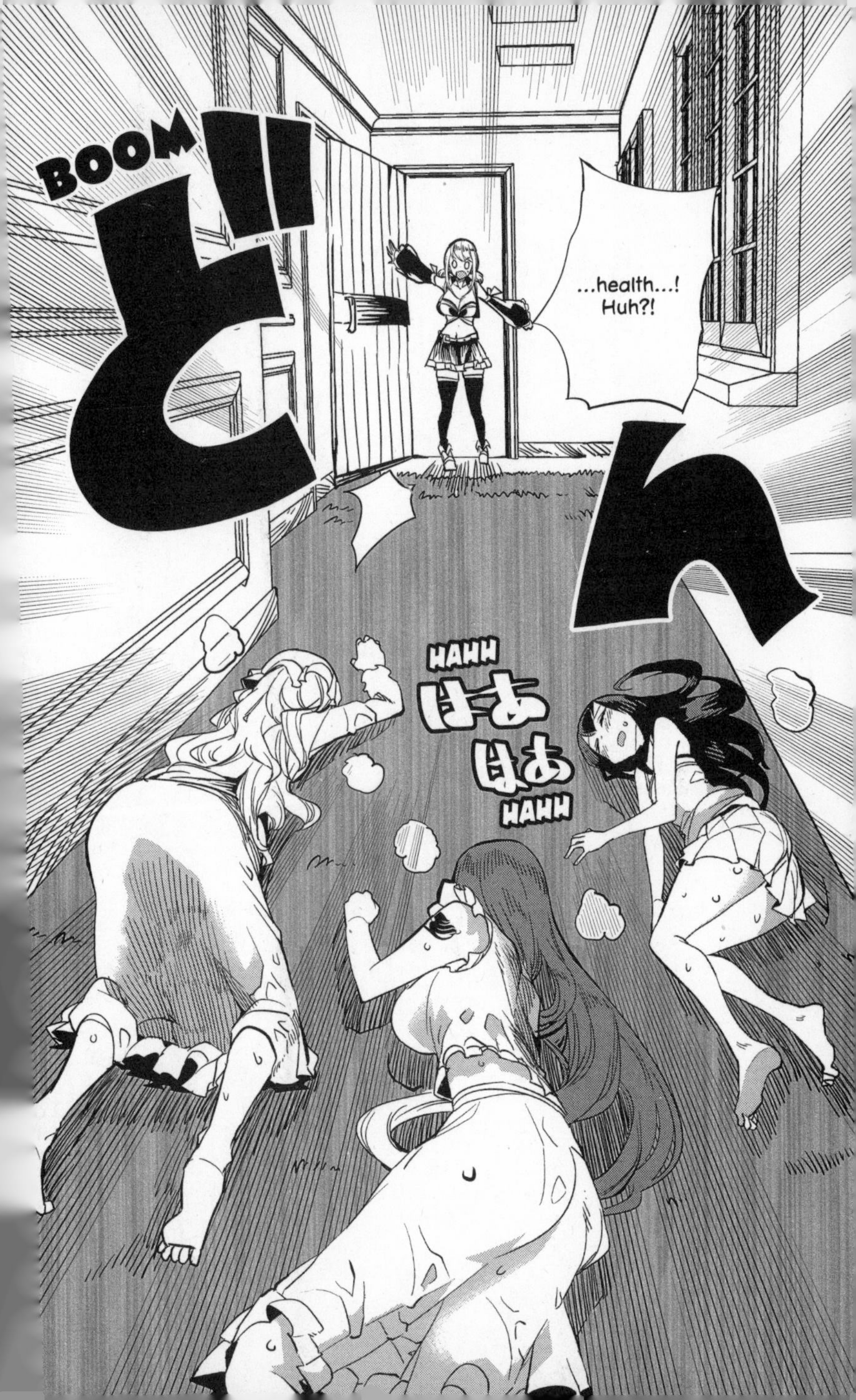
BOOM
どん!!
...health...!
Huh?!
HAHH
はあ
はあ
HAHH

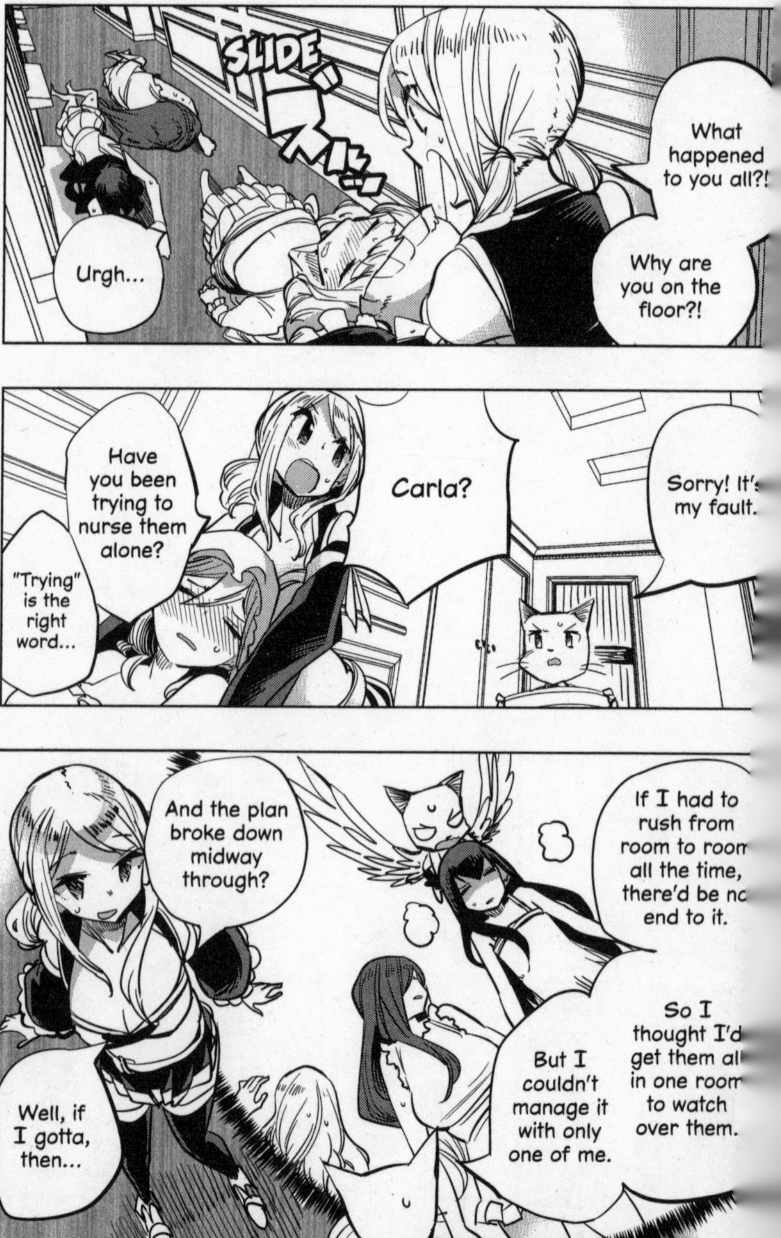

What happened to you all?!
Why are you on the floor?!
SLIDE
Urgh...
Sorry! It's my fault.
Carla?
Have you been trying to nurse them alone?
"Trying" is the right word...
If I had to rush from room to room all the time, there'd be no end to it.
So I thought I'd get them all in one room to watch over them.
But I couldn't manage it with only one of me.
And the plan broke down midway through?
Well, if I gotta, then...

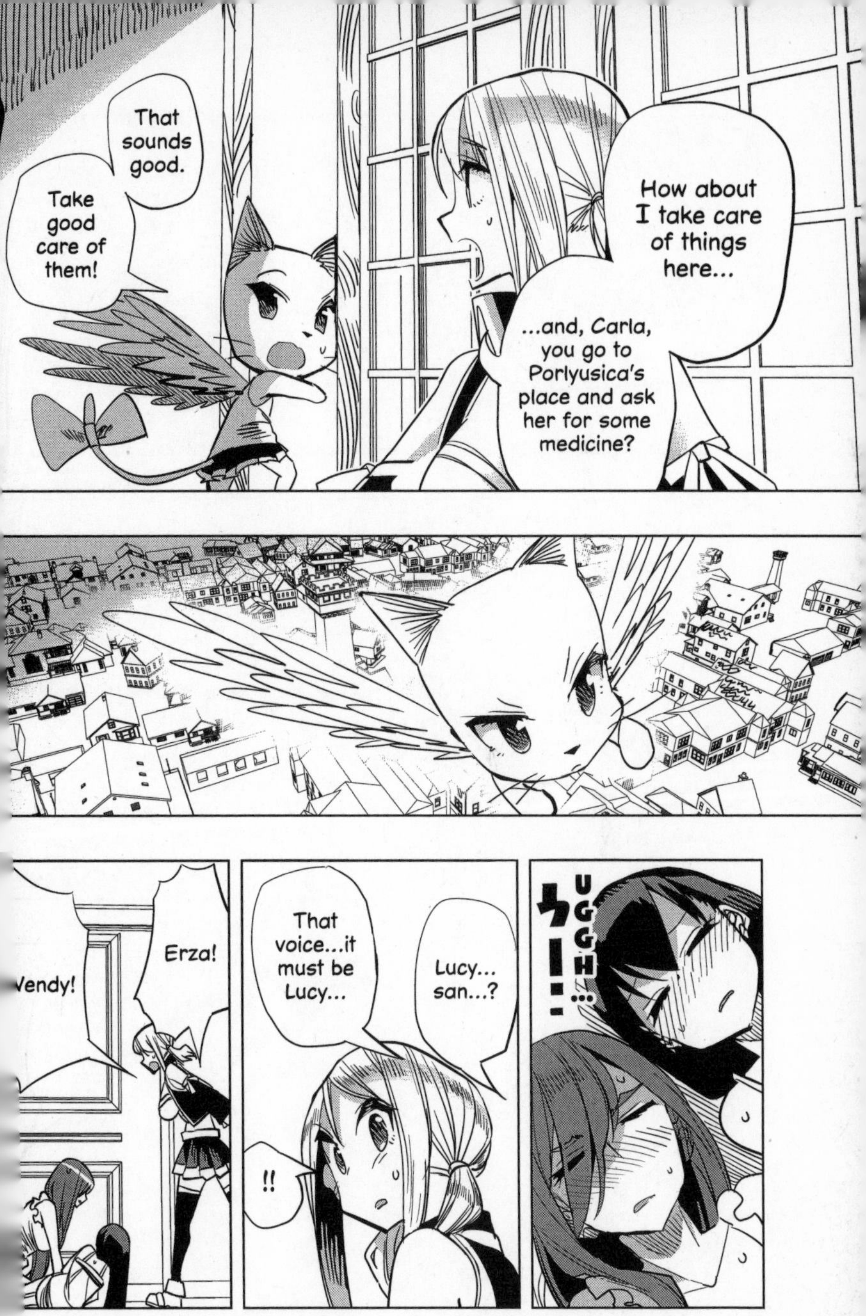
How about I take care of things here...
...and, Carla, you go to Porlyusica's place and ask her for some medicine?
That sounds good.
Take good care of them!
UGGH...!!
Lucy... san...?
That voice...it must be Lucy...
!!
Erza!
Vendy!

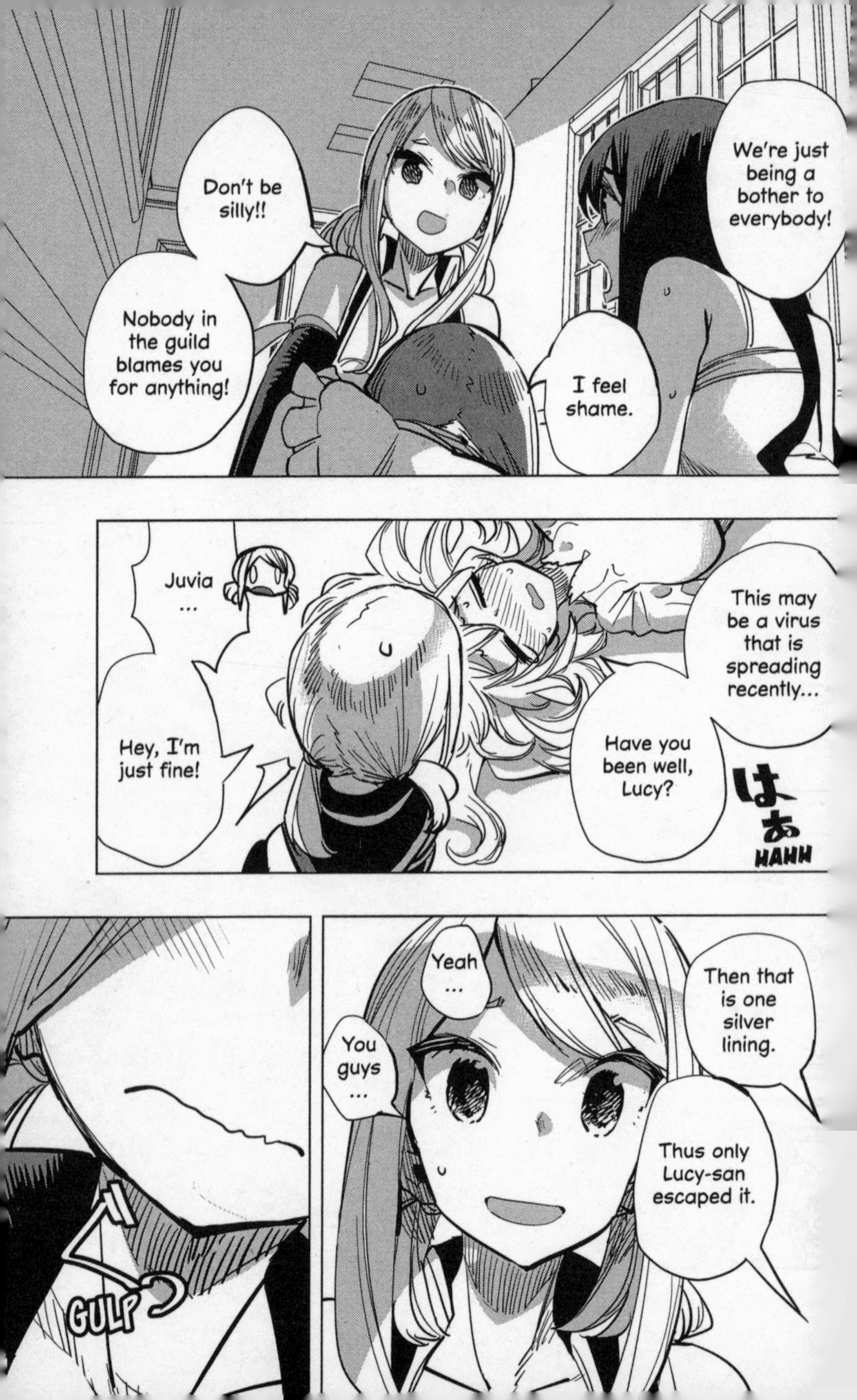
We're just being a bother to everybody!
I feel shame.
Don't be silly!!
Nobody in the guild blames you for anything!
This may be a virus that is spreading recently...
Have you been well, Lucy?
はぁ HAHH
Juvia ...
Hey, I'm just fine!
Then that is one silver lining.
Thus only Lucy-san escaped it.
Yeah ...
You guys ...
GULP

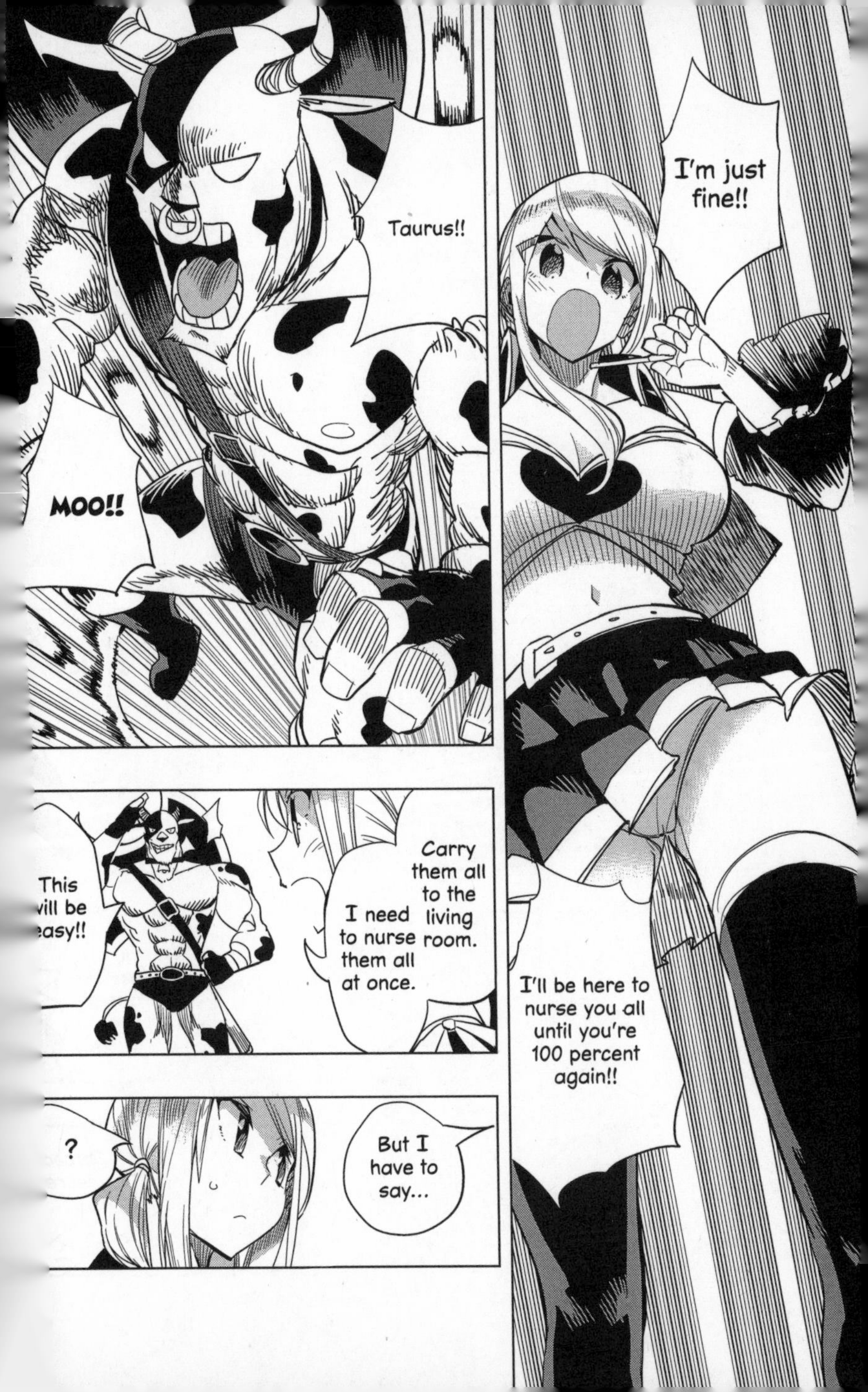
I'm just fine!!
I'll be here to nurse you all until you're 100 percent again!!
Taurus!!
MOO!!
Carry them all to the living room.
I need to nurse them all at once.
This will be easy!!
But I have to say...
?

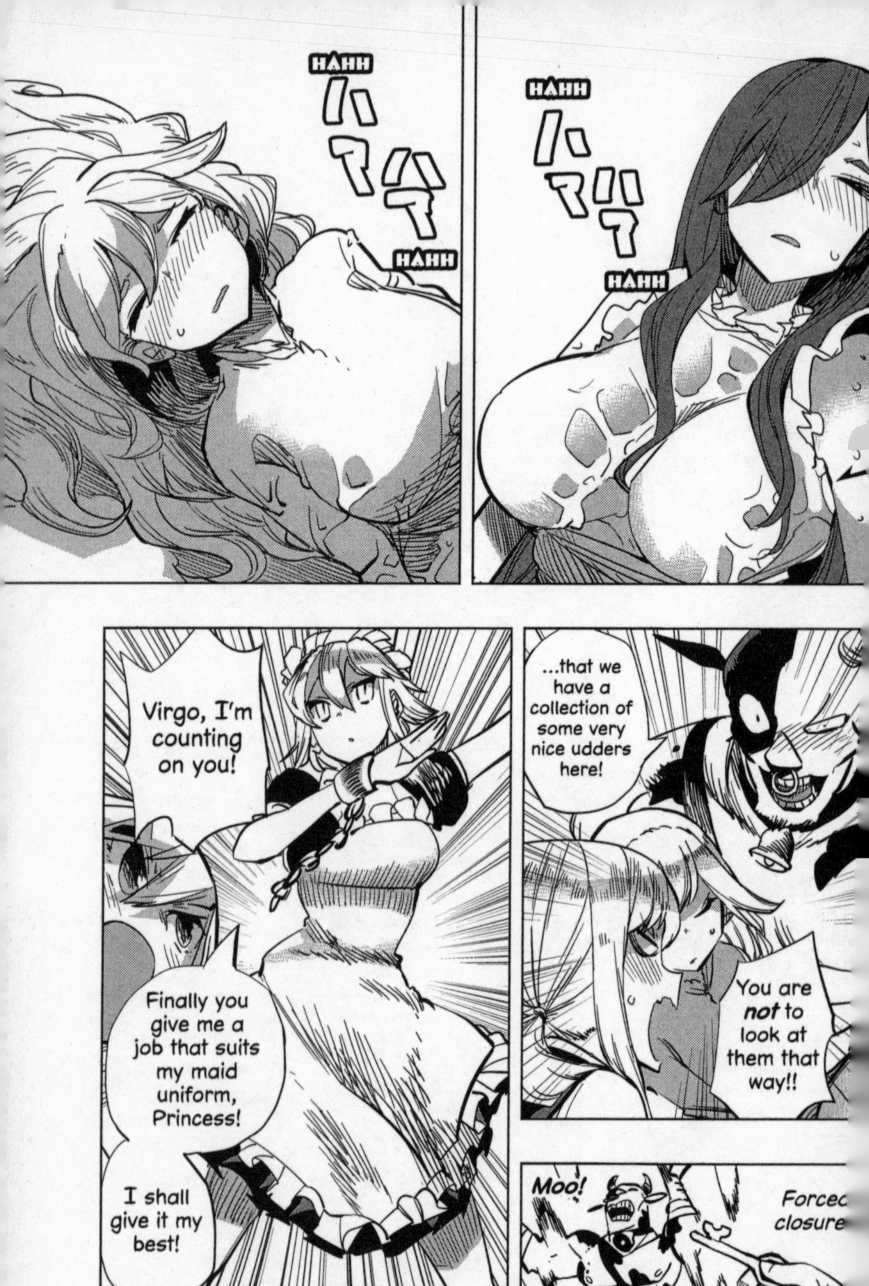
HAHH
ハァハァ
HAHH
HAHH
ハァハァ
HAHH
...that we have a collection of some very nice udders here!
You are *not* to look at them that way!!
Moo!
Forcec closure
Virgo, I'm counting on you!
Finally you give me a job that suits my maid uniform, Princess!
I shall give it my best!

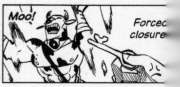

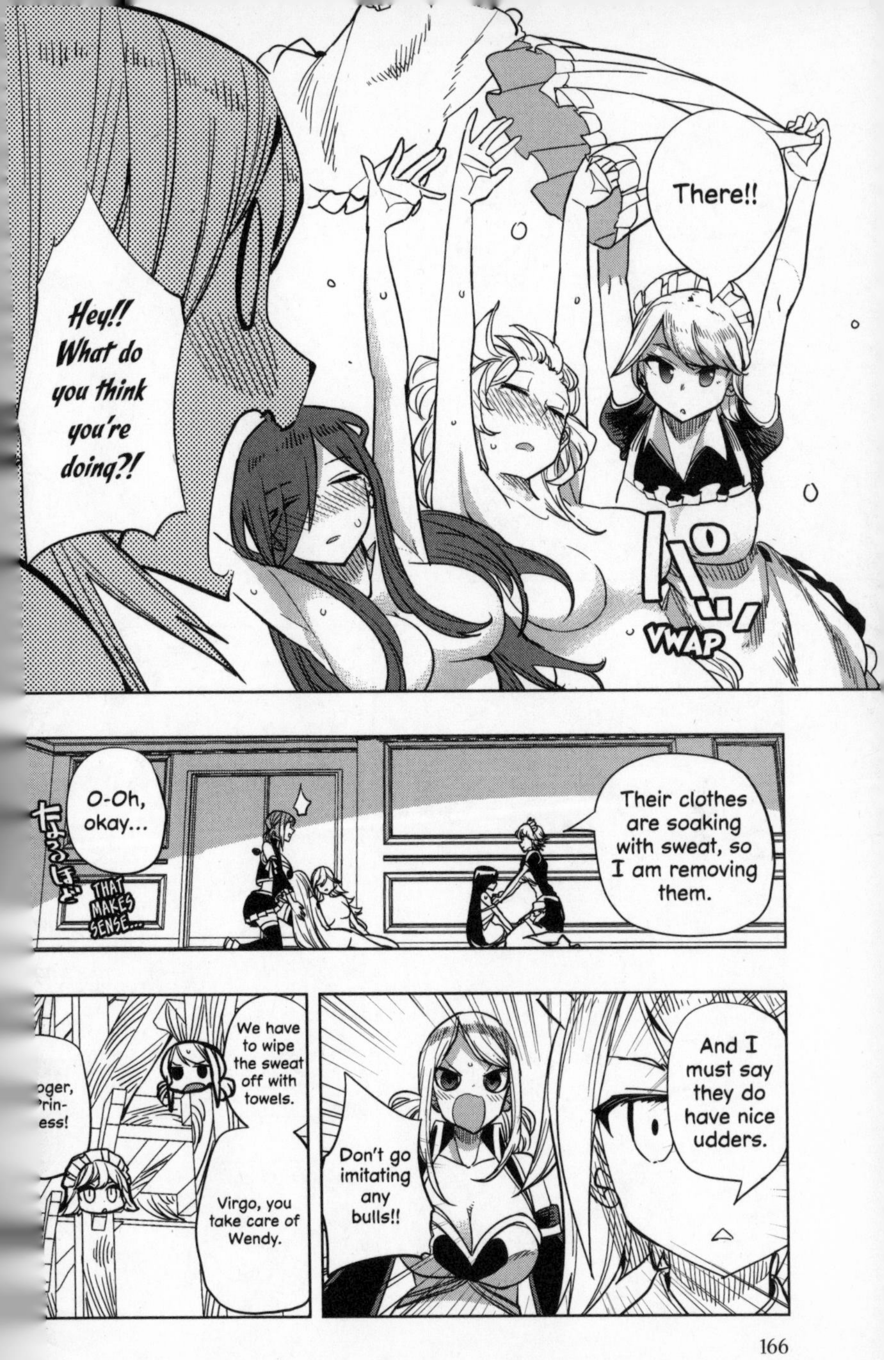
There!!
Hey!! What do you think you're doing?!
VWAP
Their clothes are soaking with sweat, so I am removing them.
O-Oh, okay...
THAT MAKES SENSE...
And I must say they do have nice udders.
Don't go imitating any bulls!!
We have to wipe the sweat off with towels.
Virgo, you take care of Wendy.
oger, Prin- ess!

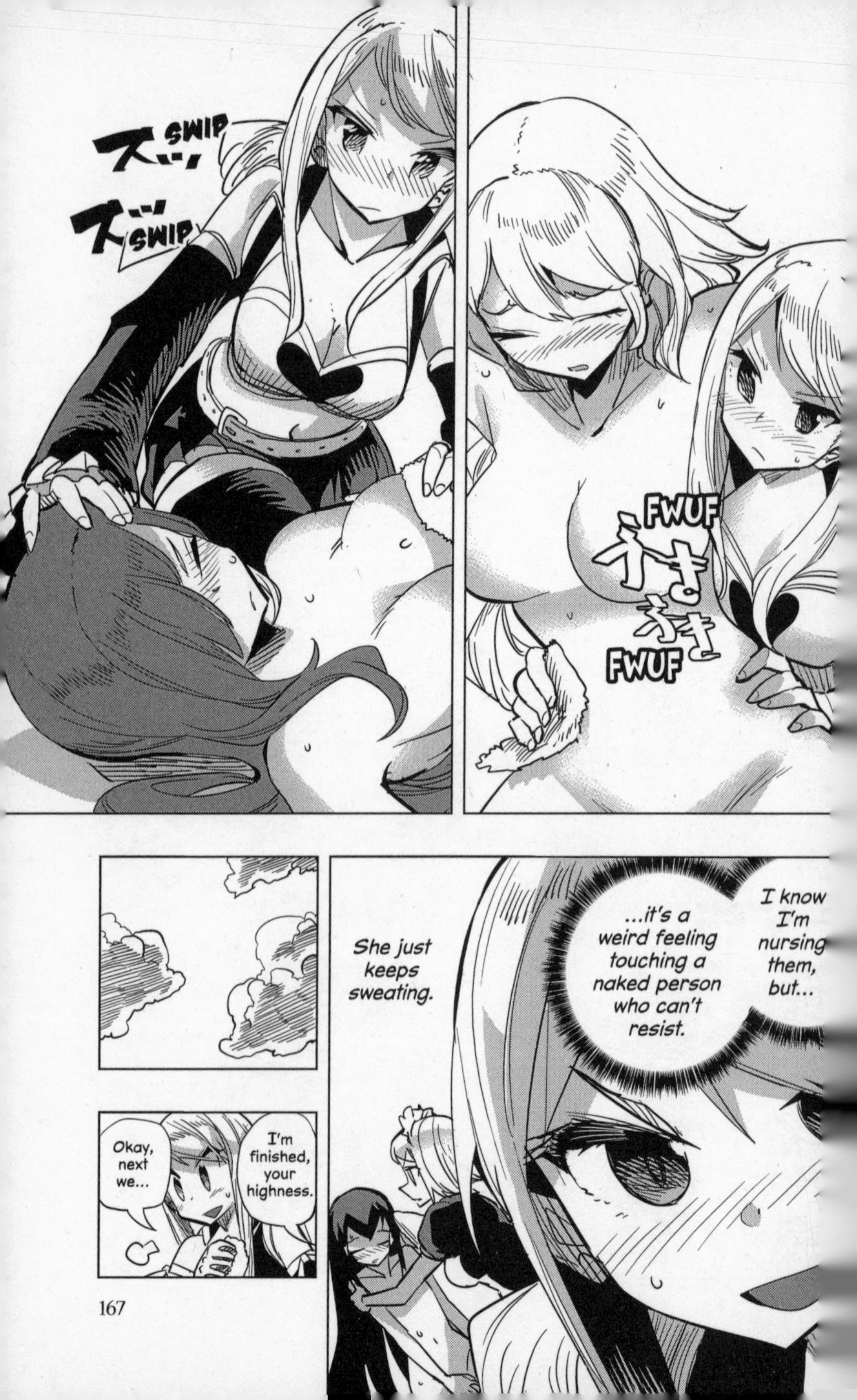
FWUF
ふき
ふき
FWUF
ス−ッ
SWIP
ス−ッ
SWIP
I know I'm nursing them, but...
...it's a weird feeling touching a naked person who can't resist.
She just keeps sweating.
I'm finished, your highness.
Okay, next we...

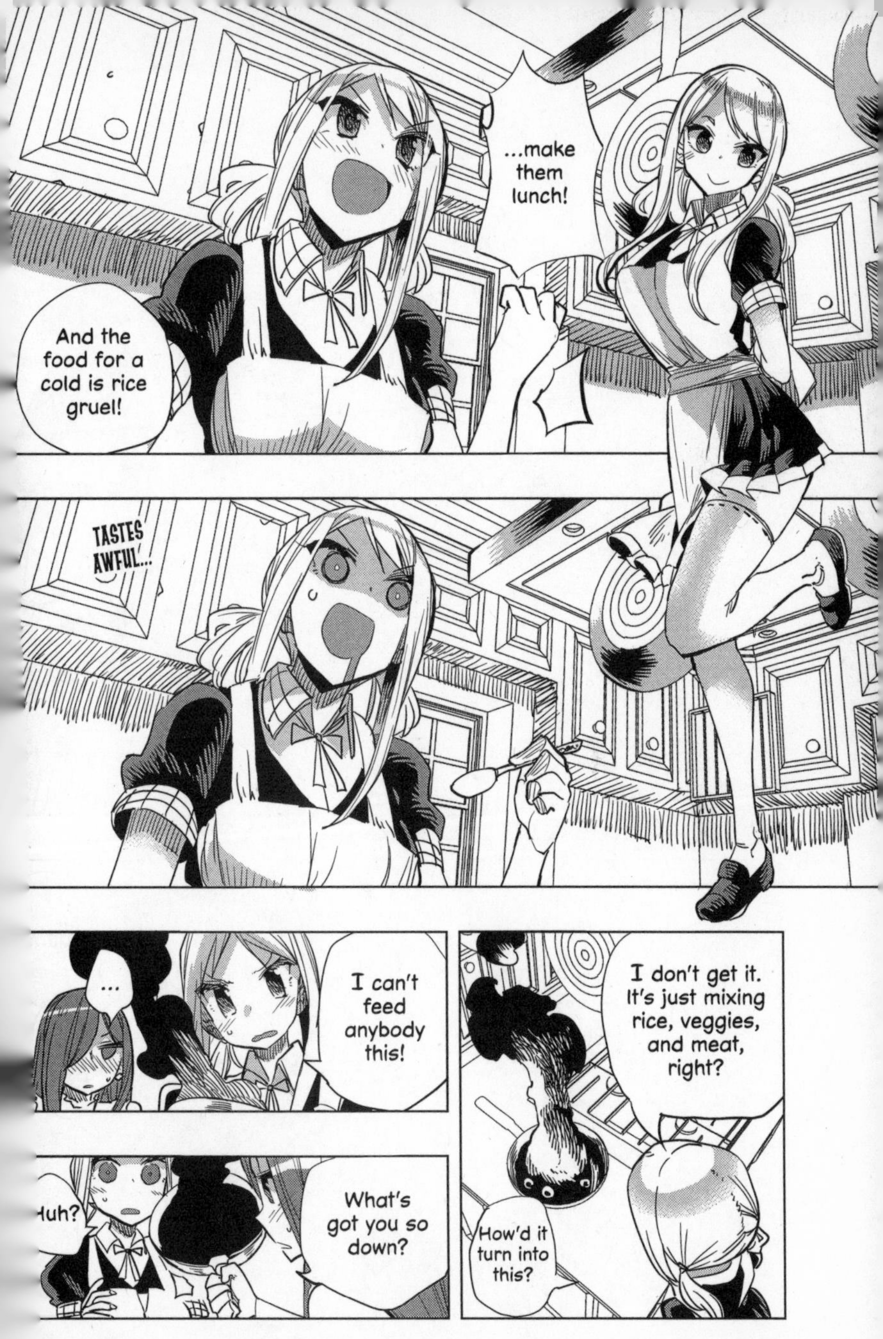
...make them lunch!
And the food for a cold is rice gruel!
TASTES AWFUL...
I don't get it. It's just mixing rice, veggies, and meat, right?
How'd it turn into this?
I can't feed anybody this!
...
What's got you so down?
Huh?

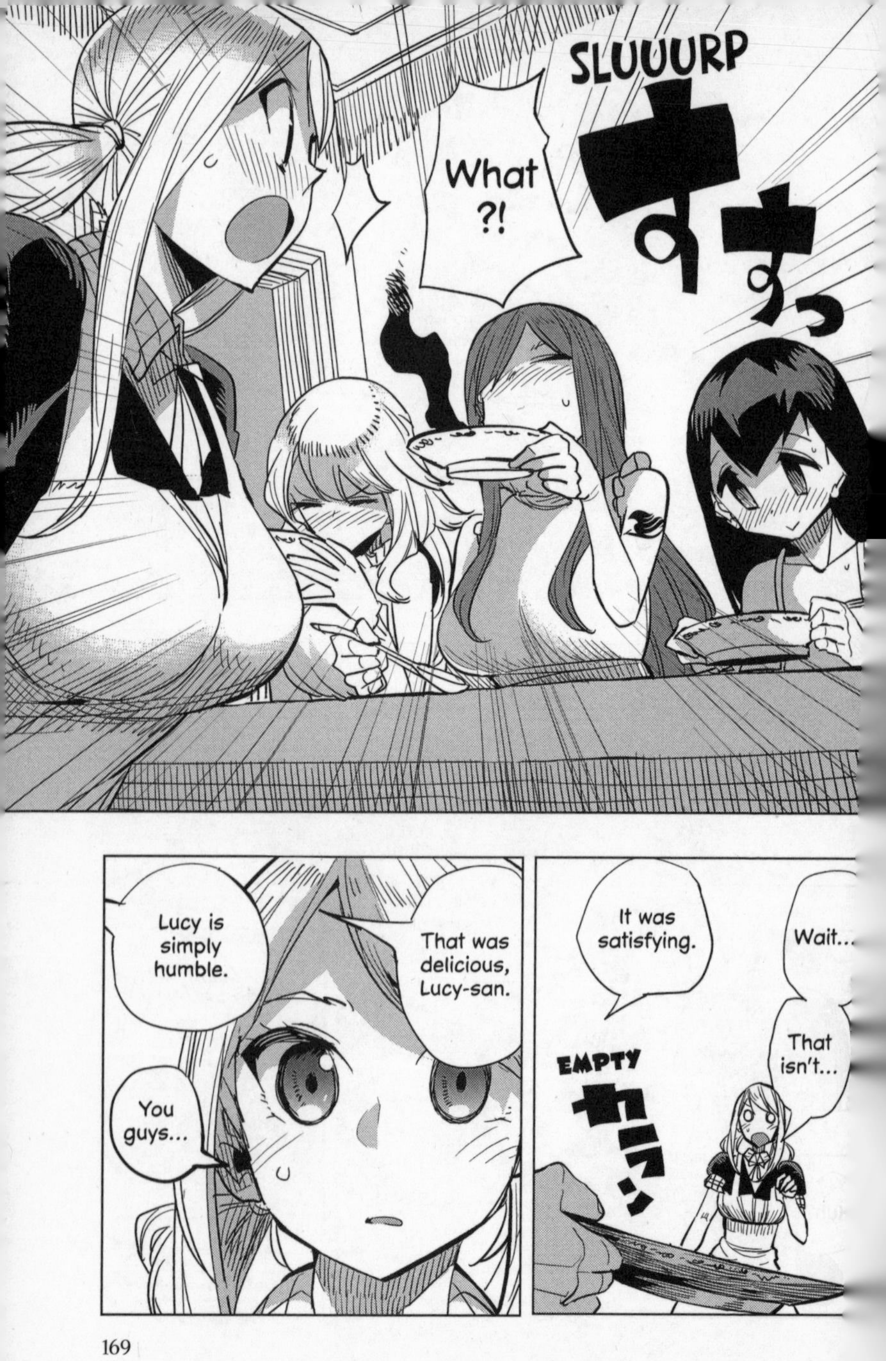
SLUURP
すすっ
What?!
Wait...
It was satisfying.
That isn't...
EMPTY
That was delicious, Lucy-san.
Lucy is simply humble.
You guys...

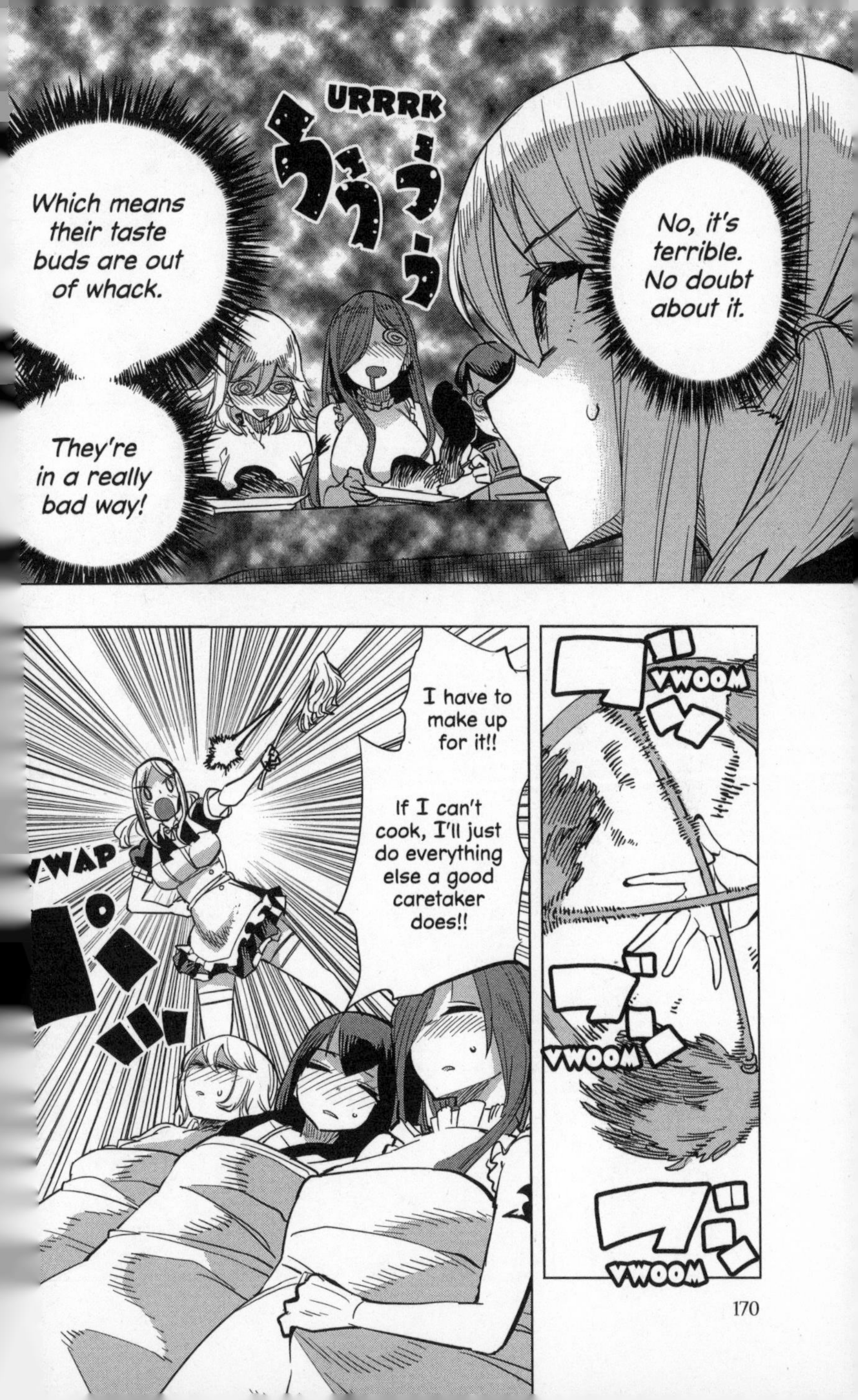
No, it's terrible. No doubt about it.
URRRK
Which means their taste buds are out of whack.
They're in a really bad way!
VWOOM
VWOOM
VWOOM
I have to make up for it!!
If I can't cook, I'll just do everything else a good caretaker does!!
WAP

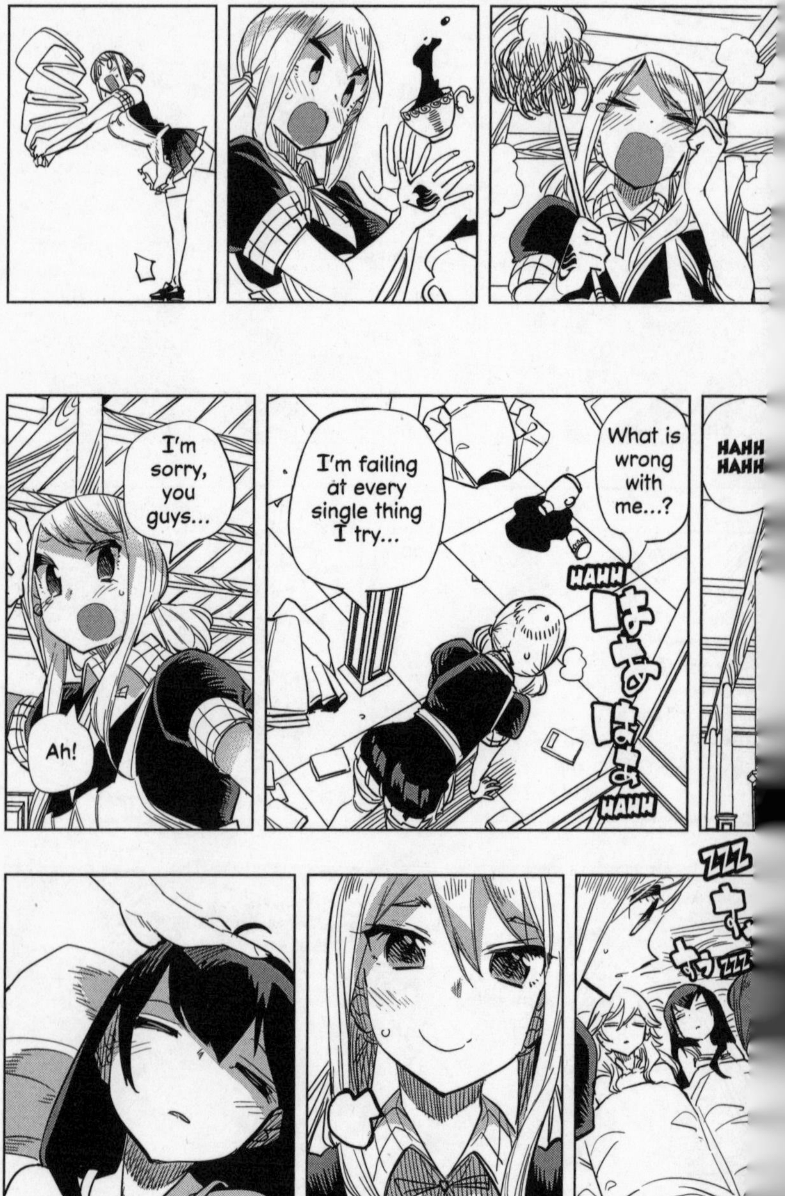
HAHH HAHH
What is wrong with me...?
I'm failing at every single thing I try...
HAHH
HAHH
I'm sorry, you guys...
Ah!
ZZZ
ZZZ

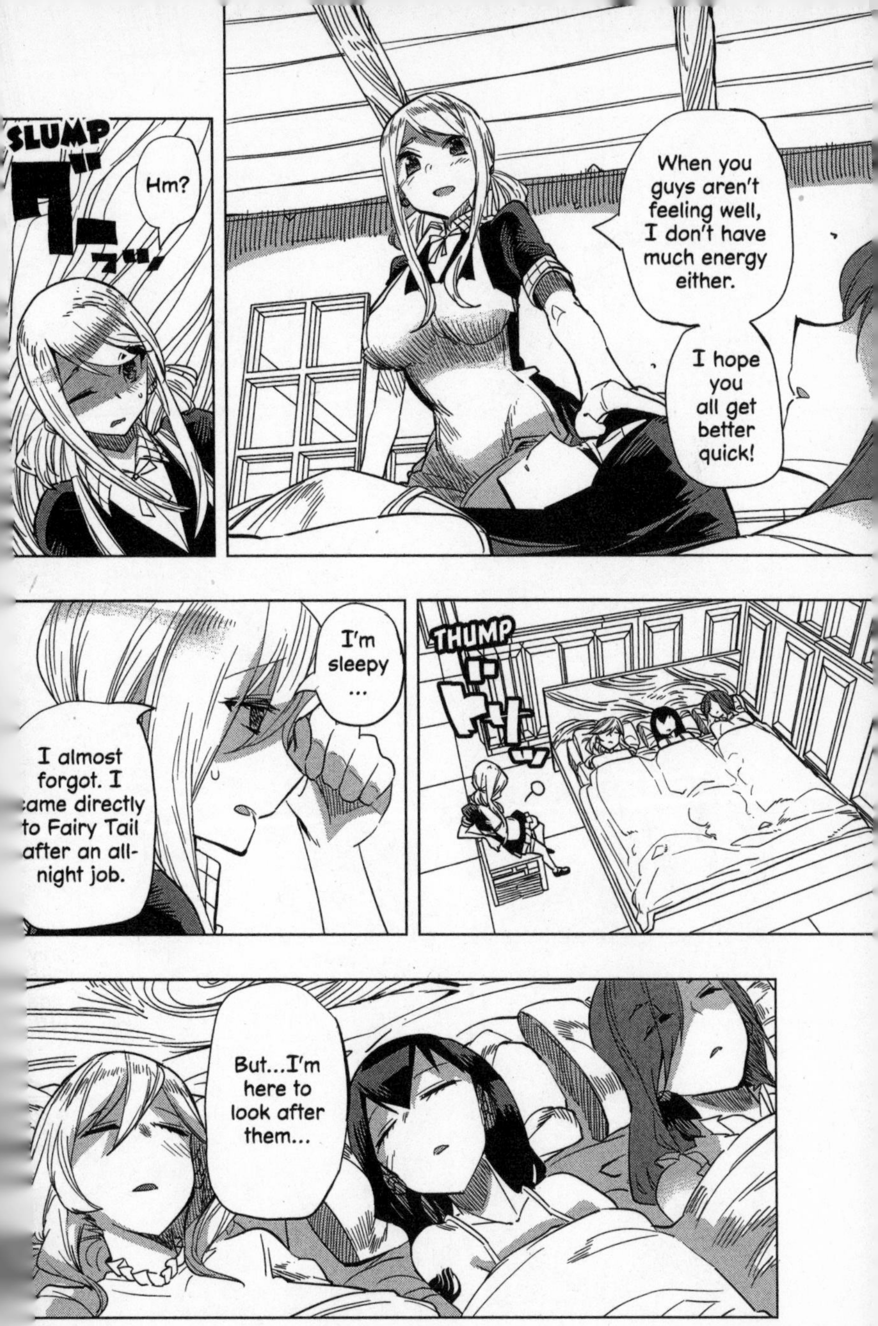
When you guys aren't feeling well, I don't have much energy either.
I hope you all get better quick!
SLUMP
Hm?
THUMP
I'm sleepy ...
I almost forgot. I ame directly to Fairy Tail after an all-night job.
But...I'm here to look after them...

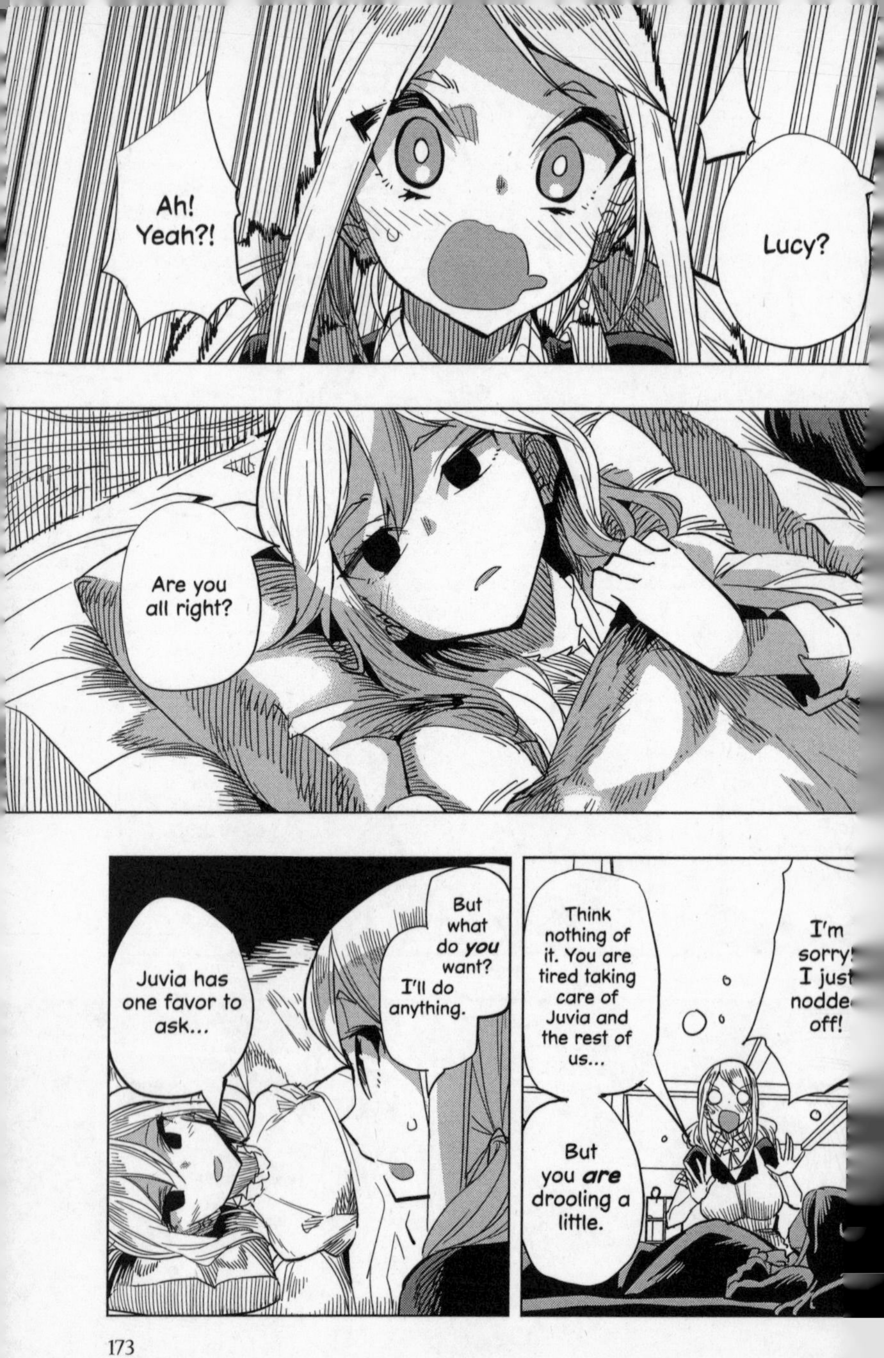
Lucy?
Ah! Yeah?!
Are you all right?
I'm sorry! I just nodde off!
Think nothing of it. You are tired taking care of Juvia and the rest of us...
But you *are* drooling a little.
But what do *you* want? I'll do anything.
Juvia has one favor to ask...

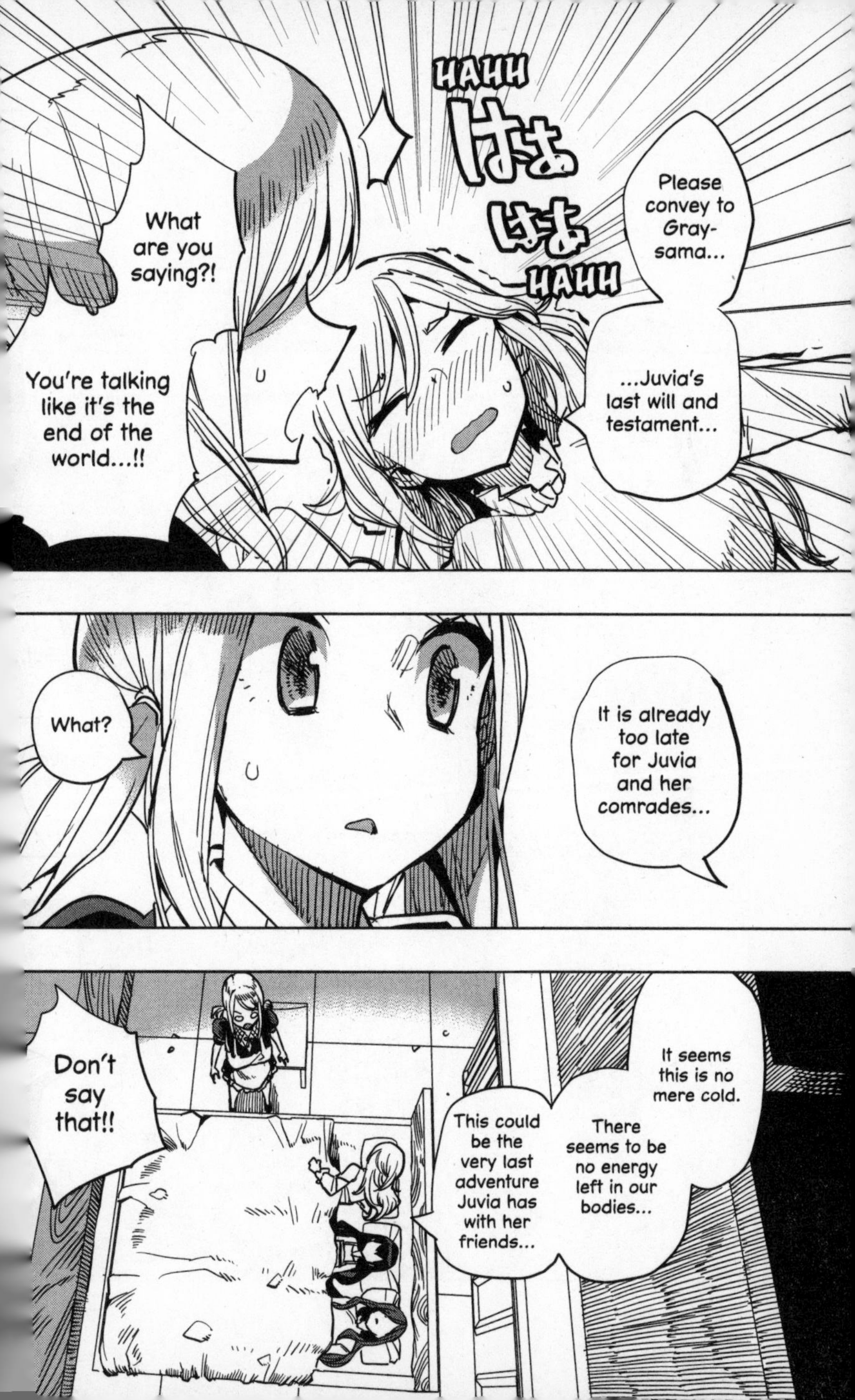
Please convey to Gray-sama...
...Juvia's last will and testament...
HAHH はぁ
はぁ HAHH
What are you saying?!
You're talking like it's the end of the world...!!
It is already too late for Juvia and her comrades...
What?
It seems this is no mere cold.
There seems to be no energy left in our bodies...
This could be the very last adventure Juvia has with her friends...
Don't say that!!

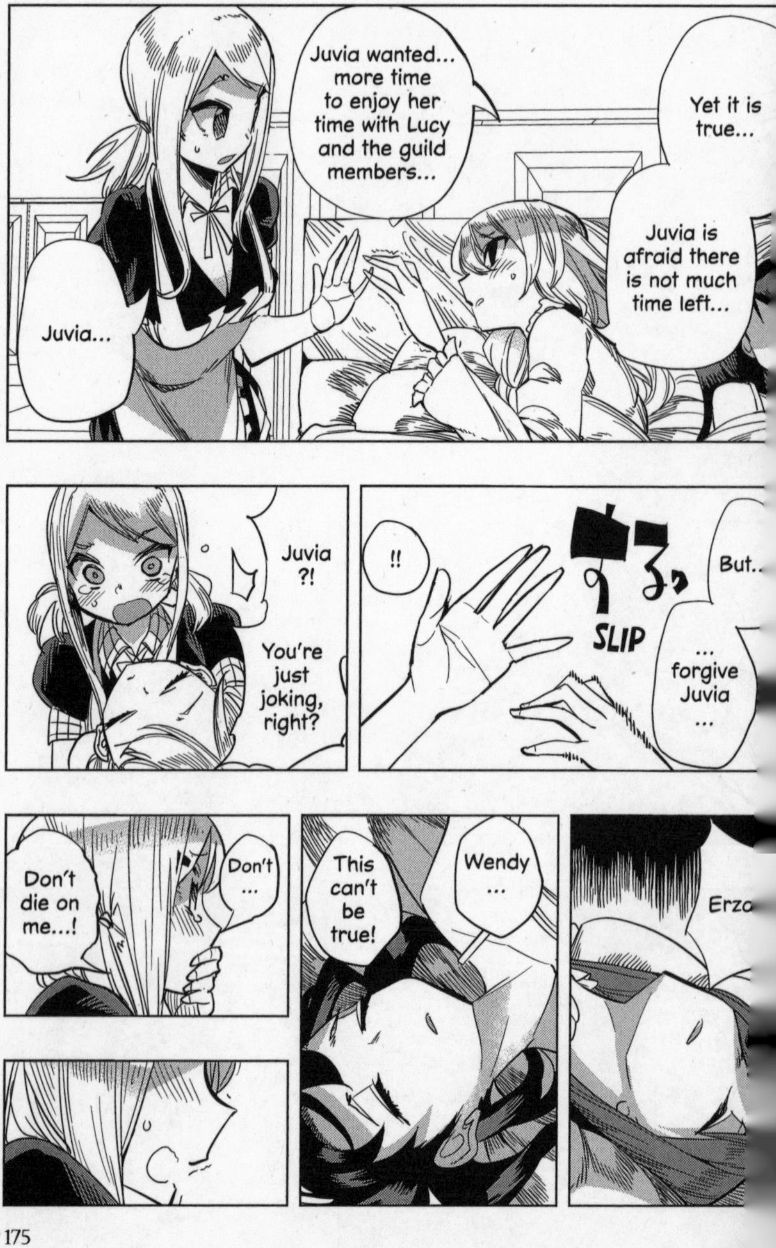
Yet it is true...
Juvia is afraid there is not much time left...
Juvia wanted... more time to enjoy her time with Lucy and the guild members...
Juvia...
But...
するっ
SLIP
... forgive Juvia ...
!!
Juvia ?!
You're just joking, right?
Erza
Wendy ...
This can't be true!
Don't ...
Don't die on me...!

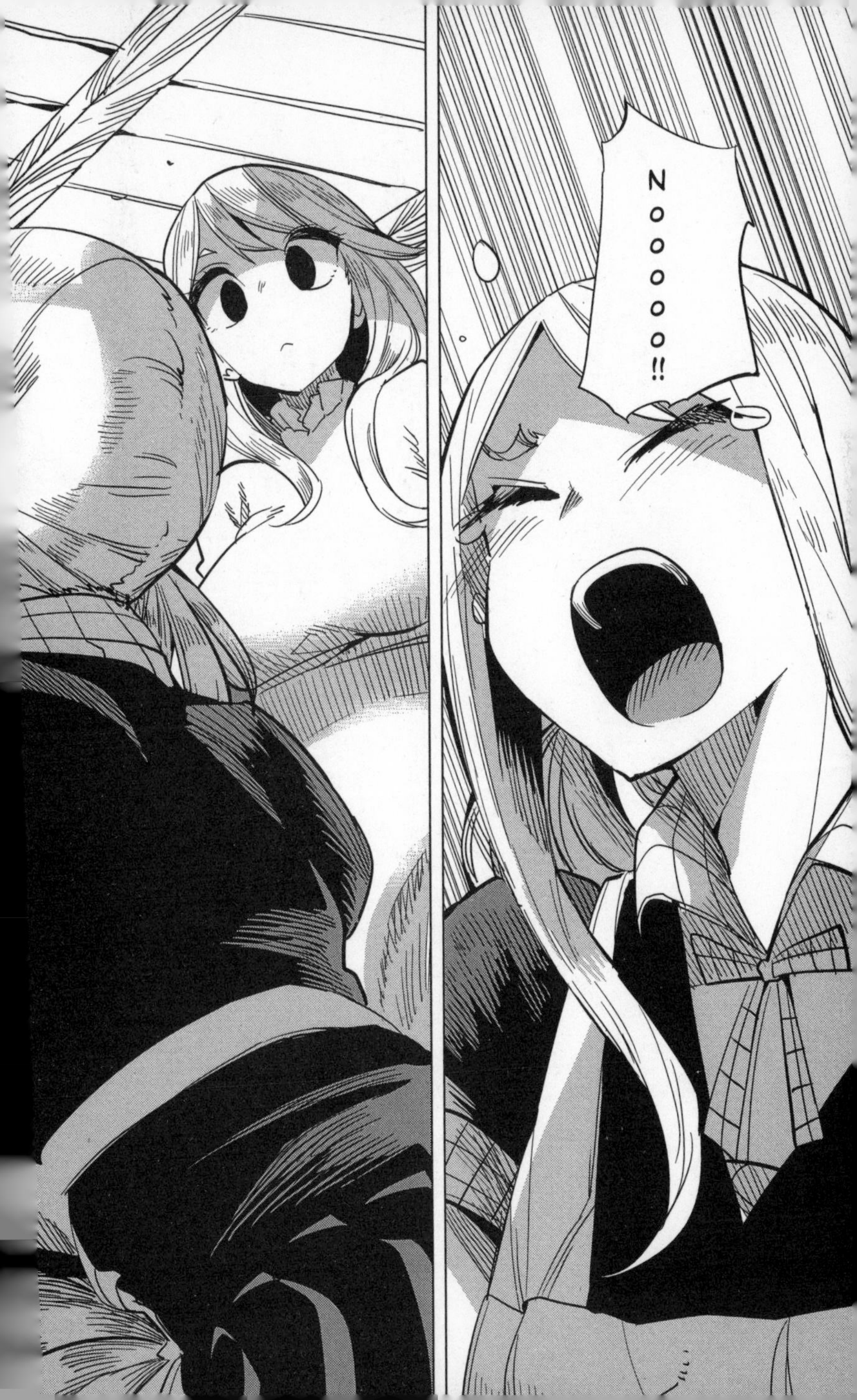
NOOOOOOO!!

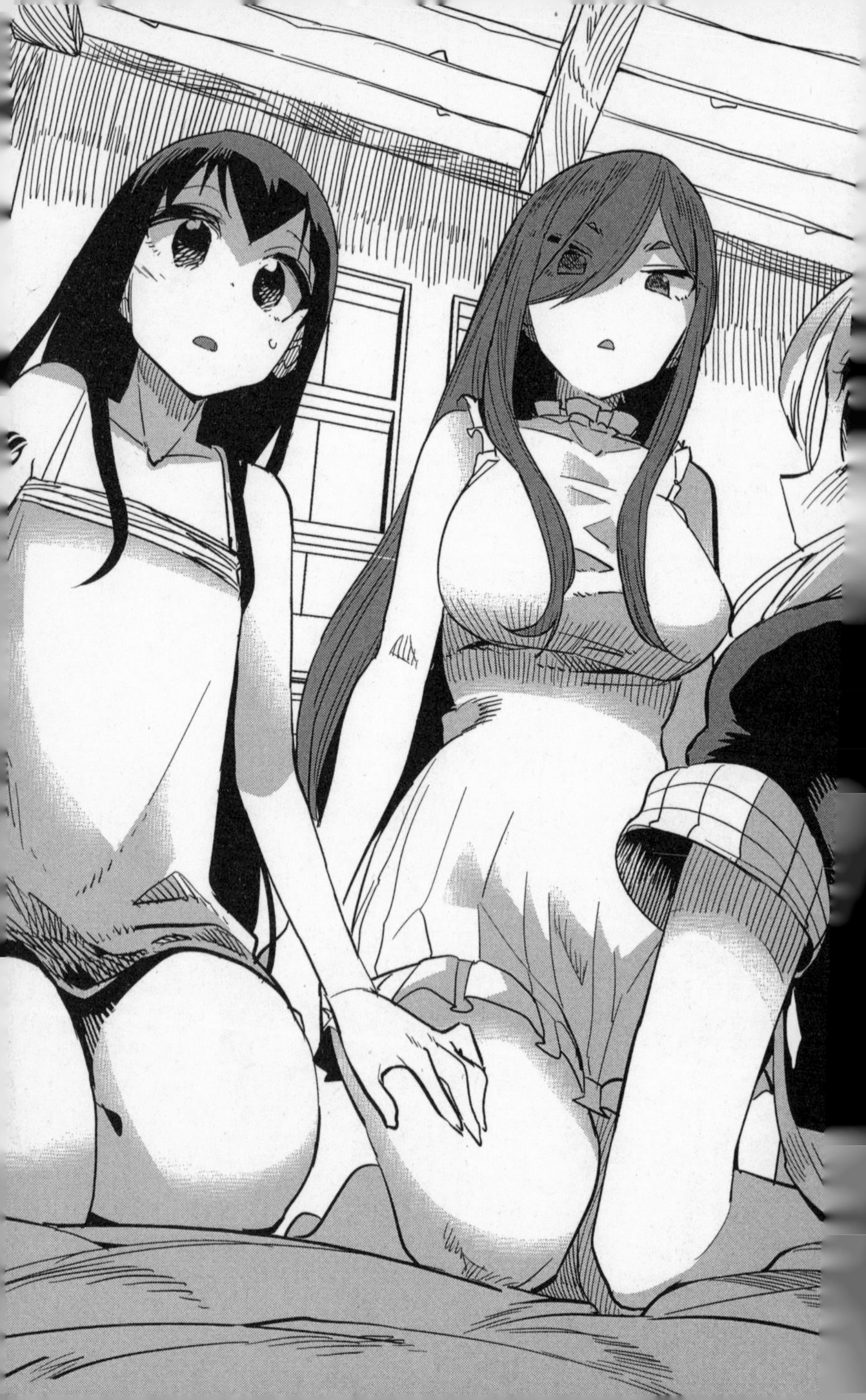

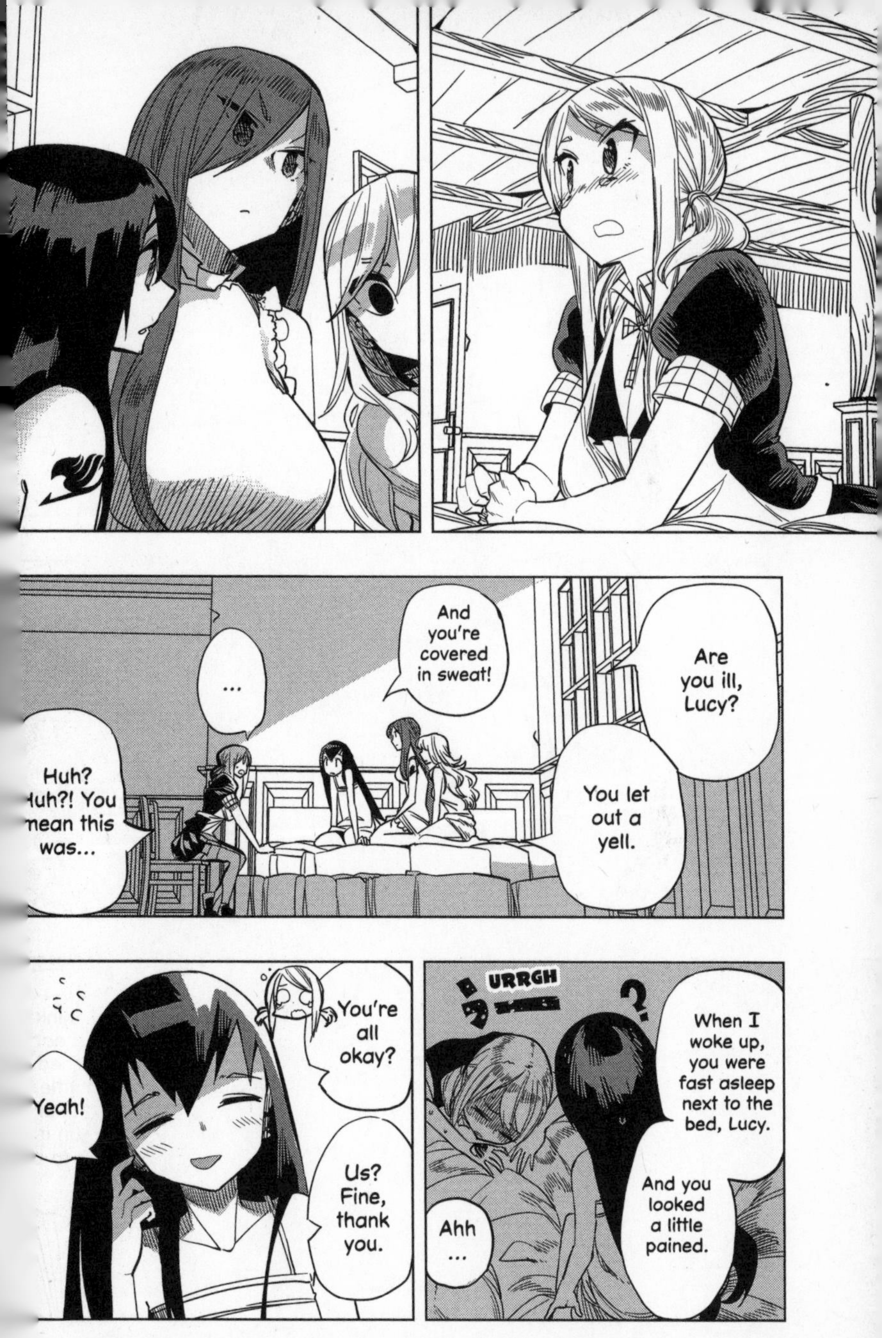
Are you ill, Lucy?
And you're covered in sweat!
...
You let out a yell.
Huh? Huh?! You mean this was...
URRGH
When I woke up, you were fast asleep next to the bed, Lucy.
And you looked a little pained.
Ahh ...
You're all okay?
Us? Fine, thank you.
Yeah!

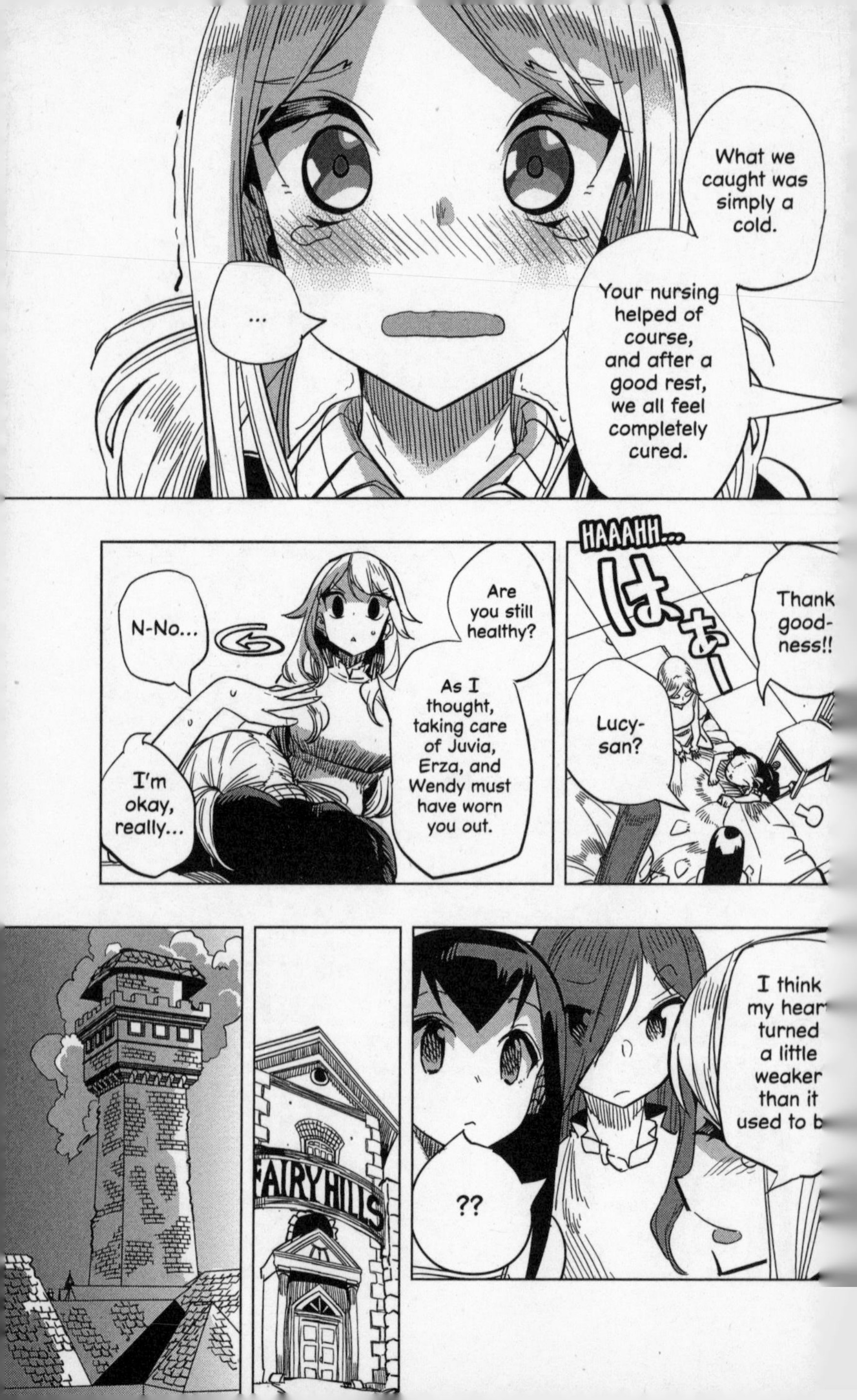

What we caught was simply a cold.
Your nursing helped of course, and after a good rest, we all feel completely cured.
...
HAAAHH...
はぁー
Thank good-ness!!
Lucy-san?
Are you still healthy?
As I thought, taking care of Juvia, Erza, and Wendy must have worn you out.
N-No...
I'm okay, really...
I think my hear turned a little weaker than it used to b
??
FAIRY HILLS

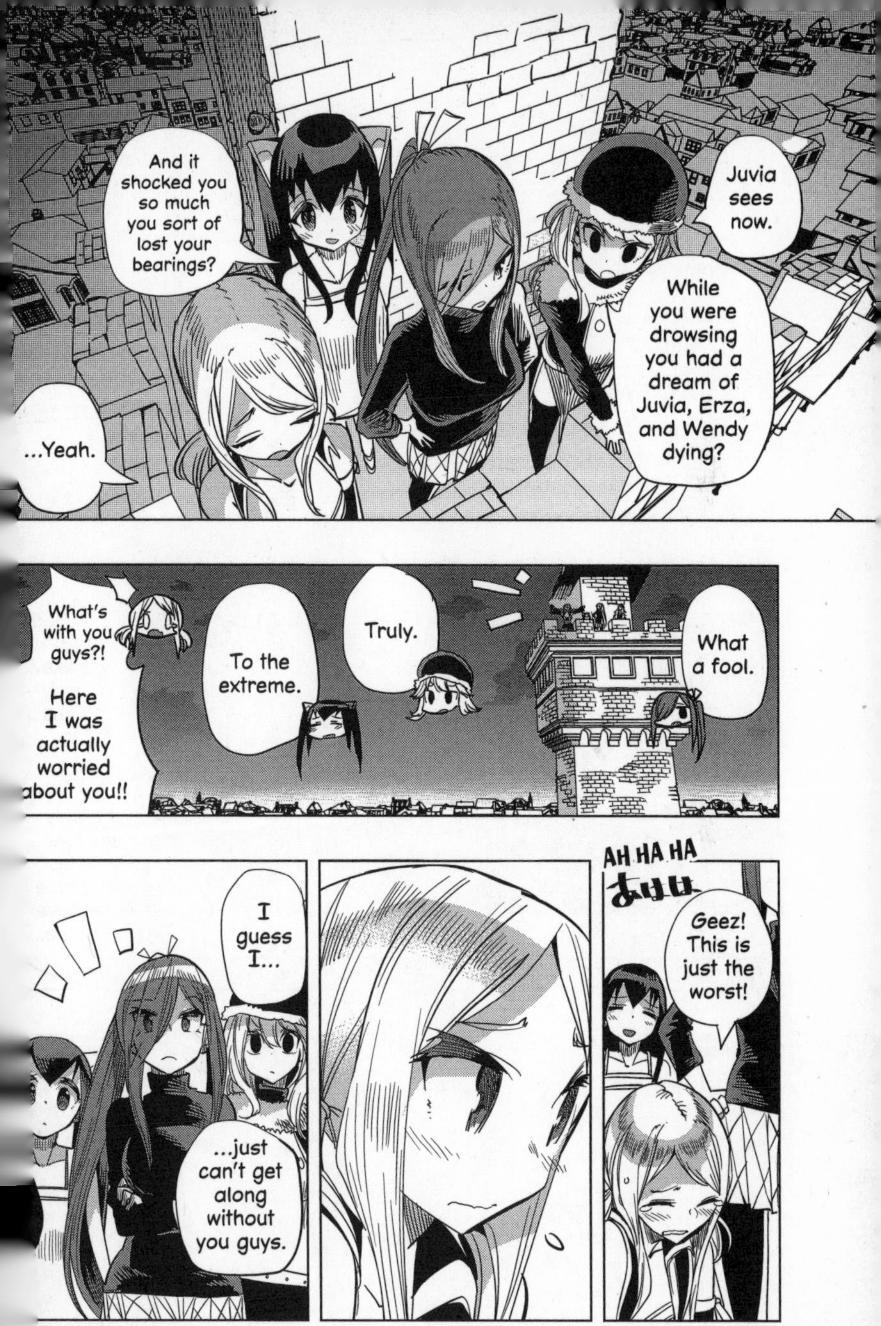

Juvia sees now.
While you were drowsing you had a dream of Juvia, Erza, and Wendy dying?
And it shocked you so much you sort of lost your bearings?
...Yeah.
What a fool.
Truly.
To the extreme.
What's with you guys?!
Here I was actually worried about you!!
AH HA HA
Geez! This is just the worst!
I guess I...
...just can't get along without you guys.

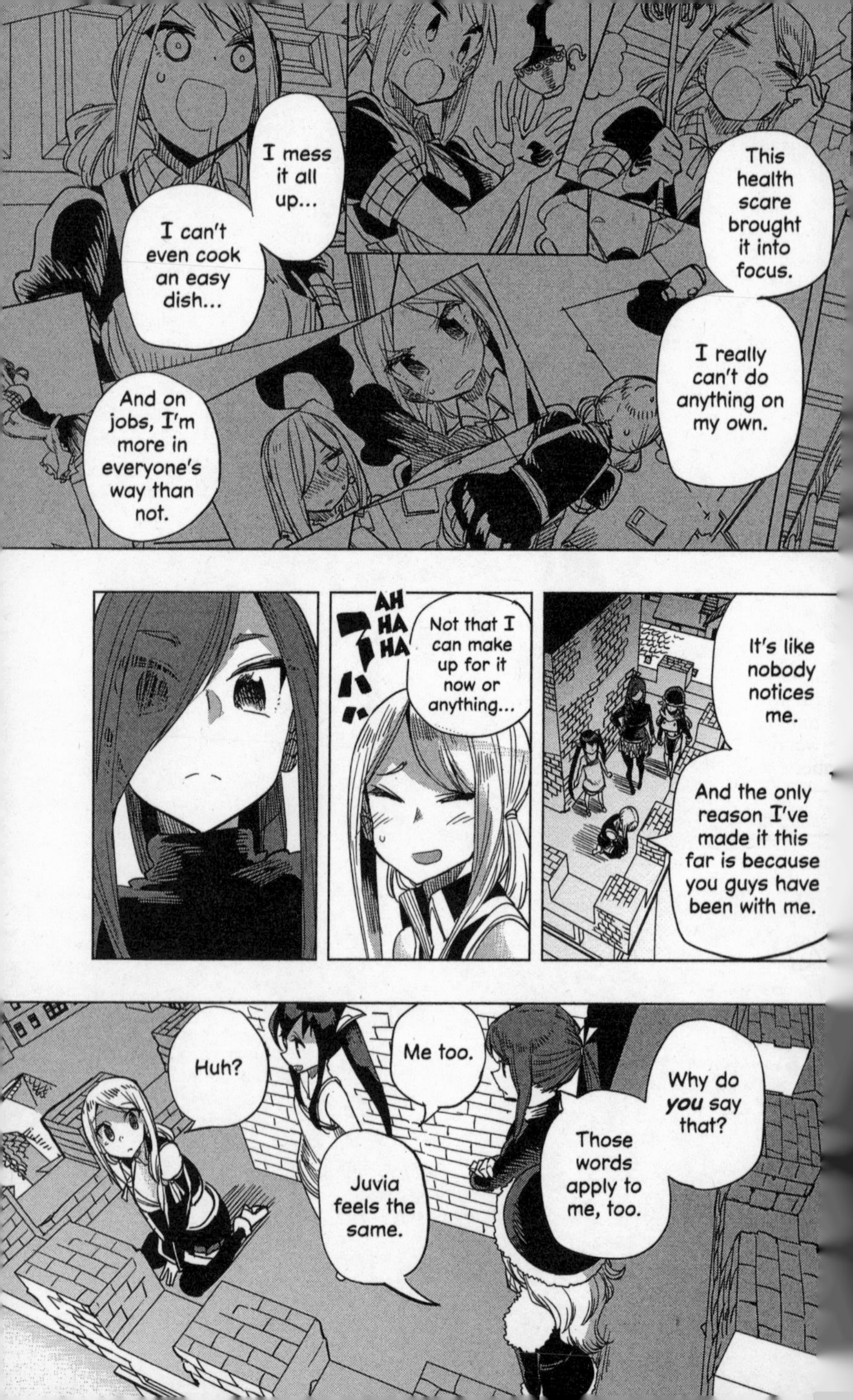
This health scare brought it into focus.
I really can't do anything on my own.
I mess it all up...
I can't even cook an easy dish...
And on jobs, I'm more in everyone's way than not.
It's like nobody notices me.
And the only reason I've made it this far is because you guys have been with me.
AH HA HA
Not that I can make up for it now or anything...
Why do *you* say that?
Those words apply to me, too.
Me too.
Juvia feels the same.
Huh?

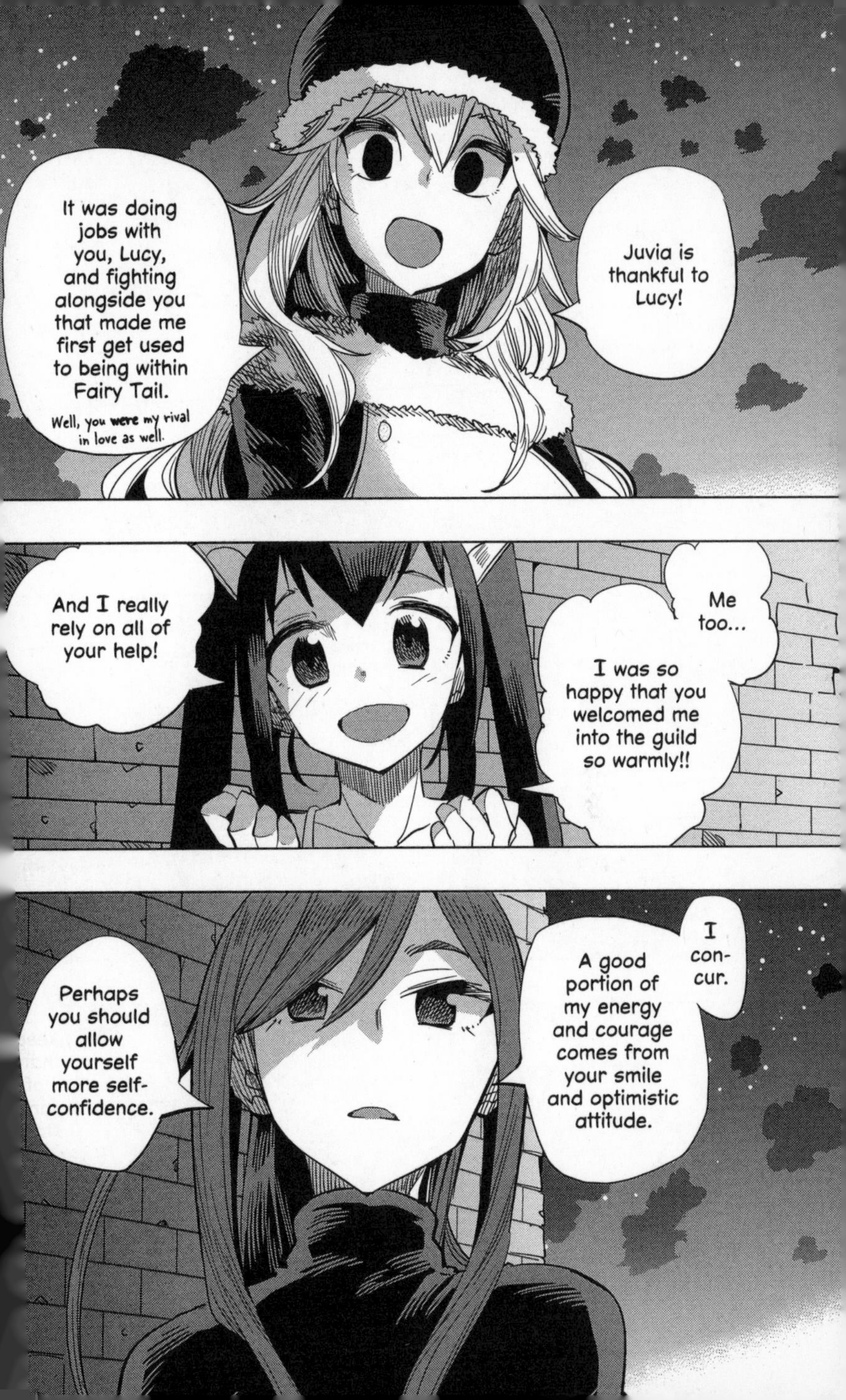
Juvia is thankful to Lucy!
It was doing jobs with you, Lucy, and fighting alongside you that made me first get used to being within Fairy Tail.
Well, you were my rival in love as well.
Me too...
I was so happy that you welcomed me into the guild so warmly!!
And I really rely on all of your help!
I con-cur.
A good portion of my energy and courage comes from your smile and optimistic attitude.
Perhaps you should allow yourself more self-confidence.

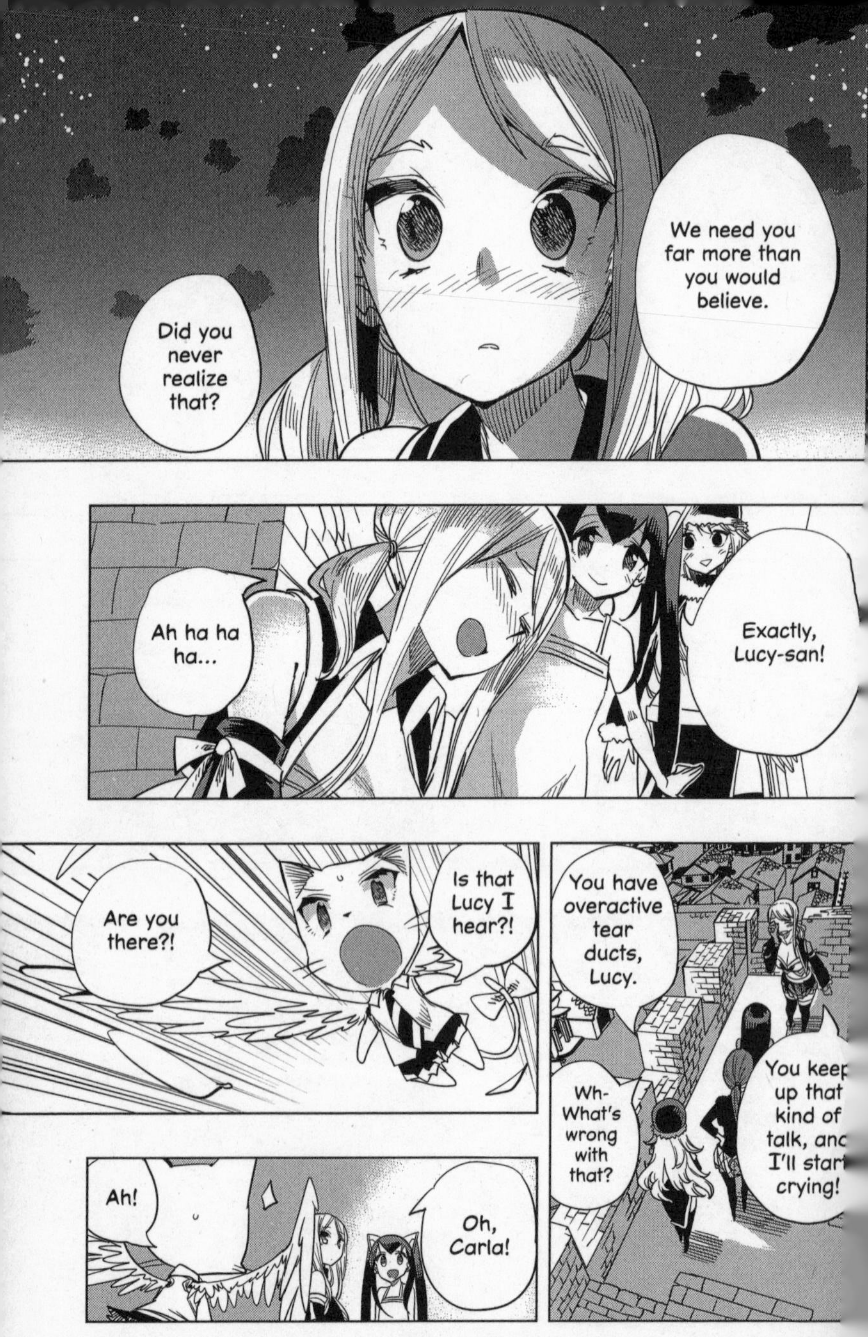

We need you far more than you would believe.
Did you never realize that?
Exactly, Lucy-san!
Ah ha ha ha...
You keep up that kind of talk, and I'll start crying!
You have overactive tear ducts, Lucy.
Wh- What's wrong with that?
Is that Lucy I hear?!
Are you there?!
Oh, Carla!
Ah!

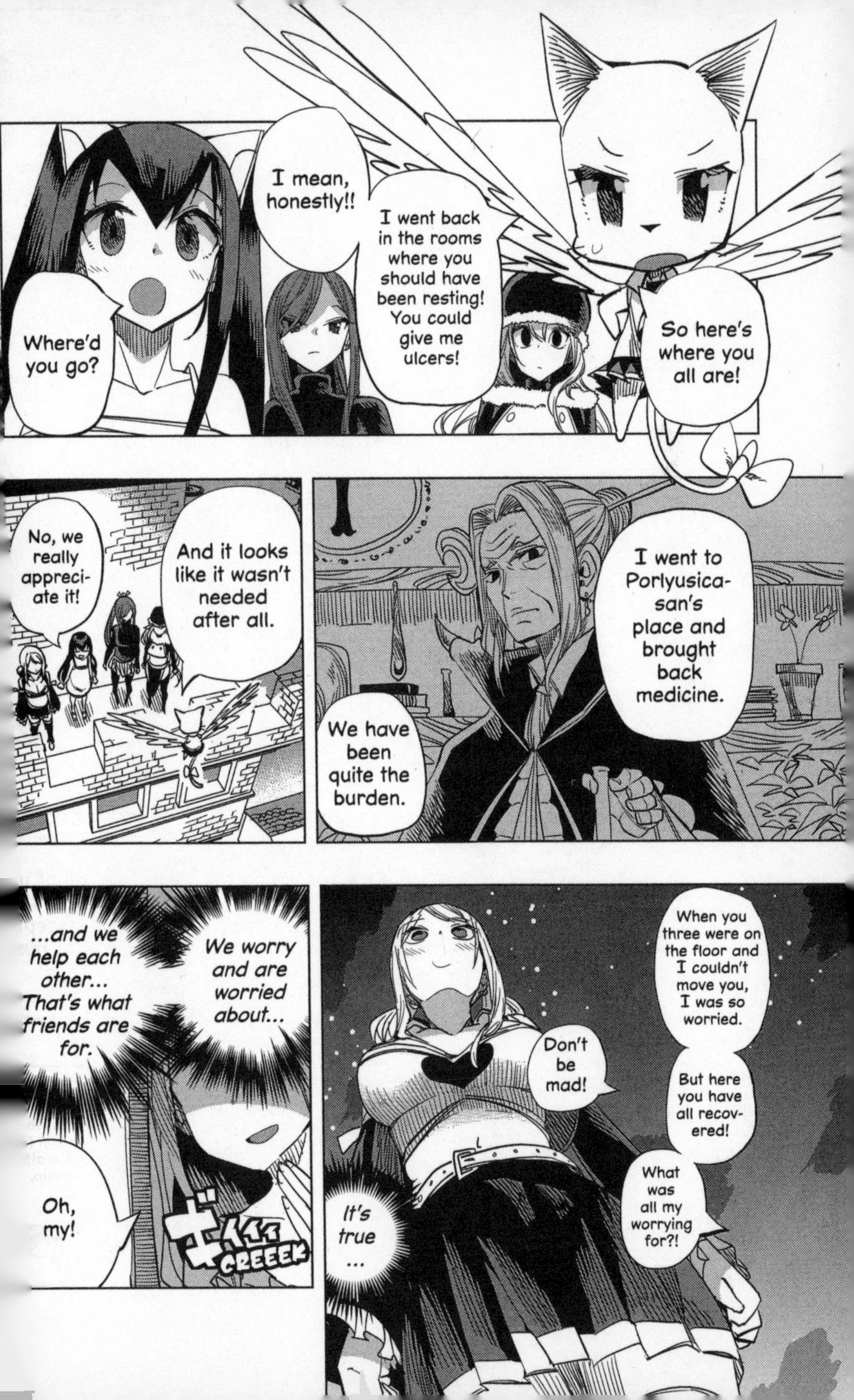
So here's where you all are!
I went back in the rooms where you should have been resting! You could give me ulcers!
I mean, honestly!!
Where'd you go?
I went to Porlyusica-san's place and brought back medicine.
We have been quite the burden.
And it looks like it wasn't needed after all.
No, we really appreci-ate it!
When you three were on the floor and I couldn't move you, I was so worried.
Don't be mad!
But here you have all recov-ered!
What was all my worrying for?!
It's true ...
We worry and are worried about...
...and we help each other... That's what friends are for.
Oh, my!
CREEEK

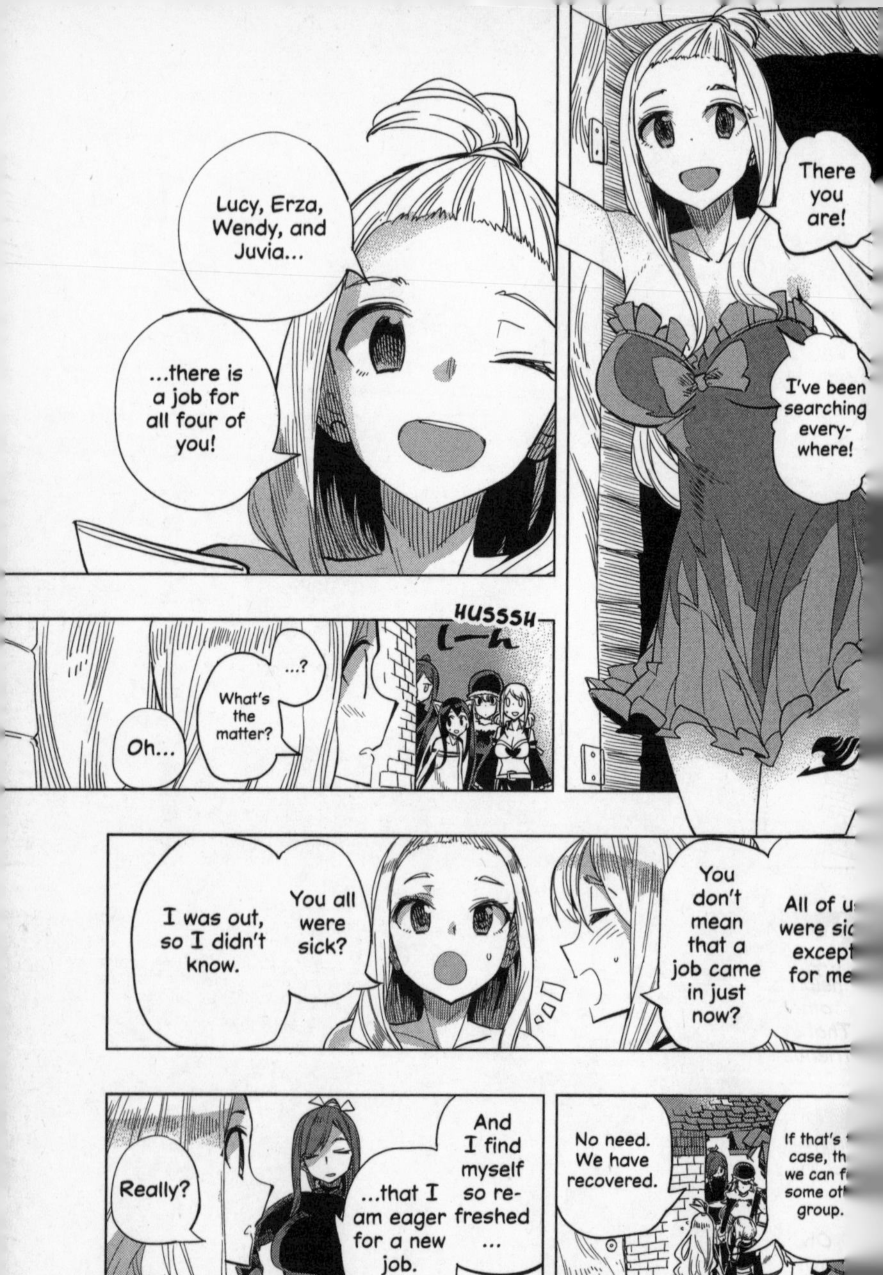

There you are!
I've been searching every-where!
Lucy, Erza, Wendy, and Juvia...
...there is a job for all four of you!
HUSSSH
...?
What's the matter?
Oh...
All of u were sic except for me
You don't mean that a job came in just now?
You all were sick?
I was out, so I didn't know.
If that's case, th we can f some ot group.
No need. We have recovered.
And I find myself so re-freshed ...
...that I am eager for a new job.
Really?

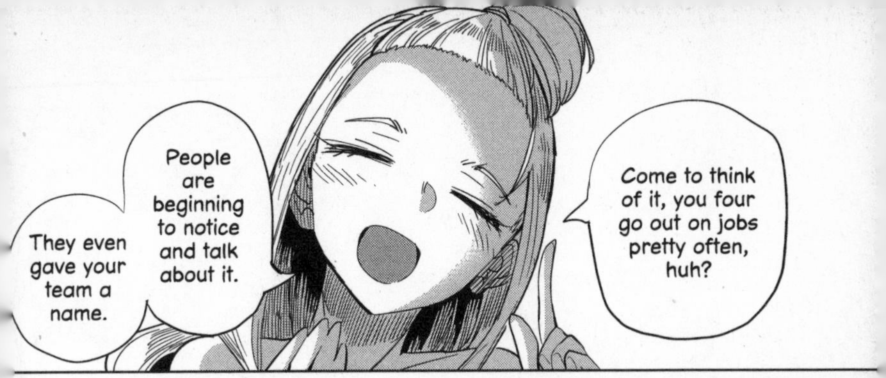
Come to think of it, you four go out on jobs pretty often, huh?
People are beginning to notice and talk about it.
They even gave your team a name.
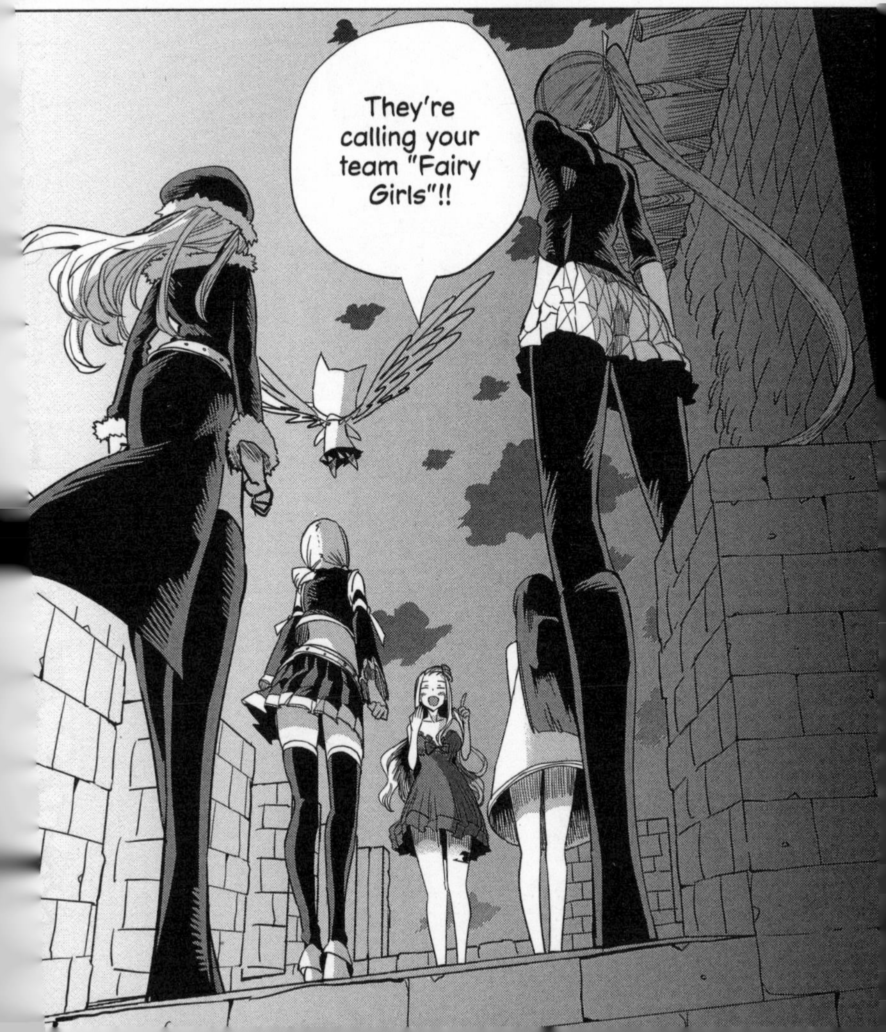
They're calling your team "Fairy Girls"!!

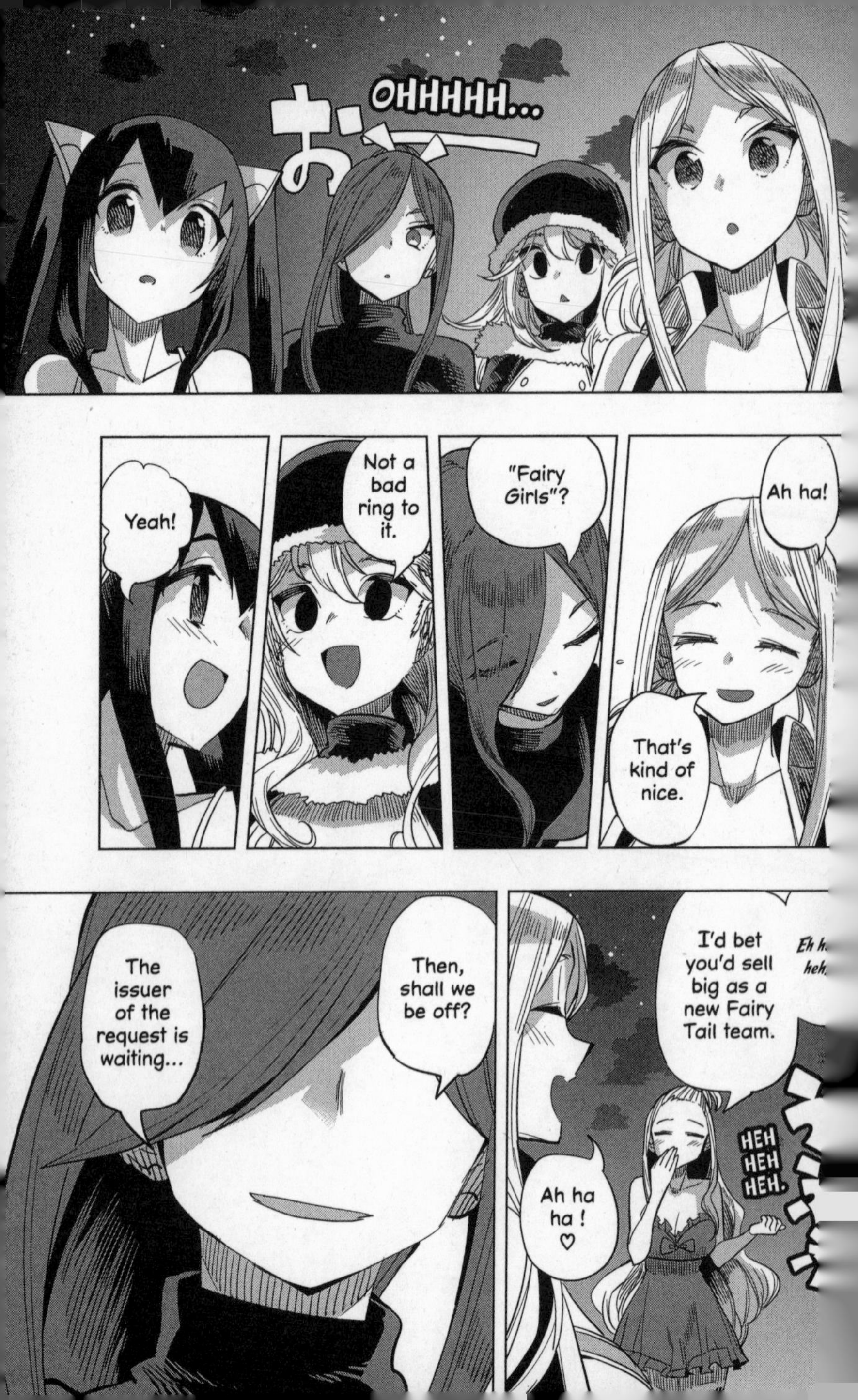

OHHHHH...
おー
Ah ha!
That's kind of nice.
"Fairy Girls"?
Not a bad ring to it.
Yeah!
I'd bet you'd sell big as a new Fairy Tail team.
HEH HEH HEH.
Ah ha ha ! ♡
Then, shall we be off?
The issuer of the request is waiting...

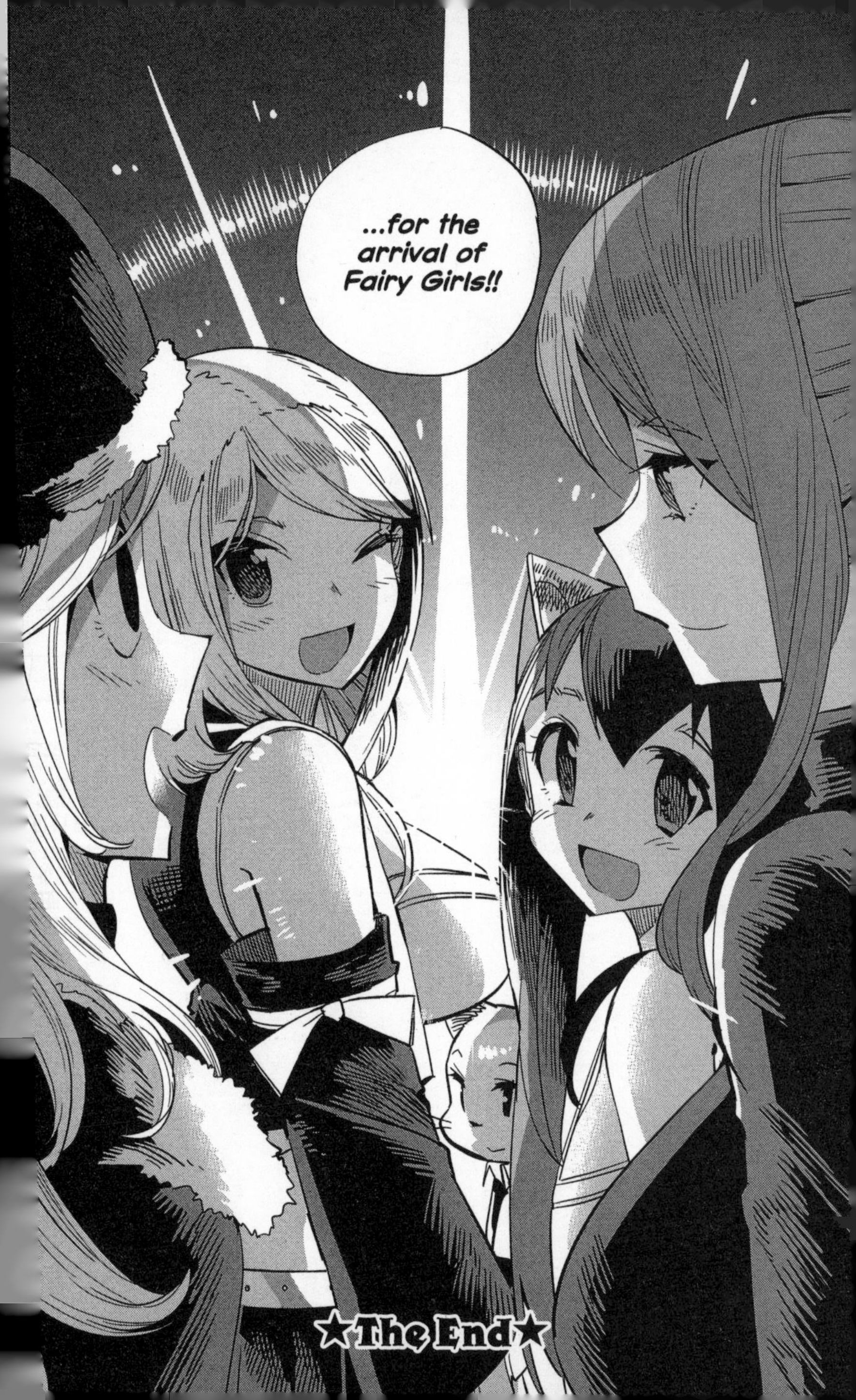
...for the arrival of Fairy Girls!!
★The End★

VILLAINS AT THE END OF THEIR STORIES

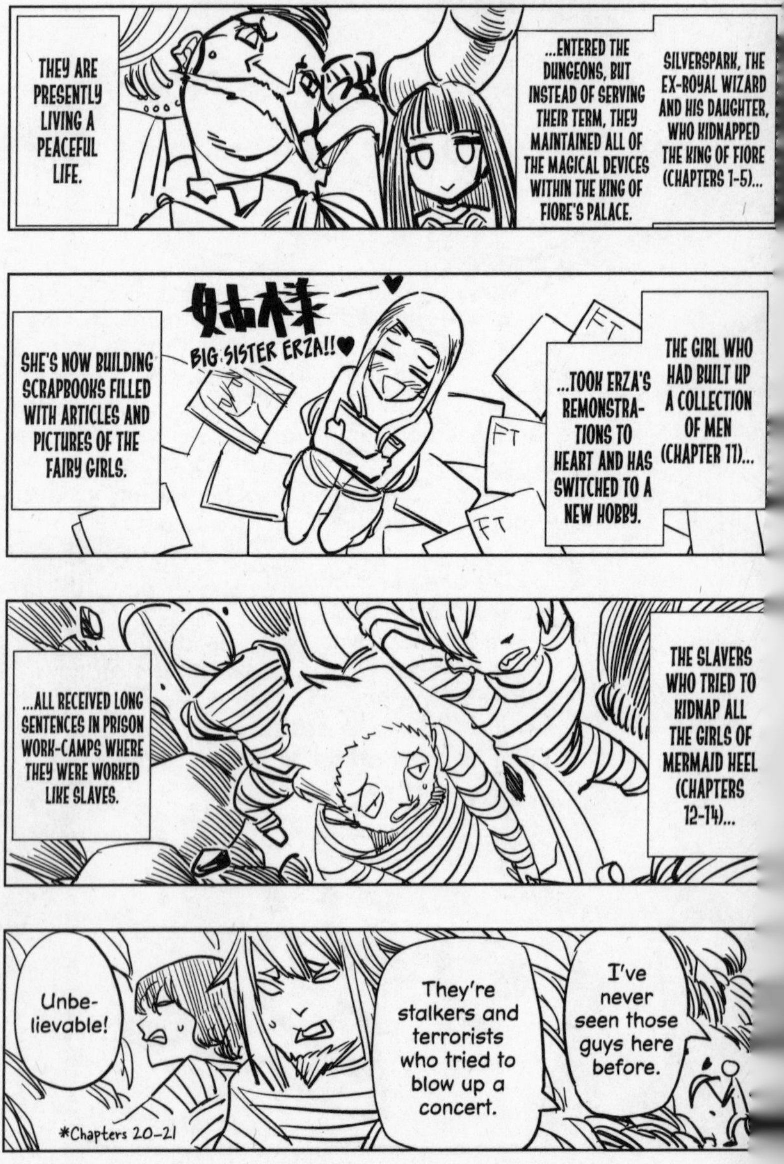

SILVERSPARK, THE EX-ROYAL WIZARD AND HIS DAUGHTER, WHO KIDNAPPED THE KING OF FIORE (CHAPTERS 1-5)...
...ENTERED THE DUNGEONS, BUT INSTEAD OF SERVING THEIR TERM, THEY MAINTAINED ALL OF THE MAGICAL DEVICES WITHIN THE KING OF FIORE'S PALACE.
THEY ARE PRESENTLY LIVING A PEACEFUL LIFE.
THE GIRL WHO HAD BUILT UP A COLLECTION OF MEN (CHAPTER 11)...
...TOOK ERZA'S REMONSTRATIONS TO HEART AND HAS SWITCHED TO A NEW HOBBY.
姉様ー♥
BIG SISTER ERZA!!♥
SHE'S NOW BUILDING SCRAPBOOKS FILLED WITH ARTICLES AND PICTURES OF THE FAIRY GIRLS.
THE SLAVERS WHO TRIED TO KIDNAP ALL THE GIRLS OF MERMAID HEEL (CHAPTERS 12-14)...
...ALL RECEIVED LONG SENTENCES IN PRISON WORK-CAMPS WHERE THEY WERE WORKED LIKE SLAVES.
I've never seen those guys here before.
They're stalkers and terrorists who tried to blow up a concert.
Unbe-lievable!
*Chapters 20-21

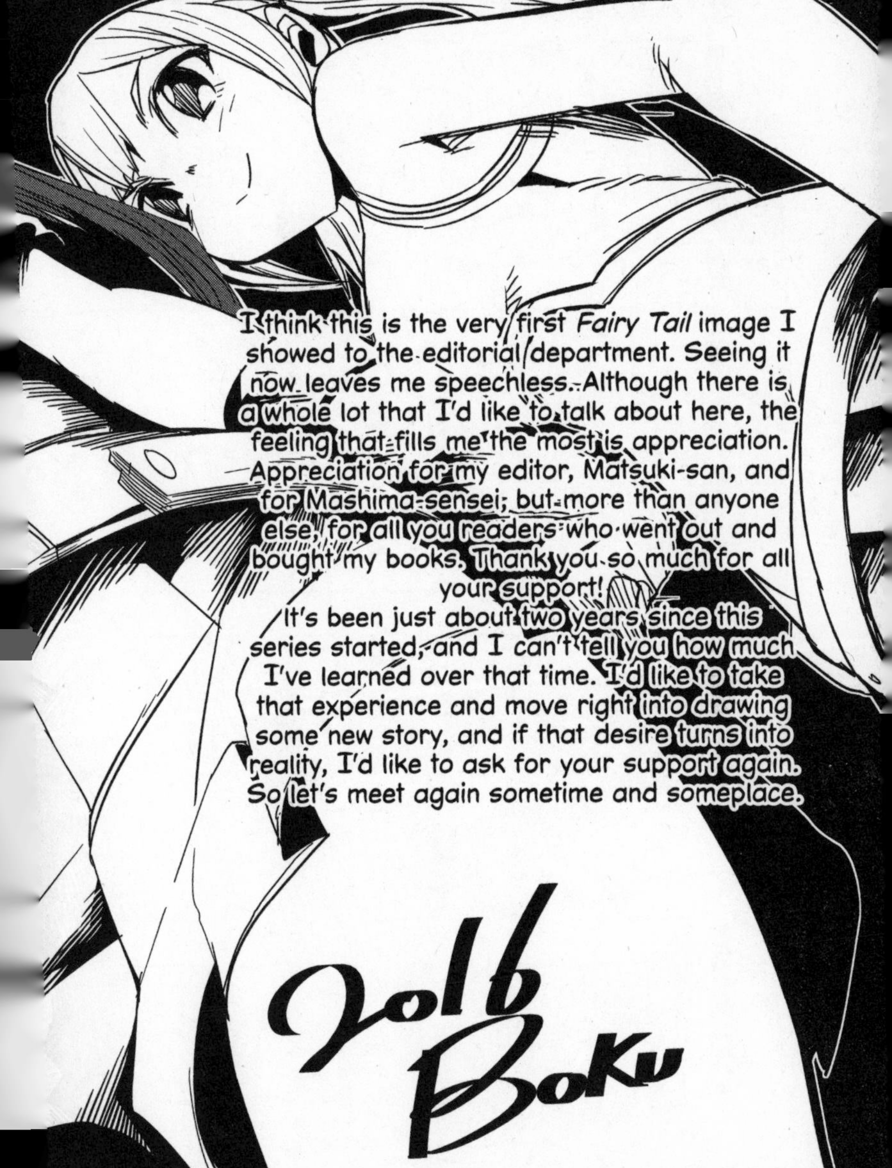
I think this is the very first Fairy Tail image I showed to the editorial department. Seeing it now leaves me speechless. Although there is a whole lot that I'd like to talk about here, the feeling that fills me the most is appreciation. Appreciation for my editor, Matsuki-san, and for Mashima-sensei; but more than anyone else, for all you readers who went out and bought my books. Thank you so much for all your support!
It's been just about two years since this series started, and I can't tell you how much I've learned over that time. I'd like to take that experience and move right into drawing some new story, and if that desire turns into reality, I'd like to ask for your support again. So let's meet again sometime and someplace.
2016 Boku

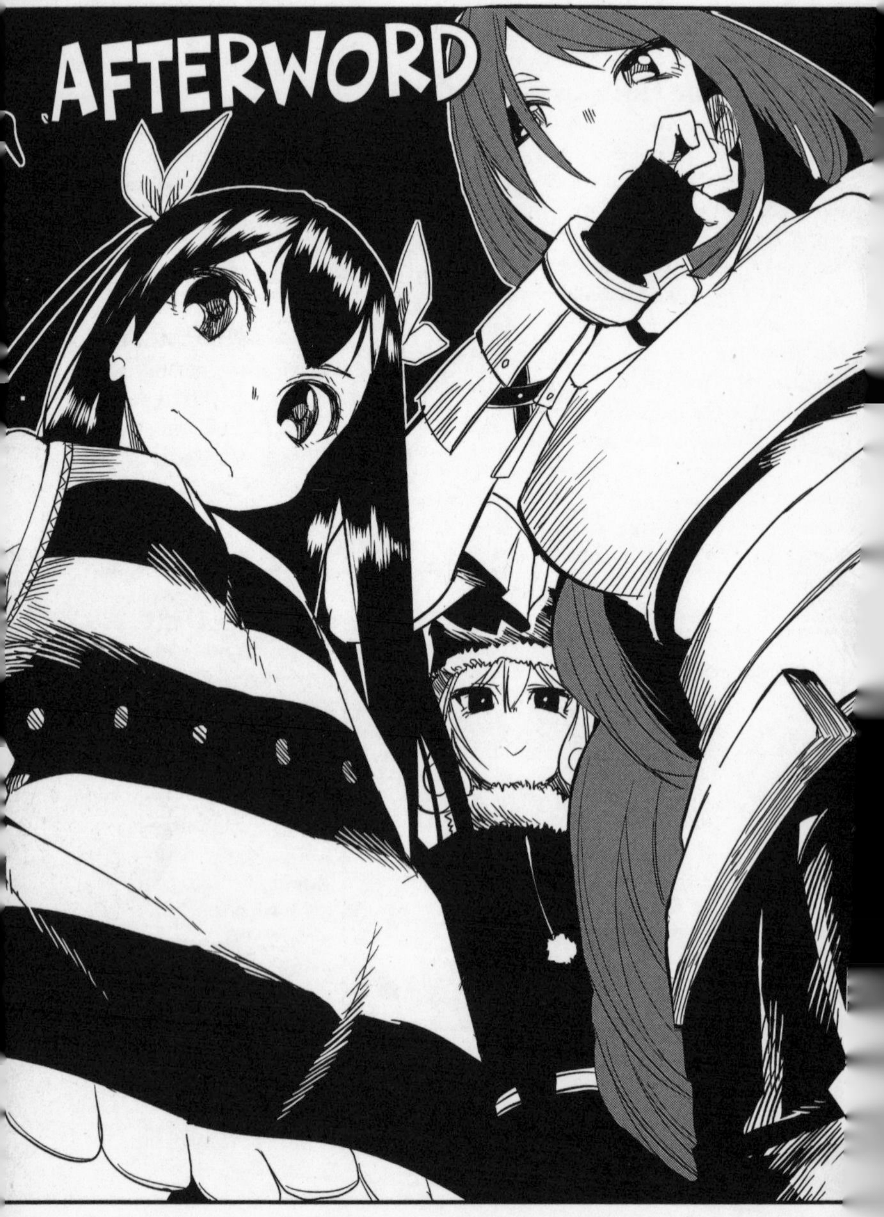
AFTERWORD

Translation Notes:

Page 101, The Hot-Springs Bath Sign

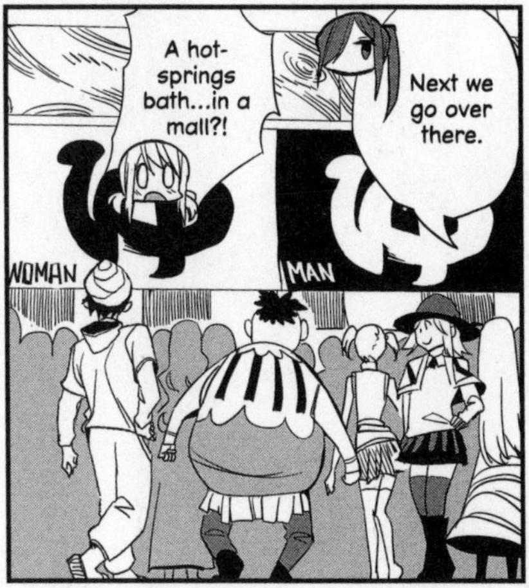
Next we go over there.
A hot-springs bath...in a mall?!
MAN
WOMAN

The Japanese word for hot water is *o-yu*, and since *o* is just an honorific, the part of the word carrying the meaning is "yu." That is why if you ever see the hiragana symbol for *yu*, ゆ on a sign, or especially a smokestack, it means the building attached to it is most likely a public bathhouse. Hot-springs bath houses also use the *yu* sign, but can also use a special symbol for hot springs (*onsen*), which is a horizontal oval with two or three wavy lines rising from it indicating steam.

Page 105, Unit

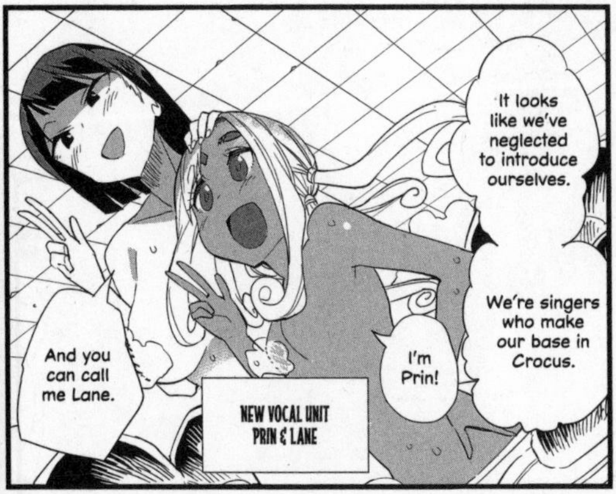
It looks like we've neglected to introduce ourselves.
We're singers who make our base in Crocus.
I'm Prin!
NEW VOCAL UNIT PRIN & LANE
And you can call me Lane.

Although most idols are solo vocalists or in vocal groups, there have been new idol divisions led by such popular groups as Exile which feature not only talented singers but also very athletic dancers as a part of the entire experience. And these have changed the vocabulary a bit from "idol groups" to "idol units." So it's possible that at the very end of the chapter (minor spoiler warning), when Prin and Lane introduce themselves as a new unit including the "Fairies," that the Fairy Girls were just there to dance and not necessarily sing.